THE HEALTHY BODY
AND VICTORIAN CULTURE

THOMAS J. WILSON PRIZE

The Board of Syndics of Harvard University Press has awarded this book the eighth annual Thomas J. Wilson Prize, honoring the late director of the Press. The Prize is awarded each year to the best first book by a beginning author.

THE
HEALTHY BODY
AND
VICTORIAN CULTURE

Bruce Haley

Harvard University Press
Cambridge, Massachusetts
and London, England
1978

Library of Congress Cataloging in Publication Data

Haley, Bruce, 1933-
    The healthy body and Victorian culture.

    Includes bibliographical references and index.
        1. English literature—19th century—History
and criticism.   2. Health in literature.
3. Physical education and training in literature.
4. Public health—Great Britain—History—19th
century.   5. Physical education and training—
Great Britain—History—19th century.   I. Title.
PR469.H42H3   820'.9'35   78-6933
ISBN 0-674-38610-8

To my mother and father

Acknowledgments

WHEN a work takes as long as this one has to finish it tends to incur many debts, both large and small. Some years ago, when the topic first occurred to me, John Henry Raleigh and Ian Watt not only urged me ahead with it but also gave helpful advice on how to approach it. As it developed into a full-length study Jack Stillinger, George Scouffas, and above all Donald Smalley generously offered practical suggestions about style and content. More recently, Brooke Hopkins, Don Bialostosky, Don Walker, William Mulder, Milton Voigt, and John Maynard have taken the time to read closely the entire manuscript or large parts of it. To all these people I should like to express my gratitude. Thanks are also due the University of Utah Research Committee for awarding me a travel grant, and to the University for an invaluable sabbatical year in England. Earlier versions of several parts of this study appeared in the *Bucknell Review* and the *Western Humanities Review*.

Finally and most especially, I should like to record here the book's enormous debt to Martha Klein Haley. She supplied the best sort of critical guidance at a time when it was most needed, and she painstakingly proofread the final manuscript. The book would not have been finished without her help.

April 1978   B.H.
Salt Lake City, Utah

Contents

PART ONE

Sound Body, Sound Mind

CHAPTER 1

Introduction:
Victorian Health

"WHOSO SPEAKS ON HEALTH," wrote George Henry Lewes, "is sure of a large audience." These words, by a distinguished Victorian psychologist, physiologist, and literary critic, appear in an essay on physical training written for the *Cornhill* in 1864. Lewes was only saying what everyone knew. No topic more occupied the Victorian mind than Health—not religion, or politics, or Improvement, or Darwinism. In the name of Health, Victorians flocked to the seaside, tramped about in the Alps or Cotswolds, dieted, took pills, sweated themselves in Turkish baths, adopted this "system" of medicine or that. Partly for the sake of Health they invented, revived, or imported from abroad a multitude of athletic recreations, and England became, in Sir Charles Tennyson's words, the "world's games-master."[1] Literary critics thought of Health when they read a new book of poems; social theorists thought of Health when they envisioned an ideal society. Victorians worshiped the goddess Hygeia, sought out her laws, and disciplined themselves to obey them.

In his *Physiology of Common Life* Lewes preached a gospel which would draw immediate assent from most readers: "No Scientific subject can be so important to Man as that of his own life. No knowledge can be so incessantly appealed to by the incidents of every day, as the knowledge of the *processes by which he lives and acts*. At every moment he is in danger of disobeying laws which, when disobeyed, may bring years of suffering, decline of powers, premature decay. Sanitory reformers preach in vain, because they preach to a public which does not understand the laws of life—laws as rigorous as those of gravitation or motion."[2] Man "lives and acts," according to him, entirely by the laws of life. A believer in what Huxley called the "physical basis of life," Lewes held that the mind and body function by the same principles and these principles are to be found everywhere in living nature. Therefore, the link between the laws of the human mind and the more general laws of nature was physiology, the study of bodily function. Like Lewes, other Victorian intellectuals insisted on the reality of a spiritual life higher than that of the body, but in one way or another they all thought physiologically: they adopted the well-knit body as their model for the well-formed mind, and the mind-body harmony as their model for spiritual health, the harmony of the self with external principles of growth and order. Total health or wholeness—*mens sana in corpore sano*—was a dominant concept for the Victorians, as important in shaping thought about human growth and conduct as nature was to the Romantics.

Physiological models have been in use since the beginning of philosophy, when man first began to consider his body separately from his mind and to speculate on the relation between the two. One's body— what he can know of himself through his senses—is a natural vehicle for envisioning what he only knows subjectively: mind or spirit. In this way "health" has long been used analogically to represent various kinds of perfection or excellence. Several factors, however, coincided to give the healthy body a special conceptual prominence in nineteenth-century thought. First, the development of physiology as a separate and distinct biological science offered hope that the laws of life could be learned in their relation to human beings. The emphasis in this science was on the wholeness of the body, on what Charles Singer has called a "synthetic study," with the organs being looked at not so much "in and for themselves as in relation to the other organs."[3] Important work was thus being done in physiological systems, particularly the digestive, respiratory, and neural, leading more and more to a concept of the whole physiological man. Second, the emergence of a physiological psychology, together with a psychological approach to medicine, fostered the conviction that the health of the body and that of the mind were interdependent. And third, a growing belief that education should develop the whole man inspired an interest in physical training as an essential part of personal culture.

All of these provided a philosophical framework for exploring the mind-body connection. Meanwhile, in the first half of the century the medical world was raising the expectation that treatment of the body could become as exact a science as knowledge of the body. Throughout the land, much money and energy was being devoted to medical care and its study. Between 1801 and 1850 more university-educated men entered the profession in Great Britain (over eight thousand) than in all of previous history. The number of practitioners was well keeping pace with the enormous growth in population.[4] This same period saw a continuing expansion of hospital facilities. Over seventy special hospitals were founded between 1800 and 1860, among them the London Fever Hospital, the Kensington Children's Hospital, and the Free Cancer Hospital, Fulham. At the beginning of the century, hospitals in England and Wales were accommodating only an average of three thousand patients; fifty years later the number had grown to eight thousand.[5]

The hospitals were providing not only more room for patients, but also expanded opportunities for the training of doctors. Especially after 1815, when the Apothecaries Act made mandatory for apprentices a half-year's experience in an infirmary, hospital, or dispensary, hospital surgeons began routinely to assume teaching duties and the larger teaching hospitals were inundated by students.[6] These places became important centers for the study of morbid anatomy when, with the Anatomy Act of 1832, all unclaimed bodies were sent to them for dissection.

Strides were being made not only in medical anatomy and physiology but also in pharmacology. Among the drugs isolated, concocted, or discovered between 1800 and 1840 were morphine, quinine, atropine, digitalin, codeine, and iodine. The nineteenth century was also a notable period in the identification, classification, and description of diseases. Scarlet fever was clinically distinguished from diphtheria, syphilis from gonorrhea, typhoid from typhus. The work of the great French physiologist Claude Bernard on the digestion established the connection between diabetes and glucose in the blood. The inventor of the stethoscope, R.-T.-H. Laënnec, wrote an important treatise in 1823 that first clearly distinguished such diseases as pleurisy, emphysema, bronchitis, and pneumonia. The English clinicians Richard Bright, Thomas Addison, Thomas Hodgkin, and James Parkinson supplied the classic descriptions for the diseases named after them.

The British public followed with keen interest these developments which seemed to promise a healthy nation. And yet, in looking around them, they could clearly see that the promise was far from being realized. In actual practice all the researchers, family physicians, apothecaries and surgeons—the whole of the medical profession—provided scant help in curing those diseases of which Victorians had been made so vividly aware. One of the rewards of bodily health, Charles Kingsley wrote, is that it "makes one unconscious of one's own body."[7] The constant threat of illness in the Victorian home made people conscious of their bodies, anxious to know how their bodies worked, and prepared to see a moral significance in the laws of life.

Nothing occupies a nation's mind with the subject of health like a general contagion. In the 1830s and 1840s there were three massive waves of contagious disease: the first, from 1831 to 1833, included two influenza epidemics and the initial appearance of cholera; the second, from 1836 to 1842, encompassed major epidemics of influenza, typhus, smallpox, and scarlet fever; in the third, from 1846 to 1849, there were occurrences of typhus, typhoid, and cholera. As F. H. Garrison has observed, epidemic eruptions in the eighteenth century had been "more scattered and isolated" than theretofore;[8] and in the early decades of the nineteenth century there had been a marked decline in such illnesses as diphtheria and influenza. Smallpox, the scourge of the eighteenth century, appeared to be controllable by the new practice of vaccination. Then, in the mid-twenties, England saw serious outbreaks of smallpox and typhus, anticipating the pestilential turbulence of the next two decades.

The first outbreak of Asiatic cholera in Britain was at Sunderland on the Durham coast during the autumn of 1831. From there the disease made its way northward into Scotland and southward toward London. Before it had run its course it claimed 52,000 lives.[9] From its point of origin in Bengal it had taken five years to cross Europe, so that when it reached the coast of Durham, British doctors were well aware of its nature, if not its cause.

The progress of the illness in a cholera victim was a frightening spectacle: two or three days of a diarrhea which increased in intensity and became accompanied by a painful retching; thirst and dehydration; severe pain in the limbs, stomach, and abdominal muscles; a change in skin hue to a sort of bluish gray. The disease was unlike anything then known. One doctor recalled: "Our other plagues were home-bred, and part of ourselves, as it were; we had a habit of looking on them with a fatal indifference, indeed, inasmuch as it led us to believe that they could be effectually subdued. But the cholera was something outlandish, unknown, monstrous; its tremendous ravages, so long foreseen and feared, so little to be explained, its insidious march over whole continents, its apparent defiance of all the known and conventional precautions against the spread of epidemic disease, invested it with a mystery and a terror which thoroughly took hold of the public mind, and seemed to recall the memory of the great epidemics of the middle ages."[10]

The cholera subsided as enigmatically as it had flourished, but in the meantime another sort of devastation had taken hold. The previous June, following a particularly rainy spring, Britain was visited by the first of eight serious influenza epidemics in the space of sixteen years.[11] In those days the disease was often fatal, and even when it did not kill, it left its victims weakened in their defenses against other diseases. Burials in London doubled during the first week of the 1833 outbreak; in one two-week period they quadrupled. Whereas cholera, spread by contaminated water, affected mainly the poorer neighborhoods, influenza was limited by no economic or geographic boundaries. Large numbers of public officials, especially in the Bank of England, died from it, as did many theater people.[12]

At that time the term "fever" encompassed a number of different diseases, among them cholera and influenza. In the 1830s the "new fever," typhus, was isolated. During its worst outbreak, in 1837-8, most of the deaths from fever in London were attributed to typhus, and new cases averaged about sixteen thousand in England in each of the next four years. This happened to coincide with one of the worst smallpox contagions, which killed tens of thousands, mainly infants and children. Scarlet fever, or scarlatina as it was then called, was responsible for nearly twenty thousand deaths in 1840 alone.[13]

Although mortality rates for specific diseases were not compiled for England and Wales between 1842 and 1846, we know that during this period there was a considerable decline in epidemics. It has been surmised that one reason was the expansion of railroad building, with the consequent increase in wage levels and a better standard of living. A hot, dry summer in 1846, however, was followed by a serious outbreak of typhoid in the fall of that year. Enteric fever, as it was then called, is a water-borne disease like cholera and tends to flourish when people are not particular about the source of their drinking water. That same year, as the potato famine struck Ireland, a virulent form of typhus appeared, cutting down large numbers of even well-to-do families. As Irish workers moved to cities like Liverpool and Glasgow the "Irish fever" moved with them. By 1847 the contagion, not all of it connected with immigration, had spread throughout England and Wales, accounting for over thirty thousand deaths. As had happened a decade earlier, typhus occurred simultaneously with a severe influenza epidemic, one which carried off almost thirteen thousand.[14] There was also a widespread dysentery, and as if all this were not enough, cholera returned in the autumn of 1848, assailing especially those parts of the island hardest hit by typhus and leaving about as many dead as it had in 1831.[15] This was the epidemic which took the lives of one-fifth of the thousand children housed at the institution for the poor at Tooting.

Diseases like cholera, typhus, typhoid, and influenza were more or less endemic at the time, erupting into epidemics when the right climatic conditions coincided with periods of economic distress. The frequency of concurrent epidemics gave rise to the belief that one sort of disease brought on another; indeed, it was widely believed that influenza was an early stage of cholera. There were other contagions, however, which yearly killed thousands without becoming epidemic. Taken together, measles and "hooping cough" accounted for fifty thousand deaths in England and Wales between 1838 and 1840, and about a quarter of all deaths during this general period have been attributed to tuberculosis or consumption.[16]

It is not hard to see why the idea of disease had such an impact in the last century. In his *Report on the Sanitary Condition of the Labouring Population of Gt. Britain* Edwin Chadwick included figures to show that in 1839 for every person who died of old age or violence, eight died of specific diseases.[17] This helps explain why during the second and third decades of the nineteenth century nearly one infant in three in England failed to reach the age of five.[18]

Generally throughout the 1830s and 1840s trade was off and food prices were high. The poorer classes, being underfed, were less resistant to contagion. Also, during the more catastrophic years the weather was extremely variable, with heavy rains following prolonged droughts. Population, especially in the Midlands and in some seaport cities and towns, was growing rapidly without a concurrent expansion in new housing. Crowding contributed to the relatively fast spread of disease in these places. The Registrar General reported in 1841 that while mean life expectancy in Surrey was forty-five years, it was only thirty-seven in London and twenty-six in Liverpool.[19] The average age of "labourers, mechanics, and servants, &c." at time of death was only fifteen.[20] Mortality figures for crowded districts like Shoreditch, Whitechapel, and Bermondsey were typically half again or twice as high as those for middle-class areas of London.

Such statistics as these not only made Britons aware of the magnitude of disease in their own time, but served as effective weapons for sanitary reformers when they brought their case before Parliament. Two reports by the Poor Law Commission in 1838, one by Dr. Southwood Smith, the other by Drs. Neil Arnott and J. P. Kay (later Kay-Shuttleworth), outlined causes and probable means of preventing communicable disease in poverty areas like London's Bethnal Green and Whitechapel. Chadwick's *Report* broadened the scope of inquiry geographically, as did a Royal Commission document in 1845 on the *Health of Towns and Populous*

Places. What we learn from these and other sources gives a depressing picture of early Victorian hygiene.

During the first decades of Victoria's reign, baths were virtually unknown in the poorer districts and uncommon anywhere. Most households of all economic classes still used "privy-pails"; water closets were rare. Sewers had flat bottoms, and because drains were made of stone, seepage was considerable. If, as was often the case in towns, streets were unpaved, they might remain ankle-deep in mud for weeks. For new middle-class homes in the growing manufacturing towns, elevated sites were usually chosen, with the result that sewage filtered or flowed down into the lower areas where the laboring populations dwelt. Some towns had special drainage problems. In Leeds the Aire River, fouled by the town's refuse, flooded periodically, sending noxious waters into the ground floors and basements of the low-lying houses.[21]

As Chadwick later recalled, the new dwellings of the middle-class families were scarcely healthier, for the bricks tended to preserve moisture. Even picturesque old country houses often had a dungeonlike dampness, as any visitor could observe: "If he enters the house he finds the basement steaming with water-vapour; walls constantly bedewed with moisture, cellars coated with fungus and mould; drawing rooms and dining rooms always, except in the very heat of summer, oppressive from moisture; bedrooms, the windows of which are, in winter, so frosted on their inner surface, from condensation of the water in the air of the room, that all day they are coated with ice."[22]

In some districts of London and the great towns the supply of water was irregular. Typically, a neighborhood of twenty or thirty families on a particular square or street would draw their water from a single pump two or three times a week. Sometimes, finding the pump not working, they were forced to reuse the same water. When a local supply became contaminated the results could be disastrous. In Soho's St. Anne's parish, for example, the feces of an infant stricken with cholera washed down into the water reserve from which the local pump drew, and almost all those using the pump were infected. Millbank Prison, taking its water from the sewage-polluted Thames, suffered greatly during every epidemic of water-borne disease.

The Public Health Bill, passed in 1848 because of the efforts of reformers like Smith and Chadwick, empowered a central authority to set up local boards whose duty was to see that new homes had proper drainage and that water supplies were dependable. The boards were also authorized to regulate the disposal of wastes and to supervise the construction of burial grounds. Simply bringing this last problem to public attention was a great service: the New Bunhill Fields burying ground in the Borough, less than an acre in size, was at this time the depository of over fifteen hundred bodies a year, though Chadwick estimated that only one hundred and ten could be "neutralized" per acre of ground. When more room was needed, the older skeletons and coffins were incinerated. The graveyard of St. Martin's, Ludgate, had long since filled, and hundreds more were interred in church vaults; the resulting stench drove away the regular worshipers from service.

Since it was widely believed that disease was generated spontaneously from filth (pythogenesis) and transmitted by a noxious invisible gas or miasma, there was much alarm over the "Great Stink" of 1858 and 1859. The Thames had become so polluted with waste as to be almost unbearable during summer months. People refused to use the river-steamers and would walk miles to avoid crossing one of the city bridges. Parliament could carry on its business only by hanging disinfectant-soaked cloths over the windows. It should have been a blow to the theory of pythogenesis when no outbreak of fever ensued from this monstrous stench. As late as 1873, however, William Budd could reluctantly report in his important book on typhoid that "organic matter, and especially sewage in a state of decomposition, without any relation to antecedent fever, is still generally supposed to be the most fertile source."[23]

Throughout most of the century, doctors can be said to have been conceptually helpless about the cause and treatment of disease. A glance at the contents of a typical volume of the Lancet (1849) tells the melancholy story: "On the Advantage of Copious Bleeding in Inflammatory Diseases"; "Report of a Case of Cholera Treated by Transfusion"; "Treatment of Cholera by Small and Repeated Doses of Calomel"; "On the Employment of Embrocations and Injections of Strong Liquid Ammonia in the Collapse Stage of Cholera." One title begins promisingly—"On the Production of Cholera by Insufficient Drainage"—but continues, "with Remarks on the Hypothesis of an Altered Electrical State of the Atmosphere."

No doubt the resistance to the theory of polluted water as a source of infection contributed to the steady prevalence of typhoid in the second half of the century as well as to the high mortality rates from cholera in epidemics as late as 1854 or 1865-6. The general cleaning up of the cities and towns, however, produced a marked reduction in deaths from typhus, a disease, as we now know, transmitted by lice. Although a systematic control of contagious disease had to await the introduction of preventive inoculation in the eighties and nineties, after mid-century the general health of the country measurably improved. In the 1850s and 1860s there came into common use such diagnostic aids as the stethoscope, the ophthalmoscope, and the short clinical thermometer. Meanwhile the employment of general anesthesia and antiseptic surgery was reducing considerably the number of hospital deaths.

Improved hygiene, diagnosis, and treatment in the past century have given people a certain emotional security even in the face of serious disease. Throughout much of the Victorian period, however, with both the causes and patterns of disease very much matters of speculation, it was difficult ever to feel comfortable about the state of one's health. The behavior of the severe contagions of the time had a special way of intensifying anxiety. They would appear, then perhaps subside for a month or two, only to reappear in the same locality or somewhere else. Also, the individual sufferer had no way of predicting the outcome of the disease in his own case. Influenza patients, observed the *London Medical Gazette* during the 1833 epidemic, "might linger for the space of two or three weeks and then get up well, or they might die in the same number of days."[24] Just as frightening was the uncertain progress of typhoid. For the first week the victim would feel listless and suffer headaches, insomnia, and feverishness. His temperature would gradually increase over this period, though fluctuating between the morning and evening hours. His stomach would be painful and distended. Probably he would have diarrhea and perhaps red patches on his skin. Typically there would be an intensification of these symptoms for a few weeks. In most cases the patient would recover, but convalescence might take additional weeks. Depending on the severity of the attack, however, and the patient's ability to resist, he might die from exhaustion, internal hemorrhaging, or ulceration of the intestine.

The beginnings of such a disease as typhoid were so mild and gradual as to be subjectively indistinguishable from, say, a cold or a moderate case of influenza, or from any of a number of nonfatal complaints. Deficiency diseases, both glandular and dietary, were but dimly understood in those days. Proper diagnosis and effective treatment of goiter, diabetes, and the various vitamin deficiencies belong to the twentieth century, as is true with allergies, many of which must also have imitated the early symptoms of acute diseases. Thousands of sufferers from eczema, hives, or asthma not only were given superficial relief but were ignorant of the nature of their maladies.

The number of unknowing victims of chronic food poisoning must also have been great. Mineral poisons were often introduced into food and water from bottle stoppers, water pipes, wall paints, or equipment used to process food and beverages. Moreover, the deliberate adulteration of food was a common and, until 1860, virtually unrestricted practice. For example, because of the Englishman's dislike of brown bread, bakers regularly whitened their flour with alum. Conditions for the processing and sale of foods were unsanitary. An 1863 report to the Privy Council stated that one-fifth of the meat sold came from diseased cattle.[25] In 1860 the first pure-food act was passed, but, as was often the case in these early regulatory measures, it provided no mandatory system of enforcement. In 1872 another act was passed, this time considerably strengthening penalties and inspection procedures. But in the meantime, and throughout most of the nineteenth century, Britons had little protection against unwholesome food and drink. We can only guess at how many tons of adulterated tea, rancid butter, and polluted meat were sold and consumed monthly throughout the kingdom.

Whenever Parliament debated some labor-reform bill, Victorians were reminded that the Industrial Revolution had brought as an unwelcome by-product the proliferation of occupational diseases. Testimony from medical investigators and workers alike included gruesome stories of "black-spittle" among miners, of grinder's rot and potter's asthma. Those looking into conditions among milliners and dressmakers found much higher than average rates of anemia, deteriorating vision, and various lung diseases caused by breathing dust and fine particles of fiber. In many places of work, ten to twelve hours a day standing or sitting in one spot, often in an unnatural position, damaged the spine, the digestion, and the circulation.

WITH THE PREVALENCE of these occupational ailments, as well as of contagions, deficiency diseases, and food poisonings, George Henry Lewes's remark that "few of us, after thirty, can boast of robust health" is understandable.[26] Their correspondence reveals that many prominent Victorians were, or thought they were, constantly afflicted. "I must get rid of this horrible condition of body," the twenty-seven-year-old Thomas Carlyle wrote; "it absolutely torments me till my soul is dark as the pit of Tophet." At thirty he was "sick with sleeplessness, quite nervous, *billus*, splenetic, and all the rest of it."[27] At thirty-four: "My health continues very uncertain; . . . I am not equal to much work."[28] At fifty-four: "Oh, it is an earnest tussle this Life of ours here below; and if a man's *body* fail him, and he get continual grinding misery of ill-health to encompass him for thirty and odd years, and drag down every step of his poor limbs—But let me not complain."[29] All of this from a man who lived to the age of eighty-five! The Carlyles had not been married long when he discovered his wife to be a fellow-sufferer. According to Harriet Martineau, Jane had "eight influenzas annually."[30] For these, and for dyspepsia, headaches, and sleeplessness she tried one cure after another, as well as a variety of doctors.

This sort of valetudinarianism seems almost the rule among Victorian intellectuals. Darwin complained so frequently of poor health that he feared becoming known as a hypochondriac.[31] Huxley variously diagnosed his own troubles as melancholic prostration, dyspepsia, affection of the liver, and hypochondriacal depression.[32] George Eliot and G. H. Lewes, like the Carlyles, found kinship in chronic debility as well as in intellectual interests, so that a trip to the seaside was a chance for both of them to pursue "zoology and health."[33] The list of the afflicted could be extended almost endlessly—to Tennyson, Spencer, Meredith, Ruskin. All of them sought Health as a kind of Holy Grail.

Health was offered in many forms. Apothecary shops carried hundreds of "specifics," drugs intended to attack particular varieties or symptoms of disease. Among the remedies for "hooping-cough" listed in the *Cyclopaedia of Practical Medicine* were opium, belladonna, digitalis, bark, cup moss, arsenical solution, nitrate of silver, oil of amber, meadow narcissus, and acetate of lead. During the second half of the nineteenth century, however, such drugs were falling into disfavor. The "specific doctor" and the apothecary were deemed not modern; they were too reminiscent of medieval alchemists.

One new and elaborate system of drugs, however, had a considerable vogue at the time. Homeopathy's principle was the old maxim, "what will cause a fever will cure a fever." The practice was curiously analogous to inoculation; homeopathic doctors carried with them cases of medicines, from which they would administer minute doses of whatever could produce symptoms resembling those of the disease being treated. Meredith flirted with the craze for a while, but ultimately rejected it. Mrs. Carlyle found a brief trial sufficient: "Homoeopathy is an invention of the Father of Lies! I have *tried* it, and found it wanting. I could swallow their whole doles' medicine-chest for sixpence, and be sure of finding myself neither better nor worse for it."[34]

There was also a considerable business to be done in panaceas. Writing in 1844, an anonymous physician termed England the "Paradise of Quacks" because anyone could sell medicines in the streets without having to buy a license or receive special training.[35] Snook's Family Pill, the Golden Pill of Life and Beauty, Dr. Coffin's Cayenne Pepper, and Parr's Life Pill (which, boasted its purveyor, "has caused me to attain my miraculous old age") were among the popular cure-alls advertised in penny-magazines and sold everywhere. Up to £40,000 yearly was spent by Thomas Holloway to advertise his Family Ointment and other remedies, a business profitable enough to enable him to found Royal Holloway College, which opened in 1886, three years after his death. The favorite quack among the well-to-do in the early part of the century was the notorious St. John Long, whose medicine was supposed to cure consumption. Long was twice-tried and once-convicted (with a fine of £250) for causing the deaths of "patients."

Perhaps the best known of the pill-sellers was James Morison, creator of the "Gamboge Pill," or, as he liked to have it called, the Universal Medicine. He began peddling his discovery in the 1820s. Within a short while, according to one of his admirers, the pill became famous for its "numerous cures . . . in all kinds of diseases, surgical cases, and mental derangements."[36] Soon Morison and his "coadjutators" had founded the British College of Health, of which the chief dispensary or sale room was in London's New Road. The college's members, called Hygeists, sold the wonder-cure throughout the country. To Carlyle, Morison and his pill were symbolic of the modern love of sham. To Matthew Arnold the College embodied the Englishman's love of "the grand name without the grand thing": "Every one knows the British College of Health; it is that building with the lion and the statue of the Goddess Hygeia before it; at least I am sure about the lion, though I am not absolutely certain about the Goddess Hygeia. The building does credit, perhaps, to the resources of Dr. Morison and his disciples; but it falls a good deal short of one's idea of what a British College of Health ought to be."[37]

The phenomenon of the Gamboge Pill is a revealing illustration of the Victorian's spirited quest for Good Health. Morison summed up his philosophy in this way: "All the lingering chronic diseases and infirmities one witnesses are only owing to not having been purged in some previous diseases, such as fevers, colds, inflammations, measles, smallpox, or lyings-in. The Hygeists make use only of one medicine, and it cures every disease radically;—the doctors prescribe a hundred different things, and they cure no disease. The patient is at best only patched up for a while;—it is impossible there can be any real cure but by sound purging."[38] The part about the doctors' inability to cure any disease was indeed the case. "The philosophy of medicine, I imagine, is almost at zero," Thomas

Arnold wrote in 1836.[39] Morison offered a solution for this unhappy state of ignorance by designating the blood stream as the bodily center of all disease. Illness was caused by "bad humours" in the blood. This was no more outlandish than the views of those "respectable" physicians who traced all diseases to the Stomach, and put their faith in Diet; or to the Skin and Lungs, and put their faith in Ventilation; or to Muscle Tone, and put their faith in Tonics.

The dispensers of drugs and elixirs belonged to what Sir William Osler has called the old schools of poly-pharmacy.[40] Those that were not homeopaths were termed allopaths—that is, they prescribed medicines which were intended to work *against* the symptoms of the disease under treatment—saltpeter for inflammation, purgatives for constipation, and so on. Philosophically, the allopaths were guided by what is really only a refinement of Hippocrates' concept of disease as an imbalance of natural elements within the body. The homeopaths regarded themselves as more modern and scientific ("the medicine of experience," its founder Hahnemann called it), but knowing virtually nothing of biochemistry they were forced to be quite dogmatic about the influence of the various drugs they used. The beginning of a truly scientific study of drugs was to come much later in the century.

Meanwhile, a large and influential body of medical opinion, having abandoned its trust in medicines, moved toward a reliance on nature therapy. Even the drug-dispensers, whether of the schools of poly-pharmacy or mono-pharmacy (as we may term the purveyors of elixir or panacea), usually included some sort of appeal to "natural law" or the "laws of nature" in their rationales. Morison claimed that in purging the blood of its "bad humours" he was only assisting Nature, which "is constantly (though silently) counteracting the vices of man, for the preservation and health of the species."[41] Homeopathy was intended to "imitate nature, which sometimes cures a chronic disease by superadding another, and employ in the (especially chronic) disease we wish to cure, that medicine which is able to produce another very similar artificial disease, and the former will be cured."[42]

And yet, however "natural" these medicines were claimed to be, doctors of what E. S. Turner[43] calls the blue-pill-and-calomel school were gradually losing ground to the practitioners of nature-therapy. Bulwer Lytton summed up the dissatisfaction with the old school: "We begin to feel the frame break under us;—we administer a drug, gain a temporary relief, shift the disorder from one part to another—forget our ailments in our excitements, and when we pause at last, thoroughly shattered, with complaints grown chronic, diseases fastening to the organs, we send for doctors in good earnest, and die as our predecessors and our rival died, under combinations of long-neglected maladies, which could never have been known had we done for the body what we do for the mind—made it strong by discipline, and maintained it firm by habit."[44]

In his belief that the only way to cure disease is to let Nature herself dispose of it, Bulwer investigated hydropathy, or the water cure. The method of systematically treating patients with a wide variety of applications of water was the invention of Vincenz Priessnitz (1801-1851), a Silesian farmer who founded a "water university" at Grafenberg in the 1820s. His idea was that man should follow the example of animals in drinking water frequently and bathing regularly.[45] This rather simple idea had an immediate appeal in England, and in the 1840s hydropathic spas began appearing across the land. Bulwer, an early convert, visited Malvern where James Wilson had built the first English hydro. After nine or ten weeks there and an additional seven under Dr. Weiss at Petersham he became sufficiently won over to write a lengthy testimonial in support of the treatment. Lewes and Eliot, the Carlyles, the Dickenses, Macaulay, Darwin, Huxley, Ruskin, and Tennyson were some of those who at least tried the cure; a number of these, like Bulwer, remained steady disciples.

Methods of treatment differed from spa to spa. (When Dr. Edward Johnson presided at Malvern he boasted some seventy-four varieties.) A typical program was that devised by James Gully. Among his procedures were the sitz bath, the shallow bath, and hot and warm fomentations. These last were applications of heated damp cloths to the abdomen, in order to reduce feverish thought by diminishing the irritating influence of stomach inflammation. The digestive apparatus could then act as a constant and natural stimulant to the brain, giving it "a sustained energy." Gully also encouraged walking and other exercise to activate the brain, the will, and the spinal cord. But the best known part of his treatment was packing the patient in damp sheets and, over these, in dry blankets. The idea was to place the patient in "a steam bath of his own making," and relieve the nerves of irritation caused by exposure to air.

At hydros like Malvern, Cheltenham, Matlock, and Leamington, water was put to almost every ritualistic use imaginable. Patients sat in it, bathed in it, had it poured over them or squirted at them, and drank it up in great quantities. For those who did not wish to remain overnight some spas made special provisions: at Grafenberg House in Hertfordshire nonresident patients could have for a few shillings per treatment a Wave

Douche, a Cold Descending Douche, a Hot Spouting Douche, a Sheet Pack, or a Condy's Ozonized Sea-Salt Bath. There was nothing remarkable about the water at hydros; it was just plain water. But people clearly preferred that to the medicinal waters at places like Bath and Tunbridge Wells, whose popularity sank considerably with the rise of hydrotherapy.

In an age of mysterious contagions and chronic complaints, when contagions and complaints were part of the same spectrum of ill-health, physicians increasingly turned to hygiene and to the *res non-naturales*—air, water, food, sleep—as the basis of their therapeutics. Sir William Osler rightly terms the 1900s the century of preventive medicine.[46] Certainly the so-called "cures" like hydropathy had more to do with hygiene than pathology. As a remedy the sitz bath was no more effective than a dose of saltpeter. But in helping restore an equilibrium of the bodily and mental systems, the total hydropathic regimen probably deserved the testimonials given by so many.

If the Victorians could not cure acute diseases, at least they could, so they felt, do much toward preventing them when the first signs of bad health began to appear. Nothing less would answer than a total regeneration of the constitution, from the outside in, and from the inside out. David Urquhart, proprietor of the Jermyn Street baths and champion of Turkish bathing for the British, saw restored health as an almost religious deliverance: "Every portion of the surface of our bodies is pierced with fountains. These fountains will run with foul water, so long as there are impurities within man, and with distilled water from the moment that these are expelled. Thus the nauseous effluvium that belongs to impurity is given us as a warning. The impurities of man come from within; the cleansing power of man also comes from himself. Disease is only filth."[47] This sort of hortatory rhetoric—an appeal to conscience as much as to reason—is typical of the Victorian literature of health. "Perhaps nothing will so much hasten the time when body and mind will be adequately cared for," Herbert Spencer wrote, "as a diffusion of the belief that the preservation of health is a *duty* . . . The fact is, that all breaches of the laws of health are *physical sins*."[48]

IN ADDITION to the immediate value of knowing the body and its laws, physiology was held to have a supplementary cognitive value. In the preface to his widely read *Philosophy of Health* Southwood Smith proclaimed that physiology should be the foundation of all study of man: "The mind is dependent on the body: hence an acquaintance with the physiology of the body should precede the study of the physiology of the mind. The constitution of the mind must be understood before its powers and affections can be properly developed and directed: hence a knowledge of the physiology of the mind is essential to a sound view of education and morals."[49] Thus, through the notion of ascending dependencies, all knowledge of man and his activities is shown to ground itself naturally in the study of the body: the physiology of the brain "depends on" that of the body as a whole; the make-up of the mind depends on that of the brain; and a person's social activity depends on the constitution of his mind. This stepping-stone approach to the study of man became extremely popular in the nineteenth century.

As a starting point in thinking about man's nature, physiology has the obvious advantage of seeming to provide an objective foundation for subjects like ethics and psychology that might otherwise remain subjective and speculative. The physiologist's claim was that when we speak of man's moral nature we necessarily deal in guesses, but when we speak of his physical nature we are dealing in verifiable facts. A physiologist is literally one who studies *physis*, or "nature." In early Greek thought the *physis* of man *was* his nature, in R. G. Collingwood's words "something within, or intimately belonging to, a thing, which is the source of its behaviour."[50] Although that does not necessarily mean the body, Hippocratic philosophy argued that in the body lay the secret of the *physis*. "Clear knowledge about the nature of man can be acquired from medicine and no other source," one Hippocratic treatise maintained, and "one can attain this knowledge when medicine itself is clearly apprehended, but till then it is impossible."[51] As the *physis* came to be more strictly identified with the body, the natural or material part of man, physiology became simply a study of bodily functions. In the nineteenth century few physiologists would argue that the body was a person's essential nature, but many insisted that knowing the body was the most direct path to knowing the man; it was at least a more certain endeavor than trying to know the mind or soul.

In his essay "On the Physical Basis of Life" Huxley called for the general adoption of a "materialistic terminology" in considering life, along with a "repudiation of materialism." Materialism, he said, involves "grave philosophical error," but "with a view to the progress of science, the materialistic terminology is in every way to be preferred [over the spiritualistic]. For it connects thought with the other phaenomena of the universe, and suggests inquiry into the nature of those physical conditions, or concomitants of thought, *which are more or less accessible to*

us, and a knowledge of which may in future, help us to exercise the same
kind of control over the world of thought, as we already possess in respect of the material world; whereas, the alternative, or spiritualistic,
terminology is utterly barren, and leads to nothing but obscurity and
confusion of ideas."[52] Huxley felt that epistemologically it is more fruitful
to consider life in its material aspect, even though we know it has a spiritual aspect as well. If we center our thoughts on those materialistic conceptions of life which are "accessible" to us, we have a means of grasping
the nonphysical world; in doing that we "repudiate" materialism. He
observed that "the most thoughtful" men of his acquaintance had
adopted that method.

The physiological model of the healthy body was, in the nineteenth
century, a common means of conceptualizing psychological health as
well as the health of the whole person, mind and body together. But even
when somatic, psychic, and constitutional well-being have been defined,
there is another kind of health which must be related to those, the one
specified in the familiar words from the *Book of Common Prayer:*

> We have left undone those things which we ought to have done;
> And we have done those things which we ought not to have done;
> And there is no health in us.

Here the word health means a life in perfect accordance with the essential
spiritual laws governing man. It is much broader than, for example, the
Latin *sanus,* from which both "sane" and "sanitary" derive, and which
suggests strictly an internal wholeness. As René Dubos has observed, the
concept of the whole man should be taken to involve not only "those aspects of the organism that make it function as an integrated structure,"
but also "the summation of all the constituents and properties of the
organism, including their individual relations to the total environment."[53] The ideal of health as holiness implies a perfect relation to one's
spiritual environment;[54] in English the words health, wholeness, and
holiness are related. Some Victorians, like Charles Kingsley, saw the
laws of health as theologically imperative; that is, to be constitutionally
whole was to be, strictly speaking, holy. Not everyone agreed with that
extreme position, but there was a general tendency to broaden the concept of health metaphysically to suggest an integration with external,
spiritual laws. Because these could not be perceived in themselves, a conceptual model was needed, a model of "health" which physiology and
medicine supplied.

Very simply defined, healthiness is a state of being which is free from discomfort or, more positively, which produces comfort. From Victorian authorities on medicine, psychology, and physiology we can isolate several elements of health which were specially stressed at the time. First, health is a state of functional and structural *wholeness.* In an organism the two are related, for a structure becomes functional when viewed as part of a living whole. For example, a heart may be structurally whole in itself, but as an organ operating satisfactorily within an organism, the body, it is also functionally sound. A human being is made up of structures—some physical, some mental. They become functional when there is some unifying principle—will, soul, character—which gives an identity to the whole. This principle transcends the purely mechanical and unifies all separate functions. The physician George Moore sums it up thus: "The body is constituted by the union of the circulatory, respiratory, assimilative, absorbent, secerning, muscular, and nervous systems, which all act together, under laws, with apparatus peculiar to each, and equally marvellous in all, for the purpose of rearing up and maintaining a complication of organized machinery pervaded and preserved by one life, and actuated by one soul."[55]

Second, since in a living organism structures are purposively functional (not just working but working usefully), the state of health is one of *telicity.* A person may be seen as whole or healthy when he acts responsibly within his environment. Archibald Maclaren, founder of the Oxford gymnasium and popular authority on gymnastic training, defined health as "that condition of the body, and that amount of vital capacity, which shall enable each man in his place to pursue his calling, and work on in his working life, with the greatest comfort to himself and usefulness to his fellow-men."[56]

Third, health is a state of *vitality,* that is, of activity, growth, and responsiveness. The healthy man is not only whole in himself and at one with his environment, he is also alive to his environment, and changes as it does. In broadest terms, Victorians conceived of health as a vital relation between the individual life and the general conditions of life. Writing in the *Cornhill,* the widely published doctor-philosopher James Hinton offered a somewhat lyrical description of this state. A man is healthy, "when his blood is in harmony with the ceaseless activities of nature; when his body is warm with the soft kiss of air, his muscles vigorous with hearty toil, his brain fertile in wise and generous thoughts, his heart glowing with generous purposes. When a man lives most out of himself, then does he truly live . . . The living body should thrill with every thrill of the wide earth, as the aspen leaf trembles in the tremulous air. Its perfectness lies in continual change."[57] The living organism is never static; without healthy movement and growth there must be unhealthy movement and growth. Discussing mental soundness, the psychologist Henry Maudsley uses a physiological analogy to make this point: "To ask that the morbid mind should stay at a certain level of degeneracy and cease to display new morbid functions would be very much like asking that a morbid growth amid healthy structures should increase and undergo its changes independently of them . . . Not to exercise and grow to the exercise of one's better nature, is to exercise and grow to the exercise of one's worse nature."[58]

These generalizations about the Victorian concept of health provide us with a working definition: *Health is a state of constitutional growth and development in which the bodily systems and mental faculties interoperate harmoniously under the direct motive power of vital energy or the indirect motive power of the moral will, or both. Its signs are, subjectively recognized, a sense of wholeness and unencumbered capability, and, externally recognized, the production of useful, creative labor.* All of this is said more simply in *mens sana in corpore sano.* Both the epigram and the long definition, however, leave open some critical questions. For example, granted that health is a harmony of mind and body leading to an ethical or spiritual perfection, how important is physical health in the whole scheme? Does physical health arise from spiritual health, or is it the other way around? If physical health is to be the model, what *sort* of health should be envisioned—strength and energy, or coordination, agility, and the capacity for growth?

The first half of this book shows how some prominent Victorian thinkers approached these questions in formulating their definitions of health. Victorian conceptions of the healthy man, which the second half of the book examines more broadly, often show the influence of Carlyle's healthy hero, Spencer's biologically perfect man, Newman's gentleman-Christian, and especially Kingsley's muscular Christian. And like those four types, they were based on *mens sana in corpore sano.* Once, while addressing some undergraduates, Carlyle used that expression and his audience burst into applause.[59] It may well be that he and they had in mind quite different conceptions of human growth and well-being. A popular interpretation of the maxim at the time, though not Carlyle's, was that training up the body assured a robust sort of mind. In this view, *mens sana* means manliness or pluck, a quality similar to physical strength or courage and dependent on them. To hold that idea went beyond a materialistic terminology and moved visibly toward materialism:

all health begins with the body, and the healthy body is no longer merely a conceptual starting point, a cognitive model for intellectual and spiritual growth, but the chief requisite in itself for human happiness and usefulness. "To be a nation of good animals," Herbert Spencer wrote, "is the first condition to national prosperity."[60] A rather simple version of the good animal, an embodiment of moral and physical toughness, became an ideal in himself and a symbol of national prosperity. Over this manly type a controversy developed in popular fiction, in the press, and in the writings of such leading literary figures as Matthew Arnold, George Eliot, and George Meredith, each of whom offered his own concept of the healthy man. Although the controversy surrounding the healthy man often focused on the symbolic figure of the British athlete, the man of strong body and strong character who "plays the game" morally as well as physically, the real issues were much broader. They involved, as Victorian considerations of health usually did, fundamental questions about the mind-body relationship and about the relation of natural law to human growth or culture.

CHAPTER 2

Mens Sana in Corpore Sano:
Victorian Psychophysiology

"THERE STILL remains in some quarters a vulgar notion that there is a natural antagonism between corporal and mental excellence." Speaking at a Liverpool college's foundation-day ceremony in 1857, W. E. Gladstone warned his listeners against such a narrow view of health and expressed his hope that neither boys nor masters would forget "manly sports" and physical education. His words received a cordial reception in the press. The *Times* editorialized: "The mind should be a good, strong, healthy feeder, but not a glutton. We have no right to despise the body, or speak of it only and exclusively as something which is vile in comparison with the mind. This language will lead astray."[1] A living article of faith to millions, *mens sana in corpore sano* was being preached in newspapers, in school chapels, and in the consultation rooms of doctors across the land. The mind cannot live without the body; neglect the well-being of one and you endanger the other. "Uncleanliness of mind and body act and react," declared a popular medical guidebook, "and perfect health of one is incompatible with an unhealthy state of the other."[2]

Not the least of reasons why these ideas were so generally accepted was the support they were receiving from men of scientific learning. During the middle decades of the last century both medical philosophy and formal psychology were showing a particular interest in the mind-body relationship. The result was to bring the two disciplines close together: at the same time that medicine was seeking psychological explanations of disease, psychology was grounding itself inductively in the study of the body.

In the early nineteenth century psychiatry and psychotherapy were undeveloped as distinct areas of study. All illness was the province of the physician, who was expected to minister to the mind diseased as well as the body diseased. The question, however, that any doctor had to face was, which diseases belonged to the *psyche* and which to the *soma?* In each case the question involved diagnosis, etiology, and treatment: (1) was the disease essentially a bodily or mental disturbance? (2) did it *arise from* a bodily or mental disturbance? (3) should it be treated somatically or psychically? The answers tended often to be a combination of the alternatives, but since the physician's chief concern had traditionally been the *physis*, the bias was usually toward physical descriptions and remedies, even for diseases which we would now consider wholly mental.

As Pedro Entralgo has shown, that bias had worked its way into medical thought over centuries. It may be traced back at least as far as the second-century Greek physician Galen, whose theories still had a surprising influence seventeen hundred years later. Entralgo summarizes the Galenic view of disease: "For Galen, 'disease' (*nosos, nosema*) is a preternatural condition (*diathesis para physin*) of the body, by virtue of which the physiological functions are affected directly . . . The illness of a person is always a condition of his body; outside of the diseased body—in the environment or in the soul—there can exist causes of disease, but not disease in the proper sense of the word. Thus, one of the *sex res non naturales*—the potential 'predisposing,' 'external,' or 'primitive' causes of Galenic aetiopathology—consists in affections of the soul. Any one of these six may, under certain conditions, serve as an external cause of disease, or may be an occasional *symptoma* of the morbid state."[3]

Galen believed that all disease was a corruption of one of the four bodily fluids, or humors, resulting in an imbalance which upset the normal communication between the mind and the body. This somatic pathology held sway throughout the Renaissance, though it was challenged in an ambiguous way by Thomas Sydenham in his classic seventeenth-century treatise on hysteria. Although Sydenham rejected a purely humoral explanation of this particular complaint, tracing it rather to a weakness of the mind, he unaccountably recommended a treatment wholly directed to the body: bleeding, purges, and blood "strengtheners."[4]

In the eighteenth century and the early part of the nineteenth, a controversy developed as to whether such "chronic" illnesses as hysteria were mental or physical in nature. After Boerhaave demonstrated that the so-called "humors" were in fact nothing else than elements or states of the blood, many physiologists turned from a humoral explanation of health and disease to one based on the nervous system. The leading figure in this movement was the Scottish physician William Cullen, whose theories had an enormous impact on medical thought. Cullen defined corporeal life as consisting in "the excitement of the nervous system, and especially of the brain, which unites the different parts, and forms them into a whole."[5] Disease, he believed, operates principally on the nervous system, either increasing its "excitability" or diminishing it, that is, producing either spasmodic or atonic symptoms.[6] Cullen's classification of mental disorders, or, as he termed them, "neuroses," had considerable influence in the eighteenth and nineteenth centuries. Of course these neuroses, like all diseases, were affections of the nervous system, but were distinguished in not resulting in idiopathic fever or local disease.

What Cullen did in identifying diseases like melancholia and mania with the nervous system was to locate them not in individual organs like the spleen, as with the old humoral pathology, but in the physical center of consciousness. In Cullen's system such diseases were still somatic, since in the eighteenth century the "nervous system" was strictly speaking a part of the body. In the nineteenth century the term came to be also applied to a person's mental state, so a "disease of the nervous system" could be regarded as either psychic or somatic.

The most important British work on this subject in the first half of the nineteenth century was James Cowles Prichard's *Treatise on Insanity and Other Disorders Affecting the Mind* (1835). In it he suggested that madness and allied diseases have a physical basis, though they should be dealt with "by moral treatment or by remedial means *suited to a disease of the mind,* often without any measures adapted to the removal of physical or bodily disorder."[7] Further, and equally important, Prichard identified the *causes* of mental illness as in many cases moral or mental: "Faulty education, an habitual want of self-control, a fickle over-sensitive character unaccustomed to and incapable of steady pursuits, the dominion of passions, vices of various kinds are among the circumstances." He dismissed the notion that madness was an idiopathic disease of the mind (that is, without secondary or predisposing diseases of the body). That notion, he stated, had been "abandoned by most enlightened physicians in England." So physicians for decades continued to search for physiological explanations and cures for neuroses. Still, the tendency was toward a more comprehensive psychotherapy, one which dealt with the mind as an entity and not simply an adjunct of the body where disease was concerned. What were termed the "moral" aspects of madness or neurosis—those relating to a person's character or habits of conduct—came to be emphasized in diagnosis and treatment as much as the physical aspects.

In Victorian fiction nervous ailments are usually depicted as arising from prolonged periods of overwork, self-doubt, and solitude. Lucy Snowe in Charlotte Brontë's *Villette* (ch. 15) must face being nearly alone during the long vacation at the school where she teaches, her only companion a helpless cretin in her care: "My heart almost died within me; miserable longings strained its chords. How long were the September days! How silent, how lifeless! How vast and void seemed the desolate premises! How gloomy the forsaken garden—grey now with the dust of a town-summer departed." The cretin, who seems to symbolize to Lucy the sense of her own inertness, becomes a tormenting emotional burden. With no vivid hope for an improvement in the circumstances of her life, Lucy at first consoles herself with the thought that God has especially chosen her for a kind of martyrdom. Then she begins building romantic daydreams around her attractive friend, Ginevra Fanshawe. Having projected her concept of her real self into the figure of the cretin, she mentally adopts Ginevra as a "heroine," a sort of ego-ideal: "One day, perceiving this growing illusion, I said, 'I really believe my nerves are getting overstretched: my mind has suffered somewhat too much; a malady is growing on it—what shall I do? How shall I keep well?' Indeed there was no way to keep well under the circumstances. At last a day and night of particularly agonizing depression were succeeded by physical illness: I perforce took to my bed." For over a week she lies in a "strange fever of the nerves and blood," able to sleep only once, and then only with the most ghastly nightmares. This is a typical pattern for what, later in the novel, Lucy calls "that strangest spectre, Hypochondria" (ch. 20), a disease of which the author had firsthand experience. There is the initial generating condition—a moral one—of fatigue, isolation, and self-consciousness; a secondary stage of crippling mental lassitude; and then bodily weakness, sleeplessness, and fever.

It is not easy today to imagine the anxiety occasioned by such an illness. Was the ailment dominantly a physical one, and if so would it follow the pattern of diseases like tuberculosis or cholera? Was it dominantly a psychological one, to follow the pattern of severe mania? In the fall of 1851 Charlotte Brontë was stricken by one of these puzzling complaints. "Before the autumn was far advanced," Mrs. Gaskell recounts, "the usual effects of her solitary life, and of the unhealthy situation of Haworth Parsonage, began to appear in the form of sick-headaches, and miserable, starting, wakeful nights." The conditions of Charlotte's life brought on these physiological symptoms which in turn, according to Mrs. Gaskell, created a depressive "mood": "Indigestion, nausea, headache, sleeplessness,—all combined to produce miserable depression of spirits." Then the melancholy sharply aggravated the physical symptoms. Charlotte wrote: "I am well aware myself that extreme and continuous depression of spirits has had much to do with the origin of the illness." Later that winter she had a fierce attack of depression followed by "internal congestion . . . and then inflammation," pains in the side, sleeplessness, slow fever, and loss of appetite. Understandably, her thoughts turned to that disease which had so recently carried off her two sisters. Much to her relief, however, her doctor informed her that her lungs had not been affected; the trouble lay only in a derangement of the liver, and could be alleviated by "medical discipline."[8]

A victim of one of these enigmatic constitutional complaints could easily become neurotic just trying to determine its source. One's incapacity for work might be both a symptom of the disease and one of its causes. So might one's indigestion. Patients never lost hope of finding, as Charlotte Brontë did, some physiological basis whose treatment would be the only way out of the vicious circle. If the disease begins with a state of psychic disorder, the restitution of health might begin with a natural and orderly physical life.

In *The Autobiography of Mark Rutherford* (ch. 3) Mark, after studying for the ministry at a Dissenting college, is sent "on probation" to preach to a congregation in the East of England. "Stimulated by the prospect" of his new life, he delivers his first sermon enthusiastically, only to discover on returning to his rooms that his faith when examined is much less secure than he had thought. This precipitates his first attack of "that most awful malady hypochondria." He develops a fixed idea that he is going mad; he prays for death; he loses all will to act. To combat this inertia a doctor prescribes stimulants, and Mark becomes dangerously reliant on alcohol. Professional help having failed him, Rutherford has to learn to deal with his hypochondria by himself. He offers the reader some practical advice in treating the disease: "The simpler and less stimulating the diet, the more likely it is that the sufferer will be able to watch through the wakeful hours without delirium, and the less likely it is that the general health will be impaired. Upon this point of health too much stress cannot be laid. It is difficult for the victim to believe that his digestion has anything to do with a disease which seems so purely spiritual, but frequently the misery will break up and yield, if it do not altogether disappear, by a little attention to physiology and a change of air."

In his case, as with Charlotte Brontë, the complaint does not disappear altogether. Hypochondria was usually chronic, that is, an abiding and integral fact of one's life. With such constitutional illnesses, states of affliction and of restored health were intermittent. The onset of the acute or critical phases of hypochondria, dyspepsia, or melancholia ordinarily occurred during periods of severe mental distress, often at times of religious doubt or doubt as to one's adequacy in filling his appointed place in life. The victim, believing that these questionings signified a breach of the state of health, felt himself destined to experience a pattern of disease before the state of health was once again temporarily restored. The pattern was one of combined existential and physiological symptoms, the two aggravating each other. As soon as one began to put his body in accord with the laws of nature, harmony of mind would ensue.

Today hypochondria is considered a disease of the mind—an imagined illness or a disposition to imagined illnesses—but in the nineteenth century it was a chronic disease of the whole person. According to Hooper's *Lexicon Medicum* (1839), it differed from melancholy in usually having "corporeal" rather than "mental" causes, commonly "a diseased condition of one or more of the digestive organs."⁹ Such a somatic etiology was then going out of fashion. Indeed, this description is a striking example of the persistence of Galenic theory. Originally the term hypochondria meant the area "below the cartilage," that is, the region between the breast-bone and the navel, containing the liver, the gall-bladder, the spleen, and so on. In Galenic medicine a disturbance in these "soft parts of the body" was thought to be caused by an imbalance in the humors. As Hooper's definition makes plain, medical science had not entirely discarded such theories in the Victorian period.

Although, according to Hooper, the source of hypochondria was physiological, the symptoms were both mental and physical. Mental symptoms were low spirits, *tedium vitae*, and misanthropy; the physical manifestations included "a troublesome flatulency in the stomach or bowels, acrid eructations [belching], costiveness, a copious discharge of pale urine, spasmodic pains in the head and other parts of the body, giddiness, dimness of sight, palpitations, general sleeplessness, and an utter inability in fixing on anything that demands vigour or courage."

Because hypochondria was regarded as a depression, both of the psyche and of the soma, cures usually involved various kinds of stimulation or invigoration. Tanner's *Index of Diseases*, a handbook for physicians, urged against the use of purgatives, sedatives, and narcotics. Instead it prescribed a variety of "strengtheners": strychnine, or nux vomica; phosphate of zinc and bark; bromide of potassium; and cod liver oil. Other remedies mentioned include "Shower bath. Sea bathing.

Turkish bath. Nourishing food. Exercise in the open air. Riding on horse-back. Physical training. Gymnastics."[10]

One victim of hypochondria, T. H. Huxley, regularly took strychnine, and also quinine, a universal remedy of the time which was used to strengthen the appetite and improve digestion. In addition, following the conventional treatment of the disease, he put great faith in exercising his body and resting his mind. "You cannot think how well I am," one of his letters reads, "so long as I walk eight or ten miles a day, and don't work too much."[11]

Hypochondria and melancholia were similar enough that often they were not clinically distinguished. Hysteria, however, was seen as an illness of a wholly different kind. In ancient medicine it was thought to afflict only women and, as its name suggests, to be centered in the uterus. Sydenham declared that this sexual differentiation was groundless, since hysteria and hypochondriasis were as alike "as one egg is to another." Although the more advanced medical thought in the nineteenth century discounted the theory that hysteria was a woman's disease, not all physicians did. Hooper's *Lexicon* stated that the ailment "comes on soon after the age of puberty; makes its onset suddenly and violently, so as to deprive the patient of all sense and voluntary motion; is accompanied with a sensation of a ball rising upwards in the throat, so as to threaten suffocation; is attended usually with much spasmodic affection; is more apt to terminate in epilepsy than in any other disease; and, on dissection, its morbid appearances are confined principally to the uterus and ovaria."[12]

Victorian medical authorities did their best to distinguish chronic mind-body complaints from one another; but doing so was a slippery business, since personal observation was so influenced by traditional conceptions. What often happened was that the descriptions were so ambiguous as to apply to almost any sort of symptoms. For example, Sir James Clark, physician-in-ordinary to the Queen, reported that with "nervous dyspepsia" the victim is sometimes very hungry, sometimes not at all hungry, sometimes diarrheic, sometimes constipated, and usually flatulent; his urine is "pale and copious." Any reader of that description might easily persuade himself he was dyspeptic. Or, given this account of "climacteric disease" (premature old age) in Beale's *Laws of Health*, anyone past middle life might feel the need to seek treatment. The ailment "is characterised by a loss of flesh in advanced life, without any obvious cause of exhaustion, accompanied by a quick pulse, and great alteration of expression of the face." Other symptoms are fatigue, headache, swelling in the legs, "but no deficiency of urine." Although the manifestations of climacteric disease were mostly physical, its origins were thought to be primarily moral. Sir James lists some of the causes as mental exhaustion, overattention to business matters, and a sedentary life coupled with "an habitual system of full living." Since the illness could be traced to bad living and an unhealthy state of mind, the best treatment, according to Beale, was "a cheerful prospect of futurity, resulting from contemplation of a well-spent life, associated with the faith and fervour of true Christianity."[13]

Such diseases as hypochondria, hysteria, dyspepsia, and climacteric disease were not psychosomatic in the modern sense of the word. They were not disorders of the body occasioned by disorders of the mind; they were constitutional complaints with physical and mental causes and symptoms, and they required treatment involving both the mind and the body. Although the trend in the nineteenth century was toward conceiving of them as essentially "moral" illnesses, the somatic bias of Galenic physiology was strong enough to affect diagnosis, etiology, and therapeutics. Galenic tradition had associated each of the four humors with its own characteristic disposition as well as its own physiognomy. By the nineteenth century medical thought had abandoned the role of humors in both psychology and medicine, but not, as some dictionaries and health manuals show, the roles of physiognomy and temperament. For example, the man of phlegmatic (or lymphatic) temperament was said to be recognized by his "light, sandy or whitish hair; light grey eyes; pallid unhealthy whiteness of skin almost bereft of hair; cold surface." He often would have a large frame and muscles, but would be deficient in strength. He was not easily aroused or disposed to exert himself. The sanguine man typically had "light brown hair, blue eyes, a fair, florid complexion." His arteries and veins were "large and superficial, and the pulse free and frequent; the body often large and tall, and inclined in middle age to obesity." His chest was unusually large, as were his thoracic organs. His "animal functions [were] splendidly developed." Although open and genial, the sanguine person lacked self-control. The bilious (or fibrous or choleric) man had black curly hair, dark eyes, a swarthy complexion, as well as "a thick, rough, hairy skin, and a strong and full pulse," a hyperactive heart, "firmness of muscle and general energy," and a stoic disposition.[14]

The melancholy man also had dark eyes, hair, and complexion, but his hair was "lank and straight, and the skin of a leaden and unhealthy hue": "It is observed, likewise, that persons of this temperament are tall, have long necks, narrow shoulders, flat breasts, long narrow heads laterally flattened, with expanded foreheads, well-proportioned countenances, small acute features, thin lips, and they are slow and sedate in their manners and habits." By contrast with the sanguine type, the melancholic possessed a slow pulse, muscles which were neither firm nor full, and a deficiency of "assimilated vigour." His disposition was nearly the opposite of the sanguine: "All the universe seems inconvenient to the melancholy man, and whether his gloomy sensibility arise from a morbid body or a mistaken view of Divine Providence, his self-complacency is alike disturbed, and he feels his individuality not as his faith dictates, but as his senses inform him, so that he is oppressed by the weight of his own helplessness, instead of casting himself with all his cares upon the Almighty." To these four categories James Gregory in the eighteenth century had added the Nervous temperament, reflecting his and the age's interest in the nervous system. People of the "nervous" type were said to have permitted their brains and nervous systems to predominate; "their blood is apt to be disordered because their digestive functions suffer from the exhaustion of their nerves, induced by study and excessive sensibility."[15] While seldom enjoying robust health, these people usually attained a good age.

With the humors theory out of favor, nineteenth-century medical authorities commonly offered systemic explanations for differences in temperament. It seemed evident, for example, that the digestive system predominated in the phlegmatic temperament, the circulatory and respiratory in the sanguine, the muscular or locomotor in the choleric, and the cerebro-neural system in both the melancholy and nervous (temperament types often not distinguished in writings of that time). This constitutional imbalance produced in each type its own "diathesis," a natural predisposition to a disease or category of diseases. Unless the mental and physical systems were brought back into balance the individual might find himself in the grip of some crippling constitutional ailment. Thus, the melancholy temperament was a "predisposing condition" to melancholia and hypochondriasis. The nervous temperament was susceptible to nervous dyspepsia, though, as one doctor observed, "Indigestion, when protracted, becomes complicated with distemper levelling the moral with the physical world—hypochondriasis, the last expression of dyspepsia and mental prostration."[16] The sanguine temperament, especially in women, was thought to be often affected with hysteria.

Dr. Beale offers this illuminating account of how temperament may morbidly influence both mind and body: "The nervous temperament is characterized by a highly developed nervous system; there is extreme sensitiveness to all impressions; the passions when evolved are impetuous, and the countenance animated and expressive; in such persons all is excitement and mobility. The great development of the nervous centres gives an intensity to the sentiments and passions, which produce considerable influence on some functions of the body, and gives rise to various derangements. When the imagination is cultivated and indulged, without due restriction by the higher power of reason, where it is allowed to run wild and carry with it the emotions and the passions, the consequences are often lamentable. Lord Byron was a grand example. With the highest endowment of the intellectual faculties, he permitted his imagination to deprive him of much happiness, and in his later writings, to render them almost unfit for perusal."[17]

The impact of the temperaments theory was so pervasive that doctors (and their patients) could never have made the sort of diagnostic and therapeutic distinctions between mental and physical ailments which is almost routine today. Fever was fever. Whether it was a contagious fever like typhus or a nervous fever like cerebritis, the treatment was the same: a medicinal or psychological depressant. The *Cyclopaedia of Practical Medicine* recommends for brain fever either general or local bloodletting as well as "active purgatives."[18] Whatever moral treatment was applied would have a corresponding effect—on the mind first, then on the body.

Not only did certain diseases display concurrent and corresponding mind-body symptoms, they also had phases in which the effects were predominantly mental or physical. A disease which began as a neurosis might pass into an acute stage which was mainly physiological and could be fatal. We are told, for example, that one could eventually die of climacteric disease.[19] Brain-fever could also hasten its victim to an early grave, as it does to both Clare and Lucy in *Richard Feverel.* Dr. Gully, the celebrated hydropath, wrote a treatise in 1880 which described three stages of "fever."[20] The first, nervous fever, is occasioned by moral causes such as business anxiety or disappointment in love, and by physical causes, of which there are only two: exhaustion and overindulgence in sex. The sufferer "finds it impossible to go on any longer, takes to his bed, and frets and tosses about it, intolerant of all and everything about him. Sleep [is] exceedingly broken and excessively dreamy, waking to a sense of intense wretchedness instead of refreshment, or else brief fits of stupor with long intervals of waking." If the victim of nervous fever assumes unwise eating habits, "so as to induce serious congestion of the organs of digestion," he will pass to a second stage, "versatile fever." From there on the morbid condition of the body may advance, with a gradually increasing "nervous loss of power," until the third stage, typhoid fever, is reached.

Admittedly not all doctors of the time would have seen typhoid and nervous fever as phases of the same disease, though the evolutionary concept of disease was very popular. As a writer in the *British and Foreign Medical Review* put it, the process begins with the person's pattern of life; to violate the laws of health in a general way is to invite specific afflictions with unpredictable consequences: "The epicure, the gourmand, the mere man of pleasure, the over-stimulated, over-cultivated woman, the anxious care-worn professional man, the toiling, striving, struggling man of business, sooner or later feels that some 'screw is loose,' that the body has been too long trifled with, and what is sown is about to be reaped. Whether it is called indigestion, liver disease, hypochondriasis, abdominal congestion, exhausted nervous power, chronic rheumatism or gout, whatever local habitation the disease may have taken, or whatever theory may be adopted to explain it, the causes have been much the same—a neglect of organic laws of long continuance, daily irregularities in small omissions or commissions, bringing the body into such a condition that some more active, more apparent, and greater cause brings on the disease. The patient himself is well aware that he has passed the Rubicon which separates him from health . . . that those vital functions which, like growth and life, had before been performed silently, unconsciously, and unerringly, go on so no longer."[21]

Since at least the predisposing condition of disease was a general falling away from a life of health, the best cure was to treat the patient as comprehensively as possible. Nature pathology, which had a widespread appeal at the time, attempts to bring the patient back to a natural state (the state of health) by "natural" means. As E. K. Ledermann recently put it, nature pathology treats the person, not the disease; it "treats patients according to the holistic principle and advocates healthy living as far as it is possible to avoid illness."[22]

This helps to explain the formidable influence of hydropathy among Victorian intellectuals, those who felt they had abused their minds and bodies by anxiety and overwork and suffered mentally and physically as a result. Hydropathy was as much a rest cure as a water cure, and the hydropath acted as both physician and psychiatrist. He was a quack in both, but the baths, the country air, the enforced relaxation, and the long walks certainly did no harm to mind-weary Victorian writers. Gully's practice was an application of the principle that physical morbidity is brought on by a morbid condition of the mind. He insisted that his patients stop reading and think little while under his care. During the troubled years between the *Beagle* voyage and completion of *The Origin of Species* Darwin was a frequent patient of Dr. Gully's. He once exclaimed happily that the treatment encouraged "complete stagnation of mind; I have ceased to think even of Barnacles!" Bulwer found especially agreeable the fact that in the early stages of the treatment the intellect was effectively put to sleep, and "even the memory grows far less tenacious of its impressions."[23]

Tennyson was one who passed from what Dr. Gully would call the moral to the physical stage of illness. In 1840 he invested heavily in a philanthropic scheme for wood-carving by machinery. Gradually he saw the project collapse, and with it his financial resources. Other personal problems developed at the same time; soon he began to suffer from a whole variety of physical complaints and gave himself up to treatment at Cheltenham Spa. In 1847 he discovered Dr. Gully and became a disciple. "It is a terribly long process," he wrote at this time, "but then what price is too high for health, and health of mind is involved with health of body."[24] Another water-patient was John Ruskin. In 1847, when his mother had interfered to sever his relations with Effie Gray, Ruskin went to Oxford for a meeting of the British Association. It was a period of severe difficulty, and after a few weeks he was on the point of nervous collapse. "I have not one moment of profitably spent time to look back to while I was here," he wrote, "and much useless labour and disappointed hope, and I can neither bear the excitement of being in the society where the play of mind is constant and rolls *over* me like heavy wheels; nor the pain of being alone."[25] It was then that he went off to Leamington for five weeks in the care of Dr. Jephson.

Nature-pathologies such as hydropathy and others which flourished a century ago are the bane of the therapeutic specialist. They arise in times of medical skepticism and lose influence only when the medical specialist displays a convincing competence in treating disease. In the latter half of the nineteenth century, with the development of psychotherapy as a separate discipline and of improved materia medica in somatic therapeutics, the various natural therapies—hydropathy, Change of Climate, kinesotherapy—fell from respectability. Diseases were parceled out to special practitioners: madness became the province of one kind of doctor and malaria the province of another.

From our perspective the older therapies may seem unanalytical and quirkish, but they approached disease in a way which some modern medical philosophers have found admirable. Using a holistic concept of health they regarded the patient as a totality of mind and body and considered the circumstances of his life as part of the whole. Victorian doctors, nature pathologists or not, were as interested in what their patients believed about themselves and in how they conducted themselves generally as in what they ate and drank. In short, they embraced what Félix Martí-Ibáñez has termed the biographical concept of disease, "which considers it a dynamic process that develops across time in the patient's life, as against the ontological concept, which considers disease an autonomous entity endowed with a natural history."[26]

WHILE VICTORIAN medicine was moving toward holism by concerning itself with "moral" causes, symptoms, and remedies, Victorian psychology was annexing physiology. In British psychology the dominant—indeed the only important—school of thought had come to center its attention on the Cartesian division of body from mind. It sought physical explanations for mental behavior and mental explanations for physical behavior, hoping to find verifiable links between the sound mind and the sound body. Metaphysical dualists after Descartes assumed that the mind, receiving sensory messages from the body, acts through the judicial agency of the will upon the body, which then influences the world of matter beyond the body. This proposition was accepted by most psychologists and physiologists, but it raised a most troublesome problem in mechanics. As Charles Spearman puts it: "On the one hand, a psyche, mind, or soul that is conscious, that knows, feels, and wills; on the other, a complex of material particles which, when the last word is said, do nothing but push and pull each other; in fact *are* nothing but pushers and pullers. Surely, such a psyche and such a body are strange bedfellows!"[27] The difficulty is in imagining two different orders of things inhabiting the same space. In a way the mechanistic approach of eighteenth-century associationist psychologists eased this conceptual problem; by reducing the mind itself to a system of pushers and pullers, this school saw the mind and body as operating according to the same sort of laws. However, associationism proved inadequate in three ways: it did not sufficiently ground itself in experiment or in physiology; it left no room for the traditional concept of the vital, conscious will; and it did not take enough notice of individual character types and behavioral characteristics. In short, it was too theoretical, too mechanistic, too inflexible. So, at any rate, the reaction to it seems to demonstrate. Such fads as mesmerism and spiritualism in the thirties and forties explored the possibilities of the dynamic will. Phrenology sought explanations for behavioral differences and, perhaps more important, tried to account for psychological patterns by using a physiological approach, by tracing disposition to the configuration of the brain, the center of consciousness.

Phrenology was in particular esteem in the early Victorian decades, even among intelligent and relatively cautious students of the mind, but in 1846 W. B. Carpenter published an essay which convincingly outlined the case against phrenology and in favor of an empirical physiological psychology. The piece, a review of Daniel Noble's *The Brain and Its Physiology*, had long-range implications no doubt unperceived by its author. Accepting the contention of phrenologists that the brain was the center of consciousness, Carpenter agreed that to map the brain was to go a long way toward charting the mind. Insisting on the singular value of comparative anatomy, he urged that something could be learned about man's nervous system by studying that of animals. Demonstrating the application of general neurology to the study of psychology, he suggested that a whole range of human activities hitherto classed as "mental" were in fact physical in nature. Carpenter's summation shows how easily the new physiological psychology could adapt itself to the old associationist terminology: "The points for which we contend are simply these:—the independent character of the sensory ganglia as the instruments of sensation and of consensual actions,—the superadded character of the cerebrum, as the organ by whose instrumentality ideas are formed and reasoning processes carried on,—and the mixed character of the emotions and propensities, as compounded of *ideas* and the *simple feelings* of pleasure and pain."[28]

Carpenter was not offering a new concept of mental activity; he was only locating activities in certain areas of the brain and nervous system. Actually there is a traditional hierarchy of the human system reflected in his account: at the bottom are the automatic (or animal) functions of the body, governed by the sensory and cerebral apparatuses together; atop these, anatomically as well as metaphysically, are the intellectual operations of the cerebrum, which in its highest role is answerable to no other part of the system. What Carpenter referred to as his "conviction of the uniformity of Nature" was thus demonstrated: mind and matter are linked by means of the nervous system. Considerations of mind shade almost imperceptibly into those of matter, yet the ultimate sovereignty of the mind is left unchallenged. Because of his eminence among physiologists Carpenter's conclusions were given considerable weight. In 1845 he had been appointed Fullerian Professor of Physiology at the Royal Institution; later he held, among other positions, the Professorship of Physiology and Forensic Medicine at University College and Hospital, London. His *Principles of Human Physiology* (1842) remained, according to Huxley, the standard English work on the subject for thirty years.[29] The fourth edition of this text (1852) contained an extensive outline of psychology, later expanded into a separate volume, *Principles of Mental Physiology* (1874), which, like the original *Physiology*, went through a number of editions.

Carpenter's importance in the field of physiological psychology was as a synthesizer and expositor of the findings of other scientists. Charles Bell, a British physiologist and surgeon, as early as 1811 had used anatomical experimentation to distinguish between the two kinds of spinal nerve roots, the sensory and the motor.[30] He further formulated the doctrine (later clarified and reinforced by the German physiologist Johannes Müller) of the specific energies of nerves, that is, that the properties of nerves themselves influence what is perceived in the mind. These discoveries had the importance of setting out the direction which the new approach to psychology was to take. The brain and central nervous system came to be regarded by most psychologists as the key to understanding the operation of the mind, at least its involvement in perception and motor activity. In the 1820s Pierre Flourens in France was publishing the results of his anatomical dissections of the brain, in which were distinguished the specific functions of the cerebrum, cerebellum, medulla, and corpora quadrigemina. These he related to the functions of the nerves and spinal cord. Müller and Marshall Hall carried out significant experiments in reflex action; Wundt, Helmholtz, and Fechner in the measurement of reactions. Broca, Fritsch, Hitzig, and David Ferrier provided a much more detailed geography of the brain and its functions.

As experimental physiology dug ever deeper into the mysteries of mind, psychologists belonging to the old associationist tradition were increasingly impressed by the results. Alexander Bain devoted a lengthy chapter of *The Senses and the Intellect* to the physiology of the brain and nerves, proclaiming that "the time has now come when many of the striking discoveries of the Physiologists relative to the nervous system should find a recognized place in the Science of Mind."[31] It now seemed clear that one could not speak knowingly about mental behavior without at least some previous study of the body. Another associationist, John Stuart Mill, was somewhat more cautious than Bain, but he did revise a passage in the 1851 edition of his *On the Logic of the Moral Sciences* (ch. iv), eliminating a respectful reference to phrenology and observing that the connection between "mental peculiarities" and variations in the nervous system "is now in a fair way of being found out."

The new psychology promised an explanation not only of personality differences, but of mental disease as well. Thomas Laycock, a pioneer in the study of unconscious cerebration, observed in his *Mind and Brain* (1860): "It appears certain that no morbid change, however minute, can take place in the body, without a concurrent change, although not cognisable by observation, in the mind. Hence it is that the Greek word for disease, *pathos*—the root of the term *pathology*—which expresses the science of disease, was also used to express mental states of suffering, and is equally the root of *pathetic*." As we have seen, the foundation for this approach to medicine was laid in the eighteenth century, with physicians like Cullen speculating that the basis of life (and of health) was in the state of the nervous system. Now physiology seemed on the verge of verifying those speculations. Benjamin Brodie, court surgeon to George IV and William IV and president of the Royal Society for thirteen years, had developed a particular interest in the way injuries to the brain can affect sensation, speech, and locomotion. By 1854 he had become convinced that "mental alienation is generally the result of some wrong condition of the body, either functional or organic."[32]

The titles of such major works as Bain's *Mind and Body*, Laycock's *Mind and Brain*, and Henry Maudsley's *Body and Will* tell their own story. As Robert M. Young demonstrates in his splendid study of the subject, in the nineteenth century "the history of research in psychology should be viewed as a development away from philosophy and toward general biology."[33] Yet, with all this research little progress was recorded in resolving the old mind-brain dilemma. Experiments dealing with the *physical* aspects of consciousness—sensation, volition, motor response—yielded no method for the inductive study of *mental* activities—imagination, intellect, emotion, will. That part of psychology which dealt with mental observations was in most cases a further systematization, thanks to Bain and Mill, of traditional associationism. Having accepted associationist explanations of the automatic nature of most mental processes, physiological psychology tried to find the bases for these processes in the material strata of the constitution, particularly in the brain and nervous system. The tendency was to accept and then try to verify the theory that human activity was fundamentally both automatic and physiological.

Beginning with sensory activity and motor response, physiologists seemed to be consigning more and more of man to the realm of natural mechanism. To some this had disturbing implications, for, as Brodie noted, a faith both in God and in man's special place in the universe had been traditionally predicated on the separate, spiritual nature of mind: "However immeasurable the distance may be between the mightiest intellect of man and that of the Deity, it must be admitted that they belong to the same mode of existence, and I do not understand how anyone who believes in the existence of a Deity can receive without hesitation the doctrine that any kind of mind can be nothing more than the result of a peculiar arrangement of the molecules of matter."[34]

To Brodie the fact that the brain changes while the mind has its own principle of stability was evidence that the two were not the same thing. Other scientists pointed out that since physiology, for all its efforts, had come nowhere near an objective account of mental activities, mind must be of a different order of things from the rest of creation. They reasoned that the only true knowledge of the mind is subjective, while what we know objectively—whatever we can see, touch, and experiment with— must be divisible, as all matter is. Since the mind is intangible, it is also indivisible and therefore spiritual. Daniel Noble expressed it thus: "If there be peculiar characteristics which more than others distinguish the conscious EGO from mere body, these, I conceive, are Spirituality and Unity of essence. Have we not the same assurance from pure consciousness, that the ME which thinks, is not material, as we have from the sense consciousness, that body is extended and an aggregate of atoms?"[35]

Noble was here falling back on the Cartesian view that while body has extension but cannot think, mind can think but has no extension, and that the evidence for mind is our consciousness of it. But the old problem inherent in the Cartesian split remained: still the mind is located in the brain; and not only is it located there, but it acts upon it in an as yet unexplained way. As Huxley put it, the mind is presumed to be able to change the body: "Thus the soul becomes a centre of force. But, at the same time, the distinction between spirit and matter vanishes; inasmuch as matter, according to a tenable hypothesis, may be nothing but a multitude of centres of force."[36] In other words, if matter is force and the active part of mind is also force, the two need not be regarded as substantially different. Huxley's tentative answer to philosophical materialism lay in a dual-aspect parallelism: mental states correspond to physical states but do not interact with them. In fact, the two kinds of phenomena may well be different aspects of the same occurrence. This position, also taken by Herbert Spencer and G. H. Lewes, came to be the dominant one among nineteenth-century physiological psychologists. The theory had a convenient application to the sorts of "nervous disorders" discussed earlier, for it obviated the whole question of whether the physical derangement causes the mental, or vice versa. Lewes offers the example of a melancholic mood: when considered subjectively it is a mental state—as such, its causes may be "disappointed affection or a fall in the Funds." However, "the same mood is also a state of the organism and considered objectively it is a change in the secretions, and an alteration of the nervous level; the sequences are in this case as exclusively physiological as in the other they are psychological."[37]

Although this new brand of dualism sought to maintain separate concepts of spirit and matter, the effect of the doctrine was to break down the distinction between the two. They are coalesced in such a way that they lose all separate identity unless for convenience's sake we want to think of them separately. Bain, who adopted the parallelist hypothesis, observed: "When physical nourishment, or a physical stimulant, restores a cheerful tone, it is not a bodily fact causing a mental fact by a direct law of causation . . . The line of mental sequence is . . . not mind causing body, and body causing mind, but mind-body giving birth to mind-body; a much more intelligible position." The chief result of the influence of parallelism was to threaten the concept of the autonomy of mind. For it was now much easier to see what Bain calls "mind-body" states as totally under the influence of bodily states than it had been under the old Cartesianism. "We find that the mental property," he declared, "in alliance with this corporeal aggregate, is remarkably susceptible to every physical effect and every trifling disturbance. In a word, mind, as known to us in our constitution, is the very last thing we should set up as an independent power, swaying and sustaining the powers of the natural world."[38]

Conservative physiologists were willing to acknowledge that *most* of the activities of the mind were automatic, as were *most* of the activities of the body. They also conceded the influence of the latter on the former. But, they held, there must also be a reciprocal influence, one which is not automatic. Carpenter stated in *Mental Physiology*, "I cannot regard myself, either Intellectually or Morally, as a mere puppet, pulled by suggesting-strings; any more than I can *dis*regard that vast body of Physiological evidence, which proves the direct and immediate relation between Mental and Corporeal agency."[39]

The issue of the Will now became crucial. On its existence depended not only a faith in the mind's power to act on its own, but also a belief in the special dignity of man and his moral nature. Without the will the mind has no self-sustaining power, no special identity, no health apart from the body's health. May we not regard the will, Noble asked, "in itself and in its consequences, as distinguishing man to an incalculable extent from the lower animals? Is it not by the agency of the will that our consciousness becomes its own object? Is it not by the same power that we analyse, and exercise control over our mental states; that we rise to abstractions and general notions, thought of causality, distinguish between virtue and vice, grasp some idea, however obscure, of the Infinite?"[40]

To the physiological psychologist the power of controlling mental states really meant the power of influencing one's *physis*, nature, or animal self. All mental states originate within either the brain and nervous system or the sensory apparatus. Therefore one has no control over their origin. Still, as Noble observed, they are "more or less governable by voluntary effort" when the mind is healthy, when "numerous and varied forms of consciousness [are] present as inducements to action from which the choices can be made."[41] The power of the will, wrote Carpenter, "is exerted in the *purposive selection*, from among those objects of consciousness which Sensations from without and the working of the internal 'Mechanism of Thought and Feeling' bring before the Ego . . . of that which shall be determinately followed up."[42] What delusions and dreams have in common, Henry Holland stated, is a weakening of the selective will, a "loss, partial or complete, of power to distinguish between unreal images created within the sensorium and the actual perceptions drawn from the external senses, thereby giving to the former the semblance and influence of realities."[43]

The will also governs physio-psychic states in restraining the passions and appetites and moderating the claims they make upon the judgment. These also are generated somatically and automatically but may be regulated when the will is healthy. Carpenter uses the analogy of "the independent locomotive power of a horse under the guidance and control of a skilled rider." To extend his analogy, the will can spur the horse as well as rein it in. As Brodie says, through volition "there is an impulse communicated from the mind to the brain, and thence to the nerves, and from these to the other organs, and producing a marked change in the direction of the latter."[44]

In these ways the action of the will *might* be seen to demonstrate the power of mind over body. All physiological psychologists described it as functioning within the neural complex, however, and the question remained: was it something separate from that complex or only an element of it? Especially in the 1860s and 1870s there was a tendency to see the will not as an abiding faculty of the mind, not in fact abiding at all. Malcolm Guthrie in an essay-review of Carpenter's *Mental Physiology* expressed a common impatience with the old-fashioned "faculty" concept of volition: "The phrase 'The Will' is a vicious term. It has two meanings.

Properly speaking, it is the succession of volitions, or volitional states; *i.e.*, the successive predominances of motives in the Emotional Volitional, or of the Practical Reason. Whatever predominates for the time being is the Will for the time being, and the succession of volitions for a life-time forming an aggregate is 'The Will' of a man; that is to say, the totality of his volitions. But it is often used as identical with one, or a combination, of human activities."[45]

A common way of describing these transient volitions was as expenditures of acquired energy or force. Henry Maudsley, who wrote widely on the volitional aspects of insanity, stated in his *Physiology and Pathology of the Mind* that "volition or will, used in a general or abstract sense, does not denote any actual entity, but simply expresses the due co-ordinate activity of the supreme centres of mental force, not otherwise than as the co-ordinate activity of the spinal cord or medulla oblongata might be said to represent its will—the faculty in both cases bring commonly an acquired one in man."[46] But even seeing these volitional states as either purely somatic or parallel with somatic states, physiology could not clearly account for them—their presence and absence, their intensity and duration. Even if an innate and permanent mind-force, a "Will," is discounted, what is the body-force which produces volitions? Some people seem constitutionally to have more capacity for decisiveness than others: where does it come from? This was only one aspect of a larger question which physiology was hard put to deal with: how do we explain physiologically the individual variations in behavior patterns? What makes one man an aesthete and another a philistine? Why does one man thrive under pressure of work and another collapse under the same pressure? Associationist psychology had given an elaborate account of *general* patterns of mental behavior, but had not adequately interpreted *idiosyncrasies of disposition*. In discrediting phrenology's anatomical approach to these questions physiologists discredited the only modern school of psychology with a somatic explanation of character traits.

The old classical theory of temperaments was still available, and in France and Germany such physiological psychologists as Wundt and Müller were assimilating the temperaments theory into the new psychology, adapting it as necessary. As A. A. Roback has noted, British psychologists have never been comfortable with classification; they "seem to fall into it as a concession." Although in his *Pathology of Mind* Maudsley spoke generally of nervous, sanguine and melancholy temperaments and acknowledged a "basis of truth" in the temperaments-psychology, he concluded that the system was too imprecise to be "of real use." Laycock, on the other hand, found the concept of temperament helpful in explaining volitional differences in terms of force: "The word 'sanguine' . . . is applied to denote the mental character of a man who, feeling intuitively the vigour of his forces, sees no difficulties in the way of attaining his projects . . . There is not only in the sanguine man a richer blood, but also a larger development of lung, and of heart and blood vessels, with a greater motor power and vital activity, so that a large amount of force is both acquired and expended in a given time."[47]

When Bain came to write his *Study of Character* he adapted the new concept of will as mind-body force to a simplified version of the doctrine of temperaments. He classified temperaments as strong or weak, masculine or feminine, with the relative amount of "spontaneous energy" being the distinguishing criterion. Women, he wrote, and men with little spontaneous energy are of the emotional, as opposed to the active temperament: "There is a physical constitution formed for emotion, and not unfrequently marked by the exterior characteristic of a rounded and full habit of body, a constitution of great vigour in the secreting organs, and less inclined to muscularity. This is one of the most probable general peculiarities of the feminine temperament, as it is a peculiarity wherein some of the other Races stand contrasted with our own." The way in which Bain conceives of spontaneous energy is a good example of parallelist thinking. Energy (or "force" or "vigor") can be seen as a purely physiological trait; it can also be seen as moral power, as when he identifies it as the source of "Endurance, Patience, Courage, and Self-Reliance."[48] It is the concept of the will formulated in ambiguously psychosomatic terminology. By making it the basis of both temperament and character, psychologists like Bain offered what seemed to be a plausible somatic explanation for personality differences.

If temperament is the original bodily and mental constitution, "character" is that plus training. It is the developed self, the superaddition of experience to the foundation of temperament through the agencies of will and intelligence. Mill tells of having "pondered painfully" the doctrine of Necessity as applied to the mind. The doctrine was, he felt, discouraging because not "morally beneficial." He could not abandon the associationist belief in the automatic nature of individual actions, but at the same time he saw it as neglecting the role of moral responsibility in human life. At length he found a way out of his dilemma. The passage in which he relates the solution is well known: "I perceived, that the word Necessity, as a name for the doctrine of Cause and Effect applied to human action, carried with it a misleading association; and that this association was the operative force in the depressing and paralysing influence which I had experienced: I saw that *though our own character is formed by circumstances, our own desires can do much to shape those circumstances;* and that what is really inspiriting and ennobling in the doctrine of free-will, is the conviction that we have real power over the formation of our own character; that *our will, by influencing some of our circumstances, can modify our future habits or capabilities of willing.* All this was consistent with the doctrine of circumstances, or rather, was that doctrine itself, properly understood."[49] This particular "train of thought," Mill tells us, not only helped him through a crisis in his own mental history, but was also "fitted to render a similar service to others."

Mill's theory of character did seem to render a service to physiological psychologists. Carpenter, for example, gave the passage just quoted a prominent place in the preface to his *Mental Physiology.* The writings of Bain and Maudsley reflect a like influence. What the physiological psychologists must have found especially appealing in the theory was Mill's distinction between "our own desires" and "our . . . habits or capabilities of willing." Although Mill appears to see these faculties as mental, some pathologists of the mind came to assign the first of them to the psyche, the second to the soma. The Victorian pioneer in the reform of mental therapy, Daniel Hake Tuke, distinguished between "the wish or desire to do a certain thing (in accordance with the etymon *voluntas*), and the power to perform it. A man wills to walk, but his will is powerless to move his legs; yet the will in the sense employed in the first clause, is in full force. It is the motor centre which is in a morbid condition or paralysed. On the other hand, when a physician says that, in a case of hysterical paralysis, the will is paralysed, he means that the very wish or desire to move the limb is wanting." In the view of physiologists the building of character acts to program, as we would say now, the first kind of will into the very structure of the nervous system, storing up through daily habit the capacity for active response in particular situations. "The strong or well-formed character which a well-fashioned will implies," Maudsley wrote, "is the result of good training applied to a well-constituted original nature; and the character is not directly determined by the will, but in any particular act determines the will." Although we cannot will a change in character, he adds, we can will a change in our circumstances "which subsequently gradually modify it."[50]

Character, then, is the complex of volitional potentialities. When it is "well-formed" in a life of decisive action, moral and intellectual decisions are made unconsciously and spontaneously through force of habit. In such decisions the "will" is little more than a predisposing condition of the mind-body, a volitional state with nothing which could be called autonomy. And yet the will which *fashions* character seems to be its own principle of authority, as both Mill and Maudsley suggest.

The Victorian concept of character offered a workable synthesis of old and new ideas in psychology. It accommodated, though in a simplified form, the classical theory of temperament; it adapted the associationist theory of mental habit to the new interest in neurology; and at the same time it found a distinct and necessary place for will and judgment in human conduct. Moral responsibility became even more imperative, for long-range decisions were seen as irrevocably implanted in the whole constitution. As Maudsley declared, the individual has "a solemn responsibility under which he is to determine rationally in himself, by help of circumstances, that which may thereby be determined in his future conduct, and in some measure in his prosperity." As in medical thought, the tendency in Victorian psychology was toward a moral physiology. The "will" and the "nervous system" having been denominated as the centers of vital growth and action, a truly psycho-physical concept of health evolved, for those centers were neither wholly mental, nor wholly physical, but both at once. The immediate cause of chronic disease was their failure in a physical sense, but the predisposing condition was their failure in a mental or moral sense. Dr. Beale wrote that *mens sana in corpore sano* was "not a mere dream."[51]

CHAPTER 3

The Thoroughly Healthy Mind:
Victorian Criticism

NINETEENTH-CENTURY moral physiology was reflected not only in the specialized language of science but in the more common vocabulary of the literary critic. In both cases morality, psychology, and health were related concerns. Macaulay traced the luxuries of Walpole's prose to an "unhealthy and disorganized mind"; Rousseau's books, wrote Carlyle, "like himself, are what I call unhealthy; not the good sort of Books"; Richard Holt Hutton found in Clough's verse an "almost morbid craving for a firm base on the absolute realities of life"; Leslie Stephen confessed that his gorge rose whenever he encountered Swift's "morbid interest in the physically disgusting."[1]

The Victorian critic believed that he should diagnose a work, looking for signs of disease or soundness, then looking further for causes of the disclosed condition. To read new poetry, Walter Bagehot declared, one must surrender his mind to the "delicate task of detecting the healthiness or unhealthiness of familiar states of feeling."[2] Today that sort of clinical vocabulary strikes us as crude and unpalatable. Behind it we sense those "unfamiliar states of feeling" whose evaluation, Bagehot tells us, is a delicate task. But more than personal states of feeling are involved here; words like "wholesome," "sound," "morbid," "diseased," when applied to an imaginative work or its author, conveyed much more than the general sense of approval or disapproval they do in common use today. They expressed a concept of the healthy mind about which there was a general accord. By exploring that concept we not only illuminate Victorian critical theory but also show how the medical and psychological theories discussed in the last chapter were evolving into a metaphysical model.

"The greatest poetry," Leslie Stephen wrote, "like the highest morality, is the product of a thoroughly healthy mind." His comparison between moral and creative excellence is not casually made. Like most Victorian critics he believed that they should be—and are in the "healthy" mind— functionally related. What F. W. Roe has said of Carlyle's critical theory may be almost universally applied: "Art is moral because intellect and morality are indistinguishable in the sound mind." Therefore it is a sign of health when all sensibilities are moral; and when the moral sense is detached from any part of the conceptualizing process it is a symptom of a deep-rooted psychic malfunction. Stephen wrote: "There are senti- ments which imply moral disease as distinctly as there are sensations which imply physical disease. Cynicism, and prurience, and a voluptuous delight in cruelty are simply abominable, whoever expresses them, and however great his powers."[3]

The "moral disease" Stephen speaks of is a deterioration of the ethical faculty, but not only that. The pathological use of the term "moral" in those days was very broad. The "moral" causes of a disease might include, say, venality or gluttony, but also anxiety and overwork. In its most general sense the moral condition was the state of the psyche in- duced by a pattern of life and a pattern of thought. Likewise, a person who was "morally insane" had of course lost the ability to distinguish be- tween right and wrong, but at the same time his other faculties were affected. His perceptions generally were unreliable. More important, his will was impaired and with it the internal, responsible direction of his own conduct. Volitional paralysis, delusion, and immorality were all symptoms of the same degenerative process. "There are states of mind," Bain wrote, "wherein all motives lose their power; an inability to remem- ber or realise the consequences of action, or a morbid delusion such as to pervert the trains of thought, will render a human being no longer amen- able to the strongest motives; the inability then ceases to be moral. This is the state of insanity, and irresponsibility." That is, in passing through what Maudsley calls the borderland between sin and madness one does not suffer different kinds of malfunction, but the same kinds with in- creased severity.[4]

In the "thoroughly healthy mind" perceptions and concepts are given shape and direction by moral volition. Health is the coordination of all living functions, and the will is the agent of coordination within the mind as it is between the mind and the body. But the will cannot effect what the mind does not conceive. If one loses the concept of his own unity, his identity, the will loses the power to realize unity and the mind becomes a loose confederation of faculties. Whatever concept a person has of himself as an individual must depend on his perceiving a unity greater than and external to himself. All organic wholes take their functional identity from encompassing wholes. The heart, for example, is a system of related functions, but the functioning heart is an entity without meaning unless the larger organic system is taken into consideration. In the same way, the functioning self only has significance within the framework of external functions—a social order, a natural order, a divine order. Purpose, growth, harmony—the conditions of internal health—are thus vitally dependent on a general perception of these qualities outside the self, and alienation is the chief condition of disease. "To be cut off," Carlyle exclaims, "to be solitary: to have a world alien, not your world; all a hostile camp for you; not a home at all, of hearts and faces who are yours, whose you are! It is the frightfulest enchantment."[5] Ruskin develops the point in *Modern Painters:* "Let [man] stand in his due relation to other creatures, and to inanimate things—know them all and love them, as made for him, and he for them;—and he becomes himself the greatest and holiest of them. But let him cast off this relation, despise and forget the less creation round him, and instead of being the light of the world, he is a sun in space—a fiery ball, spotted with storm. All the diseases of the mind leading to the fatalest ruin consist primarily in this isolation. They are the concentration of man upon himself, whether his heavenly interests or his worldly interests, matters not; it is the being *his own* interests which makes the regard of them so mortal. Every form of asceticism on one side, of sensualism on the other, is an isolation of his soul or of his body; the fixing his thoughts upon them alone; while every healthy state of nations and of individual minds consists in the unselfish presence of the human spirit everywhere, energizing over all things; speaking and living through all things."[6]

Whatever external reality the healthy mind contemplates—social, natural, or divine—it perceives not only variety, movement, and palpability, but also structure and design. To live harmoniously within ourselves we must, in Arnold's words, see life steadily and see it whole—we must take in life coherently. Victorian critics put special stress on the artist's ability to get hold of his subject mentally, to master it. Shelley's innate sensitivity, R. H. Hutton wrote, prevented him from "holding together with a strong hand the various elements of a complex problem"; Shelley's "intellect and imagination were not of a sort to master a complex whole. There was no *grip* in them." Ruskin felt that "a quality of Grasp" is visible in every great painter's work. Leslie Stephen praised

Fielding's "masculine grasp of fact" and observed more generally that "the vigour with which a man grasps and assimilates a deep moral doctrine is the test of the degree in which he possesses one essential condition of the higher poetical excellence." Bagehot praised Clough's "strong grasp of plain facts and obvious matters." According to Arnold, Maurice de Guérin "hovers above the tumult of life, but does not really put his hand to it."[7]

This ability of a poet to enclose a subject is what Arnold calls, in his essay on Guérin, poetry's "interpretative power," its capacity of "so dealing with things as to awaken in us a wonderfully full, new, and intimate sense of them, and of our relations with them." The highest, most satisfying poetry provides not only the sense of concrete, lived experience, letting us "possess the real nature of things"; it also gives us a sense of the order of things, and of our own place in that order: "I have said that poetry interprets in two ways; it interprets by expressing with magical felicity the physiognomy and movement of the outward world, and it interprets by expressing, with inspired conviction, the ideas and laws of the inward world of man's moral and spiritual nature. In other words, poetry is interpretative both by having *natural magic* in it, and by having *moral profundity*. In both ways it illuminates man; it gives him a satisfying sense of reality; it reconciles him with himself and the universe." The interpretations of science, Arnold says, convey the laws of things, but not the "intimate sense" of them. On the other hand, the interpretations of romantic nature poetry give us only that sense and leave obscure the laws of things and the laws of men. It is a poetry of intense responsiveness but it is intellectually and morally recumbent. Its intensity stirs, arouses, and temporarily enlivens, but it does not strengthen: "Assuredly it is not in this temperament that the active virtues have their rise. On the contrary, this temperament, considered in itself alone, indisposes for the discharge of them. Something morbid and excessive, as manifested in Guérin, it undoubtedly has. In him, as in Keats . . . the temperament, the talent itself, is deeply influenced by their mysterious malady; the temperament is *devouring*; it uses the vital power too hard and too fast, paying the penalty in long hours of unutterable exhaustion and premature death."[8]

Like Guérin, Keats desired (Arnold says in a letter) "movement and fulness" and pursued them at the cost of the steadying influence of coherent thought. For Arnold the excellence of a poem's essential design best indicates that its author has achieved some firm mental hold on the world. "The greatness of a poet," he writes in praise of Wordsworth, "lies in his noble and profound application of ideas to life." By *ideas*, he explains, he does not mean philosophy, but a vivid representation of life which has a moral basis, which shows us "how to live" rather than telling us about it; the wholeness of the poetic structure reflects its underlying moral structure. The poet, Arnold declares in the 1853 Preface, must be able "to think clearly, to feel nobly, and to delineate firmly."[9] When a work contains some "excellent action," some concrete and universally applicable image of life, its very firmness of delineation reveals the poet's health, his ability to think clearly and feel nobly. He has assimilated phenomena integrally as laws and represented those laws in a coherent, living action.

Like much Victorian thought the criticism of the period is dominated by this division of the objects of knowledge into things and laws. The world of things is tangible but incoherent, the world of laws coherent but intangible. The artist must reconcile the two worlds. Walter Bagehot observed that as we advance in knowledge we grow aware of a duality in the perceived universe. In addition to the "vast, visible indisputable sphere" of everyday life, we recognize an "invisible world which is altogether unlike that which we see, which is certainly not opposed to our experience, but is altogether beyond and unlike our experience." With a very Carlylean metaphor Bagehot pictured modern men as "finite beings living . . . on the very edge of two dissimilar worlds, on the very line on which the infinite, unfathomable sea surges up, and just where the queer little bay of this world ends. We may count the pebbles on the shore, and image to ourselves as best we can the secrets of the great deep."[10]

Insisting that poets *"make their image,"* Bagehot accused Clough of not doing so, of being unable to "catch up a creed" and embody it.[11] Whether a writer makes his image from the great deep or from the pebbles on the shore, his capacity for imaging shows what Bagehot calls "symmetrical genius." Some minds with "deductive abstract intellect" are gifted in lending sense to mystery. Plato was such a man. Others—Chaucer and Walter Scott, for example—have a "practical seeing sagacity," a "distinct sense of relation and combination which is necessary for the depiction of the whole of life, which gives to it unity at first, and imparts to it a mass in the memory ever afterwards."[12] Bagehot himself seemed most comfortable in the nonmetaphysical, nonmystical world of the social novel, where familiar experience was laid out in lucid patterns. He especially admired Scott's firm, clear, strong representations of "practical human society," his ability to relate everything in a novel to "the framework in which this society inheres, and by the boundaries of which it is shaped and limited." In other words, Scott's pictures are vivid in their details, clear in their general scheme. His "manly mind" imparted to these works a balance between sentiment and sense, the source of their "peculiar healthiness." "There are no such books as his for the sick-room," Bagehot says, "or for freshening the painful intervals of a morbid mind."[13]

Bagehot's image of the seashore reminds us that even as the social and physical sciences were illuminating the familiar world and making more of the world familiar, just as they were providing man with, to use Arnold's words, "the spectacle of a vast multitude of facts awaiting and inviting his comprehension,"[14] the total scheme of things seemed to many vague and incomprehensible. There was that "mysterious darkness," as Stephen called it, "which surrounds our little island of comparative light."[15] This probably explains the Victorian intellectual's urgent searching for Laws, Frameworks, Principles, Ultimate Causes, Ideas. The artist, no less than the philosopher, was held to be duty-bound to continue that search. As Bagehot observed, "the reasoning understanding and the firm far-seeing sagacity" protect the mind from "the onrush of circumstances."[16] Arnold told Clough that a poet must "begin with an Idea of the world not to be prevailed over by the world's multitudinousness."[17]

To attain a vision both comprehensive and vivid the creative mind must combine steadiness of will, strength of intellect, and clarity of perception. Critics generally believed, however, that the artist's temperament was naturally nervous, excitable, and passionate. And since his mind must be, at least in part, passively receptive to his subject, he is all the more easily overwhelmed by the mystery, movement, and variety of life. Reviewing Tennyson's *Maud*, George Brimley commented that "an innate capacity" for "weakness and misery, for crime and madness is inseparable from keen sensibility, powerful emotions, and active imagination; and if events happen which paralyse the will already feeble, turn the flow of feeling into a stream of bitterness, and present to the imagination a world of wrong and suffering, the capacity fulfils itself according to the force and direction of the events."[18] Paradoxically, then, the poet's natural susceptibility (his *diathesis*, as pathologists of the time would call it) to obsession, self-pity, and despair arises from that same energy which makes him a poet. Or as Stephen put it, "The keen sensibility which makes a man a poet, undoubtedly exposes him to certain types of disease. He is more likely than his thick-skinned neighbour to be vexed by evil, and to be drawn into distorted views of life by an excess of sympathy or indignation. Injudicious admirers prize the disease instead of the strength from which it springs; and value the cynicism or the despair instead of the contempt for heartless commonplace or the desire for better things with which it was unfortunately connected."[19] Clearly this reflects the survival and influence of the temperaments-psychology, with the notion that everyone, according to his nature, tends to be ruled by one of the physio-psychic functions. Poets are most likely to possess the nervous temperament, as Mill explains in his essay on Tennyson.[20] The true poet, he says, is endowed by nature with "fine senses": a nervous organization fitted for clear and vivid perceptions and also so made "as to be, more easily than common organizations, thrown, either by physical or moral causes, into *states* of enjoyment or suffering, especially of enjoyment: states of a certain duration; often lasting long after the removal of the cause which produced them; and not local, nor consciously physical, but, in so far as organic, pervading the entire nervous system. This peculiar kind of nervous susceptibility seems to be the distinctive character of the poetic temperament." But this "nervous susceptibility" is only the poet's native capacity. What he gains by self-culture, Mill said, is the "thinking faculty." The habits of reflection and generalization help ensure that his thoughts will be placed "in a strong light before his intellect" and impressed on his feelings. Without such training his feelings will remain intense but undisciplined as, according to Mill, Shelley's were.

What Brimley, Stephen, and Mill are saying is that conceptual disease results from a natural, or temperamental, imbalance of functions and manifests itself in delusion, passiveness, or bitterness. The creative, healthy act must then involve a strong assertion of the will, of volitional force against emotional force. The poet, Arnold says in "Resignation":

> to whose mighty heart
> Heaven doth a quicker pulse impart
> Subdues his own energy to scan
> Not his own course, but that of man.

Emotionally undisciplined poets allow into their writings, according to Ruskin, "certain expressions and modes of thought which are in some sort diseased or false." That phenomenon is the subject of the "pathetic fallacy" chapter in *Modern Painters*.[21] With the Victorian critic's usual method of arguing from assumed categories, Ruskin states that there are two "orders" of poets. The Creative poet thinks strongly and sees truly, having "a great centre of reflection and knowledge in which he stands serene, and watches a feeling, as it were, from afar off." Poets of the second, or Reflective, order have the kind of "temperament" unsuited to calmness and philosophic distance, "that of a mind and body in some sort too weak to deal fully with what is before them or upon them; borne away, or over-clouded, or over-dazzled by emotion." In periods of crisis the will gives way before an upsurge of feeling, making the mind, "for the time, more or less irrational." Cognitive distinctions between the internal self and the external world are blurred. The mind conceives a "morbid, that is to say, a so far false" idea about natural objects, interfusing them with its own emotional force. "All violent feelings have this same effect. They produce in us a falseness in all our impressions of external things, which I would generally characterize as the 'pathetic fallacy.' "

The highest creativity is the triumph of the active will over internal feelings and external objects, a victory of cognitive order over fantasy. In Ruskin's dynamic conception of life, health is seen as a process of shock and struggle, not an effortless homeostasis. The absence of morbidity in an artistic work may only reflect the absence of this creative strife, and of life itself. Therefore the pathetic fallacy, though a symptom of disease, "is in general a sign of higher capacity and stand in the ranks of being" than is an easy accuracy of perception. "But it is still a grander condition," he declares, "when the intellect also rises, till it is strong enough to assert its rule against, or together with, the utmost efforts of the passions; and the whole man stands in an iron glow, white hot, perhaps, but still strong, and in no wise evaporating; even if he melts, losing none of his weight."

Although the creative process Ruskin described pits the higher against the lower self, the ultimate product is an expression of the *whole* self, and a declaration that it stands "in due relation" with all things. Like Arnold and Bagehot, Ruskin regarded the aesthetic image as the most complete way of conveying this internal-external harmony.

A distinctive feature of Ruskin's critical theory is his view that since man and nature are vitally connected, art should incorporate both human and natural life-forms and processes. The Gothic cathedral, for example, or Gothic style generally, gives the viewer a sense of affinity with divine creation by synthesizing the various aspects of vital growth. The quality of *Savageness* or *Rudeness*, the unfinished or unperfected nature of Gothic, is "the sign of life in a mortal body, that is to say, of a state of progress or change. Nothing that lives is, or can be, perfect; part of it is decaying, part nascent. The foxglove blossom,—a third part bud, a third part past, a third part in full bloom,—is a type of the life of the world." If Savageness is the symbol of growth in all animate things, and of their imperfection at any one time, *Rigidity* embodies the energy or strength of nature. It is "a stiffness analogous to that of the bones of a limb, or the fibres of a tree." *Naturalism*, the representation of foliage, symbolizes and marks the artist's responsiveness to the "more tranquil and gentle" aspects of nature: "The green herb is, of all nature, that which is most essential to the healthy spiritual life of man."[22] So it is with all the characteristics of Gothic. One by one the unity and living force of all things are synthesized in the completed imaginative structure. For Ruskin, Gothic architecture not only expressed the vitality of nature and the sympathetic healthiness of the artist's nature, it also imparted to those who live with such architecture the sense of well-being which comes from finding one's place in the world. It offered a sense of contact with things and a sense of the unity and meaning of things.

The qualities of the artist's character are so inevitably transferred to the work of art, his own nature so directly *becomes* the nature of the work, that its forcefulness, thus implanted, must transfer itself to the audience. In Ruskin's criticism especially, the qualities of the healthy creative mind are identical with those of the healthful work of art. They are: strength and energy, growth or change, a sense of physical relationship with things in general, and a sense of the unity and completeness of things in general. Ruskin explains that the six characteristics of Gothic belong, as qualities, to the building or, as capacities, to the builder. Grotesqueness may be found in the decoration of an edifice, but it also demonstrates that the artist himself has not gained internal harmony at the cost of energy: "Wherever the human mind is healthy and vigorous in all its proportions, great in imagination and emotion no less than in intellect, and not overborne by an undue or hardened pre-eminence of the mere reasoning faculties, there the grotesque will exist in full energy."[23] That is why Ruskin calls the six characteristics of Gothic "moral elements." They are moral in the general, psychological sense described earlier in this chapter, and moral as well in their teleological potential, their usefulness.

For Ruskin these moral elements are found in the vital shapes or forms of a work, forms common to literature and buildings. To Leslie Stephen, who was a more purely literary critic, the moral aspect of a work implied in its forms may only be fully grasped by evaluating its ideas. Like Ruskin's "On the Nature of Gothic," Stephen's essay on "Wordsworth's Ethics" explores the relationship between the artist's character and the character of his work.[24] Every poem, Stephen says, though nominally a symbolic expression, is essentially a philosophy: "The symbol which the fancy spontaneously constructs, implies a whole world of truth or error, of superstitious beliefs or sound philosophy" (p. 182). Since the distinctive images in a poem reflect some system of ideas, the poet's moral soundness is most evident in the soundness of the poem's philosophy: "Once more, the highest poetry must be that which expresses not only the richest but the healthiest nature. Disease means an absence or want of balance of certain faculties, and therefore leads to false reasoning or emotional discord. The defect of character betrays itself in some erroneous mode of thought or baseness of sentiment. And since morality means obedience to those rules which are most essential to the spiritual health, vicious feeling indicates some morbid tendency, and is so far destructive of the poetical faculty" (p. 184). In poetry as in philosophy "the highest intellectual faculty manifests itself in the vigour with which certain profound conceptions of the world have been grasped and assimilated" (p. 179). So, when Stephen says we may test "poetical excellence" in a writer by "extracting the philosophy from the poetry" (p. 186), he is also saying that by the same process we may test the healthiness of the poet's character.

According to Stephen, literature's most pressing duty is the tough intellectual one of searching out a solution to "the dark riddle of life." Those not up to the task betray their cognitive helplessness by some viciousness of feeling expressed in their work. For example, "Neither Byron nor Shelley can see any satisfactory solution, and therefore neither can reach a perfect harmony of feeling. The world seems to them to be out of joint, because they have not known how to accept the inevitable, nor to conform to the discipline of facts" (pp. 195-196). Stephen praises Wordsworth not for finding *the* solution, but for finding *a* solution, which, whether true or not, at least came to grips with the problem: "Wordsworth's mode of conceiving the problem shows how powerfully he grasped the questions at issue" (p. 191). The real "issue," Stephen says, is how to reconcile experience and abstract thought. Among moral systems there are two distinct tendencies corresponding to two general classes of minds. The first class "is distinguished by its firm grasp of facts, by its reluctance to drop solid substance for the loveliest shadows, and by its preference of concrete truths to the most symmetrical of theories." The second "starts from abstract reason. It prefers to dwell in the ideal world, where principles may be contemplated apart from the accidents which render them obscure to vulgar minds." Because the weakness of the first (exemplified by Swift) is a tendency toward cynicism, and of the second (exemplified by Shelley) a tendency toward unworldliness, moral philosophy must somehow reconcile the two; it must "escape from the alternative of dealing with empty but symmetrical formulae or concrete and chaotic facts" (pp. 188-190).

The two cognitive modes which Stephen here distinguishes are roughly analogous to those already encountered in other critics: to Bagehot's "deductive abstract intellect" and "practical seeing sagacity," to Arnold's "moral profundity" and "natural magic," to Ruskin's poetry of perception and poetry of "reflection and knowledge." According to Stephen, Wordsworth was able to work out a way of reconciling reason and experience philosophically because in his own nature the two modes of perception were harmonized. Wordsworth formulated the problem as a search for "continuity" between the period of childhood, in which "we are guided by half-conscious instincts," and that of maturity when instincts are replaced by "reasoned convictions" (p. 196). Early in the essay Stephen asked how we reconcile the child's *app*rehension of experience with the man's *comp*rehension of it (p. 182). The greater part of "Wordsworth's Ethics" is devoted to the poet's solution to the problem, his view that the instincts of a young mind are (in Stephen's words) "the spontaneous products of a nature in harmony with the universe, and estimable as a clear indication that such harmony exists" (p. 198). The young healthy nature's intuitive sense of the design of things is later confirmed by the developing reason: "When the 'moral being' is thus built up, its instincts become its convictions, we recognise the true voice of nature, and distinguish it from the echo of our own passions. Thus we come to know the Divine order and the laws by which the character is harmonised are the laws of morality" (p. 224).

A man's character, then, develops in such a way that he may trust his instincts and feelings, but not be dominated by them. The graver, the more philosophical, intellectually complete vision of life is ultimately the healthier one: "And, finally, if a persistent reader should ask why—even admitting the facts—the higher type should be preferred to the lower, Wordsworth may ask, Why is bodily health preferable to disease? If a man likes weak lungs and a bad digestion, reason cannot convince him of his error. The physician has done enough when he has pointed out the sanitary laws obedience to which generates strength, long life, and power of enjoyment. The moralist is in the same position when he has shown how certain habits conduce to the development of a type superior to its rivals in all the faculties which imply permanent peace of mind and power of resisting the shocks of the world without disintegration" (p. 225).

Ultimately, to the extent that poetry offers a sound philosophy, it aids the reader's own natural evolution toward a saner, more comprehensive idea of life. The psychologist Laycock wrote that the "fundamental fact" of consciousness is an internal unity corresponding to the external unity of creation. The will, he said, is free in proportion to the mind's grasp of the coherent plan of existence: "Or we may say that a perfect rational will corresponds, as to knowledge, with the 'pure reason' of creation, as developed in the ideas of the laws of design; perfect instinct corresponds to the order of creation as manifested by the law, without any knowledge of its ideas."[25] Stephen's Wordsworth essay suggests that the philosophic training of the rational will is as necessary to spiritual health as physical training is to the health of the body. Since an untrained poet is incapable of "sound" moral philosophy, he cannot write the sort of poetry which is, to use Arnold's word, "sustaining."

The concept of the healthy mind gave the Victorian critic not only a standard of evaluation but also an analytical technique. In the biographical approach developed in the nineteenth century one worked his way backward from the poetical texture of a work—the feelings conveyed and the images laid down—to the character of the poet and thence to those "moral" conditions of his life which help shape his character. The diagnostic critical method assumed that a work of art embodies its own genesis, and what can be learned about its genesis will help explain its nature. Victorian critics, mostly following the example of Carlyle, sought to trace the condition of the work itself to its proximate cause: the author's personality. The idea that a work's style and substance directly manifest its author's temperament was grounded in the theory, found especially in German romantic criticism, of Personality as the distinctive, dynamic creative force that gives a work its individuality and shape. "Personality is everything in art and poetry," Goethe remarked in 1831; "nevertheless, there are many weak personages among the modern critics who do not admit this, but look upon a great personality in a work of poetry or art as a kind of trifling appendage." The essential nature of the artist and that of his work are identical; character and genius, Carlyle wrote, "always go together." Therefore the critic understands the artist's personality by correctly interpreting the personality of the work. As Stephen put it, "From a single phrase, as from a single gesture, we can often go far to divining the character of a man's thoughts and feelings . . . The great poet will reveal his character through a sonnet or a song." Strength of style derives from strength of personality, which in turn is grounded in the artist's moral nature. "All art being the Formative Action of a Spirit," Ruskin maintained, "whatever character the spirit itself has must be manifested in the Energy or Deed of it, and makes the deed itself Bad or Good." In short, the ultimate cause of a work's healthiness or morbidity is a moral one, and the critic, like the medical diagnostician, can usually read this moral cause in its result. In the conceptual clarity and representational fidelity of Shakespeare's plays, Carlyle discerned their author's "*morality*, his valour, candour, tolerance, truthfulness; his whole victorious strength and greatness."[26]

As THE CHARACTER of an artist's work contains the visible impress of his spirit, so does his own character manifest the spirit of the age. "The great man," Carlyle wrote, "does, in good truth, belong to his own age; nay more so than any other man; being properly the synopsis and epitome of such age with its interests and influences." Similarly Ruskin declared that "it is a constant law that the greatest men, whether poets or historians, live entirely in their own age, and the greatest fruits of their work are gathered out of their age." This harvesting he called "getting always vital truth out of the vital present."[27]

Although the spirit of the age is the natural source of the artist's creative health, his affinity with it involves certain dangers. Unusually receptive to the age's "interests and influences," drawing his energies from its energies, the artist is often the first and most dramatic victim of cultural malady. The early Tennyson's morbidity was, according to Kingsley, traceable to a weakness inherent in the times: "This modern vagueness . . . is to be found in shallow and unsound culture, and in that inability or carelessness about seeing any object clearly, which besets our poets just now; as the cause of antique clearness lies in the nobler and healthier manhood . . . which enabled Spenser and Milton to draw up a state paper."[28]

Dr. Johnson, one of Carlyle's latter-day heroes, struggled nobly against the diseased spirit of the age, but at last fell victim to it: "His fatal misery was the *spiritual paralysis*, so we may name it, of the Age in which his life lay; whereby his life too, do what he might, was half-paralysed."[29] Arnold, in the 1853 Preface terming his own age "inferior to the past . . . in moral grandeur [and] in spiritual health," counseled his fellow poets to escape its vitiating influence by contemplating the literature of an earlier time.

The belief that an era can be vigorous or lethargic, diseased or healthy, depends first on the concept of a "spirit" of the age and second on the physiological view of history that societies are organisms which follow laws of growth and decay. The spirit of an age is the principle of identity which makes possible its consideration as a whole and its relation to other ages. Mill observed in 1831 that the "spirit of the age" was a new concept and the dominant one of his time. It belongs, he wrote, exclusively to a period of change and is adopted by those who, discovering a division between their own time and the past, develop a consciousness of their age as an evolved entity with its own temper.[30]

At the time Mill's essay appeared, a keen awareness of both Change and zeitgeist coincided with an equally keen awareness of disease as a social fact. As George Rosen observed a century later, during periods of rapid transition the contrast between the observed states of things and "the standards recognized as vital by the individual" becomes especially apparent. Analogies of disease and health come to mind and are used in the social criticism emerging at such times.[31] The epidemic diseases of the 1830s and 1840s struck hardest in the depressed areas of England, pointing up the social inequality which had come in the wake of change. Some imaginative works of protest, such as Dickens' *Bleak House* and Carlyle's *Past and Present*, reflected this in their use of the symbolism of disease. By analogy as well as in fact, disease and health became the measure of social well-being in nineteenth-century thought. There was ready at hand the medical theory that physical and mental diseases were more or less natural phases of a general life-pattern. Thus, since it was believed that the pattern of life recapitulated that found in societies, periods of history were seen as states of health and disease and as stages of growth and decay. A culture, like a person, may fall into a state of disease even though the larger pattern is one of growth. Usually temporary, these phases are most likely to occur during transitions in the life pattern, when the organism seeks to adjust to a change from one stage of its existence to another stage. In "The Spirit of the Age" Mill characterized history as moving through "natural" and "transitional" stages and observed that his own period was of the latter type, "not a state of health, but, at the best, of convalescence."[32] The notion that instability is both a sign and a cause of spiritual disease is quite common in Victorian thought, especially in the writings of Carlyle. We may see everywhere, he declared, "Change, or the inevitable approach of Change . . . so that Society, were it not by its nature immortal, and its death ever a new-birth, might appear, as it does in the eyes of some, to be sick to dissolution, and even now writhing in its last agony. Sick enough we must admit it to be, with disease enough, a whole nosology of diseases."[33]

The phases of disease were believed to touch all aspects of life; their symptoms were detectable everywhere, particularly in literature, which most clearly embodies the spirit of the age. Aubrey de Vere stated: "Society having got into a morbid state, literature has to sympathize with morbidness. With the melancholy it must be melancholy, ever implying that the universe was made by mistake. Like the attendant of a wealthy hypochondriac, it must know how to talk of every symptom, tread the carpet noiselessly, and draw back the curtain pensively, not letting in a sudden light on a temple consecrated to all the maladies."[34]

In 1831, when Mill was writing "The Spirit of the Age" and Carlyle was making his observations on Change, British culture did seem ailing in all respects: political reform was stalled, literature had fallen into decline, and there was cholera. Within a couple of decades, however, all outward signs suggested that the convalescence Mill spoke of had proceeded rapidly. In its statesmen—Bright, Palmerston, Disraeli; in its popular press—the *Times*, *Punch*, the *Saturday Review*, the *Daily Telegraph*; and in its labors and amusements the period of the fifties and sixties expressed a confident vitality. On the other hand, much of the poetry of that period continued to verge on what the critics called "morbidity." This was especially true with the newer poets. Morris' *Defence of Guenevere* (1858) depicts one situation after another of despair, shame, betrayal, neurosis; a sense of bitter hopelessness pervades the whole book. Meredith's *Modern Love* (1862) is introspective, sardonic, accusatory, self-castigating. Swinburne's *Poems and Ballads* (1866) celebrates the love of death and the deadliness of love. In their relation to the temper of the times these poets seemed sequestered, like the "Children rear'd in shade" who watch the passing troops and hunters in Arnold's "Stanzas from the Grande Chartreuse":

> Action and pleasure, will ye roam
> Through these secluded dells to cry
> And call us?—but too late ye come!
> Too late for us your call ye blow
> Whose bent was taken long ago.

How does one explain a situation in which the spirit of a people and the spirit of its most original literature seem so at odds? The average Victorian of the 1850s did not feel the "sick fatigue, the languid doubt," the "strange disease of modern life" diagnosed by Arnold in "The Scholar-Gipsy." It seemed to be the occupational ailment of poets. In "The Modern Element in Literature," his inaugural lecture as Professor of Poetry at Oxford, Matthew Arnold explored this apparent contradiction. He described his time as "a significant, a highly developed, a culminating epoch" with " a copious and complex present, and behind it a copious and complex past."[35] There had been periods like it before, most notably those of Periclean Greece and Augustan Rome. What they have in common, the element Arnold calls "modern," is the presence of this "significant spectacle to contemplate" as well as the desire and freedom to make sense of the spectacle—a general intellectual awareness, an inquiring spirit, a "tendency to observe facts with a critical spirit; to search for their law, not to wander among them at random." Literature can offer to such ages an "intellectual deliverance" from facts, a way of interpreting them, a perspective. This deliverance is only achieved "when we have lost that impatient irritation of mind which we feel in the presence of an immense, moving, confused spectacle which, while it perpetually excites our curiosity, perpetually baffles our comprehension" (p. 20). Poetry's "adequacy," as Arnold calls it, in its task of deliverance depends on the total adequacy of the poet, "the most energetic and harmonious activity of all the powers of the human mind." It is not enough that the mind of the poet and the spirit of his work be alive and active, they must also be healthy, expressing both vigor and coordination, a "power of view."

The Age of Pericles, Arnold notes, has been called "a vigorous man, at the summit of his bodily strength and mental energy" (p. 23). Intellectually as well as materially Athenian society was then mature and healthy, and out of this environment arose a literature consonant with it. The works of Thucydides, Aristophanes, and above all Sophocles exhibit "the charm, the vital freshness, which is felt when man and his relations are from any side adequately, and therefore genially, regarded" (p. 29). Thus, the age of fifth-century Greece was a great "modern" epoch with a commensurately great literature. Later, with its military failures, its economic decline, and its political degeneration, Greece became "only a head without a body." Deprived of the vital social basis of its life, its literature grew detached, cynical, morally decadent. Because the age was not physically sound, it was not spiritually sound either.

By contrast the Age of Augustus was a body without a head. Outwardly more varied and alive than that of Pericles, its essential *spirit* was less sound. The poetry of Lucretius is "over-strained, gloom-weighted, morbid." That of Vergil reveals a man "of the most delicate genius, the most rich learning, but of weak health, of the most sensitive nature, in a great and overwhelming world; conscious, at heart, of his inadequacy for the thorough spiritual mastery of the world and its interpretation in a work of art" (pp. 35-36). Although the Augustan age had "energy of effort" and "fulness and movement," its literature could not encompass or give vision to the grand spectacle of facts. Paradoxically, the richer the experience which an age offers its writers for their contemplation, the greater the chance that their natural tendency to conceptual disease will be manifested: "The predominance of thought, of reflection, in modern epochs is not without its penalties; in the unsound, in the overtasked, in the over-sensitive, it has produced the most painful, the most lamentable results; it has produced a state of feeling unknown to less enlightened but perhaps healthier epochs—the feeling of depression, the feeling of *ennui*" (p. 32).

If the general life of an age is diseased or enfeebled, its thought will be also. But even a healthy "body" cannot ensure spiritual vitality, for if the mind is out of harmony with the body—if the literature of an age is not "commensurate with" its environment—the prevailing spirit or character of the age must be diagnosed as unsound. When Arnold decided to exclude *Empedocles* from the 1853 edition of his poems he did so because the feelings of the poem, the attenuated "mental distress . . . unrelieved by incident, hope or resistance," reflected too painfully the "morbid" spirit of his own time.[36]

Arnold uses what Huxley called a "materialistic terminology" to envision and give credibility to something impalpable and remote: the spirit of the age. On one level the analogic use of "health" to suggest spiritual well-being is a conceptual aid, as in this observation from Stephen's "The Moral Element in Literature": "Nobody would deny that a thoroughly healthy state of the body is the normal and most essential condition of athletic excellence. And just the same thing may be said of spiritual and intellectual health."[37] The value of such analogies is that they enable us to conceive of the mind or spirit concretely and as an entity. It is easy enough to consider them abstractly and partially, in terms of faculties, principles, and tendencies, but to comprehend them as a whole and in themselves, some sort of conceptual model is needed. In the nineteenth century people were asked to consider their bodies in a very concrete way. For the first time body-consciousness was held to be a public necessity, and people became aware of what a human body looked like inside as well as out, how it worked, and what its principles of health were. Conceptual models for the body based on sense-experience were plentiful. Now, having a somatic model, it is necessary to have a psychic model which corresponds to it logically. To think of the mind as a growing tree, for instance, makes no sense if the tree is presumed to reside in a human body. What is really needed is not just an analogy for the mind, but an analogical relationship between the mind and the body. If the mind is like the body, rather than like a mirror, or an open book, or a storehouse, and if its principles of health are similar, our conceptual model for it will not jar with what we know of the *real* mind-body relationship.

That is one value of the materialistic "terminology" as expressed in *mens sana in corpore sano:* in relating the two kinds of healthiness analogically it provides a workable model for the mind. The clinical vocabulary of Victorian critics made use of such a model, in some cases more consciously than in others. But the terminology was more than analogical. In diagnosing "character" the critic could not ignore what was common knowledge: the mind is not simply *like* the body, it is vitally related to it, and the "nature" of a poet is his whole constitution. "It seems undeniable in point of fact," Mill wrote, "and consistent with the principles of a sound metaphysics, that there are poetic *natures.* There is a mental and physical constitution or temperament, peculiarly fitted for poetry."[38]

The literal reading of *mens sana in corpore sano* was sound medical doctrine; to some it was therefore sound critical doctrine. In the case of one critic, Leslie Stephen, it was borne out by personal experience. As a boy Stephen was tall but spindly and frail. Even at the age of fourteen, Maitland records, "a long walk was too much for him," and he was seldom able to keep pace with his sturdy elder brother, Fitzjames.[39] When, in 1845, the eldest son of the family died, Mrs. Stephen became increasingly worried about Leslie's health. Doctors advised that he do less reading and thinking, more riding, rowing, and exercise in the gymnasium. Whether owing to this regimen of exercise or to normal growth, Stephen developed into a healthy, strong young man, "a great athlete in mind and body," as Sir Robert Romer has said.[40] Matriculating at Cambridge in 1849, he went in for rowing. As an undergraduate and later as Junior Tutor, he rowed in one or both of the annual spring races for ten consecutive years. His efforts as coach of the Trinity Hall boat inaugurated a long era of that school's domination of the river. Stephen pursued other sports with similar vivacity. A pioneer in athletics at Cambridge, he ran some legendary one- and two-mile races. His chief interest, however, then and throughout his life was mountain climbing. He was an early member of the Alpine Club and its president for three years as well as editor of the *Alpine Journal.* By the time he made his final ascent in 1894 he had scaled many of the most difficult peaks in Europe, his most celebrated feat being the conquest of the Schreckhorn in 1861.

Gertrude Himmelfarb has speculated that having "failed" as an intellectual, Stephen adopted the easier role of Philistine-sportsman, taking refuge in a bluff manliness and in such "crude Philistinisms" as his pronouncement linking poetry to the "thoroughly healthy mind."[41] But although in his writings and his life he may have been somewhat more consciously virile than other intellectuals of the day, his preoccupation cannot be seen as idiosyncratic, given the circumstances and interests of his time. In such a statement as the following, he only reflects a common Victorian assumption: "There are, as all moralists know, certain virtues which depend directly upon our physical organs. No man can be thoroughly healthy in mind who has a bad digestion. It is said that Calvinism was eradicated from a certain district in America simply by drainage. A thorough system of drains improved the general health, and put an end not only to agues, but to the gloomy spirit favourable to unpleasant doctrine about predestination. On the same principle, courage is intimately connected with a vigorous condition of the body."[42]

Not only did "all moralists" know about *mens sana in corpore sano*, all doctors and psychologists did too, and from it sprang a rudimentary form of psychoanalytical criticism, with its basic assumptions drawn from the physiopsychology of the day: everyone had a particular temperament predisposing him to certain kinds of physical and moral disease; the temperament was influenced by inherited constitution, but could be modified, as character, by training; and finally, the training must be both physical and mental, since mind and body were always interacting. The implication for some critics was that no analysis of character was complete which failed to take into account the subject's physical state. Aubrey de Vere's description of Shelley illustrates the approach taken: "Ill-health preyed on him till his natural sensibility had been heightened into nervous irritability. This circumstance, together with the belief that his time in this world was short, made him overtask his faculties, which were thus ever in a state of excitement."[43] Any physical singularity in a writer which might influence his character came under close scrutiny. A favorite subject was Pope, as one might expect. According to Macaulay, Pope's attack on Addison was that of a "diminutive, crooked, sickly boy . . . eager to revenge himself on society for the unkindness of nature."[44] In the same vein, Stephen termed Pope "a victim of physical as well as moral diseases," a man "writhing under some bitter mortification, and trying with concentrated malice to sting his adversary in the tenderest places."[45]

Sometimes critics drew upon traditional concepts of temperament and physiognomy. Stephen, for example, speculated on how an "athletic giant" such as Tennyson could have written so much poetry of revery. Leaving to physiologists the general issue of whether "there is any real incompatibility between athletic vigour and delicacy of nervous organization," he offered his own hypothesis about Tennyson and then about Shelley: "Your giant may be sensitive, but he carries too much ballast to be easily stirred to utterance. He is contemplative or dreamy rather than impetuous and excitable. If Shelley had put on more flesh, he might have been equally poetical, but he would not have indulged in the boyish explosions which imply an excessive mobility of the nervous system."[46] In the two poets Stephen apparently saw the typical body structures of the lymphatic and nervous temperaments and concluded that as structure is modified, so is character. The moral element of a work may be directly traced in this way to the mind-body constitution. For Ruskin the moral nature was reflected in that constitution, but, as part of the "soul," it transcended the purely mental and physical. In a lecture on art and morality he considered a particular painting, a portrait by Veronese. Noting the muscular precision and intellectual labor evident in the picture, he asked his audience whether Veronese could have continued such a fatiguing task without a sustaining joy in the creation. "And then consider," he urged them, "so far as you know anything of physiology, what sort of ethical state of body and mind that means!—ethic through ages past! . . . And then, finally determine for yourself whether a manhood like that is consistent with any viciousness of soul, with any mean anxiety, any gnawing lust, any wretchedness of spite or remorse."[47]

Ruskin's view that the "whole man" is involved in the creative act is developed at length in an appendix to *The Stones of Venice.*[48] The three parts of man, he explains, are Body, Soul, and Intellect, each of which possesses a "Passive or Receptive" as well as an "Active" faculty. Thus, "the body has senses and muscles; the soul, feeling and resolution; the intellect, understanding and imagination." In the creative process the passive or receptive faculties are engaged in sequence—the senses, then the feelings, then the understanding. This part of the process we might call conceptualization. An impression on the senses stirs the feelings, and this triggers the understanding. A concept, thus born in the mind, then awakens the active faculties, and the line of causation moves the other way, from Intellect, to Soul, to Body: the imagination, in harmony with the resolution, calls forth the action of the muscles, and the painter paints, or the writer writes. In simpler forms of activity only the lower, physical faculties might be involved; in artistic creation there is a total, sequential involvement of all three parts. In what Ruskin calls a "healthy state" of the constitution the procedure goes on unimpaired. In a "morbid" state one of the faculties assumes an excessive role, disrupting the free and natural sequence of functions. An overdeveloped intellect may impair the imagination; an overactive imagination may cripple the resolution.

Like most Victorians, Ruskin believed that healthy physical activity keeps thought from remaining within the "passive or receptive" side of one's nature by stimulating the active, affective faculties. An example of the practical application of his theory is his commentary on "Too Late," a work by the minor Pre-Raphaelite painter William Lindsay Windus. The painting, shown at the Royal Academy in 1859, depicts a young woman, apparently consumptive and near death. With her stands the lover who has reached her, the title says, too late. On viewing this dismal scene Ruskin speculated that either the artist himself had been ill or that the painting had been submitted before it was finished or that the artist had "sickened his temper and dimmed his sight by reading melancholy ballads." He then reminded young artists that "painting, as a mere physical exertion, requires the utmost possible strength of constitution and of heart. A stout arm, a calm mind, a merry heart, and a bright eye are essential to a great painter." Finally he advised them to "learn all athletic exercises."[49] One reason, according to Ruskin, why the art of earlier days was healthier than that of modern times was that people then lived more wholesomely. The ancient Greeks neither fasted nor overate, and they spent much of their time out-of-doors: "full of animal spirit and physical power, they became incapable of every morbid condition of mental emotion."[50]

Stephen often voiced similar views. In an essay "In Praise of Walking" he compared the writings of Scott and Byron, both of whom suffered from lameness. Scott's "manly nature," the source of the vividness and general sanity of his novels, he traced to the writer's love of walking, despite the handicap. Byron's affliction being more severe, he was constrained from long walking: "All the unwholesome humours which would have been walked off in a good cross-country march accumulated in his brain and caused the defects, the morbid affection and perverse misanthropy, which half ruined the achievement of the most masculine intellect of his time."[51]

IN THE CONCEPT of health Victorian criticism found its own Idea or Law, a comprehensive cognitive structure: health and disease are transmittable states of an organism's character or spirit; in the creative process they are passed from the character of the age to that of the artist and thence to the character of the work and finally, as the work finds its audience, back into the character of the age. Morally speaking, the healthiness of a work of art is its vital principle, the cause of its becoming and the essence of its purpose. Just as health engenders health, disease engenders disease: Byron's morality "may have been chiefly negative, but it was a morality of the most drastic and contagious kind."[52] A writer like Byron who isolates himself from his world by an indifference to its higher laws is himself unsound and therefore incapable of fostering soundness through his work.

The concept of health helped legitimize a moral approach to art by basing it on medical and physiological models. The relationship between morality and physical health, however, was both actual and metaphoric. Immorality was literally a disease of the whole person; but it was also, in its symptoms, progress, and effects, *like* a disease of the body. As a result of this dual epistemology we often find a conceptual ambiguity in the language of critics who relied on such models. Here is a case in point from Stephen's "The Moral Element in Literature": "To say that a man is immoral is to say that he is in some way spiritually diseased; that his mental and material organisation is somehow out of joint; that some of his instincts are defective and perverted, and therefore that the vital functions are not properly discharged."[53] Stephen is "somehow" relating immorality to "mental and material organisation." At first the connection appears to be metaphoric, though his terms—"diseased," "out of joint," "defective and perverted"—fit together so poorly as to suggest that his analogy is loosely conceived. Perhaps more than a simple analogy is intended, for he goes on to say, "What we call a fine moral sense *is proof* that the whole organisation is working soundly and is in the highest condition of intellectual training." Now the relation between morality and health is expressed more definitely: the first is a sign of the second.

Stephen had no special knowledge of medicine or physiology, but like many intellectuals of his time he had assimilated enough of the terminology of those disciplines to give his prose a vaguely scientific ring. The language hangs somewhere between physiological description and ethics, lacking the concrete definitiveness of one and the abstract definitiveness of the other. In the hands of really third-rate critics this philosophical woolliness is even more apparent. *The Fleshly School of Poetry*, Robert Buchanan's angry attack on Pre-Raphaelite writing, is notable for its sheer force of moral indignation ("Step where I may, the snake Sensualism spits its venom upon me"). It also illustrates the tendency of the clinical vocabulary to degenerate into the language of distaste, in which morbid means gloomy, unwholesome means dirty, and both of them mean disgusting. "The great strong current of English poetry rolls on," he proclaimed, "ever mirroring in its bosom new prospects of fair and wholesome thought. Morbid deviations are endless and inevitable; there must be a marsh and stagnant mere as well as mountains and wood." Of Rossetti's "A Last Confession" Buchanan complains that "the whole poem is morbid and unwholesome, and must be drunk in as a whole to leave its full bad flavour."[54]

As concepts, "health" and "wholesomeness" have here become vague positive ideals demanding a general, uncritical assent about what is right and proper. Emotive but not concrete, they have lost imaginative force and scientific reference and convey neither the image of the mind nor the idea about the mind-body connection which they did in more thoughtful criticism. Victorians thought of "mind" and "character" as dynamic moral forces, and needing to conceptualize these forces they chose physiological models as the most logical means: the laws of the body were those of the mind and the health of one was the health of the other. "So far as the poet is himself a man of healthy nature and powerful mind, he will be qualified to act as a mouthpiece of the forces that make for good, and to intensify their action."[55] Stephen wrote that, but it could have been Carlyle, Ruskin, Bagehot, or Arnold. When a Victorian critic spoke of the artist's "healthy nature" he assumed that there was such a thing as a "nature," an essential, personal entity which could be described *as a whole* and which could thus pass through discernible stages of health and morbidity. The nature, or character, was primarily spiritual, hence its moral telicity, though it involved the whole person. On those general principles most Victorian thinkers were agreed.

CHAPTER 4

Obeying the Laws of Life:
Carlyle and Spencer

IN HIS INAUGURAL address as Lord Rector of Aberdeen University, John Stuart Mill urged that physiology should be in everyone's program of study.[1] The science was immediately practical, he argued, because "the sanitary discussions of late years" had shown that knowing how the body works can lead to hygienic habits which "the most tedious and costly medical treatment so often fails to restore when once lost." Further, he went on, in its methods and its concepts physiology provides the best introduction to the study of all sciences, social as well as natural. In practice the physiologist and the sociologist learn to overcome the same obstacles, the difficulty of useful experimentation and the necessity of considering "a vast number of circumstances," all constantly changing. Physiology also familiarizes one with "conceptions which play the greatest part in the moral and social sciences, but which do not occur at all in those of inorganic nature." Among those conceptions are evolution, habit, and predisposing cause.

According to Mill, studying the body provided not only knowledge for keeping one's own body sound, but also epistemological discipline and conceptual models. In urging physiology as a heuristic point of departure he was merely reflecting an opinion about that science widely held in 1867. In the nineteenth century physiology came to occupy a central position in scientific thought. From its traditional concern with pure anatomy it was moving in two directions: through biology to a general consideration of the laws of life; and through psychology to a special consideration of the laws of mind and thus the laws of social behavior. As Mill told his audience, the proper object of all knowledge is man; therefore "physiology is the most serviceable of the sciences, because it is the nearest. Its subject is already Man."

Although Mill's position was not universally accepted, it is remarkable how many Victorian writers used some sort of physiological model to explore and relate the issues of man's place in nature, man's place in society, and the mind's place in the body. Thomas Carlyle and Herbert Spencer serve as illuminating examples. Certainly no Victorians were more influential in devising conceptual frameworks for grasping these issues. In retrospect, the two seem to stand at opposite poles of nineteenth-century thought: those ideas which comprised the fabric of Spencer's philosophy —positivism, utilitarianism, political individualism—were anathema to Carlyle, whose idealism, absolutist leanings, and veneration of the Great Man all seemed simpleminded and reactionary to Spencer. However, as F. J. C. Hearnshaw has pointed out, there was a striking similarity in temperament: "In truth neither of these two notable and typical Victorians was teachable or tractable. Both were prophets commissioned, the one by the Immensities and Infinities, the other by the Unknowable and Absolute, to instruct rather than to learn."[2] The writings of both Carlyle and Spencer resonate with the conviction of men who have understood the laws of life and framed systems of knowledge based on those laws.

CARLYLE BEGAN to work out a general concept of health in the fall and winter of 1831. As readers of George Eliot's *Middlemarch* will recall, it was a time when attention was gradually being diverted from the elections and pending reform bill to the approach of cholera.[3] On November 2, 1831, Carlyle wrote in his notebook: "All the world is in apprehension about the cholera pestilence, which, indeed, seems advancing towards us with a frightful, slow, unswerving consistency." A week later he sought to reassure his mother. The cholera, he wrote her, was "a disease of no such terrific quality" as the typhus which each year assailed Glasgow and Edinburgh; now that it had reached the coasts, "the reality which is measurable will succeed the terror which is unmeasurable."[4]

Such diseases as cholera at least had the virtue of clear visibility in their results; this was untrue of the larger national disease, of which cholera and typhus were only symptoms. For Carlyle the national health came to be a totally comprehensive issue. One could not isolate the diseases which ravaged the slums and suburbs of Britain from the social conditions which made them possible. Political and sanitary reform must be companion activities; more than this, they must be undertaken as part of a more general reformation of the nation's state of mind. What was needed was a concept of health so fundamental as to be applicable to all current concerns.

On November 17 Carlyle jotted down some notes for a new essay: "The nobleness of silence. The highest melody dwells only in silence (the sphere melody, the melody of health); the eye cannot see shadow, cannot see light, but only the two combined. General law of our being . . . Extremes meet. Perfect morality were no more an object of consciousness than perfect immorality, as pure light cannot any more be seen than pure darkness. The healthy moral nature loves virtue, the unhealthy at best makes love to it." Completed in December, the essay was given the title "Characteristics." On reflection its author considered it "baddish," though with "a certain beginning of deeper insight in it."[5] Perhaps more rigidly didactic than he liked, it did accomplish its purpose in sketching out a philosophy of health which was universal, a "general law of our being." "Characteristics" applies its concept of health to a great variety of topics, but especially to the current climate of thought, the spirit of the age. In doing so it is a diagnosis, a prognosis, and a prescription.

With "a practical medical view" Carlyle examines "the Condition of our own Era, and of man's life therein" (p. 18).[6] As he moves from point to point in his essay, from physical to intellectual to moral and finally to cultural health, his transitions reveal a man peering, scanning, viewing from a distance: "No less is this unhealthy symptom manifest, if we cast a glance on our Philosophy"; "To understand man, however, we must look beyond the individual man and his actions or interests, and view him in combination with his fellows"; "For truly, if we look into it, there is no more fruitless endeavour than this same, which the Metaphysician proper toils in." Carlyle assumes the roles of philosopher, seer, and doctor; both physician and metaphysician, he is like Goethe, the "physician of the iron age" in Arnold's "Memorial Verses," who

> took the suffering human race,
> [and] read each wound, each weakness clear;
> And struck his finger on the place,
> And said—*Thou ailest here, and here!*

Beginning with "merely corporeal therapeutics," but reminding the reader that the principles of those apply elsewhere as well, Carlyle states the central law of health, which he calls the Physician's Aphorism: "The healthy know not of their health, but only the sick" (p. 2). As long as the *"vital"* powers are functioning as they should, the body's machine sets up no "false centres of sensibility." The scattered nervous centers remain unawakened, and the only consciousness is that of the mind. This is the state which A. N. Whitehead describes in *Nature and Life*: "We find ourselves in a healthy enjoyment of life by reason of the healthy functionings of our internal organs—heart, lungs, bowels, kidneys, etc. The emotional state arises just because they are not providing any sensa directly associated with themselves."[7]

Feeling well is the condition of feeling nothing of our bodies, so that all the sensa provided by the body are those of the world external to the self. As children, Carlyle says, we seem to stand "in the centre of Nature," drawing from it and giving to it, "in harmony with it all." In a passage with Wordsworthian overtones he describes that period of life as one in which "clear tidings from without" come to the mind "unimpeded" by any sensory awareness of ourselves. "In those days, health and sickness were foreign traditions that did not concern us; our whole being was as yet One, the whole man like an incorporated Will." By *incorporated* he means, in one sense, integrated, undivided: "The perfection of bodily well-being is, that the collective bodily activities seem one; and be manifested, moreover, not in themselves, but in the action they accomplish . . . Thus too, in some languages, is the state of health well denoted by a term expressing unity [for example, Old English *hal*, healthy, whole]; when we feel ourselves as we wish to be, we say that we are *whole*" (pp. 1-2). But *incorporated* can also mean embodied, given form and substance. "Are we not Spirits," Teufelsdröckh asks in *Sartor Resartus*, "that are shaped into a body, into an Appearance; and that fade away again into air and Invisibility?"[8] The body is the divinely created manifestation of the soul, its "vehicle and implement" (p. 2); it has no reality or meaning apart from those of the spirit. Carlyle thus repudiates the Cartesian division between soul and matter, between "thinking substance" and "extended substances." Idealists see "that very division of the unity, Man, into a dualism of Soul and Body [as] itself the symptom of disease" (p. 4).

In his quite recent historical study of the mind-body issue C. A. van Peursen notes that in primitive thought, and even in Biblical and archaic Greek thought, there were no separate concepts of "body" and "mind." That particular distinction arose only with the concept of the identity of a self separate from the universe. It is evident, he argues, that "later *philosophical* distinctions relating to man (inner and outer, man and world, spirit, soul, body) could not possibly have been arrived at, did they not presuppose an underlying unity and cohesion. A philosophical account of man, nay, even the ordinary realization of individual bodily existence and a personal interior life, only become feasible when man ceases to be merged in a diffuse way with his mythico-social environment and learns to think of himself as being separate from the divine powers."[9] With the beginning of philosophical thought begins the conceptual splitting off of mind from body: this was an idea common in German Romantic thought and one of the basic assumptions of the *Naturphilosophie* school of science, among whose leaders were Schelling and Novalis. To Schelling the task of philosophy (of which science was a branch) was to reunite man and nature by showing that the laws which are seen in nature are one and the same with those which the mind conceives by itself.[10] In antiquity, he writes, "the finite and the infinite were united under a common veil." The antithesis between them, and thus between man and nature, spirit and matter, is characteristic of modern thinking "and will manifest itself time and again in science and in art until it is transcended in truly absolute identity."[11]

The answer to Cartesian dualism which Carlyle found in the writings of Schelling, Fichte, Novalis, and other Germans was that all substantial nature, including the human body, was a manifestation of spirit, a finite embodiment of the infinite. "All visible things are emblems," declares Teufelsdröckh; "what thou seest is not there on its own account; strictly taken, it is not there at all: Matter exists only spiritually, and to represent some Idea, and *body* it forth."[12]

Since the body is literally the will incorporated, its condition, its state of health or wholeness, is inseparable from the soul's. Therefore the prophet-pathologist of "Characteristics" probes inward to the intellect and finds again the same symptom: modern thinking, self-conscious, logical, speculative, has become a stranger to itself. It has lost touch with the vital source of thought, the Unconscious. "The healthy Understanding, we should say, is not the Logical, argumentative, but the Intuitive; for the end of Understanding is not to prove and find reasons, but to know and believe" (p. 5). The mind cannot comprehend itself; it cannot by logic comprehend thought, nor does the healthy mind try. "The truly strong mind . . . is nowise the mind acquainted with its own strength . . . Here as before [with respect to the body] the sign of health is Unconsciousness. In our inward, as in our outward world, what is mechanical lies open to us: not what is dynamical and has vitality" (p. 4). The tendency of thought to rely on science and metaphysics, to approach the understanding of life through analysis and speculation, is modern man's inevitable response to the loss of his totality: "all Science, if we consider well, as it must have originated in the feeling of something being wrong, so it is and continues to be but Division, Dismemberment, and partial healing of the wrong" (p. 2).

Self-sentience, dispute, and deliberation are always signs of ill-health. A recourse to anatomy and medicine reflects the body's distemper, a recourse to metaphysics reflects the intellect's. But these are symptoms. Still searching for the disease itself, Carlyle next probes the moral sphere, "the inmost and most vital of all." Here the signs are the same. Modern man is a Moral Philosopher: he dissects Virtue into virtues, the Mover, or Will, into motives. Virtue, when it can be discoursed upon, "has become aware of itself, is sickly and beginning to decline" (p. 8). The only true virtue is immediate and instinctual, the "mysterious Self-impulse of the whole man" (p. 9): "Let the free, reasonable Will, which dwells in us, as in our Holy of Holies, be indeed free, and obeyed like a Divinity, as is its right and its effort: the perfect obedience will be the silent one" (p. 8).

In his discussions of the physical, the intellectual, and the moral spheres, Carlyle returns to the idea of obedience to an ineffable power, a "vital force." In the physical sphere the force is life-energy; in the intellectual it is unconscious creation or Inspiration; in the moral it is the Moral Will. That power, in whatever form, cannot be understood, must not be questioned. The bases of health are action and silence.

As Carlyle the prophet and diagnostician surveys the course of recent history he finds the circle of free activity narrowing, that of skeptical inquiry broadening. Men do less and speculate more. Thought without action has occasioned morbidity—fantasy and volitional paralysis, the underlying symptoms of all "nervous disease." Every age provides man with some new illusory concept of himself and nature, one which has the power of destroying the freedom to act. "Alas, poor devil!" exclaims Teufelsdröckh in *Sartor*, "spectres are appointed to haunt him: one age he is hagridden, bewitched; the next, priestridden, befooled; in all ages, bedevilled. And now the Genius of Mechanism smothers him worse than any Nightmare did; till the Soul is nigh choked out of him, and only a digestive, Mechanic life remains."[13] Utilitarianism, the modern specter, propounds a view of man which deprives him entirely of a higher (or deeper) nature. It transforms him into an artificial creature of Necessity, subject to laws foreign to his true nature, laws which he cannot well understand or do anything about. Deprived of natural self-knowledge— what he knows of himself intuitively—he is stripped of the will to act. He then grows convinced that there is no such thing as will and becomes a victim of his own philosophy: "Not Godhead, but an iron, ignoble circle of Necessity embraces all things; binds the youth of these times into a sluggish thrall, or else exasperates him into a rebel; Heroic Action is paralysed" (p. 30).

At the time he wrote "Characteristics" Carlyle's thoughts were occupied with paralysis and disease. Not only was he conscious of the fever-plagued, bedridden thousands in Britain, he himself was continually beset by mysterious ailments. In one of the more hopeful letters of this period he wrote to his brother, "I believe myself to be getting yearly by some hardly perceptible degree stronger in *health*, both inward and outward: perhaps, one day, I may triumph over long disease, and be myself again!"[14] At this time also, having finished *Sartor*, he was looking about London unsuccessfully and dejectedly for a publisher. Already in his middle thirties, this fiercely ambitious man had been able to publish no substantial work. His energies seemed circumscribed as much by public indifference as by his own illnesses. Throughout the writings of this general period the persistent image of the invisible prison occurs. The philosophy of Mechanism, he says in "Signs of the Times," "like some glass bell, encircles and imprisons us," while "the soul looks forth on a fair heavenly country it cannot reach." In *Sartor*, "Invisible yet impenetrable walls, as of Enchantment" estrange Teufelsdröckh from the rest of living creation. In *Past and Present* each man is enclosed in his transparent ice-palace, "making signals and gesticulations" to his brothers, but unable to reach any of them.[15] These prisons are invisible and "enchanted" because they are merely conceptual; their walls are illusory knowledge unsupported by real faith: "Nay, after all, our spiritual maladies are but of Opinion; we are fettered by chains of our own forging, and which ourselves also can rend asunder. This deep, paralysed subjection to physical objects comes not from Nature, but from our own unwise mode of *viewing* Nature."[16] The severest, most crippling afflictions are of the soul—or at least begin there. But in the reality of things human society is spiritually coalescent: no human soul is independent of another. Therefore, having in "Characteristics" penetrated to the "moral sphere" and found more of the same symptoms but not the disease itself, Carlyle determines to "look beyond the individual man and view him in combination with his fellows." The individual soul evolves and strengthens in the "genial element" of society (p. 10): "Look at it closely, that mystic Union, Nature's highest work with man, wherein man's volition plays an indispensable yet so subordinate a part, and the same Mechanical grows so mysteriously and indissolubly out of the infinite Dynamical, like Body out of Spirit,—is truly enough vital, what we call vital, and bears the distinguishing character of life. In the same style also, we can say that Society has its periods of sickness and vigour, of youth, manhood, decrepitude, dissolution and new-birth" (pp. 11-12). Carlyle became the chief exponent in England of this holistic, physio-ethical vision. C. F. Harrold has shown, however, that this conceptual structure was already common in

German thought and literature, Richter declaring that the nineteenth century "lies upon a sick-bed," Fichte speaking of the "unwholesome self-consciousness" of the modern age, and Schlegel comparing the rationalism of British philosophy to "a man having a hale and healthy look whilst the germs of some fatal malady lie within him."[17]

The physiological metaphor of nineteenth-century historians and social critics was not, with the German idealists or with Carlyle, simply an analogy. It was a way of seeing life as an organic whole rather than as a system of correspondences. Society is not just similar in form to the individual; in Carlyle's words, it is "the vital articulation of many individuals into a new collective individual . . . a second all-embracing Life" (p. 12). The single soul embodies itself in the physical frame; the single self—body and soul—embodies itself in the social framework. If society's members fall out of health individually they do so collectively as well; if the spirit of society becomes diseased or paralyzed, so will that of its members.

In *Sartor Resartus* Carlyle details the anatomy of the body politic: government is its outward skin, the craft guilds and industrial associations its bones and muscles, and religion the "inmost Pericardial and Nervous Tissue, which ministers life and warm circulation to the whole." In society as in the self, the soul animates or invigorates. When that becomes moribund, so also does the body: "For the last three centuries, above all for the last three quarters of a century, that same Pericardial Nervous Tissue (as we have named it) of Religion, where lies the Life-essence of Society, has been smote-at and perforated, needfully and needlessly; till now it is quite rent into shreds; and Society, long pining, diabetic, consumptive, can be regarded as defunct; for those spasmodic, galvanic sprawlings are not life; neither indeed will they endure, galvanise as you may, beyond two days."[18]

Society's outward maladies, Carlyle declares in "Characteristics," are obvious enough—ignorance, hunger, poverty, revolution. But since "the Physical derangements of society are but the image and impress of its Spiritual," he asks us directly to "look within"; "while the heart continues sound, all other sickness is superficial, and temporary" (p. 22). In the unsound heart, in the unhealthy spirit of the age, Carlyle at last finds the generative disease. In every area of thought, in religion, literature, philosophy, "all seems diseased self-consciousness, collision and mutually destructive struggle. Nothing acts from within outwards in undivided healthy force; everything lies impotent, lamed, its force turned inwards, and painfully 'listens to itself' " (p. 22).

Is there a cure for such a profound, systemic distemper? Not a total cure at any rate; as Carlyle says early in the essay, quoting Novalis, "Life itself is a disease; a working incited by suffering" (p. 3). Without pain there is no life, for in essence all human life is a laborious quest for Reality or Certainty: "Man stands as in the centre of Nature; his fraction of Time encircled by Eternity, his handbreadth of space encircled by Infinitude: how shall he forbear asking himself, What am I; and Whence; and Whither?" (p. 25). Therefore, the need to discover anew some basis for knowledge "is a chronic malady . . . and perpetually recurs on us" (p. 26). Chronic diseases of the soul belong to the system. They endure, active or dormant, as long as one lives. Like Charlotte Brontë's hypochondria, they appear, disappear, and reappear. "At the utmost there is a better and a worse in it; a stage of convalescence, and a stage of relapse with new sickness: these forever succeed each other, as is the nature of the Life-movement here below." In what he calls the "World's Organisation," the stage of convalescence is marked by belief and action, the stage of sickness by doubt and inquiry: "The first, or convalescent stage, we might also name that of Dogmatical or Constructive Metaphysics; when the mind constructively endeavours to scheme out, and assert for itself an actual Theorem of the Universe, and therewith for a time rests satisfied. The second or sick stage might be called that of Sceptical or Inquisitory Metaphysics; when the mind having widened its sphere of vision, the existing Theorem of the Universe no longer answers the phenomena, no longer yields contentment; but must be torn into pieces, and certainty anew sought for in the endless realms of denial" (p. 26). With pure thought, whether religious or skeptical, "a region of Doubt. . . hovers forever in the background; in Action alone can we have certainty." Action creates an existential reality, providing the frame of mind necessary for belief. Convalescence can be hastened through work.

In his essay Carlyle follows the so-called "expectant" concept of therapeutics. This principle, arising from a general skepticism as to the efficacy of medicines, held that there was in the body a vital tendency toward equilibrium, and that a fever, for example, may simply be the body's attempt to restore its own healthy balance. Convulsions and fevers in the body are signs of pathological transition; the wise medical practitioner withholds prescription but nurses the patient and places him, as far as possible, in the healthiest conditions. In *Notes on Nursing* Florence Nightingale proposed "as a general principle" that "all disease, at some period or other of its course, is more or less a reparative process, not necessarily accompanied by suffering: an effort of nature to remedy a process of poisoning or of decay, which has taken place weeks, months, sometimes even years beforehand, unnoticed, the termination of the disease being then, while the antecedent process was going on, determined."[19]

This process is what was known, since Hippocrates, as the *vis mediacatrix naturae*. Carlyle asks whether the modern tendency toward metaphysical skepticism is not only "the symptom of universal disease," but also the "sole means of restoration and cure? The effort of Nature, exerting her medicative force to cast-out foreign impediments, and once more become One, become whole?" (p. 32). This was a view he had adopted with respect to his own and his wife's continuing maladies. Doctors had prescribed no end of medicines—mercury, opium and tartar, morphia, mustard blisters—but during the winter of 1831 he began to be dubious about these remedies. Jane was then undergoing treatment: "George Irving has been attempting to prescribe for her; she even let him draw a little blood. I rather think, however, that her faith in physicians is somewhat on a level with my own; that she will give them no more of her blood, but trust to exercise, diet, and the return of settled weather." Carlyle now believed that to put body and mind in motion was worth all the "specifics" doctors had to offer. In February 1832 he wrote to his brother Alexander that horseback riding was "the wholesomest medicine I know," and to John Carlyle that there was no help for "health of *mind*" but "action—religious action."[20]

The "expectant" treatment may be effective if the disease is only chronic, but if it passes into the acute stage, or threatens to, a stronger remedy might be needed. *Past and Present* (1843) depicts modern English society as beset by "foul elephantine leprosy," "social gangrene," and "paralysis of industry." This "social malady" is no mere reparative fever, but "Fatal paralysis spreading inwards, from the extremities, in St. Ives workhouses, in Stockport cellars, through all limbs, as if towards the heart itself" (p. 6).[21] There is both random motion and stasis, "half-frantic velocity of impetus" and "deadliest looking stillness and paralysis." Two thousand paupers sit in workhouses, another twelve hundred thousand outside, "their cunning right-hand lamed, lying idle in their sorrowful bosom" (p. 2). Sir Jabesh Windbag, the parliamentary fraud, rises momentarily on the swell of his cherished Paragraphs, then "lies stranded, sunk and forever sinking in ignominious ooze" (p. 224). An advertising contrivance, a seven-foot lath-and-plaster hat, makes its pointless circuit of London. Kilkenny cats, a whirling dervish, the melancholy "talking" meat jack, the fashionable of London chattering like Dead Sea

Apes—all show apparent signs of life, but each is immobilized in his own whirling frenzy. This spectacle is surveyed by Carlyle with that skepticism which is, according to Jean Paul Richter, "a kind of soul-dizziness that suddenly transforms our rapid movement into the entire strange world standing still."[22] In the social organism as depicted here, all movement is spasmodic, the movement of a dying man kept alive by galvanic therapy: "Industrial work, still under bondage to Mammon, the rational soul of it not yet awakened, is a tragic spectacle. Men in the rapidest motion and self-motion; restless, with convulsive energy, as if driven by Galvanism, as if possessed by a Devil; tearing asunder mountains,—to no purpose, for Mammonism is always Midas-eared!" (p. 207). Although the organism may pass from a phase of "torpor" to one of "utmost paroxysm," the signs of motion are at best a morbid or feverish energy, "a mere announcement of the disease" (p. 16). That disease is the worship of Happiness, the surrogate religion of modern man: "God's Laws are become a Greatest-Happiness Principle; . . . Man has lost the *soul* out of him; and now, after the due period,—begins to find the want of it! This is verily the plague-spot; centre of the universal Social Gangrene, threatening all things with frightful death" (pp. 136-137).

Whereas "Characteristics" tells of a society turned inward, listening to itself in morbid self-reflection and analysis, in *Past and Present* society has not even the help of anatomical or metaphysical inquiry; it has no soul to peer at or listen to. Half-aware of their illness, impatient for relief, men have turned to the charlatan, or sham-hero. The quack obliges his anxious patient by offering the hope of an administered panacea, a "Morrison's Pill":[23] "It seems to be taken for granted . . . that there is some 'thing,' or handful of 'things,' which could be done; some Act of Parliament, 'remedial measure' or the like, which could be passed, whereby the social malady were fairly fronted, conquered, put an end to; so that, with your remedial measure in your pocket, you could then go on triumphant, and be troubled no farther" (p. 23). Because the "maladies of Society" are essentially spiritual or psychological, a true cure must begin with the soul itself, with a "reawakening of thy own Self from within" (p. 232): "There will be no 'thing' done that will cure you. There will be a radical universal alteration of your regimen and way of life take place; there will be a most agonising divorce between you and your chimeras, luxuries and falsities, take place; a most toilsome, all but 'impossible' return to Nature, and her veracities and her integrities, take place: that so the inner fountains of life may again begin, like eternal Light-fountains, to irradiate and purify your bloated, swollen, foul existence, drawing nigh, as at present, to nameless death! Either death or all this will take place" (pp. 23-24).

When Carlyle declares that reform, like charity, must begin at home (p. 35), he means that it must begin not only with the individual, but within the individual's inner self, his soul. The revitalized spirit is the ultimate and only source of all revitalization, the beginning of life: "For all human things do require to have an Ideal in them; to have some Soul in them, as we said, were it only to keep the body unputrified. And wonderful it is to see how the Ideal of Soul, place it in the ugliest Body you may, will irradiate said Body with its own nobleness; will gradually, incessantly, mould, modify, new-form and reform said ugliest Body, and make it at last beautiful, and to a certain degree divine!" (pp. 189-190).

Following the general procedure of natural therapy, Carlyle proposes two methods of restoring the social organism to a state of health. One is to treat the body itself, to improve the nation's physical health. He urges the enactment of factory legislation, the building of public parks in cities, sanitary reform, and improved ease of emigration; he also advises his readers to bathe more often: "This consciousness of perfect outer pureness, that to thy skin there now adheres no foreign speck of imperfection, how it radiates in on thee, with cunning symbolic influences, to thy very soul!" (p. 234). In these various ways the body of society is purified so as to influence the soul directly, not merely stimulated with "blistery friction" (p. 37) or galvanic therapy. While the body is made hygienic, the "asphyxied" soul must be resuscitated. Parliament may pass antibribery laws, for example, but at the same time the wish to bribe or be bribed must be purged: "The death-leprosy, attacked in this manner, by purifying from without, and by rallying of the vital energies and purities from within, will probably abate somewhat! It has otherwise no chance to abate" (p. 257).

Carlyle's cure, then, is of the constitutional sort given patients at Malvern and Leamington: a "total change of regimen, change of constitution and existence from the very centre of it; a new body to be got, with resuscitated soul" (p. 36). "Once well at home," reform will "radiate outwards, irrepressible, into all that we touch and handle, speak and work; kindling ever new light, by incalculable contagion, spreading in geometric ratio far and wide,—doing good only, wheresoever it spreads, and not evil" (p. 35). The energy of disease, spreading inward from the extremities or outward from the vital organs, is random, disorderly. The energy of health is orderly, moving in "geometric ratio."

"The one healing remedy" for "this disorganic, as yet so quack-ridden" world (pp. 33, 288) is an Aristocracy of Talent. But in order to believe in real worth, people must be worthy themselves. Hero-worship begins with the liberation of the heroic in each man: "Thou there, the thing for thee to do is, if possible, to cease to be a hollow sounding shell of hearsays, egoisms, purblind dilettantisms; and become, were it on the infinitely small scale, a faithfully discerning soul. Thou shalt descend into thy inner man, and see if there be any traces of a *soul* there; till then there can be nothing done!" (p. 26). Only in the soul can be found the *vis inertiae* (p. 160), the hidden energy necessary for a return to health. Finding a notable absence of "souls" in the England of his own time, Carlyle as Editor peers into the past, into the "confused Paper-Masses" left by the thirteenth-century monk Jocelin. Here and there, he remarks, among the debris of history might be found some "human soul" (p. 38). Despite all the signs of morbidity, there is much that is still alive in England, and much that can be brought to life (p. 65). The *vis inertiae* lies in the recreatable past as well as in the uncreated future. All history is a vital continuum; the present contains the living past and the living future. The tree of life, the tree Igdrasil, has its roots among the dead, but to the historian, digging among those roots, the once dead may become living souls.

He discovers in thirteenth-century England a surprising life and reality absent from the England of his own day. Medieval England was "no mere chimerical vacuity or dreamland . . . but a green solid place, that grew corn and several other things" (p. 44). The gray town walls of St. Edmund are "an earnest fact" (p. 48). Through the words of Jocelin "we gaze into the very eyes" of the St. Edmundsbury monks and the life they live (p. 62). Revealed in the pages of the old manuscript are people at work, therefore real people. A life of labor is grounded in reality: "Show me a People energetically busy; heaving, struggling, all shoulders at the wheel; their heart pulsing, every muscle swelling, with man's energy and will;—I show you a People of whom great good is already predictable . . . By very working, they will learn; they have, Antaeus-like, their foot on Mother Fact: how can they but learn?" (p. 207). The monks at St. Edmundsbury have found the Certainty, the quest for which is the inherent disease of life. The very silence by which they go about their work is proof of their belief, "a sign of health in them": "Religion is not a diseased self-introspection, an agonising inquiry: their duties are clear to them, the way of supreme good plain, indisputable, and they are travelling on it. Religion lies over them like an all-embracing heavenly canopy, like an atmosphere and life element" (p. 60).

Active labor, performed in certainty and grounded in reality, creates reality and certainty anew. The question every man should face, Carlyle declares, is "How do you agree with God's Universe and the actual Reality of things?" No man can be healthy who is not in harmony with the laws of the universe: "This Universe *has* its Laws. If we walk according to the Law, the Law-Maker will befriend us; if not, not" (p. 25). The true laws, which Carlyle calls God's laws, are spiritual and organic, not physical and mechanical; they are the laws of "Heaven's blessed life, not Mammon's galvanic accursed one" (p. 35). We have departed from the "inner eternal Laws" and have chosen instead to take up with such "temporary outer semblances of Laws" (p. 33) as profit-and-loss, supply-and-demand, and especially the Greatest Happiness Principle.

Carlyle's emphasis on personal conversion and rebirth ("the awakening of thy own Self from within") on the knowledge of the heart, on obedience to the Law and the urgent necessity of setting one's whole life in accordance with the law—all these show the strong evangelical appeal made in *Past and Present*. So also does his belief that true healing demands first a baptism of the will. From the diary of a Clapham Sect member Noel Annan gives us this description of the evangelical discipline: "Each day Thornton examines his life according to the Commandments laid upon him by God's Book. Has he lived according to the Law? How can he amend his acts to follow it more closely? Scrutiny of his actions leads him to resolve to control his will. For the human will yearning after the pomps and vanities of the world must die and become Christ's will. The past is renounced, the old selfish private will dies, and the regenerated will takes control."[24] This approach to spiritual health is consistent with Judaeo-Christian scripture, which shows a general indifference to what we would call the etiologies, the natural causes of disease. Illnesses are fundamentally acts of God and can be cured only by a life of righteousness. When Hezekiah, having fallen sick, sets his house in order, the Lord adds fifteen years to his life. Asa "was diseased in his feet; his disease was exceeding great"; but instead of seeking Jehovah, as he should do, he looks for help from physicians. The lesson of the scriptures is clear and consistent: sickness is a sign of disobedience to the Law. When Carlyle proclaims that the only cure for the "maladies of society" is a radical "alteration of your regimen and way of life," a repudiation of quacks or false prophets, and a "return to Nature, and her veracities," he is both speaking from this scriptural tradition and reflecting the tenets of a medical theory which was fast gaining popularity. The metaphysical lineaments of natural pathology show a truly religious commitment to the ways of nature which almost exactly parallels the evangelical commitment to the ways of the Lord. The new pathology emphasized regimen, or system of living; it emphasized totality of cure, a treatment of the state of mind and the state of body. Had it been less metaphysically, more scientifically based, we could call it a psychological medicine; as it was, it was a medicine of faith.

CARLYLE'S ATTEMPT to formulate a "general law of our being," a law describing man equally well as a physical, a psychological, and a moral or social creature, was being paralleled at the time in the empirical sciences. Noting the "rapid progress of generalization in the physical sciences," W. B. Carpenter speculated in 1838 that soon "one simple formula shall comprehend all the phenomena of the organic world" and hoped that the same simplification of laws might occur in the organic sciences.[25] To his contemporaries Herbert Spencer seemed the man who came closest to fulfilling the dream of a truly unified scientific knowledge. Like Comte, but with much greater comprehensiveness, Spencer tried to postulate a true religion of science by setting out, as a basis of total faith, a complex law meant to explain the relations of all phenomena.

In *First Principles* (1862) Spencer stated his objections to the two major philosophical schools of his time. The German school—the followers of Fichte, Schelling, and Hegel—mistakenly believed that what was beyond direct consciousness—the absolute nature of things—could be grasped. The English empirical school, on the other hand, concerned itself rightly with the relative rather than the absolute, but not, as it should, with "those aspects of the relative which are embodied in mathematical formulae, in accounts of physical researches, in chemical analyses, or in descriptions of species and reports of physiological experiments." German philosophy was too much concerned with ontology, while English philosophy was not experimentally based. Spencer credited Comte for unifying science and philosophy by putting "into a more coherent form" the knowledge gained in the natural sciences.[26]

The tendency of nineteenth-century positivism was to distrust precisely the kind of intuitive synthesis Carlyle used in formulating his law, preferring to found its system of knowledge on the objectively verifiable laws of the physical sciences. The positivists distrusted abstract metaphysics, arguing that even in matters of human behavior, development, and morality, what we usually regard as debatable or mysterious can be explained perfectly well by laws we already know and understand. The positivist pursued that sort of reductionism which, in Jacquetta Hawkes's words, investigates the world and tries to control it by "breaking down its vast complexities into smaller and smaller parts." In *Man Adapting* René Dubos relates how considerations of health and disease were increasingly reductionistic in the latter half of the nineteenth century. The laws of health were narrowed to those of physiology, and those of physiology to those of biology, chemistry, and physics.[27]

Through this methodology of reducing and simplifying laws positive philosophy sought a scientific comprehensiveness. It sought a synthesis of knowledge through a synthesis of laws. The technique is illustrated in this passage from Comte: "The whole social evolution of the race must proceed in entire accordance with biological laws; and the social phenomena must always be founded on the necessary invariableness of the human organism, *the characteristics of which, physical, intellectual, and moral, are always found to be essentially the same, and related in the same manner, at every degree of the social scale.*"[28] As an epistemological method, this might be called discovery by analogy; the idea is to apply strictly the verified laws of the "advanced" sciences to those branches of knowledge which are in a relatively immature state. One moves from discipline to discipline by establishing and then applying certainties, rather than deductively applying laws as Carlyle did.[29] Yet the conceptual models discovered by the two methods could be remarkably similar. By 1850 Spencer had developed this physiological model for society: "When . . . the citizen contemplates the relation in which he stands to the body politic—when he learns that it has a species of life, and conforms to the same laws of growth, organization, and sensibility that a being does—when he finds that one vitality circulates through it and him, and that whilst social health, in a measure, depends upon the fulfillment of some function in which he takes part, his happiness depends upon the normal action of every organ in the social body—when he duly understands this; he must see that his own welfare and all men's welfare are inseparable. He must see that whatever produces a diseased state in one part of the community, must inevitably inflict injury upon all other parts."[30]

Like Carlyle, Spencer defined health as organic wholeness—the harmonious operation of functions. Both writers saw all organisms as governed by some universal set of laws, and both saw "one vitality," as Spencer phrased it, motivating all organic creation. The crucial differences lay in how the two writers understood the laws of wholeness and the laws of vital movement. Spencer's ambitious plan for a "synthetic philosophy" covering all branches of science was grounded in a belief that "the laws of life are essentially the same throughout the whole organic creation."[31] Early in life he became convinced of a principle which was always to form the basis of his epistemology, that all organisms develop by evolution. From there it was a matter of adding other elementary principles—the "persistence of force," the development from homogeneity to heterogeneity, and other ideas borrowed from biology and physics, until he was able to arrive at his famous statement of the Law of Evolution: "an integration of matter and concomitant dissipation of motion; during which the matter passes from an indefinite incoherent homogeneity to a definite coherent heterogeneity; and during which the retained motion undergoes a parallel transformation." Spencer defines life, then, as a movement from confusion to order and from indefinite simplicity to definite complexity. He saw all organisms, including the social organism, as passing in their evolution from "indeterminate arrangement to determinate arrangement." Functions within the organism become more and more defined, and both the organism and its functions more and more "individuated": units become separate and distinct, though mutually dependent, and their functions in the organism undergo the same transformation: "this growth of an organism, of which one portion cannot be injured without the rest feeling it," as well as the concurrent segregation and dependence of functions, "may all be generalized under the law of individuation. The development of life generally, may be described as a tendency to individuate—*to become a thing*."[32]

The principle of Individuation in Spencer's organic analogy was derived from Coleridge's influential *Essay towards the Formation of a More Comprehensive Theory of Life*, a work largely plagiarized from German sources.[33] Coleridge argued that organisms grow and function not by any special vital force, but by the same forces operating throughout the inorganic world. However, in the living body these forces are "individuated" —they are stored and used to serve its own organic separateness, its character as an individual. What is true of the living body as a whole is true of organs within the body: they, too, in their specialized and definite use of natural forces, become individuated. Then, in the process of degeneration, this individuality of structure and function is gradually lost: "The advancing destruction of the organic compounds, blurs the minute structure—diminishes its distinctness. From the portions that have undergone most decay, there is a gradual transition to the less decayed portions. And step by step the lines of organization, once so precise, disappear." In the decadent stages of society, Spencer affirms, social ties are loosened, classes and subclasses dissolve, and with actual revolution "organized society lapses into an unorganized aggregation of social units."[34]

That sounds like the world of Carlyle's *Past and Present:* disease or degeneration in society is characterized by a loss of wholeness and a dispersal of energy. The principle of wholeness, however, is radically different in Spencer's concept. To Carlyle, only a general, unified growth of the organism can assure the vitality of its separate members. To Spencer, the health of the total organism depends on the unimpeded growth of its parts; that is, although individuals in a society must "conform to the moral law" and live in "mutual dependence," they can only develop into moral creatures individually and without constraint: "The ultimate man will be one whose private requirements coincide with public ones. He will be that manner of man, who, in *spontaneously* fulfilling his own nature, *incidentally* performs the functions of a social unit; and yet is only enabled to fulfil his own nature, by all others doing the like."[35]

Those historians and sociologists most influenced by Spencer's analogy tended to apply the idea of physiological individuation as a social principle. Spencer called this principle the law of equal freedom: "*Every man has freedom to do all that he wills, provided that he infringes not the equal freedom of any other man.*" H. T. Buckle's *History of Civilization in England* (1857 and 1861), arguing that a nation's historical importance depends on "the degree to which its actions are due to causes springing out of itself," defines a healthy civilization as one in which the growth and movement of individuals has been little impeded by the power of aristocracies, sects, and rulers. Buckle's history is organized as a physiological study, first of the healthy, English model, then of diseases which afflict various continental civilizations. "The foundation of all pathology," he reasons in the beginning of his second volume, "must be sought in an observation, not of the abnormal, but of the normal functions of life." Therefore, "in order to understand the way in which the diseases [of France] were aggravated by the quackery of ignorant rulers, it was necessary to understand the way in which the health [of England] was preserved by being subject to smaller interference, and allowed with greater liberty to continue its natural march."[36]

J. W. Draper devised an even more elaborate physiological schema, one which, he claimed, "commends itself to the intellect of man by its majestic grandeur." Chemist, physiologist, and historian, Draper read an abstract of his theories to the British Association for the Advancement of Science in 1860, then published them in augmented form in his *History of the Intellectual Development of Europe* (1863). The thesis of this work is that "Social advancement is as completely under the control of natural law as is bodily growth. The life of an individual is a miniature of the life of a nation." In both kinds of life the stages are infancy, youth, maturity, and old age. Like Buckle, Draper argues that the signs of healthy maturity in a society are intellectual freedom and the resulting advancement of knowledge and that this law of social health, like all natural laws, is undeviating and therefore predictable: "The laws of nature never vary; in their application, they never hesitate, nor are wanting."[37]

When Spencer began applying the doctrine of Persistence of Force to his conceptual synthesis, the effect was to change the model radically. In *Social Statics* the "law of life" underlying his organic metaphor is a *condition* of growth common to individuals and societies. With the doctrine of Force he found a *thing* which sustained all life. Force became the real link between the divisions of the universal system—between the inanimate and animate, the vegetable and animal, the animal and human, the body and mind, the self and society. The concept provided Spencer with the key to evolution, the constant, universal factor in evolutionary change: "Evolution becomes not one in principle only, but one in fact. There are not many metamorphoses similarly carried on; but there is a single metamorphosis universally progressing, wherever the reverse metamorphosis has not set in."[38]

Here again, as with Individuation, the concept was borrowed and adapted rather than invented by Spencer. By the 1850s dynamism, the theory that force or energy is the basis of all phenomena and phenomenal change, was becoming widely accepted in scientific philosophy as a way of correlating the principles of physics, physiology, and psychology. An influential statement on the correlation of mechanical and physiological forces was set forth in a paper read by Carpenter to the Royal Society in 1850. In it he rejected the purely chemical and mechanical explanations of life processes popular since the seventeenth century, as well as the vitalistic explanations proposed in opposition to mechanism. Vitalism held that there was a "vital agency" or "anima" which inhabited all animate beings, distinguishing them from things governed exclusively by mechanical or chemical principles, those of motion and matter. Taking note of recent discoveries by Faraday and others in the transformation of modes of *mechanical* energy, Carpenter concluded that Force in its various forms was the governing principle throughout the natural universe. Although "vital force" is different from mechanical force, he found a clear, intimate correlation between the two: "Starting with the abstract notion of Force, as emanating at once from the Divine Will, we might say that this force, operating through inorganic matter, manifests itself in electricity, magnetism, light, heat, chemical affinity, and mechanical motion; but that, when directed through organized structures, it affects the operations of growth, development, chemico-vital transformation, and the like; and is further metamorphosed, through the instrumentality of the structures thus generated, into nervous agency and muscular power."[39]

Having correlated Mechanical and Vital forces in this way, it was but a small step for physiological psychologists to incorporate Mind force into the system. Thus, Carpenter speaks of the Physical Forces of inorganic nature, the Vital Forces of organic nature, and Mind Force, which properly belongs to man alone. What he calls Nerve Force is the highest form of Vital Force, and he believes the purpose of mental physiology is to show the relation between Nerve Force and Mind Force within the individual. Laycock makes a similar distinction between "vital energy" and "mental energy," the latter being manifested during operations of the body which involve consciousness—"feelings, ideas, motives, and the like."[40]

Life, then, is the process by which energy evolves into ever more sophisticated and potent forms, just as matter evolves into compounds of greater and greater complexity. By conceiving of the universe as a system of forces manifesting themselves in matter, and evolving along with matter, dynamism constructs a scheme whereby Man, Nature, and the Absolute become parts of a grand Unity. Commenting on Carpenter's Royal Society paper, James Hinton noted that while the notion of a unique and separate vital force had been put to rest forever, at the same time were revealed "the proofs of a profounder harmony in nature": "Life is strong, because it is dependent; immortal, because it draws its being from a perennial source. All things minister to it. The tender organic frame needs no self-preserving power from within, because all the natural powers are its servants. The earth and air and distant orbs of heaven feed it with ceaseless care, and supply, with unfailing constancy, its wants. Life is in league with the universal forces, and subsists by universal law." The human organism and inorganic nature obey the same "universal law." And for the physiological psychologist, that law applies to mind and body alike. "May we not . . . already perceive," Maudsley asks, "what advancing knowledge must ever render more clear, how the conscious mind of man blends in unity of development with the unconscious life of nature? . . . Idealism and realism blend and are extinguished in the intimate harmony between the individual and nature."[41]

Some scientists nurtured the hope that force or energy might be comprehended in itself, but Spencer insisted that we can only know it in its effects, and in its patterns of behavior, its laws. For example, human nutrition changes the external physical energy in food into physiological energy. From physiological energy derives mental energy, and this in turn is transformed back into internal physical energy. Or, more directly and immediately, some physical force outside the body—a sound, for instance—will be translated by the brain into mental force and thence into physical. There is, therefore, "a correlation and equivalence between sensations and those physical forces which, in the shape of bodily actions, result from them. And yet these are but specialized manifestations of a general something called Force, a something which man is at a loss to comprehend: "By the Persistence of Force, we really mean the persistence of some Cause which transcends our knowledge and conception. In asserting it we assert an Unconditioned Reality, without beginning or end."[42] We may be conscious of the force of our minds as we are of our minds themselves, that is, subjectively, and we may be conscious of the force of our bodies in an objective way. Since these forces behave identically, we know that the same principle is operating throughout. "It is one and the same Ultimate Reality," Spencer observes in *Principles of Psychology*, "which is manifested to us subjectively and objectively. For while the nature of that which is manifested under either form proves to be inscrutable, the order of its manifestations throughout all mental phenomena proves to be the same as the order of its manifestations throughout all material phenomena."[43]

Since things cannot be known in themselves, their various manifestations as force are "modes of the Unknowable." Just how one manifestation produces another is an enigma, as enigmatic as the nature of things. How "a force existing as motion, heat, or light can become a mode of consciousness" is a mystery "impossible to fathom . . . We can learn nothing more than that here is one of the uniformities in the order of phenomena." What we can know about living creation are the patterns or laws of life. The same patterns are visible in the social organism but in a more complex form: "Whatever takes place in a society is due to organic or inorganic agencies, or to a combination of the two—results either from the undirected physical forces around, from these physical forces as directed by men, or from the forces of the men themselves."[44] Therefore the study of man should begin with a knowledge of the laws of force. In training a child, for example, if we keep in mind that "the amount of vital energy which the body at any moment possesses is limited," we will not be inclined to tax this energy by overworking him at his studies.[45]

For Carlyle the primal energy, though a mystery in itself, is best understood as a spiritual vitality manifesting itself in matter. For Spencer that mysterious energy is best understood as a physical vitality manifesting itself at times as mind; he, like Huxley, preferred the materialistic terminology. "We do not sufficiently realise the truth," Spencer writes, "that as, in this life of ours, *the physical underlies the mental*, the mental must not be developed at the expense of the physical."[46] Since mental capacity depends directly on physical energy, "the first requisite for success in life is to be a good animal." Or, to state it more broadly, for a man to develop at his most advanced level, he must see to it that his growth at every level is a thoroughly "natural" one, in accord with the processes of development observable everywhere in nature. In effect, this is the thesis of his very influential *Education: Intellectual, Moral, and Physical*, a collection of essays which appeared separately in various journals between 1854 and 1859.

In the essay which serves as the introduction to his book Spencer asks, "What Knowledge Is of Most Worth?" To answer this he proposes a descending scale of importance for all human activities, beginning with those which directly promote or ensure self-preservation and ending with "those miscellaneous activities which make up the leisure part of life, devoted to the gratification of the tastes and feelings."[47] The purpose of education is to *"prepare us for complete living"*; therefore, for the average man, "the desideratum is, a training that approaches nearest to perfection in the things which most subserve complete living, and falls more and more below perfection in the things that have more and more remote bearings on complete living" (p. 36). Spencer systematically examines his five categories of human values—self-preservation, self-maintenance, parental duty, citizenship, and "the refinements of life"—as to whether, in each case, a scientific education or a literary and artistic one provides the better "knowledge as guidance." For self-preservation, a study of physiology and hygiene is the most useful: "We infer that as vigorous health and its accompanying high spirits are larger elements of happiness than any other things whatever, the teaching how to maintain them is a teaching that yields in moment to no other whatever" (p. 43). For self-maintenance or "the gaining of a livelihood" science again is the more practical, especially mathematics, physics, chemistry, biology, and sociology. Likewise in the third category, parental duty, a knowledge of "the laws of life" is the "one thing needful," and classical learning has little value: "When a father, acting on false dogmas adopted without examination, has alienated his sons, driven them into rebellion by his harsh treatment, ruined them, and made himself miserable, he might reflect that the study of Ethology would have been worth pursuing, even at the cost of knowing nothing about AEschylus. When a mother is mourning over a first-born that has sunk under the sequelae of scarlet-fever . . . it is but a small consolation that she can read Dante in the original" (p. 63). The duties of citizenship are best learned by studying sociology, a discipline based on biology and physiology. And even accomplishment in "the refinements of life" is best begun with scientific training, for "without Science there can be neither perfect production nor full appreciation" (p. 75).

Having thus demonstrated science to be the most useful Knowledge as Guidance, Spencer is able to "treat with comparative brevity" the two approaches to education with respect to their value as Discipline. "It would be utterly contrary to the beautiful economy of Nature," he observes, "if one kind of culture were needed for the gaining of information and another kind were needed as a mental gymnastic" (p. 84). Since science teaches "the meanings of things" rather than "the meanings of words" (p. 93), the most important mental faculties—memory, judgment, the moral powers, and even the religious sense—are best strengthened in their direct application to reality: "Everywhere throughout creation we find faculties developed through the performance of those functions which it is their office to perform; not through the performance of artificial exercises devised to fit them for these functions" (pp. 84-85). When Spencer uses botanical comparisons throughout *Education* to speak of mental development, it is not simply a rhetorical device; it reflects his belief that man and plant belong to the same order of creation, and both obey, or should obey, the same laws. His metaphors imply a real, not an imagined relationship: "the mind like the body has a predetermined course of evolution . . . it unfolds spontaneously" (p. 113). "Architecture, sculpture, painting, music, poetry, etc., may be truly called the efflorescence of life" (p. 73).

In explaining why aesthetic or literary culture must always "yield precedence" to a more practical culture, he develops one of these metaphors at length: "A florist cultivates a plant for the sake of its flower, and regards the roots and leaves as of value, chiefly because they are instrumental in producing the flower. But while, as an ultimate product, the flower is the one thing to which everything else is subordinate, the florist very well knows that the root and leaves are intrinsically of greater importance; because on them the evolution of the flower depends. He bestows every care in rearing a healthy plant; and knows it would be folly if, in his anxiety to obtain the flower, he were to neglect the plant"

(p. 73). This analogy reflects two interesting aspects of Spencer's way of seeing human development. First there is his explicit conclusion that the well-being of the flower depends on that of the rest of the plant. Although he does not tell us very specifically what in human nature corresponds to "root" and "leaves," it is clear that he is suggesting a hierarchy in which the elements most essential from the standpoint of "life" are to be developed first and nourished most carefully. To prepare for complete living means, most fundamentally and urgently, to be able to live at all. The inevitable correlative of this is that, in any education, concerns for health must predominate.

Another implicit assumption is, to put it plainly, that a plant is a plant. Perhaps with his analogy Spencer has a geranium in mind, but what would happen to his argument if *we* have in mind a cucumber vine? If he fails to take into account individual variations it is because his mind is not so much analytical as systematic; it prefers to contemplate correspondences rather than differences. Sometimes this leads him into strange passageways. For example, "As the child's features—flat nose, forward-opening nostrils, large lips, wide-apart eyes, absent frontal sinus, &c.—resemble for a time those of the savage, so, too, do his instincts" (p. 206). Or do we need evidence, Spencer asks, that a vegetarian diet is unhealthful? We might "contrast the stolid inactivity of the graminivorous sheep with the liveliness of the dog," or the root-and-berry-eating Bushmen of Australia with Europeans, whom they are "quite unable to cope with" (pp. 237-238).

Spencer also relies on animal analogies, particularly in his essay "Physical Education," where the comparisons are mainly to the care of livestock and pets. Why is it, he asks at the beginning of his discourse, that most men show an interest in the breeding, training, and raising of animals, but few in the rearing of children? "Infinite pains will be taken to produce a racer that shall win the Derby: none to produce a modern athlete" (p. 222).[48] Such comparisons reflect Spencer's confidence in the scientific "principle" as a means of understanding complex problems by their similarity to simpler ones. In certain ways people are like animals. Since our knowledge of animals is founded "on the established truths of modern science," our first task in training people should be to apply these truths: "It is time that the benefits which our sheep and oxen have for years past derived from the investigations of the laboratory, should be participated in by our children" (p. 223).

Behind all of this is his absolute faith in the "beautiful economy of Nature," the "inherent self-sufficingness" of the "constitution of things" (pp.

84, 111). Nature works when allowed to, when not interfered with; the evolution of forms and energies is its normal course. Just as we have learned not to swaddle babies tightly and not to use artificial discipline in prisons, we have learned that a natural system of education is the best one. In the same way that in medicine "the old 'heroic treatment' has given place to mild treatment, and often no treatment save a natural regimen," we should adapt our educational methods to "that spontaneous unfolding which all minds go through in their progress to maturity" (p. 111).

What is true of the mind is true of the body. The emphasis in "Physical Education" is on hygiene—nutrition, proper clothing, exercise, and ventilation. The principle is equally valid when applied to the social organism. In *The Study of Sociology* Spencer condemns the "must-do-something" impulse of politicians and economists, their urge to interfere with normal social development. In medicine, he argues, as in political theory, a belief in specific remedies is a sign of primitive thinking: "The question with the modern physician is not as with the ancient—shall the treatment be blood-letting? Shall cathartics, or shall diaphoretics [agents to induce perspiration] be given? Or shall mercurials be administered? But there rises the . . . question—shall there be any treatment beyond wholesome regimen? . . . Is is not probable that what in the individual organism is improperly, though conveniently, called the *vis mediacatrix naturae*, may be found to have its analogue in the social organism?"[49]

That force which in its manifold forms inspirits nature, man, and society is persistent. Evolution of any organism is naturally assured if nothing is done to misdirect that force. An organism, Spencer declares in *First Principles*, is a "dependent moving equilibrium," dependent on its environment for the resupplying of the motive power it dissipates in the process of equilibration. Again, the natural tendency of the organism to maintain its balancing of functions in the course of its growth constitutes the healing power of nature.[50] So, like Carlyle, Spencer repudiates the efforts of philosophical quacks and meddlers. But Carlyle increasingly conceived of the social organism and its individual members as so enfeebled by disease that a radical cure was needed—not just what Spencer calls a "wholesome regimen" but also a "radical universal alteration," a purifying and strengthening of body *and* soul together, a heroic effort to free the heroic will in men. Quite simply, Spencer could not have believed in the purification of the moral will, because he did not believe in the will as an entity. The will was not, to use Bagehot's wry phrase, "an extraordinary incoming 'something,'" but in Spencer's words a "simple homogeneous mental state, forming the link between feeling and action."[51] It was not an initiator of energy, but simply a condition in which one form of energy changed into another kind.

According to Spencer's evolutionary schema, lower and simpler forms continually develop into higher, more complex forms; homogeneous, general functions develop into heterogeneous, specialized functions. But in any one organism at any one time the vitality of the higher functions derives directly from that of the lower. Therefore, when he says that "vigorous health and its accompanying high spirits are larger elements of happiness than any other things whatever" (p. 43), he only means that man's general well-being depends first of all on the well-being of his body. If we give the plant plenty of light and water, the flower will bloom of its own accord.

CHAPTER 5

Types of Healthy Christianity:
Newman and Kingsley

ADVOCATES OF A utilitarian approach to learning have traditionally stressed physical training and a knowledge of what Spencer calls the laws of life. In the beginning of his *Education* John Locke declares, "How necessary *Health* is to our Business and Happiness: And how requisite a strong Constitution, able to endure Hardships and Fatigue, is to one that will make any Figure in the World, is too obvious to need any Proof."[1]

John Henry Newman probably knew the passage; at least he knew the work, for in the seventh discourse of his *Idea of a University* he quotes from it another passage in which Locke asks whether it is not ridiculous that a child destined for employment in trade must learn Latin, a language he will soon forget. Newman replies: "I say, if a Liberal Education consists in the cultivation of the intellect, and if that culture be in itself a good, here, without going further, is an answer to Locke's question; for if a healthy body is a good in itself, why is not a healthy intellect? And if a College of Physicians is a useful institution, because it contemplates bodily health, why is not an Academical Body, though it were simply and solely engaged in imparting vigour and beauty and grasp to the intellectual portion of our nature?"[2] In effect Newman's treatise is an expansion of that argument; it is an attempt to show that university education has no other purpose than the health of the intellect and that only a liberal university education fulfills that purpose. He begins his sixth discourse with a crucial discussion of terms: "It were well if the English, like the Greek language, possessed some definite word to express, simply and generally, intellectual proficiency or perfection, such as 'health,' as used with reference to the animal frame, and 'virtue,' with reference to our moral nature" (p. 110). He goes on to say that of the English words that come to mind, none seems entirely apt. Some, like "talent," "genius," and "ability," apply to man's natural self, which he calls the "raw material" of education. Others, like "judgment," "taste," and "skill," refer to the practice of the mind. Still others—"knowledge" and "science," for example—refer to possessions of the mind, and so they will not do. What he wants is a word applicable to a condition of the mind, a high and excellent condition. Newman here is looking for not only a word but also a concept of intellectual excellence as well as a concept of health analogous to it. He draws out his analogy with characteristic meticulousness, and in defining one concept he also defines the other.

If intellectual perfection is not the practice of the mind, then neither is physical perfection the practice or activity of the body, not, for example, work, as Carlyle declares. Nor is it the natural condition of the body, as Spencer would have it. Newman's three-part analogy emphasizes the condition of health and the cultivation of that condition, as well as of virtue and intellectual excellence. The university's business is "to make this intellectual culture its direct scope, or to employ itself in the education of the intellect,—just as the work of a Hospital lies in healing the sick or wounded, of a Riding or Fencing School, or of a Gymnasium, in exercising the limbs" (p. 111). The healthy state of mind is achieved by systematic training and, when lost, restored by systematic therapy. Its perfection depends on help from without.

As the discourse unfolds, so does Newman's analogy. The mind, he says, is often thought to be a container of knowledge; a narrow mind contains a little of it, and an enlarged mind a great deal. But in reality the mind is more than a container. It has a life and constructive power of its own, just as the human body does. Education should consist, therefore, not just in the passive reception of new ideas but in "the mind's energetic and simultaneous action upon and towards and among those new ideas." It is "a digestion of what we receive" (pp. 118, 119).

An accumulation of physiological metaphors reinforces the impression of the mind as a live thing, capable of growth or debility. In some of these it is like a hand or arm: the university teaches the intellect to "reason well in all matters, to reach out towards truth, and grasp it"; "We must have a grasp of principles"; the perfected intellect has "philosophical reach" (pp. 111, 123, 135). Sometimes the mind is described as an organ for seeing: "The bodily eye, the organ for apprehending material objects, is provided by nature; the eye of the mind, of which the object is truth, is the work of discipline and habit"; "We require intellectual eyes withal, as bodily eyes for sight" (pp. 135, 128). And on one occasion

Newman combines the two metaphors. The man who mistakes data for knowledge "may not see with his mental eye what confronts him; he may have no grasp of things as they are" (pp. 134-135).

It is just this power of grasp, this organic functionalism, which distinguishes human from animal consciousness. With the beast, sensations remain only sights and sounds, whereas man's intellect "seizes and unites what the senses present to it; it grasps and forms what need not have been seen or heard except in its constituent parts . . . In a word, it philosophizes; for I suppose Science and Philosophy, in their elementary idea, are nothing else but this habit of *viewing*, as it may be called, the objects which sense conveys to the mind, of throwing them into system, and uniting and stamping them with one form" (p. 65). The mind perceives and takes hold of experience, then shapes it, as the hands of a sculptor might shape wet clay, into a formal design, a unified structure of knowledge, a philosophy. Or, as the eye of the painter creates design, the mind fulfills its function in composition. And just as the bodily organ strengthens and enlarges itself in the work it does, so the organ of the mind grows. Education's chief value is that very growth.

To attain its perfection, its comprehensiveness and unity, the mind must be systematically brought to bear on comprehensiveness and unity. It takes on the formal qualities of what it deals with. Although liberal studies would not seem to be "useful" as Spencer understands that word, they have a more immediate usefulness than those which Newman calls servile. They help us not to preserve our lives or make our living, but to attain full development as human beings. Typically, Newman clarifies the nature of liberal mental pursuits by comparing them with liberal physical ones: "I say, there are exercises of the body which do receive that appellation. Such, for instance, was the palaestra, in ancient times; such the Olympian games, in which strength and dexterity of body as well as of mind gained the prize. In Xenophon we read of the young Persian nobility being taught to ride on horseback and speak the truth; both being the accomplishments of a gentleman" (p.95). Such activities, Newman explains, are liberal in that they are "self-sufficient and complete"; they do not seek to "minister to something beyond them." He continues: "You will see what I mean by the parallel of bodily health. Health is a good in itself, though nothing came of it, and is especially worth seeking and cherishing . . . The parallel is exact:—As the body may be sacrificed to some manual or other toil . . . so may the intellect be devoted to some specific profession; and I do not call *this* the culture of the intellect. Again, as some member or organ of the body may be inordinately used and developed, so may memory, or imagination, or the reasoning faculty; and *this* again is not intellectual culture. On the other hand, as the body may be tended, cherished, and exercised with a simple view to its general health, so may the intellect also be generally exercised in order to its perfect state; and this *is* its cultivation" (pp. 145-146).

This growth is what Newman calls, in *Grammar of Assent*, man's "progress with relation to his perfection and general good."[3] Every creature, he explains, has a "principle of vitality . . . which is of a sanative and restorative character, and which brings all its parts and functions together into one whole." Every being, then, has an inherent principle which drives it toward formative growth. What characterizes man, in contrast with brute creation, is that man alone is born "with nothing realized." Other creatures are born complete, their natures perfected; man is a potential, and creates himself: "This is the law of his being, which he cannot escape; and whatever is involved in that law he is bound, or rather he is carried on, to fulfil." Therefore, both the formative growth and the equilibrium of health are teleological; they answer a predestined purpose inherent in the organism itself. Physiological models ordinarily include some principle of operation, an explanation of how the organism works—what makes it grow, move, change. Carlyle and the German nature philosophers argued a pantheistic, spiritual vitalism. They assumed that the "vital force" was Idea evolving in matter. Spencer, along with most of the English physiologists, similarly rejected cold mechanism, but, in William Coleman's words, "in general favored a less shrill form or forms of vitalism."[4] Newman's "principle of vitality" represents a third answer to mechanism, one altogether different from the other two and, like so many others in Newman's writings, Aristotelian.

Aristotle's idea, which was later adopted by Thomist philosophers, was that every living thing had a principle or tendency to actualize itself, to realize its own particular nature. This he called the soul, or *pysche*. Thus, Newman says in the *Idea of a University* that the soul is "a living principle" in the human frame, "acting upon it and through it by means of volition" (p. 55). Inferior beings have their own kind of soul, according to their nature; only man, however, has a "rational soul." Therefore man's special entelechy, or "indwelling perfectability," as one writer has translated it, is the formal actualization of his mind.[5] The formal actualization of the body is merely the entelechy of the animal part of him. So for Newman, as for Aristotle, the health of the being is more or less equivalent to the condition of its growth or formation, the particular condition of the organism in relation to its own ideal of perfection. Since man's entelechy must involve intellectual perfection, his health *as a human being* must be measured according to this standard. However, one point distinguishes Newman's model from those of the various "vital force" groups: the health of the organism has less to do with its accumulated and usable fund of energy than with its formal excellence. Education, he says, "brings the mind into form,—for the mind is like the body. Boys outgrow their shape and their strength; their limbs have to be knit together, and their constitution needs tone. Mistaking animal spirits for vigour, and overconfident in their health, ignorant what they can bear and how to manage themselves, they are immoderate and extravagant; and fall into sharp sicknesses. This is an emblem of their minds" (p. xxxiii). This is why healthy growth—culture—needs plenty of external help. Whereas Spencer writes that "the mind like the body has a predetermined course of evolution . . . it unfolds spontaneously,"[6] Newman argues man's "moral certainty of his losing his soul if left to himself."

Obviously the disagreement here involves two related questions: considering man as a rational or spiritual being, are the laws of nature adequate to his fulfillment? and despite the analogic resemblance, is the mind of a different order of things from the body, or is it only a sort of evolution of the animal self? Although Newman and Spencer both seek to extend knowledge by means of analogy, their methods are quite dissimilar, and the difference helps illuminate their approaches to these questions. Spencer assumes that because the same principles operate throughout creation, the same laws can be used to explain everything. The mind, for example, though substantially different from the body, obeys the same laws. The Aristotelian Newman, on the other hand, argues that each order of things has its own principle, and although the various principles might bear a formal resemblance to one another, they are not to be confused. Therefore, while knowledge may supply the mental equivalents of physical health—"strength, energy, agility, graceful carriage and action, manual dexterity, and endurance of fatigue" (p. 746)—resemblance must not be mistaken for identity: "moral and spiritual agents belong to another, not to say a higher, order than physical" (p. 48).

Thus Newman uses analogy as much to stress differences among various "orders" in nature as to suggest similarities. As Ludwig Edelstein has shown, this particular use of the physiological analogy was in common use among ancient Greek writers, especially Aristotle.[7] In the *Rhetoric*, for example, Aristotle declares that health is a good in itself, then adds: "the virtues also must be a good thing; for those who possess them must be in a sound condition, and they are also productive of good things and practical."[8] The comparison is used to make clearer the value of virtue, and not to suggest that virtue and physical health are equally important. Throughout the *Idea of a University* Newman insists on this vital distinction. It would be extravagant, he says, for a doctor to claim that "bodily health was the *summa bonum*, and that no one could be virtuous whose animal system was not in good order" (p. 78). Newman pursued that point in his address to the Catholic University medical students. It would be vanity, he cautioned his listeners, to believe that the laws of their profession are absolute. After all, "bodily health is not the only end of man, and the medical science is not the highest science of which he is the subject. Man has a moral and a religious nature, as well as a physical. He has a mind and a soul; and the mind and soul have a legitimate sovereignty over the body, and the sciences relating to them have in consequence the precedence of those sciences which relate to the body" (p. 378).

In so strongly asserting the separateness of the soul and the body, and the "legitimate sovereignty" of the first over the second, Newman was confronting a firmly rooted tradition of utilitarian thought. As he was writing the *Idea of a University* he had before him Macaulay's well-known essay on Bacon.[9] He must have been struck by the prominent place given to medical science in that essay, which is an attack on the "ancient philosophy" and its "impractical" view of man, as well as a defense of Baconian or inductive philosophy and the practical benefits it has given the world. Macaulay's thesis is that the philosophy of the Greeks and Romans, instead of helping man control his natural environment, "tended to raise the mind above low cares, to separate it from the body, to exercise its subtilty in the solution of very obscure questions."[10] So to Plato, for example, "the science of medicine appeared to be of very disputable advantage." By contrast, Bacon "vindicated the dignity of that art by appealing to the example of Christ, and reminded men that the great Physician of the soul did not disdain to be also the physician of the body" (p. 380). Later, Macaulay observes, the Epicurean and Stoic rightly measured the quality of experience according to the criteria of pain and pleasure, but ignored that very science which could best decrease pain and increase pleasure. He imagines a follower of Epictetus and a disciple of Bacon traveling together. Discovering a town devastated by smallpox, "The Stoic assures the dismayed population that there is nothing bad in small-pox, and that to a wise man, disease, deformity, death, and loss of friends are not evils. The Baconian takes out his lancet and begins to vaccinate" (p. 386). Throughout the essay modern induc-

tive philosophy is represented as dynamic, direct, and fruitful, and ancient philosophy as lost in barren controversy; the first is a path and the
second a treadmill. And not only the philosopher, Macaulay says, but
also the "plain man" of today shows the influence and shares the benefits
of the philosophic revolution. He responds, for example, to an attack of
indigestion by taking plain, positive action. "He has never heard Lord
Bacon's name. But he proceeds in strict conformity with the rules laid
down in the second book of the *Novum Organum*, and satisfies himself
that mince pies have done the mischief" (p. 391).

It would take an essay longer than Macaulay's to sort out all the sim-
plifications and distortions he makes in his headlong romp through the
history of philosophy. Though cleverly argued, the essay evolves from a
narrow and dubious assumption—that philosophy can do much to increase physical comfort but very little in a direct way to improve our
souls. Therefore, he says, it is better to be a shoemaker than the author of
On Anger, since shoes have kept dry the feet of millions, whereas Seneca
has never helped anyone keep his temper (p. 366). Repeatedly Macaulay
returns to the point that the physical necessities of life and the creature
comforts are more useful objects of study than the improvement of the
soul. His chief target here is Plato, who in the *Republic* tells us that the
body has "less of truth and reality" than the soul, and therefore what
serves the body's needs is less true and real than what serves the soul's.
Physical culture, Plato argues, must be kept subordinate to intellectual
culture, lest the lower activity obstruct the higher. "Excessive care of the
body" interferes with a person's duties both at home and at his work.
"Worst of all . . . it is prejudicial to learning of all kinds and to thought
and meditation." This position was also taken by Aristotle, who declared
that physical and intellectual education must not be carried on simultaneously. "It is not right," he says, "to do work with the mind and the
body at the same time. The two different sorts of work tend naturally to
produce different, and indeed opposite, effects. Physical work clogs the
mind; and mental work hampers the body."[11]

In urging that the mind has a legitimate sovereignty over the body,
Newman reflects this classical humanist tradition. Both Plato and
Aristotle viewed education as a vertical process in which the lower faculties are trained first, then the higher. The temperament, whose gentle
and spirited sides are developed by music and athletics respectively, is
shaped by habits formed early, the intellect by education administered
late. The system set out in the *Ethics* has been summarized by W. L.
Newman: "To train the whole nature, but to train each part of it succes-

sively and in the order of its emergence, and to train each part with a view to the higher element which emerges next, and all with a view to the development of reason—that is the broad scheme of education which Aristotle lays down here."[12]

Both Plato and Aristotle caution against developing in young men a barbarian toughness through excessive physical training. In the *Politics* Aristotle accuses the Spartans of turning their youth into savages "by imposing rigorous exercises, in the idea that this is the best way of fostering the virtue of courage." Similarly Plato argues that "unmitigated athletics produce a sort of ferocity." To avoid this warping of the temper, physical training must be "carefully regulated" at all stages of life. A healthy body, Plato insists, cannot in itself produce a healthy mind, though the sound mind "has power in itself to make the bodily condition as perfect as it can be."[13]

Edith Hamilton has remarked that the love of games among ancient Greeks illustrates their special concept of happiness, "the exercise of vital powers along lines of excellence in a life affording them scope." However, for a variety of reasons, by the time of the Socratic philosophers athletics had fallen into some disrepute, and the tendency, at least among philosophers, was to emphasize what Matthew Arnold calls "play of mind." Education was pointed toward developing and freeing the reason, toward making the body subservient to the soul. In his *Ethics* Aristotle specifies the qualities of the excellent man, the equivalent and model of Newman's man of philosophic habit. A life of virtue, he says, produces happiness, and happiness is a quality not of the body, but of the soul, the distinctive feature of man. Since happiness consists in the activity of soul in accordance with the best and most complete virtue, the most useful activities are those which develop virtue in the individual. A state of virtue is a good in itself; it also produces virtuous action just as a state of health produces healthy activity. "Wisdom produces Happiness, not in the sense in which medicine produces health, but in the sense in which healthiness is the cause of health."[14] In his *Rhetoric* Aristotle enlarges on this similarity between excellence of mind and of body, while carefully distinguishing the two. Among those things which "must necessarily be good" are "Happiness, since it is desirable in itself and self-sufficient, and to obtain it we choose a number of things. Justice, courage, self-control, magnanimity, magnificence, and other similar states of mind, for they are virtues of the soul. Health, beauty, and the like, for they are virtues of the body and produce many advantages."[15] The Aristotelian concept of health is identical with that reflected in *The Idea of a University*. It is specifically what Aristotle calls a bodily virtue, distinct from the virtues of the soul like justice, courage, and magnanimity; but it is like virtue of the soul in that as a state of potentiality or readiness it is both a good and conducive to good.

By the end of the seventh discourse Newman has demonstrated that although we do not have a name for the intellectual equivalent of physical health we do have the ideal, one passed down from thinkers of Greek antiquity. It is an ideal parallel with, but superior to its counterpart, and the university should devote itself to it exclusively. This is a task arduous and exacting, but productive of those faculties absolutely essential to the perfection of the human nature: "the force, the steadiness, the comprehensiveness and the versatility of intellect, the command over our own powers, the instinctive just estimate of things as they pass before us, which sometimes indeed is a natural gift, but commonly is not gained without much effort and the exercise of years" (p. xxxiii).

In Discourse VIII, however, Newman turns to the limitations of such an education. Although philosophy can perfect the mind and thus perfect human nature, it does not raise the mind above nature (p. 165). There is yet even a higher ideal of perfection which might be called the health of the soul. Enlarging the mind brings to it the awareness of perfection as an ideal, but without religion this awareness induces pride, against which the gentleman's only safeguards are shame and modesty. Relying solely on instincts cultivated by moral philosophy, he abhors vice as a matter of taste. Knowledge "generates within the mind a fastidiousness, analogous to the delicacy or daintiness which good nurture or a sickly habit induces in respect of food; and this fastidiousness, though arguing no high principle, though no protection in the case of violent temptation, nor sure in its operation, yet will often or generally be lively enough to create an absolute loathing of certain offenses" (p. 166). Such a refinement has a daily usefulness which, Newman acknowledges, religion cannot emulate. In the cultivated mind there is a modest, continual striving against the baser parts of our nature. Knowledge "is capable of resting on the mind, and taking up its familiar lodging with it, and engrossing it, and . . . thus becomes a match for the besetting power of sensuality, and a sort of homoeopathic medicine for the disease" (p. 165). Like homeopathy, secular philosophy can supply a benign stimulant to cure a malignant fever; "it expels the excitements of sense by the introduction of those of the intellect" (p. 165). In so doing philosophy and the frame of mind it induces yield a useful but superficial treatment for what Newman calls the "moral malady." At their best they provide "an irresolution and indecision in doing wrong, which will act as a *remora* [an instrument for keeping broken bones in place] till the danger is past away" (p. 166). Or it can supply a specific remedy "sufficient to cure the particular moral disorder, and to prevent its accesses ever afterwards" (p. 167). But by instilling merely an aesthetic distaste for vice, secular philosophy cannot effect a systemic cure: "Deformity is its abhorrence; accordingly, since it cannot dissuade men from vice, therefore in order to escape the sight of its deformity, it embellishes it. It 'skins and films the ulcerous place,' which it cannot probe or heal" (p. 179). Secular training ministers to the mind and body, but only through religion can the soul achieve the state of health. The Church "aims at regenerating the very depths of the heart . . . She is curing men and keeping them clear of mortal sin" (p. 180). The philosophic habit, the highest attainment of the gentleman and the proper aim of the university education, has among its most "beautiful," its most "winning" qualities that of modesty, but it cannot in itself love *humility* and thus stops short of spiritual perfection. Just as English has no word for the classical conception of intellectual excellence, "ancient civilization had not the idea, and had no word to express" the Christian concept of humility. Modesty, an admirable and valuable social grace, is only counterfeit humility. True humility is "to feel and to behave as if we were low; not, to cherish a notion of our own importance, while we affect a low position" (p. 182).

As the trained body is an assistance to education, so the trained mind is to religion, but the ultimate goal of man's development must always be kept in mind. To stop with philosophy, the perfection of one's human nature, is little better than stopping with physical health, the perfection of his animal nature. All the qualities attained by the man of philosophic habit are, like modesty, but the *natural* counterparts, and thus inferior, to the qualities of the holy man. Intellectual perfection "is *almost* prophetic from its knowledge of history; it is *almost* heart-searching from its knowledge of human nature; it has *almost* supernatural charity from its freedom from littleness and prejudice; it has *almost* the repose of faith because nothing can startle it; it has *almost* the beauty and harmony of heavenly contemplation, so intimate is it with the eternal order of things and the music of the spheres" (p. 123; italics added).

Not surprisingly, Newman's thoroughly healthy man turns out to be a Christian as well as a gentleman. It is worth comparing this model of the Christian gentleman with Carlyle's model of the healthy hero. A hero, Newman says, need not be a gentleman (p. 96). If we review the pantheon of figures in *Heroes and Hero Worship* we glimpse personages of great force, endurance, and single-minded integrity, but we see little in the way of winning modesty, grace, or simple charity. Carlyle's Hero is a Man equipped by nature to deal with Mankind. Newman's gentleman is a man equipped by his education to deal with men: not a transcendent figure, but one whose ordinary mental talents have been refined and strengthened. His typical qualities, such as "good sense," "sobriety of thought," and "steadiness of view," are not alien to Carlyle's healthy hero, but Newman certainly emphasizes strength, energy, and action less than does Carlyle. These differences reflect contrasting concepts of health. Newman's concept, like Aristotle's, is of an approachable but not attainable ideal of excellence, a state of purity and harmony which makes right action possible. Carlyle's concept of health is more dynamic. To recall Newman's distinction, it stresses practice rather than condition. Since the individual cannot perceive his own condition of health, his soundness is only manifest in healthy action.

Victorians sought a concept of health which was environmental in a broad sense, which took into account the individual's responsiveness to elements, both physical and psychological, in the outside world. Carlyle's concept implied that sort of relationship in relating internal unity to unity with the world at large. His hero is not only healthy in himself, he is also the true healer, one whose word "is the wise healing word which all can believe in."[16] Being whole himself, he helps create wholeness. Newman's man of philosophic habit, with his "connected view or grasp of things" (p. xxxiv), also can live in accord with the most universal principles. But he remains a man of capacity rather than active energy. Like his personality, his actions are modest. "He is mainly occupied in merely removing the obstacles which hinder the free and unembarrassed action of those about him" (p. 185). Even the Church develops in him but a fine potential: "She is putting souls in the way of salvation, that they may then be in a condition, if they shall be called upon, to aspire to the heroic, and to attain the full proportions, as well as the rudiments, of the beautiful" (p. 180).

Carlyle's emphasis on the Will as the center of health, and consequently on heroic action as proof of health, gave to his concept an appeal not shared by either Spencer's positivist concept or Newman's classical concept: it identified health with an active, vigorous life, and therefore with personal power and self-creation. According to Whitehead, these values are absolutely essential to any idea of "life": "Process for its intelligibility involves the notion of a creative activity belonging to the very essence of each occasion. It is the process of eliciting into actual being factors in the universe which antecedently to that process exist only in the mode of unrealized potentialities. The process of self-creation is the transformation of the potential into the actual, and the fact of such transformation includes the immediacy of self-enjoyment."[17]

Carlyle's hero and Newman's gentleman are presented as models of healthy manhood. There is little of the gentleman in Carlyle's model and less of the hero in Newman's. But they share this quality: as figures for general emulation both leave something to be desired. They are, to put it simply, remote. Admittedly an emblem of perfection (though not the highest perfection), the man of philosophic habit is an ideal type, who, for example, "never inflicts pain." Carlyle's hero seems distant from us because of his extraordinary natural qualities; he has something of the saint, but more of the deity. Newman describes the type in Discourse VI: "There are men who, when in difficulties, originate at the moment vast ideas or dazzling projects; who, under the influence of excitement, are able to cast a light, almost as if from inspiration, on a subject or course of action which comes before them; who have a sudden presence of mind equal to any emergency, rising with the occasion, and an undaunted magnanimous bearing, and an energy and keenness which is but made intense by opposition. This is genius, this is heroism" (pp. 122-123).

Carlyle made the unified, assertive will the basis of his concept of health. Like electrical force or any other natural energy, it is visible not in itself but only in what it accomplishes. This manifestation in work is its realization and only true reality. Still, Carlyle never held that the heroic or healthy will must "incorporate" itself in bodily heroism. The Carlylean hero is "featurely," to use Bagehot's term, in personality alone; in other respects he may well be unprepossessing. The hypochondriacal Cromwell in *Heroes and Hero Worship* has "an outer hull of chaotic confusion," but "a clear determinate man's-energy working in the heart of that." The same inner force is evident in the scrofulous Dr. Johnson. "A healthy soul," Carlyle declares, "imprison it as you will, in squalid garrets, shabby coat, bodily sickness, or whatever else, will assert its heaven-granted, indefeasible Freedom, its right to conquer difficulties, to do work, even to feel gladness."[18] In physique, manner, way of life—in all visible things—the Hero "has had to cramp himself into strange shapes." Because his energy is of the mind, it is manifested in spiritual or psychological influence. Thus, the healthy man has a firm ethical and psychological relation with the human world about him; that is his health as well as the proof of his health. Here is a pattern for human conduct and, as Newman once wrote, "instances and patterns, not logical reasonings, are the living conclusions which alone can have a hold over our affections, or can form the character."[19] And how much more forceful it is to take this dynamic concept and embody it physically, to provide an instance or pattern which is also a clear image of the healthy life. In his life and in his writings one of Carlyle's disciples, Charles Kingsley, offered just such a living embodiment to the Victorian public.

KINGSLEY's rough-and-tumble debate with Newman is best understood by reading the correspondence between the two as well as Kingsley's pamphlet *"What Then Does Dr. Newman Mean?"*—and of course Newman's *Apologia*. Walter Houghton has isolated some of the larger philosophical issues that arose. The questions posed in the course of this famous controversy were many and varied, but there was one very important topic which was only debated obliquely: Kingsley's muscular Christianity. To support his original attack on Newman and Roman Catholicism, Kingsley found an old sermon in which Newman stated that Christians, *in times of persecution*, must exercise a self-restraint which will "give them the appearance of being artificial" and make them seem "wanting in openness and manliness." With his usual disregard for fine points, Kingsley read the passage as "telling Christians that they will always seem 'artificial,' and 'wanting in openness and manliness.' " In reply Newman argued that Christ's example of meekness, passiveness, and innocence was a better alternative to man's natural tendency to rely on "carnal inducements" and "physical and material force," and he pointedly cited "muscular Christianity" as an example of reliance on physical and material force. In one sense the issue came down to whether a Christian should be manly or gentlemanly, and whether he should follow his natural bent or restrain it. "There have been Protestants," Newman observed in *Grammar of Assent*, "whose idea of enlightened Christianity has been a strenuous antagonism to what they consider the unmanliness and unreasonableness of Christian morality, an antipathy to the precepts of patience, meekness, forgiveness of injuries, and chastity."[20] These words were published in 1870; the original war of letters and pamphlets took place in 1864. But even long before that time Kingsley and his muscular Christianity had attracted the censure of a variety of critics. When the Newman controversy broke out, he had had seven years' experience in debating the issue.

In an age weary of introspection the Canon of Eversley was just the sort of man to attract an immediate following. He seemed to be thoroughly at home in the universe, delighted to be alive and certain of his purpose for living. As preacher, lecturer, novelist, and poet he "made his image," as Bagehot would say—an honest, strong, clear image. He conveyed a sense of familiarity with all sorts of topics: Chartism and the Church of Rome, Saint Paul and sea anemones. Ideas, people, and natural objects alike were to him vivid and immediate, "presences plain in the place." He had blunt, outspoken views on them individually and in combination, and his views often were rapid in the forming: "Physiognomy, which has been a study of mine for years, gave me certain opinions of ____ the first day that I ever saw him, which said, 'that man and I, unless utterly changed—more changed, perhaps, than he will ever be in this mortal body,—can never be friends." In brief, Kingsley was the embodiment of the bluff, English way of dealing with things, the virile way. This style or habitude was what most people took muscular Christianity to mean, though certain philosophical convictions underlay what Fitzjames Stephen called "a school of feeling rather than thought."[21]

In his *Education* Spencer noted that the appearance of this school signified a new concern for health in the raising of children. "The topic," he added, "is evidently ripe for discussion."[22] Kingsley himself, by nature combative, loved controversy and did indeed feel that the topic was ripe for discussion. Unfortunately, even by 1859 when Spencer wrote that, Kingsley's own role in the discussion had been defined by others. The term muscular Christianity was not his; he hated it and tried his best to disengage himself from it, but with feeble success.

Apparently Kingsley's novel *Two Years Ago* had inspired the coining of the phrase in 1857. T. C. Sandars, discussing the work in the *Saturday Review*, observed: "We all know by this time what is the task that Mr. Kingsley has made specially his own—it is that of spreading the knowledge and fostering the love of a muscular Christianity. His ideal is a man who fears God and can walk a thousand miles in a thousand hours—who, in the language which Mr. Kingsley has made popular, breathes God's free air on God's rich earth, and at the same time can hit a woodcock, doctor a horse, and twist a poker round his fingers."[23] Although on the whole friendly to the author and his novel, Sandars did tend to lapse into that spirit of amiable jocosity which Kingsley was to find so aggravating. Kingsley also had to contend with the graver stance of reviewers like Fitzjames Stephen. In an *Edinburgh* review of *Tom Brown's School Days* Stephen noted that muscular Christianity seemed to be a product of Kingsley's "deep sense of the sacredness of all the ordinary relations and all the common duties of life, and the vigour with which he contends for the merits of a simple massive unconscious goodness, and for the great importance and value of animal spirits, physical strength, and a hearty enjoyment of all the pursuits and accomplishments which are connected with them." Stephen had no quarrel regarding the sacredness of ordinary tasks and relations, but simple massive goodness, he argued, was a poor response to life's knottier problems; the mind's faculties, not the body's, were most in need of training and refining: "No doubt strong muscles and hardy nerves are of incalculable importance, but they derive that importance from the mind, of which they are the servants."[24]

Kingsley felt pressed to answer such criticism. He complained by letter in October 1858 to the author of a recent review which had used that "painful, if not offensive, term, 'Muscular Christianity.' " Kingsley knew of only one sort of Christianity, he told his correspondent, that which purposes to transform each man into Christ's likeness and to consecrate mankind, "body, soul, and spirit," to His service. He aimed only to tell strong and healthy men that they too can serve God, even though they are not quick-witted or highly educated. Kingsley always sensed a special destiny in the fact that his family tree had produced more soldiers and sportsmen than scholars. What if it *had* pleased God, he asked the reviewer, that he "should have been born and bred and have lived ever since in the tents of Esau? What if—by no choice of my own—my relations and friends should have been the hunters and fighters?" The story of Esau and Jacob was to occur to Kingsley often in this context. His one idea in life, he declared to F. D. Maurice, was to "tell Esau that he had a birthright as well as Jacob."[25] In the preface to the fourth edition of *Yeast* he wrote that his novel was mainly addressed to "poor, rough Esau, who sails Jacob's ships, founds Jacob's colonies, pours out his blood for him in those wars which Jacob himself has stirred up—while his sleek brother sits home in his counting-house, enjoying at once 'the means of grace' and the produce of Esau's labour . . . Esau has a birthright; and this book, like all the books which I have ever written, is written to tell him so." In the parable from Genesis, Kingsley saw symbolized the eternal division of mankind—the two camps, divided partly along economic lines: Esau was the tailor laboring in London sweatshops or the dispossessed farmer making his living by poaching; more generally he was any man—sportsman, soldier, or worker—whose view of life was not complex or sophisticated and who relied more on physical action than on intellect. Kingsley believed that the clever could take care of themselves; his ministry, as he conceived it, was speaking out for "healthy animalism." "I have to preach the divineness of the whole manhood," he wrote Maurice in 1863, "and am content to be called a Muscular Christian, or any other impertinent name, by men who little dream of the weakness of character, sickness of body, and misery of mind, by which I have bought what little I know of the human heart."[26]

Kingsley believed that in his own case the gift of health was a divine one, a kind of miracle which had conveyed to him his special calling. He could well sympathize, he told the reviewer in 1858, with the man whose life had been nothing but a struggle with bodily weakness, for his own life had been like that for fifteen years. "But what if, when God gave me suddenly and strangely health of body and peace of mind, I learnt what a priceless blessing that *corpus sanum* was, and how it helped, humiliating as the confession may be to spiritual pride—to the producing of *mentem sanam?*"[27] The certitude of his belief in *mens sana in corpore sano* was the evangelical faith of a man who had labored to a state of grace both physically and mentally. Though very energetic as a child, he was given to frequent breakdowns in health. Twice he was afflicted with brain fever and was subject to violent attacks of croup (which he was to blame for his lifelong stammer). At grammar school he was strong, active, and physically courageous, but too uncoordinated and sensitive to criticism to be any good at games. Ironically it was in searching for "peace of mind" that he found the gift of health. While at Magdalene College, Cambridge, he began to devote himself more and more to physical exercise. He took up rowing and developed the habit of long walks: twenty-five miles a day was, his wife later recalled, "a real refreshment" to him in those days as well as later. (He once made the distance from Cambridge to London—fifty-two miles—in a single day, starting out early in the morning and arriving at nine in the evening.) He also found time for riding, shooting, and fishing. To some extent all this was done to gain relief from the intellectual demands of university life. Once, during examinations, he walked ten miles down the Cam and back for some pike-fishing. His "panacea for stupidity and over-'mentation' " was "a day in a roaring fen wind."[28]

This constant, strenuous exercise was so exhilarating that Kingsley soon felt in danger of succumbing wholly to it, of indulging in it as in strong drink. It was an anodyne not only to the rigors of study, but to a state of depression caused by a separation from his future wife, Fanny Grenfell, a separation enforced by her parents. On his return to Cambridge in the fall of 1842, she writes, he "became reckless, and nearly gave up all for lost: he read little, he went in for excitement of every kind —boating, hunting, driving, fencing, boxing, duck-shooting in the Fens, —anything to deaden the remembrance of the happy past, which just then promised no future." The mania for action also arose from a severe testing of his religious convictions caused by a general disenchantment with churchmen and with the religious commonplaces of the day and, surprisingly, an attraction to the Oxford movement and even to Rome itself. There was always in Kingsley's nature a strong ascetic bent, which for a time found appealing an idea he attributed to Catholics and Tractarians, that of despising the flesh and all other things material. His own continual, spontaneous discharging of physical energies, and the pleasure which that gave him, he came to regard as immoral. In February 1841 he wrote to Fanny: "I strive daily and hourly to be calm . . . I have refused hunting and driving, and made a solemn vow against cards . . . You cannot understand the excitement of animal exercise from the mere act of cutting wood or playing cricket to the manias of hunting or shooting or fishing. On these things more or less most young men live. Every moment which is taken from them for duty or for reading is felt to be lost— to be so much time sacrificed to hard circumstance."[29]

Kingsley's problem was that while he mistrusted those impulses of the body which called the mind away from reflection and the sterner duties of life, he also despised the sort of pallid asceticism which he associated more and more with evangelical and Roman Catholic theology. "Manicheeists" (his name for believers in bodily self-denial) encouraged a contempt for ordinary human relations, including sexual relations, stemming from their contempt for the body: "In their eyes man is not a spirit necessarily embodied in and expressed by an animal; but a spirit accidentally connected with and burdened by an animal. The animal part of them only is supposed to be human; the spiritual, angelic or diabolic, as the case may be. The relations of life are supposed to be properties only of the animal part, or rather adjuncts of them. The ideal of man, therefore, is to deny, not himself, but the animal part which is not himself, and to strive after a non-human or angelic state. And this angelic state is supposed, of course, to be single and self-sustained, without relations, except to God alone."[30]

Kingsley wanted some philosophical justification for those instincts which told him that the life of a clergyman was compatible with married life and with that of a sportsman. He found it in the works of Carlyle, which convinced him of "the Perfect Harmony of the Physical with the Spiritual Universe."[31] Kingsley's notion of the healthy hero was most directly influenced by three of Carlyle's ideas: the body is an expression of spirit, and therefore the obedience to healthy impulse is a sign of constitutional harmony; the state of health is a knowledge of the laws of nature and a compliance with these laws; and heroism is a life of action made possible by observing the laws of health. As a matter of fact, he deviated from Carlyle significantly on every one of these points, though possibly he never grasped that fact.

The basis for Kingsley's philosophy of "healthy materialism" appears to have been the essay on the German idealist Novalis, included among other of Carlyle's works sent to him by Fanny in 1841. Especially interesting to Kingsley in his current state of doubt was Novalis' attitude toward the material world of Nature. "He loves external Nature with a singular depth," Carlyle had written; "nay, we might say, he reverences her, and holds unspeakable communings with her: for Nature is no longer dead, hostile Matter, but the Veil and mysterious Garment of the Unseen; as it were, the Voice with which the Deity proclaims himself to man." Novalis believed, as Carlyle did also, that matter and spirit were one, that matter was but the visible projection of spirit, and that it was therefore indivisible as spirit is, a "self-subsistent universally connected Whole." Thus the body of man is the highest spiritual revelation. In a passage quoted by Carlyle in this essay and also in *Sartor Resartus* Novalis declared: "There is but one Temple in the World; and that is the Body of Man. Nothing is holier than this high form. Bending before men is a reverence done to this Revelation in the Flesh. We touch Heaven, when we lay our hand on a human body."[32] From such passages Kingsley drew his strong conviction in the wholeness of man. Should we not "learn to love all things, all men—not as spirits only . . . but—as men and women, of body, soul, and spirit, made each one being, and therefore all to be loved?"[33]

Kingsley came nowhere near adopting the "Transcendental Philosophies" of Carlyle's Teufelsdröckh, the "humour of looking at all Matter and Material things as Spirit."[34] It was enough for him to believe that the body and the spirit were both divine: "There has always seemed to me something impious in the neglect of personal health, strength, and beauty, which the religious, and sometimes the clergymen of this day affect . . . I could not do half the little good I do do here [at Eversley], if it were not for that strength and activity which some consider coarse and degrading . . . How merciful God has been in turning all the strength and hardihood I gained in snipe shooting and hunting, and rowing and jack-fishing in those magnificent fens to His work."[35]

Believing now that the state of health was the absolute harmony of mind and body, Kingsley readily accepted Carlyle's view that self-consciousness, or any intellectual consciousness which threatened that harmony, was a disease. Fitzjames Stephen was no doubt right in suggesting that anti-intellectualism was an inevitable corollary of Kingsley's reverence for the body. A widely read man himself (senior optime in mathematics and a first in classics at Cambridge), Kingsley never misprized formal study, but he did believe that thought without action was unhealthy. In 1842, when Fanny was tormented by religious perplexity, he advised her: "We may think too much! There is such a thing as mystifying one's self! Mystifying one's self is thinking a dozen thoughts to get to a conclusion, to which one might arrive by thinking one—getting at ideas by an unnecessarily subtle and circuitous path: then, because one has gone through many steps, one fancies one has gone deep . . . The consistent Christian should have no second thoughts, but do good by the first impulse."[36]

Kingsley was a man of strong and manifold opinions, but he cannot be said to have had a keenly speculative mind. When he reached a verdict on some issue he rejoiced in the certainty it gave him. As one reviewer wrote, "The impulsiveness which is the chief characteristic of his mind is exactly the kind of impulsiveness which makes a man delight in athletic exercises, in communion with animals, and in combating a certain amount of physical difficulties."[37] Nor did Kingsley resent being called impulsive, holding as he did that an act of impulse signified the divine accord of flesh and spirit. If the will is noble, he told Fanny in 1843, the unreasoned act represents "the highest state of harmony and health, the rare moments of life, in which our life is not manifold, but one—body and soul and spirit working together!" To equate health with wholeness in this way, as Kingsley often did, was to affirm both the separateness and the interdependence of flesh and spirit. The state of health exists "when the will is noble," when it is above nature, above the body, and therefore receptive to divine promptings rather than merely to the transient whim of bodily desire. "Where a man acts from impulse, it is because the flesh is at harmony with, and obeys, the spirit." Kingsley sometimes suggested that all impulses are noble, and at other times that some are more noble than others. The way to evaluate an impulse, he said in one letter, is by its effect. Does it, we should ask ourselves, lead to good or evil? "If to good, it, like every other good gift, is from God. If to evil, it is your fleshly will impelling itself, not the spirit at harmony with the spirit, and the spirit with the flesh."[38]

In Kingsley, as in Carlyle, health is an ethical state of constitutional well-being, equivalent to righteousness.[39] Insofar as man is a moral agent, having free will and being capable of divine inspiration, he belongs to the spiritual world and must live according to spiritual laws. But man also is a part of the physical world, and must live according to its laws. Kingsley insisted on this dualistic epistemology, on the existence of two worlds, each with separate laws: "The spiritual world—I beg you to fix this in your minds—is not merely an invisible world which may become visible, but an invisible world which is by its essence invisible; a moral world, a world of right and wrong." Roman Catholics, he believed, mistakenly assume that objects in the physical world—sacramental bread, for example, or statues—possess extraphysical qualities. The tendency to confuse the physical with the spiritual was the basis of all superstition: "But Himself?—Who can see Him? Except the humble and the contrite heart, to whom He reveals Himself as a Spirit to be worshipped in spirit and in truth, and not in bread, nor wood, nor stone, nor gold, nor quintessential diamond." We can understand the laws of the physical world objectively and intellectually; our cognition of the laws of the spiritual world is entirely subjective, though it is gained through action in the physical world. In other words, by acting morally, man expresses the godlike in himself: "This is healthy materialism, for there is a truth even in materialism. The man has hold of a reality who says—'This earth is, after all, to me the great fact.' God is the great fact, objectively, in the pure truth of things; but He can only become the great fact to us, subjectively, by our acting on the truth, that matter, and all its ties—so interwoven with our spirits and our spiritual ties that it is impossible to separate them—that this earth, I say, is the next greatest fact to that of God's existence, the fact by which we know Him."[40] One comes to know God forcefully, that is to say subjectively, by living an active, Christian life, not by studying nature for evidence of a grand design. If he makes the error of believing that the ethical basis of human life is to be found in natural law, "he is doomed forever to be the slave of his own needs, enforced by an internecine struggle for existence."[41] The study of nature may, far from teaching moral theology, "unteach it." To his "dear master," F. D. Maurice, Kingsley wrote: "I have long ago found out how little I can discover about God's absolute love, or absolute righteousness, from a universe in which everything is *eating* everything else—infinite cunning and shift (in the good sense). Infinite creative fancy it does reveal; but nothing else, unless interpreted by moral laws which are in oneself already, and in which one has often to trust against all appearances, and cry out of the lowest deep (as I have had to do)—Thou art not Siva the destroyer. Thou art not even Ahriman and Ormuzd in one . . . There is something in me—which is not nature, but Thou must have taught me

—which cries and will cry: Though Thou slay me, as Thou hast slain world on world already—though I and all this glorious race of men go down to Hades with the ichthyosaurs and the mammoths, yet I will trust in Thee."[42]

In Kingsley's writings the laws of nature seem, on the one hand, ethically neutral—they are the laws of growth and decay, of life and death: "By the very same laws by which every blade of grass grows, and every insect springs to life in the sunbeam, she kills, and kills, and kills, and is never tired of killing." On the other hand, for man, the percipient creature, the laws of nature are prescriptive and judgmental. Because they are one manifestation of "the express will of God," to violate them is to abandon in theological terms the state of righteousness: "Evil, as such, has no existence; but men can and do resist God's will, and break the law, which is appointed for them, and so punish themselves with getting into disharmony with their own constitution and that of the universe; just as a wheel in a piece of machinery punishes itself when it gets out of gear."[43]

Like Carlyle and Spencer, Kingsley held that being healthy demands obedience to the laws of nature. However, as Mill pointed out in his essay on nature, that demand invites confusion: "To bid people conform to the laws of nature when they have no power but what the laws of nature give them—when it is a physical impossibility for them to do the smallest thing otherwise than through some law of nature, is an absurdity." The problem, he suggested, lay in mixing up one notion of law— "what is"—with another notion—"what ought to be." Mill himself argued that we can only make a choice among natural laws by placing ourselves in circumstances wherein the more beneficial ones operate more strongly than the others. Kingsley, however, never worked his way through the issue. He never really squared his belief that *all* laws are the express will of God with his formula that we should, "if need be, counteract one with another."[44]

The tendency to speak of the "laws of nature" as observable regularities and as prescriptions, Mill observed, derived from the writings of popular physiologists like George Combe, who regarded the benefits of physiology as so manifest that securing them was an absolute duty. An enthusiastic reader of Combe, Kingsley may have drawn his evangelical attitude toward "nature" partly from his writings, but it is likely that the chief influence was once again Carlyle. In his writings Carlyle uses the word *nature* in several ways. Sometimes it simply means the material and visible world, but when he speaks of the "laws of nature" he usually means the spiritual laws *behind* nature, laws which may seem to conflict with the perceived regularities in the behavior of matter: "Where are the Laws of Nature? To me perhaps the rising of one from the dead were no violation of these Laws, but a confirmation; were some far deeper Law, now first penetrated into, and by Spiritual Force, even as the rest have all been, brought to bear on us with its Material Force." For one with sufficient insight to grasp these hidden, spiritual laws there is no contradiction between "what is" and "what ought to be." They must inevitably be obeyed, since they govern the course of things with unfailing uniformity. Therefore, the "laws of nature" are synonymous with what *will* happen as they manifest themselves in time. For example, unless England undergoes a revolution of spirit, Carlyle wrote, political revolutions will follow one after the other: "The Laws of Nature will have themselves fulfilled. That is a thing certain to me."[45]

When Carlyle declares that we must, at our peril, obey these laws he means that we must not be beguiled by such artificially conceived laws as self-interest and supply-and-demand or by the laws of physical phenomena. But when Kingsley calls for obedience to the laws of nature he is referring, quite simply, to those laws governing the physical world. With regard to human welfare the most urgent ones are those pertaining to physiology and hygiene: the laws of health. As one of his contemporaries put it, Kingsley became "the apostle of cleanliness."[46] When the cholera epidemic in the summer of 1849 reached Eversley where he was Rector, he exhausted himself working among the parishioners and finally had to retire to Devonshire for a rest. Within a month, however, he was back in the parish. That autumn, with the cholera menace at its severest, he worked resolutely in London and in the country, and at Eversley preached three famous sermons on the subject. He also began assembling material on London's water supply. In October he wrote to his wife from Chelsea: "I was yesterday with George Walsh and Mansfield over the cholera districts of Bermondsey; and, oh, God! what I saw! people having no water to drink—hundreds of them—but the water of the common sewer which stagnated full of . . . dead fish, cats and dogs, under their windows. At the time the cholera was raging Walsh saw them throwing untold horrors into the ditch, and then dipping out the water and drinking it!!"[47]

Kingsley remained active in the cause of sanitation, raising money, gathering statistics, and, in 1854, giving evidence before the House of Commons on the unhealthful conditions of the cities and on the low pay of medical officers. A letter to Lady Harding in 1859 reveals characteristic motives in his absorption with sanitary reform—a predilection for the tangible rather than the abstract, and a weariness over theological and political dispute: "I am going to throw myself into this movement. I am tired of most things in the world. Of sanitary reform I shall never grow tired. No one can accuse a man of being sentimental over *it*, or of doing too much of *it*. There can be no mistake about the saving of human lives, and the training up a healthy generation. God bless you all and all good ladies who have discovered that human beings have bodies as well as souls, and that the state of the soul too often depends on that of the body." To him the laws of health were both inexorable and clear: lack of exercise led to flabbiness of body; poor sanitary conditions led to disease. Of these laws there was total certainty, and to help disseminate them was an absolute imperative. "It is duty," he told the members of the Ladies Sanitary Association, "one of the noblest of duties, to help the increase of the English race as much as possible, and to see that every child that is born into this great nation of England be developed to the highest pitch to which we can develop him in physical strength and beauty, as well as in intellect and in virtue."[48]

Once Kingsley, in his early reading of Carlyle, began to feel the full force of the idea that the body is the temple of the living God, his natural enthusiasm for the physical life led him to direct his concept of health toward matters pertaining to that temple. For Carlyle the source of health and disease was the spiritual environment in which man lived—the zeitgeist. For Kingsley, amateur sportsman, naturalist, and physiologist, the source of health and disease was the body and those things which influenced it. From that assumption it was but a short step to glorifying the body, which many accused him of doing.

Kingsley was to disclaim any belief that the heroic Christian life had to be a muscular one. Reading his novels and essays, however, one can hardly blame a critic like W. R. Greg for declaring, "He himself is endowed by nature with a vigorous and exuberant organization, is a sportsman, a fox-hunter, an athlete, and would probably have been a gladiator if he had not been a Christian. He revels in the description of every species of athletic exercise and desperate strife. Accordingly all his heroes are men of surpassing animal strength, all bone and muscle, marvels of agility, boiling over with exulting and abounding life, and usually miracles of physical beauty likewise."[49] Throughout his writings the range and intensity of Kingsley's athletic interests are manifest: in the descriptions in *The Heroes* of Jason's boyhood training in wrestling, boxing, and hunting; in the impassioned account of the Cambridge boat-race in *Alton*

Locke; in the vivid fishing and fox-hunting scenes in *Yeast;* and in the two prose rhapsodies on field sports in "Chalk Stream Studies" and "North Devon."

In "North Devon" Kingsley records an imaginary conversation with an artist, who asks him whether one must pursue sport in order to be noble and manly. No, he replies, not if he is sufficiently gifted in intellect; however, the mass of men have neither natural nobility nor "manly physical training." He assures his friend that "ever since the days of the Persians of old, effeminacy, if not the twin-sister of cowardice and dishonesty, has always gone hand in hand with them. To that utter neglect of any exercises which call out fortitude, patience, self-dependence, and daring, we attribute a great deal of the low sensuality, the conceited vulgarity, the want of a high sense of honour, which is increasing just now among our middle classes; and from which the navigator, the engineer, the miner, and the sailor, are comparatively free." Thus anyone can attain nobility by training himself to be manly. Endowing the Carlylean healthy hero with a visibly robust body, Kingsley divested him of his mystery. Although, according to Carlyle, some potential for heroic action lies within every man, the Hero himself is a transcendent figure, "above thee, like a god." The great man both embodies his age, the "synopsis and epitome" of it, and stands apart from his age, "aloft, conspicuous . . . serene, unaltering." Nowhere in Kingsley's writings appears this mystic figure of extraordinary gifts. Instead of the hero he speaks of heroism and the heroic, birthrights of everyone: "There is no limit to the capacities of every human being to form for himself or herself a high and pure ideal of human character; and, without 'playing fantastic tricks before high heaven,' to carry out that ideal in every-day life." In an essay on heroism he gives as an example of this ideal Thackeray's Henry Esmond, who conquered the brutalizing circumstances of his age by "holding fast throughout to honour, duty, virtue. Thus, and thus alone, he becomes an ideal eighteenth-century gentleman, and eighteenth-century hero."[50]

The qualities of the hero and those of the gentleman are thus merged in a higher type, the gentleman-hero, the muscular Christian. Significantly, Kingsley sees Esmond as "holding fast" to these qualities, rather than seeking to develop new ones. When he says that Esmond is "true to the light within him" we sense immediately the difference between manliness and the gentlemanliness defined by Newman. The man of philosophic habit has, Newman says, "illumination," not an inborn, infallible guide for conduct, but a cultivated, steady, comprehensive vision of things which makes for right conduct. One of the most revealing exchanges in the Newman-Kingsley controversy occurred over just this point. In a lecture published in 1850 Newman remarked that a man might be just, generous, honorable, and conscientious "not from a supernatural power, but from mere natural virtue." What, Kingsley wanted to know, was wrong with natural virtue? "Every good gift and every perfect gift comes down from God above. Without Him no man does a right deed, or thinks a right thought."[51] In other words, every natural gift *is* a grace, and one needs only to "hold fast" to these to lead a manly and righteous life. Spiritual health is no more than natural health in its total moral and physical sense.

When Kingsley preached the "divineness of the whole manhood" he envisioned that wholeness as a divine state, a unification of mind and body which themselves partook of the divinity of nature. Therefore, the "noble impulse," the action of the whole man, was proof of righteousness. The implications of that view are far-reaching indeed. If mind and body are truly one, then the virtues of both are attained simultaneously, not at different times and by different means, as Newman and Aristotle said. One need not attend a university to form a manly character; he need only attend a school where games are played. "Games conduce not merely to physical, but to moral health," Kingsley wrote; "in the playing-field boys acquire virtues which no books can give them; not merely daring and endurance, but, better still, temper, self-restraint, fairness, honour, unenvious approbation of another's success, and all that 'give and take' of life which stand a man in good stead when he goes forth into the world, and without which, indeed, his success is always maimed and partial."[52]

PART TWO

The Healthy Man

CHAPTER 6

The New Era:
Victorian Sport and Training

As HE PONDERED the subject of cholera in 1831, Carlyle wrote: "This is not the era of sport, but of martyrdom and persecution. Will the new era never dawn? It requires a certain vigour of the imagination and of the social faculties before amusement, popular sports, can exist, which vigour is at this era all but total inanition."[1] For him that lack of vigor was the "moral malady" of a nation possessed with its own infirmities. In those days, however, people lacked not only the spirit but also the opportunity to play. A mandatory full-day's work on Saturday was the standard; and such was the influence of stern Evangelical groups that Sunday games had been effectively barred throughout England. The Society for the Suppression of Vice had taken for its special calling the keeping of the Sabbath pure of sinful romping, for example, "the shameful practice of rowing-machines and boat races."[2] Those who resisted were threatened with prosecution in the courts.

In 1802 William Cobbett had complained of the modern puritan's "hostility to rural and athletic sports; to those sports which string the nerves and strengthen the frame, which excite an emulation in deeds of hardihood and valour, and which imperceptibly instill honour, generosity, and a love of glory, into the mind of the clown."[3] There were few sports in the first half of the nineteenth century whose popularity extended to "clown" and gentleman alike. The word "sports" itself was then likely to call to mind the outdoor pleasures of the relatively wealthy "sporting types." Field sports—shooting, hunting, and angling—were viewed by most people as hobbies for men of leisure. Blood sports—horse or coach racing, boxing and cock-fighting—were regarded as somewhat improper, either despite or because of their popularity among wealthy, "fast" young men; devotees were often the subject of satire (Jem Osborne in *Vanity Fair*) or simple comedy (Jerry Hawthorn and Corinthian Tom in Pierce Egan's *Life in London*). Athletic sports such as cricket and football were mainly the recreations of children and (especially during fairs and festivals) of rural folk.[4] Most gentlemen left them behind at school.

Even at mid-century those contests to which the modern newspaper daily devotes hundreds of column inches were not taken very seriously. Outside the schools and universities only cricket was played on a more or less regular, scheduled basis, and the only common interscholastic and intervarsity sports were cricket and rowing. Although these had a fairly constant following, they never drew large crowds. Occasionally some unusual athletic event would create a sensation—a boxing match, perhaps, or a pedestrian contest between a foot-runner and a man on stilts—but since spectators were interested mainly in placing wagers, such spectacles were actually not far removed from the interest in the turf or in cock-fighting.

Such was the situation in 1850. The time was soon to come when Englishmen would be converting their back lawns into tennis courts, making yearly assaults on the Alps, and packing the grandstands at rugby matches. What happened in the next thirty years or so can only be described as a national mania, perhaps the most widespread and long-lasting of any in the Victorian Age. Commenting on one of its manifestations, track-and-field athletics, the *Saturday Review* observed in 1869, "Englishmen may be slow to entertain novelties, but when the first disinclination is overcome, they usually go to the opposite extreme, and prosecute them with extraordinary ardour and persistency."[5]

Perhaps the most striking change in outdoor contests between 1850 and 1880 is the growth in number and variety. In its 1855 edition *The Boy's Own Book*, a popular manual of pastimes, listed under Athletic Sports only cricket, archery, gymnastics, fencing, driving, and riding. In the 1880 edition football, hockey, and baseball had been added, as well as golf, shinty (a form of field hockey), croquet, trocat (lawn billiards), rackets and fives, tennis and pallone, lawn tennis, badminton, lacrosse, bowls, broadsword and singlestick, bicycling, dumbbells and Indian clubs, boxing, and wrestling.[6] Some of these, like broadsword and singlestick, were centuries old, but most either had been introduced to England within the previous twenty-five years or had become both respectable and popular in that time.

Anthony Trollope's *British Sports and Pastimes* (1868), an anthology of sporting essays, is instructive because of the recreations it omits as well as those it includes. The subjects covered are horse-racing, hunting, shooting, fishing, yachting, rowing, Alpine-climbing, and cricket. Trollope explains some of the omissions in his preface, giving us some notion of how the various sports were regarded at the time. Prizefighting, for example, had so declined in popularity by 1868 that he felt wholly justified in excluding it. Football, on the other hand, had "hardly as yet worked its way up to a dignity equal with that of Hunting and Shooting, or even with that of Cricket and Boat-racing." Coursing he excluded because of his admitted prejudice; golf because of its limited following; croquet because it was "too delicate, too pretty, too refined"; tennis and rackets because they were games rather than sports; track-and-field athletics because they had "fallen short of the necessary dignity."[7] The distinction Trollope makes between tennis as a game and cricket as a sport might seem obscure now, but in those days games were often thought to be diversions like tip-cat, stool ball, and the current novelty, croquet— activities which, offering no special physical challenge, were suitable for children or women. Such a categorical distinction is revealing: "sport" was by its very nature a pursuit to be taken seriously; it was *manly*. Trollope's idea of ranking these activities according to their relative "dignity" was fairly representative of the views of educated Victorians in the sixties. Sport could now be part of the business of life, not just a respite from it.

The most respectable of popular Victorian sports throughout the century was cricket.[8] For one thing, there was no question of its pedigree. The Hambledon cricket club, patronized by an impressive contingent from the nobility, had been formed as early as 1750, and was preeminent until its demise in the 1790s. One of its patrons, the Earl of Winchelsea, helped Thomas Lord start up the Marylebone Cricket Club at White Conduit Fields, where the first match was played in May 1787. The first University match was held in 1827; the annual series dates from 1838. From the fifties to the seventies cricket was sovereign among sports. From county field to village green its popularity as a game to be played or watched was unrivaled. The period saw the rise of exhibition cricket, with touring groups like the All-England Eleven and its chief rival, the United All-England Eleven. Cricket also became international with the first test matches. In 1856 the *Saturday Review* noted that the number of clubs in the land had doubled in the past twenty years, and at that time the age of expansion for the county clubs was just beginning.[9] By 1885 the Marylebone Cricket Club had between two and three thousand members and an annual income of £15,000.

The man in this era who embodied cricket at its best was the legendary

W. G. Grace. A huge, colorful figure on the field, the black-bearded "W.G." changed the emphasis in the game from bowling to batting. Though a prodigious bowler, his most remarkable records were at the bat, where during one seven-year period he averaged more than a thousand runs. He was a prime attraction wherever he played and was without question the greatest Victorian sporting hero.

The interest in cricket was by no means limited to adult play. In 1880 Edward Lyttelton observed that, whereas at Eton-Harrow matches thirty years before the number of spectators was barely sufficient to encircle the grounds at Lord's, "now such is the importance of the annual pageant that it affects the duration of the London season."[10] On the first day of the 1864 match spectators numbered "upwards of 10,000, the number of carriages being truly wonderful." That year for the first time rope barricades were deemed necessary, and by 1867 it was clear that something must be done about the crowds, so a new grandstand was erected. By the 1870s, with attendance at Lord's approaching 38,000 for some matches, a turnstile had to be added, and officials found it necessary to open the gates as early as 5:00 A.M. The Oxford and Cambridge match of 1883 attracted 46,000, a record still unbroken.

Although cricket has always been among the most conservative of British sports, generally resisting innovation, the game was enlivened at this time by a number of changes which did much to widen its appeal. The technique of roundarm bowling was legalized in 1844 and of overhand bowling in 1864. With the faster pitched ball came the need for greater agility, so the tendency in adult cricket now was toward younger players. John Bayley, a slow roundarm bowler of an earlier period, had come to prominence only in his forties and was still playing in important matches at the age of fifty-six. Significantly, one 1810 match between a "young" and an "old" team placed the upper age limit of the young team at thirty-eight; by the 1860s a county player that old was uncommon.

Another change was in dress. The picturesque but impractical high beaver hat of the thirties and forties was replaced by the snug cap known as the billycock. Uniform shirts became general and, as protection against the "fly-about uncertainty" of the faster ball, so did gloves and leg padding. Partly to reduce that uncertainty, wickets were carefully maintained for the first time in the sixties. Also field boundaries were introduced. As the game became speedier and the fields better managed, the element of spectacle also grew, with the audience contributing as much as the players. The Eton-Harrow match was especially colorful, the ladies appearing in partisan hues, with light or dark blue dresses, gloves, parasols, ribbons, and rosettes.

If the Eton-Harrow and Oxford-Cambridge cricket matches were high-lights of the summer season, no spring event was greeted with more enthusiasm than the University Boat Race, which became an annual oc-currence in 1856.[11] Held on the Thames between Putney and Hammer-smith, this race was one of the splendid pageants of the year. Not only hundreds of rowboats, but also screw launches, panting lugs, and paddle steamers would crowd the river, all of them, the *Times* reported, "heavily freighted." There were also wherries, canoes, and coal barges; houses on both sides of the river were crammed with spectators, and the banks lined "many deep."[12] Before the race, boathouse owners ran advertisements in the papers offering platform tickets for ten shillings and balcony tickets for five shillings.

The excitement on the river was often intense and the crush enormous. In 1859 the race ended prematurely when one boat was swamped by a steamboat full of spectators which had drawn too near. This and other instances of crowd interference caused officials to hold the race the next year at 8:30 A.M., in order to discourage attendance. After the 1873 race the *Times* reported laconically the spectator casualties admitted to West London Hospital, Hammersmith: "Two patients suffering from extensive scalp wounds; one patient suffering from severe injury to ankle-joint; one fractured base of skull; one lacerated nose. Fifteen patients also admitted as in patients, but having been attended to by house surgeons, were sent to their homes. Considering the immense number of people who witnessed the boat race, it is considered remarkable that there was not a greater number of accidents."[13] There would have been more had not the police kept the towpath clear of those spectators on horseback who in previous years had ridden down pedestrians or sent them into the ditch, and had not police boats kept unskilled rowboaters off the course. So great was the continuing interest in this event that in 1880 as many people were turning out to watch the varsity boats in practice as had seen the race itself twenty years before.[14]

Press coverage of the University Boat Race may be said to mark the beginning of modern sporting journalism; never before had athletic con-tests been written about so extensively. As the first of the mass-spectator sports, rowing was news. The *Sporting Gazette* ran day-by-day reports of the training of the crews, beginning with their arrival at Putney. One Cambridge crew was described as "an exceedingly fine and well-made set of men [who] with one or two exceptions, looked the perfection of what condition ought to be a week before an important race." They were taller than the Oxford rowers, the journal added, but "not so well developed about the back and loins." The *Gazette* also chronicled the daily activities of the crews, and one year devoted a special story to a photograph, which could be purchased by readers, taken of the Oxford men.[15] The *Times*, which gave over generous blocks of space to the event, developed a peculiarly solemn reporting style appropriate to the occasion. It wrote of the "gallant struggle" of the 1869 Cambridge crew which soldiered on despite having lost one of its members to an attack of quinsy.[16] On the 1859 Cambridge crew's gamely maintaining stroke after being swamped, the *Saturday Review* declared, "The spirit which sustained the losing, sinking Cambridge crew throughout the contest was the same which held the slopes of Waterloo a long summer day, and it will again be manifested, tenacious and indomitable as of old, whenever any enemy shall dare to arouse it."[17]

With the help of such writing, the oarsman of the period became a recognized figure of admiration, even of awe. In the fervent though ungainly prose of those sporting columns appear the beginnings of the heroic reporting style: "A more gallantly disputed struggle, with frequently alternating leads, is seldom seen, and was anticipated by few."[18] Legends were also constructed by partisans looking nostalgically back to their university days. What did it matter to the author of the "Lay of the Seven Oars" that the shorthanded 1843 crew celebrated in his poem had probably aroused the interest of very few at the time:

> From the Thames their oar-track fades,
> Other Champions wield the blades;
> But on the flood of Time 'tis bright,
> An ever broad'ning line of light.
> In Memory of their fame, I vote
> We call the Great Bear the Seven-oared Boat,
> To which to sink 'tis never given.
> For what heroes ever in the stars of heaven
> So well have earned a place as the glorious Seven?[19]

The University Race was only part of a general renaissance in rowing. During the forties scholastic rowing had suffered a decline, but a decade later meets between the various public schools became annual. The formation of the London Rowing Club in 1856 and its winning of the Henley Challenge Cup the following year helped make Thames rowing a fixed institution. For the next twenty-five years this sport rivaled all others in the phenomenal growth of its popularity. Professional scullers like Kelley and Sadler competed for substantial cash prizes made up from on-the-spot wagers. The championship of the Thames in 1860, won by Chambers of Newcastle, included a prize of £200. Challenges like the following appeared regularly in *Bell's Life:* "If the Nottingham Trent Crew think that they would have any chance for the final heat at Derby, the Manchester crew will row them for £50, and row at Nottingham, without expenses; or will stake £50 to £30 if they will row at Manchester."[20]

Even in amateur races the prizes were not inconsequential. The amateur awards for one race held on the Thames in 1860 included a sculler's boat, a claret jug, and a scarf pin. Sometimes even the expectation of prize cups (which could be worth a great deal) led to bad feeling and bickering. In 1860 at the Barnes and Mortlake Amateur Regatta, the West London Club, having appeared when neither of their opponents did, rowed over the course at the umpire's instructions, expecting to be awarded the cup. When the other two crews arrived they too rowed the course. Officials decided to have the race rowed again another day, much to the disapproval of the *New Sporting Magazine*, which reported the event.

Rowing was among the most physically demanding of sports, requiring a strict training regimen of diet and exercise. The London Rowing Club of the sixties would begin to train six weeks before a race, rowing every evening and three times a week in the morning; there were morning rubdowns; meals were limited to stale bread and beef or mutton (pork was banned). Bishop Wordsworth of St. Andrews, an originator of the University Boat Race in 1856, recalled that in those days "Very underdone meat, bread, and good sound beer or porter was considered the proper diet; and running at top speed early in the morning was one of the things much relied on."[21]

With all his training, the oarsman *looked* the athlete; one could not mistake him. This was even more true of that new species of sportsman, the track-and-field athlete, who became, with the aid of journalism, the Victorian embodiment of the hero as Strong Man. Here is a contemporary account of a hammer throw in the first Athletic Sports between Oxford and Cambridge: "He held the bottom of the handle with the grip of a vice in both hands, extending them above his head. The firm set muscles, at the top of each arm, were visible beneath his shirt. For a few seconds he stood in this position, getting the perfect poise of the hammer; then he lowered it, waltzed around three times very rapidly, and, stopping just short of the line, let the unwieldy instrument loose. It had travelled upwards of 27 yards when it fell to the ground, ploughing up the turf."[22]

ATHLETICS IN THE modern sense is wholly a product of the middle Victorian decades.[23] Running competitions had been common throughout the early part of the century, but in those days they were relatively un-organized. Professionals ran with amateurs, some of whom competed under assumed names. Records of times and distances, when kept, were far from reliable. No attempt was made to standardize the events: en-trants would run or walk over whatever course happened to be available —and for whatever prize could be collected. The first regularly organized athletic meet was held in 1849 at the Royal Military Academy, Wool-wich. During the next ten years the schools and universities began to hold interscholastic and intervarsity competitions, and by 1860 athletics had become an important part of school life. By this time the meets were featuring hurdles, weight-throwing, and jumping, as well as several kinds of flat racing. On Sunday, March 5, 1864, competitions were first held between Cambridge and Oxford on the spongy grass surface of a wet cricket field at Christ Church. The hundred yards was won in 10½ seconds, the mile in 4 minutes, 56 seconds, the high jump at 5 feet, 5 inches. Those early times and distances are all the more surprising when we consider the conditions prevailing. There was no hard-surface track. When the pole vault was introduced, the vaulter used a hardwood pole with three spikes at the bottom. After running to the bar, he would im-plant the pole in the ground, then climb up it and vault over in a sitting position.

A greater difficulty was likely to be the crowd who, having paid to enter the colorful flag-festooned area, could not be restrained from run-ning onto the track as each race ended and mobbing the runners in what some members of the press regarded as a dangerous way. There were bizarre interruptions, as when Edward Colbeck in the 1868 English cham-pionships ran the quarter mile in just over fifty seconds, despite having collided midway through the race with a sheep which had wandered onto the track and which stood, an observer recalled, "amazed at the remark-able performance which the runners were accomplishing." (At that, his time for the event remained the unbroken standard for thirteen years.)[24]

In 1864, the same year that the first University meet was held, the newly formed Mincing Lane Athletic Club (later the London Athletic Club) conducted its first open meets. Within two years organized ama-teur athletics, now divorced entirely from professional competitions and exhibitions, were being held in towns and rural areas throughout En-gland. In an age which loved physical achievement and manliness, these contests were especially well suited to develop the cult of the athlete, now certain his performances would be chronicled by journalists. Colbeck's sheep-hindered 440 was well-recorded, as was the dead-heat between

Lang and Richards in the mile at 4:17 ¼, a record which stood for sixteen years. Perhaps the best known of the university athletes was the Oxonian M. J. Brooks, first to clear the high-jump bar at 6 feet. In 1876, after having jumped 6 feet, 1/8 inch three weeks earlier, he delighted a crowd of ten thousand at Lillie Bridge by clearing 6 feet, 2½ inches and then, for show, going over at 6 feet while wearing a top hat.

Interuniversity sports drew enormously; a crowd of four thousand was not exceptional. At the sports held in 1885, over five hundred Oxonians traveled to the meet on a special train added for the occasion by the London and North Western—this despite the fact that it was during final examinations. The scene at these events was always one of gaiety, even though the mid-March weather was often nasty. Multicolored banners were strung up with "England expects . . . " and other slogans on them. Journalists were there in force, having gained free entrance with their press cards (grandstand seats were one shilling for women and two shillings, sixpence for men).

Meanwhile professional pedestrianism had lost none of its appeal. In a typical race of that day, well-advertised beforehand in the sporting papers, two men would meet on a country road. A level stretch, say of three hundred yards, would be found, and a starter and referee appointed. Spectators, knowing something of the runners' reputations and speculating on their present physical condition, would lay down bets, the runners would toe the scratch, and the race would proceed. The referee decided any close finish, invariably sparking noisy arguments in the crowd. Racing that involved any sort of novelty was especially popular. One ten-mile race featured two Indians and two white men, another included nine Mexican women. In the seventies long-distance walking was the rage. In 1876 an American named Weston walked 109 miles and 832 yards in twenty-four hours. Some days later he walked a similar distance in the same time, afterwards addressing the spectators (at Agricultural Hall, Islington) and thanking them for the fair play he had received. Then he concluded with a cornet performance of "God Save the Queen." Events of this kind retained their old nomenclature of pedestrianism. When a number of running, jumping, and throwing events were held at a single meet, they were collectively called athletics, or athletic sports, or games, the uncertainty of terminology reflecting the newness of the phenomenon. The *Saturday Review* argued against calling them "games," on the principle that the *playing* of games had little in common with "the grim struggle of a mile race."[25]

An even grimmer struggle characterized another Victorian innovation, mountaineering.[26] As a sport, mountain climbing is said to date from the ascent of the Wetterhorn by Alfred Wills in 1854, with the "golden age" extending from that year to 1865, when Whymper climbed the Matterhorn. Of the thirty-nine European peaks surpassing 13,000 feet in height, British climbers mastered thirty-one. These men were "mountaineers" in a new sense of the word; they were competitors, rather than merely, in the older sense, sojourners in mountains. The founding of the Alpine Club in 1857 signaled a new attitude toward mountains. A mountain was no longer regarded only as a sublime object or as a place of simple recreation, but as a challenge to man's courage. Mountaineering was, in the words of Leslie Stephen, "a sport to be put beside rowing, cricket, and other time-honoured sports of Englishmen."[27]

The growth of this activity was truly impressive. With only twenty-eight members to start with, the Alpine Club grew tenfold in two decades (though some of its members, like Matthew Arnold, cannot be said to have been serious about the sport). Soon this and other climbing groups claimed a total membership of several thousand. By 1867 all the important peaks of the Alps had been exhausted and the English mountaineers turned to the Caucasus, thence to the mountains of America and New Zealand, and finally to the Himalayas. Their exploits could be followed in the pages of the *Alpine Journal*, begun in 1863 as a "record of mountain adventure and scientific observation." Public interest is attested to by the success of *Peaks, Passes, and Glaciers*, in which Alpine Club members recounted their adventures. The book went into five editions before the first year was out, leading to a second series in 1862.

Whereas mountaineering, like cricket, rowing, and athletics, gained a sufficient respectability simply from the large numbers of intellectuals and professional men engaged in it, football was a sport striving to overcome its class associations.[28] Unlike cricket it had neither a fashionable London residence nor the patronage of fashionable people. Trollope's remark in 1868 that it was too undignified to be written about seriously is a fairly clear indication of its status. From the Middle Ages there apparently never was a time when football lacked considerable popularity among working people, and very few times when it was not condemned by the authorities. The traditional Shrove Tuesday games, said to have begun in 1175 in the London Fields and soon played throughout England, were banned in 1314 by proclamation of Edward II on account of the "great noise in the city caused by hustling over large balls, from which many evils may arise, which God forbid." Richard II proscribed the game because it diverted young men from the study of archery. In 1579 John Wonkell of Durham County was found guilty of playing football and sentenced to a week in prison, after which he had to do penance in church. In 1583 a gloomy pamphlet foresaw the end of the world because "devilish pastimes" like football were being played on the Sabbath, "causing necks, legs, backs, and arms to be broken, eyes to start out, and noses to gush out with blood."[29]

Like most popular recreations, football had a history of persecution on religious, utilitarian, and humanitarian grounds. In the nineteenth century festival football succumbed to a combination of these pressures and underwent a general decline. Its revival took place in the schools. Although certain headmasters like Shrewsbury's Dr. Butler disapproved of the game as only "fit for butcher boys," it was generally allowed, for the playground game was a much tamer variety than the free-for-all, marketplace and narrow-street style practiced in towns and villages. Just as each school over the centuries had developed its own peculiar slang and customs, each also nourished its individual sort of game, with features sometimes governed more by the eccentricities of the various playing fields than by any rational design. The most radical innovation, that of carrying the ball, emerged at Rugby. Since most of the other schools still prohibited this practice, the sport began to take two distinct forms.

By 1863 a number of football clubs had been formed, mainly in London and mainly of Old Boys from various schools. That year, led by players at Cambridge, a committee drafted standardized rules of play. It was then that the Rugby partisans seceded over the question of handling the ball, as well as over an impending resolution banning "hacking" (kicking at the ball—or perhaps, in the concealment of a scrum, at an opponent's shin). One supporter of this practice said that "hacking was the true football game" and that if abandoned, "all the courage and pluck of the game would be at an end."[30] The two kinds of football developed independently. The majority of teams, adhering to the more traditional style of play, made up the new Football Association (whence "soccer," originally university slang for "assoc.") In 1871 the cup competition was inaugurated with a cup costing £20, subscribed to by all the clubs. Altogether there were fifty clubs by this time, a fivefold increase in four years. With the beginnings of "cup-fever" in 1873-4, when there were twice as many entrants as the year before, association football was clearly becoming the most popular national sport. The beginnings of professionalism came in the 1880s when some clubs were expelled for paying players. Through rule changes at the opening of the 1885-6 season professionals were allowed to compete under certain specified conditions, including local residency.

Meanwhile, in 1871, the year of the first cup competition, seventeen clubs and three schools formed the Rugby Union. They drafted rules which, among other provisions, put an end to hacking, tripping, and "scragging" (throttling). The determination of conservatives to keep the "gentleman-amateur" character of the game occasioned another secession, this time by the northern clubs, who in 1893 formed the Northern Union, which later became the Rugby League.

As THE SPORTING mania continued, games were devised for those who because of sex, age, or state of fitness were unable to compete in rough sports.[31] According to its "inventor," Major Walter Wingfield, lawn tennis could be "played in the open air in any weather by people of any age and both sexes." His original name for it, Sphairistikè, came to little, as did his suggestion that during a hard frost the net could be set up on ice and the players provided with skates, though he did apparently realize some profit on the patented outfits he sold. The set costing £6 included "best selected" bats, the £5 one had "second quality bats, very good," and the £3 15s. one contained "third quality ditto, strong and useful for Schools and Regiments." Among his customers were the Prince of Wales, the Duke of Edinburgh, the Crown Princess of Prussia, and various other British and foreign notables.[32] Lawn tennis quickly achieved wide popularity. A writer in the *Edinburgh Review* declared it "the most perfect of games" to play and a pleasant one to watch as the ball was being "patted to and fro in lofty arcs by pretty young ladies, tripping gracefully to the simple strokes which complaisant young gentlemen run about to recover from their random directions and make easy to return."[33]

The social aspect of tennis (*Punch* had the inevitable puns on "love" and "court") was also a feature of the new pastime, badminton, a game believed to have been adapted by the Duke of Beaufort from the older battledore and shuttlecock. Neither tennis nor badminton, however, attracted as much enthusiasm as croquet, a game first played in Ireland in 1852 and soon brought to England. After a Bond Street merchant failed in marketing it, the Messrs. Jacques, purveyors of various kinds of games, took it up with great success. In 1866 the first tournament was held, with the best players from the Midlands competing at Evesham in Worcestershire. The prize was a gold and silver cup. The winner, a Mr. Whitmore, organized an all-comers tourney the next year, the same year that the All England Club was formed. Shortly after, this group purchased four acres of ground near the Wimbledon station and, as was the case with nearly all Victorian sports, old or new, standardized rules were drawn up. "Spooning" (pushing without an audible knock) was forbidden, as well as "tight croquet" (putting one's foot on his own ball when knocking away the other player's ball). Until tennis came in, croquet was *the* outdoor game for everybody. Some, like Captain Mayne Reid in his early croquet manual, found far-reaching benefits: "Its rules are so varied, so rational, that the intellect is constantly kept on the alert,— never summoned to a painful stretch, and never allowed to subside into an equally painful inaction."[34] The *Gentleman's Magazine* ran a series of articles on "The Science of Croquet," with helpful illustrations depicting "vicious stances."[35]

While croquet was being celebrated in music hall songs and lampooned in *Punch*, what came to be known as "rinkomania" started to take hold. Roller skates had been patented in England in 1823, but the wheels of the early models were metal and set in a line from toe to heel, so the going was too hard to make skating any real pleasure. In 1859 a skate was developed with vulcanized rubber wheels; but these too proved inadequate since any amount of weight pressed them out of shape and made rolling impossible. Although various rinks were opened around London, there was not much fun in skates that would stop suddenly, pitching the skater onto his face. Then in 1863 J. L. Plimpton, an American, patented a revolutionary device which prevented the convergence of the rollers and permitted the skater to steer himself and turn easily. After achieving popularity in the United States the novelty traveled to England, and in 1874 a rink was opened at the Corn Exchange in Brighton. Prince's rink in London soon became the most fashionable in the land, and within a few years there were dozens of rinks in London alone. Prince's boasted four thousand members, of whom three thousand attended on a single day. A comic poem of the time tells of the loyalty of rinking enthusiasts to their sport:

> "Croquet," said they, "has had its day,
> Lawn tennis is so so,
> While archery is out of date
> And badminton is slow.
> Skating's the thing, they all did sing,
> And rinks are found to 'go.' "[36]

In the seventies all these sports had to make room for yet another: golf. The first English course established by Englishmen was at Westward Ho in Devon. In 1878 the annual match between the two universities was inaugurated. The golfing vogue spread, one writer recalls, faster than any other of the new amusements, and "there were districts in England where a person's moral character was considered of less importance than the ease and precision of his swing."[37]

The list of Victorian sporting novelties is long. Bandy, or ice-hockey, was introduced to London in 1860 at the Crystal Palace. In 1870 the London Swimming Organisation established regulations for a game variously called "football in the water," "water handball," "aquatic handball," and "water polo." Although the height of the cycling craze was in the nineties, its start coincides roughly with rinkomania. In the early days the few eccentrics riding awkward-looking high-wheelers were scorned as "cads on casters." Their machines were somewhat uncomfortable with their wooden wheels, but when the rubber tire came in the sport began to catch on. By 1874 the editor of a handbook on cycling could boast: "Ten thousand people have assembled at one time to witness a Bicycle contest, and the best manufacturers are in arrears with their orders for machines."[38] In 1875 the London Bicycle Club held its first meet at the Lillie Bridge Grounds in West Brompton. The major event was a twenty-five-mile race between the best riders of that club and those of the Cambridge Bicycle Club, the prize a silver cup worth £20. Even before that, however, there had been exhibitions by professional riders like Daniel Stanton, who in October 1874 tried to go one hundred miles in eight and a half hours. After ninety-six miles he was exhausted, and though attempts were made to revive him with brandy, tea, and sponge cake, he had to be helped from his machine.[39]

As a writer in *Macmillan's* observed, the young men of that day seemed "possessed by a perfect mania for every species of athletic contest."[40] Underlying much of that was the Victorian spirit of self-improvement, expressing itself now in physical terms: the March of Mind was giving way to the March of Body. With the opening of Archibald Maclaren's celebrated Oxford University gymnasium in the autumn of 1859, the age of training may be said to have begun. The building and its equipment were regarded as a modern wonder. The *Illustrated London News* printed a picture of the interior and an account of Maclaren's method of scientifically determining the physical condition of each person entering the program so that "exercises may be adapted to that part which is defective." By one machine he could "measure the depth of chest at any point."[41] Throughout the country the construction of other gymnasiums followed in short time, one of the most marvelous at Liverpool in 1865 at a cost of £14,000. For some reason London was late in acquiring such a facility, and Lord Morley, writing in 1866, argued in favor of "half-a-dozen such halls as that which Mr. Maclaren superintends at Oxford," places which "would make London a perfect sanatorium for hard-worked mortals who are compelled to live there the greater part of the year."[42]

The coining of the word "calisthenics" (from the Greek "beautiful strength") shows that, however new the training procedures, the classical ideal of harmonious development was always kept in mind. The *Illustrated London News* urged the adoption of special devices for "calisthenic exercises" then being used in India: "Besides the great recommendation of simplicity, the Indian Club possesses the essential property of expanding the chest, and exercising every muscle in the body concurrently, and we believe it will be found well worthy of attention for all who are interested in giving to the young men of Great Britain strong arms to second the purposes of strong hearts."[43]

THE COMBINED interest in training and athletics spawned a number of local athletic clubs in England and of national confederations which held giant meets. A typical festival, staged in Birmingham in 1867 by the National Olympic Association, was inaugurated by a procession to the grounds led by the band of the First Warwickshire Rifle Corps and a fife and drum band from Shropshire. Men of the Birmingham Athletic Club marched in their club uniforms—white trousers and shirts with blue facings, straw hats with blue ribbons, and silver badges picturing an eagle and the motto "Strong and Free." The competitions followed an address by Mr. Brooke of Much Wenlock on the importance of physical education.

Such festivals, which could draw hundreds of competitors and thousands of spectators, featured a great variety of muscular activity. A meeting at Manchester's Broughton Race Ground in 1867, with the mayor presiding, provided two days of competitions. On the first there were fencing, gymnastics, boxing, putting the twenty-four-pound shot, vaulting, Indian club and dumbbell exercises, single-stick, throwing the cricket ball, pole-leaping, and throwing the sixteen-pound hammer. The second day was reserved for pedestrian events: races, jumping, and leaping. Large meets like this were given detailed and sometimes critical coverage by the sporting press. Of the boxing matches at Manchester the *Athletic Review* editorialized, "We should advise some of the gentlemen who competed in this contest to keep their tempers more under control. Showing their teeth and hitting hard is not boxing."[44] Generally, however, decorum seems to have been maintained. On the second day of the Liverpool Festival of the Athletic Society of Great Britain a man whose dress was deemed too skimpy was made to wear a coat in the walking race. The *Athletic Review* commented: "If the published programme of any contest requires that a shirt or guernsey and trowsers or knickerbockers should be worn, it is only fair to enforce this rule. And we think it very desirable that such a rule with regard to dress should be adopted generally and strictly enforced. It is by no means an edifying sight to see competitors come to the scratch in tights or fleshings and scanty drawers."[45]

The general air of conviviality at these huge festivals was tempered by one of profound purposefulness. Addressing the opening of the Liverpool meeting of the Athletic Society of Great Britain, its founder, John Hulley, reminded his listeners that sport had its serious side: "Physical education is the great fact of the nineteenth century. The opposition to it has sunk from the general to the individual. The nation has accepted it. All over the country athletic festivals are being celebrated; and these afford evidence of which it is impossible to mistake the bearing. They must convince every unbiassed mind that we are just entering upon a new phase of national development. May the time soon come when weakly, misshapen men, and sickly, hysterical women will be the exception and not the rule among the inhabitants of our towns and cities."[46]

This new mood inspired a wealth of periodical literature to chronicle its manifestations. *Bell's Life*, one of the older sporting journals, is a useful indicator of the change in national habits. It had begun by concerning itself principally with the turf and the ring, and with field sports. By the mid-sixties, in addition to racing, boxing, coursing, and pigeon-shooting, it contained a two- or three-column "aquatic register" (yachting, rowing, and swimming) and pages devoted to wrestling, football, cricket, and other athletic sports. It assigned a special reporter to witness and write up public school cricket matches.

Many of the older and newer publications were cautious in abandoning the traditional concept of "sport." Although *Baily's*, a monthly started in 1860, attended to the whole range of outdoor pastimes, it first gave over pages of its Gallery of Sporting Characters to other than turf figures in 1865, when it officially recognized the cricketer R. A. H. Mitchell. The *Sportsman*, issued four times a week, included reports of football matches but leaned more toward the "sporting" interests in the older sense of the word. Some periodicals, on the other hand, were springing up specifically dedicated to being as comprehensive as possible. The *Athletic Review and Journal of Physical Education* promised in its first issue (July 2, 1867) that "all events connected with Athletics, Yachting, Rowing, and manly sports generally, both home and abroad, will be critically reported, and accuracy assured in names of competitors, and details of competitions hitherto unattainable." Despite its hopeful prospectus, however, and its reasonable price of 3d., it managed only a couple of issues.

With so many rivals in the field, new sporting magazines sometimes tried to achieve success by broadening their appeal. The *Sporting Gazette* reviewed drama, music, and literature as a sort of bonus. When the industrious Beeton enterprise started up its *Journal of Travel, Sport, History, and Romance* in December 1867 it offered a generous miscellany of subjects at an equally generous price of one penny. The first issue announced that the magazine's "special object" would be to foster the "new and promising game" of lacrosse, "to diffuse information respecting the clubs formed for playing it, to discuss and settle its yet undigested laws, and to advance its interests generally." Unfortunately the first winter *Beeton's Journal* was published was so severe as to discourage lacrosse or any other new outdoor game, and the journal, expiring more or less with the old year, did not see what became of the sport in England.

Aside from these publications which were issued monthly, weekly, or even more often, mention should be made of the many almanacs or annuals which began to appear in the sixties. *The Athlete* (a publication read by George Meredith) chronicled the year's events in athletic sports, promising in its first number (1866) that in its pages competitors "will not only find their own performances accurately recorded, but will be able to compare them with members of other clubs." The *Cricketer's Almanac* offered a similar service, as did the *Oarsman's Companion and Rowing Almanac*, which featured steel-plate portraits of famous rowers and a detailed map of the Oxford-Cambridge rowing course. The *Football Annual* did not begin until 1873, reflecting the somewhat delayed popularity of that sport.

In reading the back pages of these annuals we are reminded that sport was becoming profitable not only to players and journalists, but to a variety of entrepreneurs. For example, Kent and Lewis, Athletic Clothing Manufacturers, advertised in the first issue of the *Football Annual* that they were prepared to outfit football, cricket, and rowing clubs, as well as colleges and schools, with "football jerseys, knicker hose to match, the same in caps, running drawers, etc. Hand-knitted perspirers, elastic belts and garters, straw hats, bands, sashes and canvas shoes suitable for all sports."

Within a very few decades, sports had become much what they are today: a universal recreation and a prime means of achieving health, fame, and of course income. "As a medium for the circulation of money," reads the title page of Harry Sargent's *Thoughts upon Sport* (1895), "and as a national benefactor, Sport stands unrivaled among the institutions of the kingdom."[47] Rinkomania, athletic festivals, cycling—it all seems genial, innocent, and healthy. If a healthy life is marked by an unconscious, free vitality, a liberation of the animal spirits from the pleasure-denying authority of the conscience, then all this activity must be a sign of health. At first glance it appears to have little in common with Carlyle's notion of the healthy life of moral strenuousness, and even less to do with that intellectual perfection which Newman regarded as analogous, and superior, to health.

The sport-loving Britons of the later Victorian period may strike us as trying to free themselves from the stringent, demanding notion of Carlyle's that health, wholeness, and holiness mean the same thing. The truth, however, was that every step of the way, Victorian spokesmen for Conscience, Work, Improvement, and Mind-over-Matter had much to do with creating and channeling the new spirit. Sport could never have become institutionalized in the nineteenth century without the approval of institutional authorities; it could never have become sanctified without the assent of religious spokesmen who argued that health as a principle of moral betterment was fully compatible with healthy activity as simple amusement or relaxation. Lord Shaftesbury, appointed to the newly created Board of Health in 1848, became a propagandist for health in both of its aspects, fighting for sanitary improvements, playgrounds, physical education, gymnasiums, and athletic festivals. Playgrounds, he declared, "are greatly beneficial as having a moral effect in affording wholesome amusement, relaxation, and pleasure. Depend upon it that the mind must occasionally be amused, as well as the body cared for."[48] The source of this statement is significant. An influential Evangelical reformer, Shaftesbury maintained that adults as well as children need the sort of mental diversion supplied by popular sports. At mid-century the puritanical opposition to games which had incensed Cobbett fifty years earlier was now found only in reactionary religious zealots. Sports were no longer regarded as hindering moral development; the next step was to argue that far from limiting that development, they aided it.

CHAPTER 7

Growing Up Healthy:
Images of Boyhood

"UNQUESTIONABLY, the time of life at which you are arrived, and more particularly the younger boys among you, is, in itself, exceedingly dangerous. It is the time, beyond all others in life, when temptation is great, and the strength of character to resist it exceedingly small . . . It is a great matter, too, that your bodies, at your time of life, so far outgrow your minds;—that your spirits and bodily strength are so vigorous and active, while your understandings are, in comparison, so feeble."[1]

Thus the boys in Rugby chapel were addressed on the perils of being young and healthy. The speaker was Thomas Arnold, the man said to be responsible for making "earnestness" the guiding principle in Victorian Public School education.[2] When he took over the headmastership of Rugby in 1828, Arnold may well have been justified in holding such a low opinion of boyhood with its "spirits and bodily strength." Although Rugby was no worse than any other public school, it was afflicted with the same ills which had brought censure upon all of them—physical bullying, stealing, poaching, excessive drinking, and of course "immorality." All of Arnold's celebrated reforms were directed at one educational aim: to make of his boys an image of "godliness and good learning."[3] To further this goal he took the unusual step of assuming the chaplain's duties as well as those of headmaster. His most influential reforms included turning the sixth form into a disciplinary body by making prepositors of all its members; eliminating abuses of fagging by restricting the privilege to the sixth form; using, when efficacious, other sorts of persuasion than flogging; and quickly expelling troublemakers from the school. It was this series of regulative changes and the philosophy underlying them that gave Rugby its special character.

Arnold's practices in managing the Rugby pupils reflect his stated conviction that he could only hope to make Christian men, for he despaired of making Christian boys.[4] The sixth form ruled by right of general maturity; they were an aristocracy of seniority and moral eminence. Arnold wished government to be placed in their hands rather than, as was often the case in schools, left to the physically strong and aggressive. Younger boys—those, say, of ten or twelve—because they had not had their characters shaped, were wholly reliant on external direction; and Arnold well knew from the history of Rugby and other schools that this meant compliance with the schemes and standards of the older boys rather than with the authority of the masters. Perceptively he argued that youngsters are the slaves of custom, tending through "fear and outward obedience" to enter into the practice of "combination," a tendency which gave him special anxiety. Distrusting the motives of boys in groups, he encouraged individual motivation, "the obedience of the heart and the understanding."[5]

Manliness for Arnold was a matter of doing what was right without being told, and to develop manliness was his pedagogical aim. This philosophy was wholly consistent with his religious latitudinarianism, which held that bases of conduct and guides to belief should be an inner response to the spirit of Christianity rather than, as with the "Judaizing temperament," reliance on doctrine, ritual, or ecclesiastical authority.[6] Therefore, he encouraged self-discipline and self-motivation as the means of building Christian character. Here one peculiarity of the English public school—age diversity—worked to his advantage. The public school is a society of varying capabilities, and Arnold made this fact the basis of his prepositor system. The youngest child in the school must have seemed notably helpless and helpworthy to those in the upper forms, who, if they could be discouraged from bullying him, might learn to take responsibility for his welfare. Also, if Arnold asked of the morally weaker younger boys to submit to the mild indignities of fagging or the greater indignities of corporal punishment, he demanded of the sixth form absolute integrity and accountability. When George Hughes, elder brother of the author of *Tom Brown*, refused to expose a wrongdoer he was quietly but swiftly expelled.

Because Arnold declared that the qualities he looked for in a Rugby student were, in order of importance, religious and moral principles, gentlemanly conduct, and intellectual ability, he has been identified with pedagogic anti-intellectualism. But if he believed that character and good behavior were the highest goals of a public school, he was just as firm that these could be acquired only through the maturing of the mind. "I am satisfied," he once wrote to a former pupil, "that a neglected intellect is far oftener the cause of mischief to a man than a perverted or overvalued one."[7] He especially warned his boys not to harbor the notion that physical fitness was the one thing needful: "If you were born in a station, in which you would be called upon to work chiefly with your hands hereafter, then the strengthening of your bodies, the learning to be active and handy, to be bold and enduring of bodily pain and labour, would be your special duty, over and above that common duty of love to God and to man, which belongs to every age and every condition alike. But, as it is, you will be called upon to work chiefly with your minds hereafter; and although it is very true, that the mind works but feebly when the body is sickly; and that, therefore, you are called upon, like all other persons, to make yourselves, as far as you can, strong and active, and healthful and patient in your bodies; yet your especial call is rather to improve your minds, because it is with your minds that God calls upon you to work hereafter."[8]

Arnold himself was physically active as a young man. While a private tutor at Laleham, before going to Rugby, he shared with the pupils his zest for strenuous play—leaping, swimming, walking with them, always feeling that this sort of lighthearted recreation was the best way to maintain rapport. In the same spirit, no doubt, he undertook to teach his own children cricket. But he never seems to have adopted a serious attitude toward games; quite the opposite, as shown in this pleasant sketch of him by one of the Laleham boys: "Who that ever had the happiness of being at Laleham, does not remember the lightness and joyousness of heart with which he would romp and play in the garden, or plunge with a boy's delight into the Thames; or the merry fun with which he would battle with spears with his pupils?" Arnold had enjoyed himself like a boy, he recalled when he left Laleham. Looking forward to Rugby, he reflected that he was not afraid of work if he could get proper exercise; "but I want absolute play, like a boy, and neither riding nor walking will make up for my leaping-pole and gallows [a contraption built to climb up and slide down], and bathing, when the youths used to go with me, and I felt completely for the time a boy as they were."[9]

This desire to be a boy from time to time is not at all inconsistent with his view of boys as "naturally inferior . . . morally and intellectually," or with the searching earnestness of his mind at chapel sermon.[10] He looked on youthful play as, in the strictest sense, recreative. It belonged to a wholly different realm of life from work; therefore, he insisted that it be totally free, amoral, nonintellectual. A walk along a road is not true exercise if the walker considers or discusses "subjects of interest." "A skirmish over the country is a very different thing, and so is all that partakes of the character of play or sport."[11] Since the greater part of a man's life should always demand intellectual and moral discipline, occasionally to feel "completely for the time a boy" is to release oneself from mental responsibility when it is not specifically called for. The natural object of the body's consciousness is itself, expressed in healthy play. The proper object of the mind's consciousness is something totally outside itself and is found in work.

Arnold regarded young boys as by nature neither good nor evil. They were simply without character and thus susceptible to immorality. All in all, he seemed to have viewed boyhood and adolescence as times of trial, the successful endurance of which was the cultivation of a healthy manhood. "What especial cloud hangs over our life's current," he asked the boys in the Rugby chapel, "that the stream here will ever be dark and sullen, while on its earlier or later course it is either bright and lively, or the purity of its waters is lost to the distant view in the breadth and majesty of their volume?"[12] Intellectual innocence is what makes the stream in infancy "bright and lively"; that same innocence, when coupled with the physical capabilities for sinning, turns it "dark and sullen" in boyhood. "I always fear," Arnold wrote, "that, where the intellect is low, the animal part will predominate; and that moral evils will increase, as well as intellectual proficiency decline, under such a state of things."[13] This is why the "spring and activity of youth" often seemed more distressing than "the shouts and gambols of a set of lunatics." Juvenile robustness, especially when combined with wealth or position, too often resulted in a neglect of inward examination and moral self-improvement. It was the special opportunity of the public school to encourage that inner moral development which was at once substantial and abiding. With the unprivileged—the poor or the old—righteousness might be stimulated externally, by their economic privation or physical suffering; "but with boys of the richer classes, one sees nothing but plenty, health, and youth; and these are really awful to behold, when one must feel that they are unblessed."[14]

That image of boyhood was well conveyed in "Rugby Chapel," Matthew Arnold's elegy on his father: "Those who with half-open eyes / Tread the borderland dim / 'Twixt vice and virtue." But, with his distrust of youthful spirits, was Dr. Arnold guilty, as some critics claimed, of seeking to quench them prematurely, of shepherding the boys too quickly through that dim borderland? In the preface to the sixth edition of *Tom Brown's School Days* Thomas Hughes answered the charge that his former mentor had turned out "a set of young square-toes, who wore long-fingered black gloves and talked with a snuffle." On the contrary, he insisted, Arnold taught that "boyishness in the highest sense is not incompatible with seriousness,—or earnestness, if you like the word better."[15] No doubt Arnold did believe that, though with the qualification that the two should never be confused. The peculiar charm of *Tom Brown* is that it depicts a boy's world where happy spontaneity and grave meditation merge. Unlike most juvenile fiction of the time, it asserts that work and play, duty and pleasure, do not necessarily conflict: a boy can enjoy himself and live an upright life at the same time.

Hughes's original conception of *Tom Brown* has been recounted by J. M. Ludlow. Hughes and some friends were chatting when "the talk fell on children's books, and Hughes said that he had often thought that good might be done by a real novel for boys—not didactic, like *Sandford and Merton*—written in a right spirit, but distinctly aimed at being interesting."[16] Until *Tom Brown* appeared in 1857, Thomas Day's *Sandford and Merton* was regarded as *the* boy's book, having maintained that eminence for over seventy years.[17] It tells of the moral education of young Tommy Merton by a village clergyman, Mr. Barlow, and by Tommy's naturally virtuous friend Harry Sandford. By observing Harry's exemplary conduct and listening to Mr. Barlow's edifying stories Tommy undergoes a substantial improvement in character, a change for which he shows himself grateful as he finally takes leave of his playmate at the book's conclusion: "Should I ever be tempted to relapse, even for an instant, into any of my former habits, I will return hither for instruction, and I hope you will again receive me."[18] This tale, with its unremitting sanctimoniousness, may well be what Hughes refers to in *Tom Brown's School Days* as a "kid-glove and go-to-meeting-coat picture" of a boy's education.[19] By contrast, Hughes accepts boyhood on its own terms, has sympathy with it. He addresses his readers as "young sirs" or "gentlemen," as if he were a sixth-former addressing the lower-fifth, or an "old boy" (as he calls himself on the title page) addressing pupils still in school. His tone is alternately serious and high-spirited, but never condescending.

With *Tom Brown* Hughes gave the English schoolboy a new respect. A few years after the novel's appearance a *Blackwood's* reviewer hailed its author as "the Columbus of the world of schoolboy romance." There was a time, the writer recalled, when adult society tolerated the schoolboy, "as it tolerates poor relations or cynical maiden aunts—either for the sake of antecedents or future expectations"; but now, thanks to Hughes, this figure had become a hero.[20] Hughes succeeded in discovering and charting the world of boyhood because he thoroughly believed in its existence: a separate and definable stage of life different from childhood and adolescence, distinct in its outlines, unique in its perils and promises, but with more promise than peril.

When the story begins Tom is still a child, living a wholly supervised life, guided solely by the adults around him: his mother and father, his nurse, and his rheumatic mentor, old Benjy. With no one his own age to play with, he grows increasingly restless and mischievous. Only when the schoolmaster agrees to let some of the best pupils out early to play together does Tom begin to pass into boyhood, the "second act" of his life, conquering "the step which all real boys so long to make; he had got amongst his equals in age and strength, and could measure himself with other boys; he lived with those whose pursuits and wishes and ways were the same in kind as his own" (p. 41).

With boyhood moral development begins. Education then occurs chiefly outside the classroom and home. During this period Tom is constantly testing himself, usually in games, within various groups of his peers: "Prisoner's base, rounders, high-cock-a-lorum, cricket, football, he was soon initiated into the delights of them all; and though most of the boys were older than himself, he managed to hold his own very well. He was naturally active and strong, and quick of eye and hand, and had the advantage of light shoes and well-fitting dress, so that in a short time he could run and jump and climb with any of them" (p. 42).

When the "regular games" are finished for the day, the village boys turn to other "trials of skill and strength"—pony riding, marbles, and especially elbow- and collar-wrestling. At the private school where Tom is first sent, the chief testing ritual is "mud-patties," a sort of king-of-the-hill. And, at Rugby, Tom encounters big-side football, hare-and-hounds, and more cricket. By means of these games and some occasional fistfights he finds his natural place in the world of boys.

One function of play has been described by René Dubos in terms appropriate here: "Play can be regarded as the chief method children use for securing the kinds of sensations and perceptions out of which they construct their private reality. In other words, the child is a selector of environment before he becomes a solver of problems."[21] Quite literally, for Tom and his friends play is a way of selecting environment: "Besides their home games, on Saturdays the boys would wander all over the neighbourhood; sometimes to the downs, or up to the camp, where they cut their initials out in the springy turf, and watched the hawks soaring, and the 'peert' bird, as Harry Winburn called the gray plover, gorgeous in his wedding feathers; and so home, racing down the Manger with a roll among the thistles, or through Uffington-wood to watch the fox-cubs playing in the green rides; sometimes to Rosy Brook, to cut long whispering reeds which grew there, to make pan-pipes of; sometimes to Moor Mills, where there was a piece of old forest land, with short browsed turf and tufted brambly thickets stretching under the oaks, amongst which rumour declared that a raven, last of his race, still lingered; or to the sand-hills, in vain quest of rabbits; and birds'-nesting in the season anywhere and everywhere" (p. 43). Though untutored, these forays are educational adventures in discovering, in naming, and especially (with the symbolic act of cutting initials in the turf) in achieving an identity in relation to surroundings.

To the boy out of school the world seems boundless; with the school games, on the other hand, geographic boundaries are assumed, as are other rules of play. When Tom first arrives at Rugby he asks his new friend East, who is explaining the "mysteries" of football to him, "But how do you keep the ball between the goals? I can't see why it mightn't go right down to the chapel." East explains, "Why, that's out of play . . . You see this gravel-walk running down all along this side of the playing-ground, and the line of elms opposite on the other? Well, they're the bounds. As soon as the ball gets past them, it's in touch, and out of play. And then whoever first touches it has to knock it straight out amongst the players-up, who make the two lines with a space between them, every fellow going on his own side. Ain't there just fine scrummages then! and the three trees you see there which come out into the play, there's a tremendous place when the ball hangs there, for you get thrown against the trees, and that's worse than any hack" (p. 72).

Not only is sport a way of relating to the natural environment, it is a means of assimilating the group ethic and understanding group expectations. There is a common understanding about limits; they are a matter of general assent, and to accept them is to accept the customs of one's society. As George Herbert Mead has written, "The game is . . . an illustration of the situation out of which an organized personality arises. In so far as the child does take the attitude of the other and allows that attitude of the other to determine the thing he is going to do with reference to a common end, he is becoming an organic member of society. He is taking over the morale of that society and is becoming an essential member of it."[22]

If play is the means by which a boy defines his role and status within his own world, and also his means of defining that world itself, it can also be a way of challenging the more complex ethics of the adult world and of maintaining his identity as a boy. This is its intrinsic limitation. One of the few pleasures of the dismal private school Tom attends early in the book is the half-holiday at Hazeldown, a wonderland of field mice, humble-bees, sand martins' nests, and blue and gold butterflies. On one of these visits, temporarily out of sight of the school usher, he strays into the village to buy some toffee. Since the village has been "especially prohibited," he is flogged on his return to school. At Rugby, Tom increasingly challenges such boundaries, most of which are arbitrary, set by custom and agreement. One of them is the Avon River, where only the school side is permitted the boys for their fishing and swimming. One day Tom and some companions cross to the far bank, take up and reset their night fishing lines, and are caught by a keeper who takes Tom back to the school in hand. When he admits to Dr. Arnold that he knows "the rules about the banks" he is ordered flogged the next morning. A mere three weeks later he and East manage to scale the walls of the School and carve their initials on the minute hand of the great clock. They get off with a minor punishment but are soon in trouble again, this time for going to a town fair against orders, and Tom once more receives a flogging.

The "second act" of Tom's young life is a time of unconscious ethical adaptation, as it should be. Conscious choice plays little part in the process. According to Dubos, the element of decision is what a child's play chiefly lacks: "Free will . . . can operate only if there is first a motive, and this in turn implies the existence of some belief to provide the basis of choice. Individuality thus becomes more complex and also better defined as a person continues to develop. Adult man is *par excellence* the creature who can eliminate, choose, organize, and thereby create."[23] By the time Tom reaches the lower-fourth at Rugby it is clear that the process of moral growth has been stalled by the absence of real choice. As he "breaks bounds" more and more, Dr. Arnold begins to worry about his not "gaining character and manliness" (p. 154). As Dubos says, the exercise of choice depends on the "existence of some belief." Reading Carlyle had impressed upon Hughes the idea that the will to believe needs some human object of faith. When Tom Brown finally leaves Rugby he is "a hero-worshipper, who would have satisfied the soul of Thomas Carlyle himself" (p. 268).[24] By then Tom's hero is Dr. Arnold, though all along he has been a worshiper of heroes. While using games to test himself socially, he discovers that although he is more capable than most of his companions, there is usually one boy more worldly and athletic than he.

Tom immediately fixes on this boy as his hero. In his village Harry Winburn, "the quickest and best boy in the parish," takes on this role. Harry
was, says Hughes, "the Crichton of our village boys. He could wrestle
and climb and run better than all the rest, and learned all that the schoolmaster could teach him faster than that worthy at all liked" (p. 38). At
the private school Tom's new hero is "one of the bolder spirits," a lad
who persuades him "to break bounds and visit the martins' bank." This
unnamed youth is "indeed a desperate hero in the sight of the boys" (p.
48). When Tom arrives at Rugby, he is no sooner off the tally-ho coach
than he encounters East, "one of the young heroes" he sees standing when
the coach drives up. "Great in the character of a cicerone," East shows
Tom around the quadrangle and School-house hall. Tom cannot help
"admiring and envying" such an attentive and experienced guide, and he
is overawed when East begins to explain the mysteries of football. Characteristically, Tom measures himself against his new friend by engaging
him in a spontaneous foot-race, to show him that "although a new boy
he was no milksop."

East, like the others, is only a conditionally acceptable hero. His per-
spectives and values are wholly those of the boy's world: " 'That's the
chapel, you see,' said East, 'and there just behind it is the place for fights;
you see it's 'most out of the way of the masters, who all live on the other
side and don't come by here after first lesson or callings-over' " (p. 70).
The worldliness of Tom's early heroes is totally that of boyhood games
and customs; it is acquired and passed on without vision or moral effort.
The time comes when Tom must view himself in relation to a larger,
more heterogeneous world. The "turning-point," as Hughes calls it, of
Tom's Rugby career is the appearance at the school of the serious and
pious young Arthur, whom Dr. Arnold gives into Tom's charge. The two
boys complement each other: whereas Tom is hale and strong, "straight,
hard, and springy, from neck to ankle," Arthur is "frail and delicate,
with more spirit than body." While Tom has the Brown family's instinctive sense of fairness, and will always defend smaller boys from bullies,
he lacks Arthur's grounding in Christian principle. Tom teaches Arthur
football and cricket, Arthur teaches Tom piety; they both become muscular Christians. Gradually Tom assimilates the Arnoldian spirit of
"manliness and thoughtfulness," and along with it an unconditional faith
in his headmaster: "It had taken eight long years to do it, but now it was
done thoroughly, and there wasn't a corner in him left which didn't believe in the Doctor" (p. 268).

Hughes believed that an important part of development was the process of assuming heroes appropriate to one's stage in life, then discarding them when passing into another stage. The process continues until the highest form of hero-worship, Christian faith, is attained. At the novel's end Tom has not quite reached that point. We see him kneeling in the chapel, his mind totally occupied with thoughts of his dead teacher: "And let us not be hard on him, if at that moment his soul is fuller of the tomb and him who lies there, than of the altar and Him of whom it speaks. Such stages have to be gone through, I believe, by all young and brave souls, who must win their way through hero-worship, to the worship of Him who is the King and Lord of heroes" (pp. 275-276).

One's life, Hughes adds, is made up of such "mysterious human relationships" as that of the hero and admirer. At any one time they are the totality of significant experiences which constitute one's character. Therefore, while one may move from one relationship to the next, the experience itself remains implanted. Every phase of life, with its heroes, its customs, its recreations, is incorporated into the next phase. Thus, although *Tom Brown* is essentially a tale of boyhood, it begins with a leisurely "look at the life and environments of the child." For if the child is father to the man, a fortiori "he must be father to the boy" (p. 15). In the tradition of the Victorian biographical novel Hughes wishes to show how much of the child *and* the boy dwell in the grown man: a vital connection with one's past is necessary to the wholeness of his character, so the past must be actively assimilated in the present if one is to grow up healthy.

An assumption of metaphysical organicism, like that of its counterpart theory in physiology, is that growth, or *vital* change, is an integration of structures, of functions, and of functions and structures. As this view developed in the nineteenth century it embraced the additional proposition that in the healthy organism all phases of existence interinvolve. In our own time Ernst Cassirer has written: "When dealing with the problem of organic life we have, first and foremost, to free ourselves from what Whitehead calls the principle of 'simple location.' The organism is never located in a single instant. In its life the three modes of time—the past, the present, and the future—form a whole which cannot be split up into individual elements."[25] What is true of the individual life is true also of the organic life of a society. For a people to lose memory of the past means losing touch with what they have been and therefore part of what they are. "In these racing railroad times," Hughes tells his readers, "you don't know your own lanes and woods and fields . . . And as for the country legends . . . they're gone out of date forever" (p. 5). So he urges young cosmopolitan travelers to return home periodically.

Berkshire's Vale of the White Horse, where Tom is reared, contains "sacred ground" where heroes and history lie buried. The landscape "teems with Saxon names and memories" (pp. 7, 11). Unlike Wessex in Hardy's *Mayor of Casterbridge,* history in the Vale is not simply buried skeletons: community memory enlivens it through tradition. Once again Hughes reflects the influence of Carlyle, who declared in *Sartor Resartus* that if in a single generation men stand woven together, "not less indissolubly does generation with generation. Hast thou ever meditated on that word, Tradition: how we inherit not Life only, but all the garniture and form of life?"[26]

The sense of communal tradition so sadly absent from modern England in *Past and Present* is expressed in *Tom Brown*'s Vale of the White Horse by the "veasts," those festivals by which each village celebrates the opening of the parish church centuries before. There are sack races, donkey races, wrestling, back-swording, and jingling matches (in which blindfolded contestants pursue a man wearing a bell around a rope-enclosed ring). These games, like everything about the veasts—the feast cakes, the ginger and raisin wine, the penny peep show—are traditional, charming, and simple. "We are easily pleased in the Vale," Hughes remarks (pp. 22-23).

The values of social coherence and continuity gave the Vale of the White Horse a special place in Hughes's imagination. Two years after *Tom Brown* he published a casually but lovingly assembled story, *The Scouring of the White Horse,* about a city clerk who vacations in the Vale during one of the veasts. The high point of the festival is the games, and Hughes tried to show, as he did in *Tom Brown,* how authentically English these games were: uniting all classes in a single activity, they symbolized the British democratic spirit. Class prejudice and the desire for personal glory are left behind as people compete only for their county or parish: "The object of wrestling and all other athletic sports is to strengthen men's bodies, and to teach them to use their strength readily, to keep their tempers, to endure fatigue and pain. These are all noble ends, my brethren. God gives us few more valuable gifts than strength of body, and courage, and endurance . . . We ought to cultivate them in the right ways, for they are given us to protect the weak, to subdue the earth, to fight for our homes and country if necessary."[27] In brief, the old festivals reflect the true character of muscular Christianity as both Hughes and Kingsley wanted the term understood.

Despite his fondness for these old "veasts," Hughes did not view their inevitable passing regretfully. The modern indifference to them is a "good sign," he says, "if it be that the time for the old 'veast' has gone by, that it is no longer the healthy, sound expression of English country holiday-making; that, in fact, we as a nation have got beyond it, and are in a transition state, feeling for and soon likely to find some better substitute" (p. 31). He adds that whatever equivalent modern society finds for the popular rituals of the past must engage the total man, appealing to his love of play as well as his desire for work, and to his physical as well as his moral self. There must be something "to try the muscles of men's bodies, and the endurance of their hearts, to make them rejoice in their strength." Too often the modern schemes of social reformers ignore these goals, "and the consequence is, that your great Mechanics' Institutes end in intellectual priggism, and your Christian Young Men's Societies in religious Pharisaism."

Not many years before he wrote *Tom Brown* he had ventured to put these ideas into practice in a unique contribution to the Christian Socialist Movement. In 1854 F. D. Maurice opened the Working Men's College in Red Lion Square, London. Although all the classes had already been provided with teachers, Hughes felt that he could be helpful: "I had been much struck . . . by the awkward gait and unhealthy look of almost all our pupils. Many of them were strong big men . . . but there was scarcely one amongst them who seemed to have the free use of his arms and legs. Round shoulders, narrow chests, stiff limbs were, I submitted, as bad as defective grammar or arithmetic, quite as easily cured, and as much our business if we were to educate the whole man."[28] Agreeing that a program of physical education was needed, Maurice protested that the cost of adequate space and the purchase of such equipment as horizontal and vertical bars would strain the school's budget. Hughes settled for teaching a boxing class. He was confident of his credentials, having been "President" of the sixth-form room at Rugby during boxing nights and having taken lessons while at Oxford from the "Flying Tailor," a former prizefighter and short-distance runner. The classes flourished and soon the sport became the center of social evenings. Much to Hughes's delight, other physical recreations began to take hold as well: a cricket club was begun, and a gymnasium was outfitted with those parallel and horizontal bars earlier considered an impossible luxury.

In the program of sports at the Working Men's College, Hughes seems to have found a modern equivalent for the "veasts," a means of combining the work of social amelioration with the play of simple recreation and submerging the individual in the common will. In *Tom Brown* the public school games also served as the "better substitute." On the playing field, as house is matched against house and school against school, personal ambitions are forgotten in the fellowship demanded by first-rate team play. Cricket is a noble game, one of the masters exclaims to Tom, as the two stand watching a match: " 'The discipline and reliance on one another which it teaches is so valuable, I think,' went on the master, 'it ought to be such an unselfish game. It merges the individual in the eleven; he doesn't play that he may win, but that his side may.' 'That's very true,' said Tom, 'and that's why foot-ball and cricket, now one comes to think of it, are such much better games than fives or hare-and-hounds, or any others where the object is to come in first or to win for oneself, and not that one's side may win' " (p. 260).

Pure play of the sort Arnold insisted on is protected from meanings external to itself: a "transnatural, fragile, limited perfection," as Kenneth Schmitz writes.[29] Play becomes less pure in this sense, however, the more it is identified with group concerns. In *Tom Brown* the public school sports like cricket and football are consciously value-laden. Through the maintaining of customary rules and styles of play they help hold together the spirit of the school, and they have educative value in creating habits of pluck and fairness which carry over into adult life. Tom "could never play on the strongest side with any heart at foot-ball or cricket, and was sure to make friends with any boy who was unpopular, or down on his luck" (p. 244). The business of life is managing oneself properly in a physically and morally demanding world; because that business is like a game, sport is one way of preparing for it. "Man is a militant animal," Hughes wrote in *Notes for Boys*, "and he is the most manly who with dauntless, but not heedless front swings onward to face dangers and difficulties, and, one obstacle being surmounted, braces himself to overcome another. Our campaign of life is like the ascent of some many-turreted mountain: as each peak that had seemed the summit is conquered, yet loftier pinnacles are seen to rear themselves beyond."[30]

Viewed in this social context the games in *Tom Brown* assume those qualities Auden has assigned to genuine ritual: a merging of the aesthetic or pleasurable with the ethical or dutiful.[31] Still, while ritualized they are not institutionalized. That is, while they express ethical meanings they are not in themselves necessary to the welfare of society as a whole, either the society of Rugby or that of England. Therefore, they are not compulsory. Sport becomes institutionalized when its cultural function is formulated and codified and when custom is replaced by fixed rule.[32] That did finally happen in Victorian public schools, but though Hughes's power of myth-making might have helped the process along, he can hardly be accused of advocating institutionalized sport. The games are managed not by the school authorities but by the boys themselves, and they seem to be managed entirely by precedent. In the football game the boundaries of the field are casual to say the least, and so is the time boundary: the game comes to a halt when the clock strikes five. The boys do not wear uniforms (that practice, Hughes tells us, belongs to the future). "Fifty or sixty boys in white trousers, many of them quite small," take on "a huge mass opposite" them. While the match goes on we are chiefly aware of push and struggle, plenty of individual spirit but not much group discipline, despite an authorial comparison to "the column of the Old Guard" at Waterloo.

Dr. Arnold's role in such scenes is that of a benignly disposed spectator. Nowhere in *Tom Brown* is it suggested that he actively promoted games or saw any moral value in them, or that at Rugby he did more than watch them, as his biographer Stanley recalls, "with unaffected interest."[33] When young Thompson dies of fever the Doctor tells the boys he found "nothing painful" in seeing them playing cricket that day. And Pater Brooke reminds the School-house players after the football game that the headmaster has never tried to put an end to sports: "he encourages them; didn't you see him out to-day for half-an-hour watching us?" (p. 92). When *Tom Brown* appeared, however, reviewers assumed that it had been Hughes's intention to picture Arnold as a muscular Christian, and a sort of controversy developed over the accuracy of that depiction. The *Quarterly* declared that the "bold and manly games, so peculiar to the public schools of England . . . were earnestly and wisely encouraged by Dr. Arnold, who throughout his life found in violent exercise, pursued with a boyish enthusiasm, an anodyne to his severe mental labours."[34] On the other hand, Fitzjames Stephen's review in the *Edinburgh* noted the strangeness of making Arnold out to be "the patron saint of athleticism" and added that judging from his letters, "the exuberant animal spirits of the boys filled him with a sort of sorrow."[35] The *North British Review* argued that Arnold's "censorial eye" was attracted by youthful spirit "in all its phases except the athletic."[36]

However tolerant or intolerant he was of youthful energy, whether he encouraged its expression in school games or simply allowed it, the ultimate goal of Arnold's system of education was to develop manliness, by which he meant maturity of mind, not body. Boyhood recreations belonged to a different realm of experience from school attendance or chapelgoing, just as the body belonged to a realm different from the mind and was inferior to it. In *Tom Brown* the chapel and the football "close" are united by identity of purpose as well as physical proximity. Muscularity and Christianity find a common field, and the foundation of true manliness is youthful pluck and vigor. Tom Brown "had nothing whatever remarkable about him except excess of boyishness; by which I mean animal life in its fullest measure, good nature and honest impulses, hatred of injustice and meanness, and thoughtlessness enough to sink a three-decker" (p. 106). Youth has its own moral wisdom, learned in games rather than in books. Firmly assimilated in boyhood, it may be drawn upon throughout one's life. When you see Rugby products, Hughes declares, "the mark by which you know them, is, their genial and hearty freshness and youthfulness of character. They lose nothing of the boy that is worth keeping, but build up the man upon it."[37]

Tom Brown was written with the conviction that a healthy manhood incorporates within it the preceding phase of life, that of boyhood with all its pluck and enthusiasm. Frederic Farrar's *Eric*, which appeared the next year, 1858, seems to have been written with a view to repudiating that phase altogether. Its theme is that with boys, brutality and self-indulgence are not just the inherent traits of the few, or the temporary weaknesses of the many, but the natural and constant possession of all. "I have often fancied," Farrar muses dolefully, "that there must be in boyhood a pseudo-instinctive cruelty, a sort of 'wild trick of the ancestral savage,' which no amount of civilization can entirely suppress."[38] *Eric; or Little by Little* shows us how a boy's life is full of grave and unforeseeable hazards and is almost no fun whatever. The novel's purpose, the author explained in the preface to the twenty-fourth edition, was "the vivid inculcation of inward purity and moral purpose, by the history of a boy who, in spite of the inherent nobleness of his disposition, falls into all folly and wickedness, until he has learned to seek help from above."[39] Surely the story of little Eric at Roslyn School is as dismal a moral lesson as was ever composed! Even before he gets there he is given a taste of what life is like. He enters a grammar school run by a man who is "a little wrong in the head." Ultimately the master reaches the point where he must announce to the children, "Boys, go, I am mad!" and has himself committed to a lunatic asylum.

At Roslyn a train of daily misfortunes befalls Eric. Although some of these spring from his own moral degeneration at the school, many result from the viciousness of his schoolmates, and some appear to be no one's fault at all. As the title suggests, Eric suffers his moral decline by stages. By an early error in judgment he fails to protest when he hears indecent words spoken in the dormitory. Although the author calls upon divine influences to protect the boy ("Open his eyes that he may see the fiery chariot of angels who would defend him, and the dark array of spiritual foes who throng round his bed"), Eric is unequal to the occasion and does not speak out. Worse behavior follows: smoking, cribbing, drinking brandy, and borrowing money. Finally he is forced to leave the school after being wrongly accused of stealing the cricket-equipment funds. He hires on aboard a cattle-ship where, mistreated by captain and crew, he nearly dies. The floggings he receives are only part of his distress: "His sense of refinement was exquisitely keen, and now to be called Bill, and kicked and cuffed about by gross-minded men, and to bear their rough, coarse, drunken talk, and sometimes endure their still more intolerable patronage, filled him with deep-seated loathing."[40] Eric manages to survive the voyage, but on returning home he learns that his mother has died of grief over his brother's accidental death at Roslyn and his own disappearance from the school. This news is unendurable and he too dies, destined for a "land where there is no more curse."

For decades *Eric* competed with *Tom Brown's School Days*, though neither book's existence seemed to damage the sales of the other. By the end of the century *Eric* had gone through more than fifty editions. Nearly as successful were Farrar's three other schoolboy novels: *Julian Home*, *St. Winifred's*, and *The Three Homes*. All were in much the same vein. *Julian Home* tells the story of a simple boy named Hazlett who is tempted away from school to London, a world of danseuses, cards, and gin, by "the clever, and gay, and handsome Vyvyan Bruce." Julian tries to lecture him, but Hazlett is already beyond moral reach: "As the weeks went on, his ill-regulated passions grew more and more free of the control of reason or manliness, and he sank downwards, downwards, downwards, into the most shameful abysses of an idle, and evil, and dissipated life."[41]

The success of Farrar's novels was not to be measured merely by what his son and biographer called "the vulgar standard of sales." The critics, to be sure, were unkind, though Farrar pointedly ignored "the odious 'Press,' " and the "unchristian tone" of its reviews. His gratification came from personal testimonials regarding the efficacy of his books' moral teachings. Letters reached him from all over the world. One correspondent, identifying himself as "Secretary of a very influential Literary Class, and that moreover in connection with a Churchman's Club," wrote to say that the stories "give tone, health, and vigour to the spiritual frame, and feed the lamp of Shekinah with oil pure as crystal." A student declared, "I like Eric's nature and the pieces of poetry in it immensely, and I am sure those to whom I have lent it have also enjoyed it."[42]

It is in the context of such popularity that muscular Christianity's plea for a more liberal notion of health must be heard. Farrar's emphasis on refinement of manners, purity of mind, and delicacy of behavior is in striking contrast to the ethical activism of Hughes. The exquisite attitudes with which the boys at Roslyn hold each other's hands and call one another "dear" spring from the same hyperactive sensibilities which make shame and grief occasions for emotional self-indulgence rather than self-improvement. In a treatise on mental disease the psychologist Maudsley declared, "A healthy mind, like a healthy body, should lose the consciousness of self in the energy of action. By introspection and self-analysis, especially as they are inculcated as a religious duty upon persons who, from bodily or other causes, are inclined to excessive susceptibilities, a morbid egoism is fostered, which is sometimes mistaken for an awakened conscience."[43] That "energy of action," so prominent in *Tom Brown*, is a seldom-rewarded trait in Farrar's novels. If a boy shows any real spirit or daring he is usually courting disaster, and the best boys are ordinarily the quiet ones. At Roslyn School, for example, two separate groups emerge, the physically precocious and the morally precocious. As captain of the cricket eleven, the ill-starred Eric belongs to the first. The other ones go in for intellectual pursuits and try, "by every means in their power, to counteract the pernicious effects of the spreading immorality."[44]

Farrar himself began his career in the public schools in 1854 with a short period of service as assistant master at Marlborough. Hopelessly unathletic, he was out of place at Marlborough, where the sporting fever was just then taking hold. "Boys are stern and keen judges of their instructors," Sir Edwin Arnold has written, "and those who were smitten with the modern passion for athletics did not always find Farrar enthusiastic enough about cricket, football and the out-of-door portion of an English boy's upbringing."[45] Soon Farrar left to become assistant master at Harrow, then returned to Marlborough later in his life for an unsuccessful tenure as headmaster. Throughout these years he was delivering lectures and writing papers on education. Significantly, he became known not only as a disciple of Dr. Arnold but also as an enemy of what he termed the "mania of muscularity." It was regrettable, he once declared, that "a boy should spend *all* his energies and *all* his admiration on the attainment of those corporeal attributes in which, let him do his best, the brute and the savage will beat him still."[46]

Considering Farrar's suspicion of the youthful, untutored mind, his misgivings about the typical recreations of boys are understandable. A bullying episode in *St. Winifred's* leads the author to describe the essential nature of boys as "an absorbing selfishness, a total absence of all tenderness and delicate consideration."[47] The inference to be drawn from his novels is clear: the time between infancy and adulthood is one of grave moral trial in which the dark, unappetizing susceptibilities emerge as a frightening wilderness of temptations. In *Tom Brown* there is no depravity. And although Hughes's Rugby is not without its pitfalls, it also opens broad avenues for the enjoyment of life.

Studying fiction which deals with a child's emergence into adolescence can tell us much about the author's view of the capacities of man—both the good and evil inherent in man and visible at the precise time of his social apprenticeship. If we take *Tom Brown* and *Eric* as initiation fables—and it is probably safe to see most boy's fiction in this light—Farrar's view of life seems by comparison extraordinarily puritanical. For him the public school, which carries the child to the threshold of adult life, is far from Edenic; there is almost no innocence and very little of the joy of discovery that Tom Brown finds at Rugby. If *Eric* has a Garden, it is in the unspoiled mind of the infant before he experiences much of anything. When told by his mother that there are some children who do not like to say their prayers, the as yet uncorrupted Eric remarks, "How unhappy they must be! I shall *always* love to say my prayers"; then he travels off to school, leaving the Christian refinements of home for life among the savages.

Eric is the *Clarissa* of juvenile fiction, denouncing the very sins whose portrayal gives it piquancy. This element in Farrar's novels was not missed by a reviewer of *Julian Home* in *Every Boy's Magazine* (1862), who noted that while the scenes of temptation in the book had verisimilitude, the interest attaching to them was "not wholesome, or even attractive in its kind,—we seem to move too much in an atmosphere of vice when among such company." The peculiar temper of these books, in which sin and death are appealing and repellent at the same time, is closer to the spirit of Swinburne's *Poems and Ballads* than to that of Arnold's sermons. Hugh Kingsmill wittily observes that they are the sort Arnold might have written had he taken to drink.[48]

When Hughes was at work on *Tom Brown* there were two quite distinct traditions in instructional children's fiction. One was the openly utilitarian story (exemplified by *Sandford and Merton*), which tried to encourage moral reflection by appealing not to fear but to reason. Although didactic, this type of story was neither grim nor sensational. Farrar's novels drew on another tradition, the darkly pious stories of unhappy lives and happy deaths to be found in such as *The Child's Maga-*

zine and Sunday Scholar's Companion, pinched little duodecimo periodicals where the only joy is religious joy. They featured missionary tales, poems on the deaths of children, and stories like "The Happy Blind Girl" and "The Dying Sunday Scholar." In these cheerless publications the life of a child is so troubled that when it is over for him ("not dead, but gone to Heaven") the reader feels a warm relief.

THE CONTINUED popularity of Farrar's books and of that general sort of fiction throughout the century shows that the struggles of the soul and the terror of inner experience must always have an appeal for the young mind. But the era of *Tom Brown* was primarily one of liberation from guilt. The boy, or young man, was now treated not as a morally inferior creature but as one whose recreations and natural outlook on life might be respected. The Beetons' successful *Boy's Own Magazine*, begun in 1855, differed from *The Child's Magazine* in the same way that *Tom Brown* differed from *Eric*. That is, it was the reader's "own." It fashioned itself according to his expected interests. In the fifties and sixties dozens of magazines appeared which featured "boys" in the title, ranging from the hastily done up *Boy's Leader*, a 1/2d. pulp weekly illustrated with cheap woodcuts, to E. J. Brett's lavish *Boys of England; A Magazine of Sport, Sensation, Fun, and Instruction*. This latter was one of the most ambitious enterprises of its kind, with serialized stories, puzzles, charades, "Crackers for the Ingenious," and a page of sports under the direction of the current rowing hero, Henry Kelley. Within six months of its first appearance *Boys of England* reached a circulation of 150,000 a week, and newsdealers were hard pressed to keep issues in stock.[49]

What such publications had in common, and what made them sell, was the adventure story. "Our aim," announced *Boys of England*, "is to enthrall you by wild and wonderful but healthy fiction." Stories of buccaneers swarming over ships' railings or of serpents dropping from trees onto boy-explorers were wild and wonderful in that they offered an exotic change from the schoolroom or back garden, healthy in that the more acutely disturbing realms of experience were excluded. G. A. Henty specialized in adolescent heroes who, according to his biographer, "were not so much boys as men, saving this, that he kept to the boy life, and never made them sickly by the introduction of what an effeminate writer would term the tender passion." On one occasion when Henty did touch on this subject, having a boy of twelve kiss a girl of eleven, he received "a very indignant letter" from a dissenting minister.[50]

The heroes of the new boys' fiction were uncomplicated but clever;

they were energetic; and above all they were visibly healthy. Preparing for their foreign adventures, the Hardy boys in Henty's *Out on the Pampas* undergo a regimen of tough exercise: "They both widened across the shoulders, their arms became strong and muscular, and they looked altogether more healthy and robust."[51] On the other hand, Jack Martin, one of the "indefatigable trio" of R. M. Ballantyne's *The Coral Island* and *The Gorilla Hunters*, is described in the first chapter of the latter novel as having already "grown to a size that men seldom attain without losing in grace infinitely more than they gain in bulk, but he had retained all the elegance of form and sturdy vigour of action that had characterized him as a boy. He was fully six feet two inches in his stockings, but so perfect were his proportions that the great height did not become apparent until you came close up to him. Full half of his handsome manly face was hid by a bushy black beard and mustache, and his curly hair had been allowed to grow luxuriantly, so that his whole aspect was more like to the descriptions we have of the old Scandinavian Vi-Kings than a gentleman of the present time".[52]

As the hero of the later Victorian boys' novel passes into manhood there is little change in him other than in size, strength, and worldly wisdom. He is still the strapping pagan who learns the lessons of life by himself, who is gifted by nature to be at home in nature. A world of action is no place for the "muff" (the timid, unenthusiastic boy), warns the narrator of *The Gorilla Hunters*. "Let muffs, therefore, learn to swim, to leap, and to run. Let them wrestle with boys bigger than themselves, regardless of being thrown . . . Let them learn to leap off considerable heights into deep water, so that, if ever called upon to leap off the end of a pier or the side of a ship to save a fellow creature, they may do so with confidence and promptitude."

The notion conveyed by the boys' adventure story of the fifties and sixties is that life is largely made up of physical challenges which differ from those of the playing field only in degree of hazard. The public-school world *of Tom Brown* and *Eric* is small and relatively stable. Its moral laws are comprehensible and a boy's initiation must involve the process of comprehending them. By contrast, the world of the adventure story is so vast and variable, so impossible to grasp as a whole, that a young man must provision himself with self-cultivated values and talents before he enters it. Physically and morally he is on his own, and, since the highest morality is quick action, to a large extent his physical health becomes his moral health.

CHAPTER 8

Anarchy and
Physical Culture

THE YEAR *Tom Brown's School Days* came out, authorities suspended the Eton-Harrow matches at Lord's because the young players were falling victim to the wilder pleasures of the London "season." Reporting that decision, the *Saturday Review* expressed its hope that the suspension would soon be lifted: "It is in these sports that the character of a boy is formed. It is from them that the readiness, pluck, and self-dependence of the British gentleman is principally caught. 'Waterloo,' said the Duke, was won at Eton.' "[1] In 1857 that line of thought was quite new but was catching on everywhere: the function of a public school was to turn out gentlemen; a gentleman was a man of character; character consisted of readiness, pluck, and self-dependence; and these virtues were best learned on the playing field. As a philosophy of culture or education it would not have appealed much to Dr. Arnold, nor, as we shall see, did it appeal to his son. One reason why it was becoming identified with the Doctor was that certain of his disciples were even then implanting it in schools across the land. These men—among them Cotton at Marlborough, Benson at Wellington, and Butler at Haileybury—discovered that the philosophy worked two ways: if games could impart character to a boy, they could do the same to a school.[2]

Founded in 1843 to give education to the sons of clergymen, Marlborough College provides a clear example of the power of a single headmaster in furthering a school's reputation through athletics. In the forties there was little emphasis on games at Marlborough. Football was played, but on a makeshift field where a pile of coats represented a goalpost. Anyone who showed up could play, but since very few showed up, the sides were small by later standards. Most of the boys seemed to prefer playing leapfrog or fly-the-garter, or looking for birds' nests, or simply climbing trees. As at most schools there was trouble with neighboring farmers over poaching and forays into poultry yards. Discipline was maintained with the cane, which was "always on the go."[3]

Gradually the enmity between pupils and masters, never really absent, increased to the point that in 1851 an actual rebellion occurred. The boys marched on the headmaster's room and, after standing outside and assaulting him verbally, began smashing windows. For a week all discipline vanished. Desks and windows were destroyed; fireworks were tossed into hearths near which masters were standing; an unpopular sergeant was knocked down and pummeled and the racquets court set ablaze.[4] To restore order the governors of the school hired the Reverend George Cotton, a close friend of Arnold's and the "grave young master" of *Tom Brown's School Days*. Cotton adopted the prefect system and gave authority to the sixth form. He also began to organize games, bringing in assistant masters who were zealous in this task. The first school cricket professional, James Lillywhite, was engaged in 1853. Cotton arranged cricket matches with Rugby and Cheltenham, he had new fives courts built, and after introducing into his school the Rugby football rules, he developed that sport so that eventually the house games saw the whole house participating, and usually housemasters as well. The changes brought manifold benefits to the school. A decline in bullying and an increase in morale were accompanied by a rise in Marlborough's athletic prestige. By 1859 five of its graduates were playing on the Oxford cricket eleven and Marlborough teams were on a par with the best in the land.

Cotton's success was matched at Wellington by E. W. Benson (later Archbishop of Canterbury). Although never actually a pupil or assistant master of Arnold's, Benson did attend King Edward VI's School, which was at the time headed by a former Arnold master, James Prince Lee. Later, after taking a degree at Cambridge, he was given a position as assistant master at Rugby, where Arnold's influence was still strong. In 1859, when the Queen inaugurated Wellington College, Benson was named its first headmaster. With his aloof manner and his occasional outbursts of wrath, he was unlike Arnold personally, but he had assimilated the fundamentals of his method. He placed great reliance on the prefect system, even going to the length of having the prefects wear a sort of uniform—tall hats and white canes. At first the prefects were resisted; Benson once had to cane some of the younger boys for ducking one of them in the boating lake. Eventually, however, the system took hold, much to the delight of Benson's friend and neighbor, Charles Kingsley.

Unlike Arnold, Benson was not athletic. Partly because of this and partly because it would violate "the dignity of his vocation as Head Master," he never took an active part in games. But he recognized their value in maintaining discipline, and one of his first projects at Wellington was to see that cricket and football fields were laid out. He even helped clear away heather for a hockey field. Always believing in a judicious delegation of authority, he set up the Upper School Meetings in imitation of the Rugby Levee.[5] By this means the members of the upper school were given management of the games fund and the power of planning athletic schedules.

Though originally planned by the Prince Consort as a military academy, Wellington soon took its place, in accordance with Benson's design, "among the Public Schools of England."[6] Certainly the eminence it achieved in sport contributed to this new status. Like Marlborough, Wellington found in games one way of asserting its identity as a public school and actively rivaling Winchester, Harrow, and the other older schools. For a Wellington player to be accepted as a peer by the captain of football at Eton was to be accepted as a peer in social status as well.

In 1862, three years after the founding of Wellington, Haileybury School was started on the grounds of the East India College near Hertford. According to the original prospectus, it was intended "for the Education of the Sons of the Clergy and Laity of the Home and Eastern Counties, though not confined to them" and was to be "conducted on the same principle as Marlborough and Rossall." The first headmaster, A. G. Butler, was if anything a more spirited supporter of games than Cotton or Benson. Soon after the opening of the school he added a guinea to each boy's fee to raise £530 for a new cricket field. But football was his great love. He and several assistant masters, all Rugbeians, built up the game at Haileybury according to the Rugby rules, and two years after the school's founding, compulsory football was introduced. Butler arranged everything. He would even determine who was to play on the big side, usually not giving his reasons except to the newer boys. Like his assistants, he was fond of joining in the games, and was remembered for his exceptional left-footed dropkicks. If he was standing in front of the goal, the boys, no matter how far away, would always dropkick the ball, out of respect to him.[7] One might suppose that the boys would rather be left to themselves, and that such participation by the headmaster would have a dampening effect on the game, but apparently such was not the case. The bumptious master was usually welcomed by boys used to stern fathers and strict teachers. When a game was on, he would sometimes appear in his cap and gown, stand impatiently watching for a while, then shed his academic garb: "[His] figure presenting to view an immaculate shirt and a pair of red braces would be seen dashing into the fray, now emerging triumphant with the ball held aloft and at another moment bowled over in the mud like the humblest forward, eventually retiring from the field with great detriment to his clothes but none to his dignity".[8]

Butler's use of his staff to organize games was far from unique. In fact, at some schools special masters were employed to give direction. There were two cricket professionals at Rugby, another man teaching racquets, a gymnastics master, and a swimming teacher. In 1866 a new assistant master hired at Eton introduced a "new era" of cricket there. He was R. A. H. Mitchell, an Etonian who also had been a star on what became a legendary Oxford team. Mitchell's memorable contribution at Eton was to organize the sport thoroughly. Wasey Sterry explains: "Before he came to Eton as a Master in 1866, there was practically no coaching at all. If you could not bat or bowl by nature you were never taught, and you must learn to correct your faults by the painful experience of finding out what their effect was. There used to be, it was true, professional bowling, but, as a general rule, all the professional did was to bowl with dogged accuracy, anything beyond that was not in his line."[9]

Inspired by the new athleticism among the masters, a new ruling class emerged among the boys. What Arnold had feared came to pass: influence flowed to the sporting set, who constituted an elite with considerable authority and prestige. As early as 1864, when the Public Schools Commission looked into this matter among others, it found that at Eton the captain of the boats was the greatest man in the school, the next in precedence being the captain of the Eleven.[10] At Harrow, where cricket was supreme, the Eleven were easily distinguishable by their school dress —white flannel trousers, flannel coat with brass buttons, and white waistcoats also with brass buttons. And, as against the white straw hats worn by the rest of the boys, the cricketers were permitted black and white.

Such pupil-run organizations as the Rugby Levee, the Philathletic Club at Harrow, and the Eton Society (which came to be controlled by athletes) betokened a new aristocracy not based on social rank. This no doubt made it easier for progressive headmasters to break down divisive snobbery within the schools and tended at least to reward energy and capacity rather than position and charm. In the long run, however, the replacement of one sort of elect by another proved no less disruptive. At

Wellington, for example, the Upper School Meetings fell under the domination of the "caps," the football team members who were gaining more and more ascendancy in the school life.

In the early days of the games movement, when it was more or less under the control of all the students, foreign visitors would often comment favorably on the manly individualism of the English schoolboy. In *German Letters on English Education* (1851), Dr. L. A. Wiese observed that the aim of the public schools was "the formation of strong individual character" and that games had as large a role in that as did the curriculum. The Comte de Montalembert described this sort of education as "at once classical and manly." He approved especially of the rural aspect of public school life, noting that when not actually in class the boys roamed unsupervised through the countryside. The effect of such early emancipation was that in the mass of children "life, health, and intelligence overflow with a sort of expansive and respectful serenity, which is not met with among the pupils of our scholastic barracks."[11]

Gradually, however, that free and unsupervised aspect of public school recreation began to disappear. Supported by the athletic factions among the students, many school authorities began to require participation in sports. At Harrow there were "school compuls," or compulsory games, three times a fortnight. By 1880 at Marlborough games were obligatory each day of the week. At Wellington, Saturday football was made compulsory by Benson's command; with the very large sides, many boys never got to handle the ball, and those who did not want to play were made to appear anyway; when the game was on they would "walk around the field, mostly muffled up in rugs."[12]

From the viewpoint of the headmasters, compulsory games were seen as a convenient means of supervision. When Edward Thring went to Uppingham in 1853 he decided to ensure that the boys were kept busy out of classes as well as in them. On the principle that "every boy can do something well," he devised occupations for all tastes—carpentry, games, music, gymnastics. "These are the weapons," he wrote, "with which we anticipate sensual evils, and ward off their attacks, and reduce them to a minimum."[13]

Schools in Dr. Arnold's day were much freer places in many ways than they were to become. Arnold tried to encourage self-discipline and then dealt personally with any troublemakers or malingerers. Later headmasters sought to prevent trouble by keeping the boys occupied all the time. As football replaced birds'-nesting, and then as it became mandatory, something of the "expansive and respectful serenity" must have disappeared from the boys' countenances. One can imagine being a new boy at Clifton College and hearing the following words spoken by the headmaster, who seemed centuries old: "In this atmosphere you are expected to imbibe a love for manly tastes and pursuits; something of an active, enduring, persevering spirit; something of a true contempt for effeminacy and indulgence, and torpid do-nothing idleness. The more sickly and morbid elements of character are purged out of men by the discipline of such a life as yours."[14] This kind of cold-bath heartiness may have been intended as bracing, and no doubt it was to the earnest, but it must have made many a wonder-smitten boy of ten want to be home again. Arnold could never have made the speech nor could Tom Hughes have approved it; it is as alien to the former's stern but tender nature as to the latter's amiability. Yet the speaker was John Percival, a product of the Rugby system.

In the sixties and seventies games in the public schools were seen as an integral part of education, a means of tempering the character as books were a means of expanding and disciplining the mind. Hely Hutchinson Almond, defending "Football as a Moral Agent" in the *Nineteenth Century*, began by asking pointedly what French boys talked about when English boys were discussing football. He then continued to this hopeful assertion: "It is an incalculable blessing to this country that such a sport is so enthusiastically beloved by almost all that part of boyhood whom Nature has endowed with strong passions and overflowing energies. Its mere existence and the practical lessons which it preaches are worth all the books that have been written on youthful purity."[15]

Naturally this attitude was hard on the silent, reflective boy, the daydreamer or young eccentric. A writer in the *Quarterly*, reviewing schoolboy novels, felt that it was only right that it should be so: "What is to become of yon pale, apathetic, listless-looking boy, possessed of no animal spirits to impel him to amuse himself, no popular qualities to attract invitations from companions? . . . As he grows older, he is delighted to find that by sneaking in a corner or lying at his length in a boat, with the forbidden 'weed' in his mouth, he can earn the reputation for being 'fast'! What a boon, though an unwelcome one, it would have been to him had he been forced into the cricket-ground or the foot-ball field before he was entitled to choose for himself!"[16]

In the sixties and after, there was a determined effort to eradicate "idleness." Edmond Warre of Eton testified to the Public Schools Commission that he had done his best to stop "idling in boats": "We have a staff of watermen who are posted at different places to prevent them from going down into certain backwaters and back streams, but the idling about is, I think, the worst fault connected with boating. The object . . . has been to infuse a sort of energy into it, so as to make them really row in order to be able to row well." Clement Dukes, physician to Rugby School, observed in 1883 that the idle boy is the bane of every school: "The boy who does not join in games, but swaggers and lounges about, should, after failing to *make* him take part in them, be weeded out and got rid of, before he has the opportunity of corrupting others through his idleness and the evil it engenders."[17]

If that was the prevailing idea at Rugby in the 1880s, the spirit of games at the school had changed radically, unless the picture given in *Tom Brown* is inaccurate. But even when that novel came out, a reviewer was led to muse, "Sensualism, both at school and in the world, is found to lie among the quieter natures." What that writer called "sensualism"— mainly homosexuality and masturbation—was regarded as a problem of unsurpassed importance in Victorian schools. Edward Thring at a confirmation spoke "solemn warning" of the "devil work of impurity," warning that he would expel anyone found guilty of it.[18] In a letter-survey on the "solitary vice," conducted quietly in 1883 by Edward Lyttelton, assistant master at Eton, a reply was received from Dr. Andrew Clark that the majority of boys were addicted to it; Sir William Jenner placed the figure at 80 per cent while Dr. Pusey estimated that only ten boys in a hundred were guiltless. Lyttelton himself felt sure that if the "solitary vice" were eradicated, the "dual vice" would also disappear. But how does one make a start? Speaking to a group of headmasters, he confessed that the old solution, "plenty of occupation for body and mind," was proving inadequate and that boys would have to be continually warned on the subject.[19]

Lyttelton himself was brought up to believe in the value of games as a preventative for indecency. On the death of Edward's father, George William, Baron Lyttelton, there was found among his papers a model from which he composed letters to each of his sons on their leaving for school. It concerns "the sin" which, though he refrains from mentioning it, is clear enough, since he remarks of it that although "the woman's guilt is the greater," the man cannot "act in this way" without sharing her culpability: "I dare say I had as strong passions as anyone else: but I never fell into vice, not once, nor did it ever occur to me as a question of *possibility* at all. As a safeguard against this sin, besides the religious ones . . . I will mention two. One is constant occupation of mind or body or both . . . Both of the above are important: but I believe that occupation of mind is the most so. But plenty of healthy exercise, and temperate habits, so as to go to bed rather tired and likely to sleep quietly is of great use. The other aid is the prospect of marriage."[20] The Lyttelton brothers, all of them Etonians, appear to have taken seriously the advice on healthy exercise. In 1872 the cricket Eleven at Eton had three Lytteltons on it, four others having been members previously. Certainly Alfred was the most notable athlete in the family. He was amateur tennis champion in 1882 and seven times member of the England cricket team. While at Eton his personal demeanor was as exemplary as his cricket play. Edward recalled that "though he was in the very midstream of boy life exposed to all its various elements, some at that time poisonous, some barbarous, some splendidly healthy, there was a dominating manliness about him which did not exactly rebuke vice, but banished it, and all diseased talk about it, from his company."[21]

As the public school came to be regarded as a conservatory for learning such manliness, and as games came to be regarded as the uniquely British aspect of the public school, it was natural that games and British manliness would become synonymous. "The physical training of a public school," a *Quarterly* reviewer stated in 1860, "is by no means the least important part of the system: combined with the field-sports of the holidays in after-life, it goes far to make the Englishman what he is."[22] One reason for the general respect given this view was the pervasive nationalism of the time. The ten-year period following the Crimean War witnessed a number of inflammatory incidents affecting Britain's relations with other countries and her own dominions. Some of these affairs were much more serious than others, but all contributed to the spirit of jingoism at home. In 1856 there was a brief war with Persia over the possession of Herat on the Indian border; the following year the Sepoy rebellion broke out in India; in 1858 the attempted assassination in London of the French Emperor and Empress by some Italian refugees resulted in stern threats by French military officers and an answering mood of hostility in England. The "French scare" grew the following year with the Emperor's decision to go to war with Austria. The Chinese campaign of 1859-60 was the delayed result of the *Arrow* incident in 1857. The *Trent* and *Alabama* incidents nearly drew England into the American Civil War. In 1865 concern for the rights and welfare of British subjects abroad was aroused by the Jamaica uprising and by the imprisonment in Abyssinia of a number of Britishers, an act which resulted in the Abyssinia War of 1867-68.

The accumulated effect of these episodes was to prolong for a decade the jingoistic mood of the Crimean War. When the Secretary of War authorized the creation of the Volunteer Corps in 1859, 119,000 men joined within four months. British pluck was demonstrated in force of numbers. John Bullism was a natural development in a period receptive to the thought that the Briton was braver, more generous, and more open-hearted and honest than his counterpart abroad. The sentiment was satirized in *H.M.S. Pinafore* (1878):

> A British tar is a soaring soul,
>   As free as a mountain bird,
> His energetic fist should be ready to resist
>   A dictatorial word.
> His nose should pant and his lips should curl,
> His cheek should flame and his brow should furl,
> His bosom should heave and his heart should glow,
> And his fist be ever ready for a knock-down blow.

What better evidence could be found of the relation of British grit to British sport than the fact that the dominance of home athletes over foreign rowers, cricketers, and mountaineers had become routine? British climbers ruled the Alps; British rowers swept the international regattas; British cricketers overmatched their Australian and American rivals. Writing in the *Lancet*, Robert Farquharson commented that, aside from their gymnastics, the Germans and the French were sedentary peoples, while the Americans lived in such "hygienic unwholesomeness" that, with their "inferior physical development . . . their active minds frequently devour their bodies." He further cited the firsthand evidence of Sir Charles Dilke that most athletic sports were despised in America. "The prospect is not bright," Dilke is quoted as saying. "Year by year Americans grow thinner, lighter, and shorter lived." Farquharson added his own evidence: the defeat of the American rowers at the International Regatta, "purely on account of want of staying power."[23]

A familiar character in schoolboy stories of the time was the fatuous French master incapable of anything more strenuous than kite-flying. Of one such figure the narrator of *Ernest Bracebridge* declares, "Had he been an Englishman, we might have despised him for not playing cricket or football, but we thought it was only natural in a Frenchman."[24] In *The Boys of Bircham School* the fantastic French master is seen to be foolish and inept in his love affairs and even more so at cricket. When he tries sculling he capsizes his boat and must be saved from drowning by one of the stronger boys. Once ashore the Frenchman is treated with deserved contempt, while the rescuer is met with "such cheers as were, years afterwards, when their lungs became stronger and their faces bearded and bronzed, repeated amid the grey smoke of battle, and told the foe that the sturdy Briton was gathering for a final and overpowering charge . . . a cry that but one nation uses; and those that cause it by a brave action may well feel proud of receiving for a reward the hearty English 'Hurrah!' "[25]

Nor was it only in boy's fiction that the link between British games and British manliness was perpetuated. A *Times* leader of 1868 described the University Boat Race as alive with "that instinct which urges every Englishman to be as good as his neighbour, and which keeps up the whole nation at least on a par with other nations."[26] In an age of general confidence such sentiments fed a national sense of smugness or, when combined with patriotic idealism, a national sense of destiny. The Duke of Wellington did not, we now know, claim that the battle of Waterloo was won on the playing fields of Eton.[27] But the authenticity of the "Wellington mot," as it was sometimes called, was accepted by almost everybody, and the myth inspired a sort of lugubrious pride. It is hard to say when the story got started, but it is at least as old as the Comte de Montalembert's remarks on Eton in 1856: "The Duke of Wellington, when he returned in the decline of his days to this beautiful spot, where he had been brought up—recollecting the plays of his youth, and finding the same precocious vigour in the descendents of his old playmates and friends, he exclaimed aloud—'*It is here that the Battle of Waterloo was won.*'"[28] Archibald Maclaren, founder of the Oxford gymnasium, tells the story even more dramatically, recounting as if from personal memory that "the grand old warrior, in the evening of his days, with a glistening eye and trembling lip, confessed, as he watched the Eton boys scoring their innings in *their* field—the field that led to his—'It was here that Waterloo was won.'"[29]

Sometimes those who distinguished themselves by military valor were credited with having been more accomplished and admired as schoolboy athletes than had really been the case. One notable example is Captain William Hodson of Hodson's Horse, hero of the siege of Delhi and "the best blade in India." According to Thomas Hughes, his schoolmate at Rugby, he was not especially adept or enthusiastic on the playing field.[30] Even so, Hodson came to be singled out as an exemplary product of Dr. Arnold's advocacy of "moral and physical force," a man who "carried his hare-and-hounds into his country's service."[31] That part of the Hodson legend appears to belong to the same realm of created history as the stories of Arnold and the Rugby close and Wellington and the Eton playing fields.

The assumption underlying such myths is that the game teaches lessons in independence and daring, in short, develops character. Boys on the continent had their school gymnastics, but that was not the same. A contributor to *The Field*, a sporting quarterly, drew a comparison between the French lycée product, overworked with thirteen hours of study a day and given for recreation nothing but the regulated exercises of the gymnasium, and the English lad, who was supplied with time for voluntary athletic sport. The French youth is "pale and worn, his limbs badly formed, his body without proper development, either elongated and thin, or stunted and obese, weak in either case. Mentally he is without decision, feels himself lost in the wide world, and detests law and order. On the other hand, an English youth, on finishing his school or University career, usually possesses a clear complexion and well-proportioned figure; is able to shift for himself should circumstances compel him to do so; and is proverbially a law and order loving member of society."[32] These remarks proclaim an ideal of health, and another of education. More broadly, they imply a concept of personal and social culture in which a nation's health is seen to depend on the cultivation of healthy constitutions in its citizens. By its nature the English public school with its games was fitted to play a leading role in this cultural destiny.

As generally persuasive as that philosophy of culture turned out to be, it was from the first challenged by a number of Victorian intellectuals. Does the robust Englishman's ability to "shift for himself" really equip him for life? Might not a too-exclusive concentration on that side of his upbringing cripple him functionally in other ways and result in only a semblance of culture? And may not a nation, beguiled by such narrow educational goals, itself develop only a counterfeit culture? In the writings of Matthew Arnold such questions were prominent concerns in which the public school game had a considerable symbolic importance.

ARNOLD's interest in the issue was partly personal. He and Thomas Hughes had been schoolmates and had remained friends in later years. Memories of those Rugby days, he told Hughes, always recalled to him "the glory and exploits . . . of youth, and strength, and coolness." On the other hand, he was disappointed with the picture of Rugby life in *Tom Brown*. He felt that the novel gave a one-sided view of his father, virtually ignored the school's educational aims, and implied that public schools should turn out healthy animals, teach them manners and rectitude, and supply them with social contacts.[33] Whatever role *Tom Brown* had played, Arnold believed that public schools had become "precious institutions where, for £250 a year, our boys learn gentlemanly deportment and cricket." The fault lay not with the games themselves, but with the educational importance attached to them. In the English mind "the playing-fields are the schools."[34]

Arnold's duties as a school inspector made these concerns professional as well as personal. In 1864 he published "A French Eton," an account of his visit to the private school at Sorèze, France. The Public Schools Commission had just recently issued its report, with a well-publicized denunciation of public school athleticism, so what he had to say about games and recreation in the French schools had a special topicality. Not much of "A French Eton" is devoted to athletics, and most of what is favors the English system. At a typical French lyceum the gymnastics court is spacious, "but it is a poor place indeed—poor in itself and poor in its resources—compared with the *playing-fields* of Eton, or the *meads* of Winchester, or the *close* of Rugby."[35]

At Sorèze, Arnold found a greater stress on physical education than at the lyceums. He was shown a stable with twenty riding horses, a fencing hall, a shooting gallery, and an armory "full of guns and swords." Even so, "all this is in our eyes a little fantastic, and does not replace the want of cricket and football in a good field, and of freedom to roam over the country out of school-hours." Toward the end of his essay, he paused to ask what effect the "ardour for amusement and enjoyment" was having on the education of public school boys in England: "What gives to play and amusement, both there and at the universities, their present overweening importance, so that home critics cry out: 'The real studies of Oxford are its games,' and foreign critics cry out: 'At Oxford the student is still the mere school-boy'?" He concluded that for an aristocracy this consuming passion for recreation "tends to become enervative and weakening," that the culture of the upper-class in England had declined, and that "this declension, though natural and venial, impairs its power."[36]

Four years later Macmillan published a reprint of Arnold's report to the Taunton Commission. *Schools and Universities on the Continent* quickly sold out its edition of 750[37] and provoked an attack in the *Quarterly* which was to have a direct bearing on the writing of *Culture and Anarchy*. Once again Arnold's references to athletic exercises in the continental schools were few and brief, and his comparison between British games and French and German gymnastics was a balanced one. He felt gymnastics were probably more beneficial to the health of German boys, who are confined to their studies all day, but less "animating and interesting" than English school games. In his chapter on the French lycées he observed: "Certainly, the boys, at their quarter-hours or half-hours of recreation, seem to enjoy themselves with great spirit, and their gymnastics are probably a better physical training for the short time they have to give to exercise than our boys' amusements would be; but they did not, in general, to my thinking, look so fresh, happy, and healthy as our public-school boys."[38] Surely these words did not show a partiality toward the continental system, nor did his subsequent observation that English schoolboys would do poorly in such constraining exercises. To the *Quarterly*, however, such passages—indeed the whole book—seemed un-English and snobbish. The magazine had always been in the vanguard of the games movement, and there was also more than a little chauvinism in its pages.

The review's author had an ambiguous relationship with this developing controversy. He was Oscar Browning, then assistant master at Eton and later a well-known Cambridge don. Throughout his life he was among the most vocal critics of athleticism. He had in 1862 drawn up a memorandum for the Public Schools Commission, a document whose central theme was the overemphasis of sport at those institutions. Years later, in a monograph written in 1888, he reflected, "Tom Brown's School-days represents the heroism of the forties,—the high-water mark where boyish enterprise and independence reached their height under the influence of manly recognition. During the last quarter of a century, games have become a serious business, instead of the wholesome distraction of public-school life. They are organized as elaborately as the work."[39]

It was not uncommon to find Victorian intellectuals like Browning ready to defend the role of sports in British life while opposing their solemnization. At Eton he refused to direct the boys in their games, thus passing up an easy path to popularity. On the other hand, he had made his own inspection of French secondary schools, noting especially the absence there of "the essential qualities of an English Public School education—freedom, manliness, self-reverence, self-knowledge, self-control."[40] In the course of his survey, while expressing some doubts as to its accuracy, Arnold had related the opinion of a *pension* master that French boys held up longer during long walks than did English boys. Inferring that Arnold approved the comment, Browning bridled at this supposed attack on "our English games": "But whatever superiority exists in boyhood certainly disappears in after life. It it were not so, the Alpine Club would long ago have passed into non-existence, and we should see Frenchmen scaling Monte Rosa and the Matterhorn, and Englishmen riding with parasols up the Montanvert."[41]

Arnold's statement that English boys preferred the freedom of games to the discipline of gymnastics could easily appeal to the British belief in hearty individualism. Even here, however, Browning took Arnold's words as a slur on his countrymen: "But what can show more complete subjection to rule than the training of a Harrow boy for the Eleven, or an Eton boy for the Eight? They both require perseverance, industry, and a surrender of individual will to corporate action far more than gymnastics. Mr. Arnold, we suppose, would reply that it is the 'Celtic element' in a school that secures the victory at Henley or at Lord's."[42] In his review, Browning's defense of free and hearty athletic rivalry was directly followed by a long vindication of public school examinations, which Arnold had termed a "preposterous violation of the laws of life and health."[43]

Arnold's turn to reply on both issues came when he wrote the preface to *Culture and Anarchy*. A sardonic passage in the first edition (deleted later) applauded the "manly self-confidence" with which Browning had offered his own case to illustrate the success of the public-school housemaster system, and that of his brother "as evidence that to train and race little boys for competitive examinations is a good thing."[44] Although there is no mention whatever of the "English games" controversy, Arnold's ironic language obviously alluded to it. The same rhetorical stance is maintained throughout the book. The enemies of culture suppose themselves manly; in the confidence of being right they achieve a formidable energy of will. The "stout main body of Philistinism" (p. 61), the Barbarians with their "staunch individualism" (p. 102), the Populace with their "hands and sinews" (p. 65)—all possess that "manly self-confidence" evident in Browning's review. Each sect, party, or class in modern England can be depended on to cultivate only that side of its nature which seeks to "choose out forms for itself and fight for existence, swelling and spreading till it swallows all other spiritual sides up, intercepts and absorbs all nutriment which should have gone to them, and leaves Hebraism rampant in us and Hellenism stamped out" (p. 21).

Like Carlyle, but with decidedly anti-Carlylean conclusions, *Culture and Anarchy* diagnoses a modern, national ailment, the "diseased spirit of our time" (p. 184), whose manifestations are provincialism, sectarianism, dogmatism, specialization, and smugness. His remedy is the cultivation of more sweetness and light: beauty and intelligence. In an age of bustle and push these qualities are not much favored, and for espousing them Arnold admits to having been ridden hard by "the believers in action, who are so impatient with us and call us effeminate" (p. 212). We have encountered such instances of rugged impatience earlier, most notably in the works of Kingsley and his mentor Carlyle. In "Characteristics," for example, Carlyle had argued that too much time is spent in an "unprofitable looking behind us to measure the way we have made," whereas the "sole concern" should be "to walk continually forward, and make more way."[45] Almost as if replying to that passage Arnold declares that "our Puritans, ancient and modern, have not added to their care for walking staunchly by the best light they have, a care that that light be not darkness; . . . they have developed one side of their humanity at the expense of all others, and have become incomplete and mutilated men in consequence" (p. 11). We continually have to ask whether the light we have is the best one, or else we have no way of knowing whether the "intense energetic absorption in the particular pursuit we happen to be following" is an obedience to a higher law, calling forth our morally best selves, or an obedience to whim, calling forth our "ordinary selves" and making a virtue of robustly pursuing the most proximate goal.

Culture, as Arnold defines it, is the study of an inward, general, and harmonious expansion of all our powers. Anarchy is Doing as One Likes. The modern Briton esteems, first of all, "doing" rather than becoming, movement rather than inward growth. This activism is represented as a national trait, "the old story that energy is our strong point and favourable characteristic rather than intelligence" (p. 129). He also esteems individualism, the strong action of the self or the "one," and this inhibits a general, cultural expansion; the national habits of dissenting and protesting have fostered sectarian jealousies within the social structure as well as between political parties and religious denominations. Finally, the Briton insists on pursuing what he "likes," acting on simple, unreasoned preference; in this he neglects the rational, orderly, and therefore harmonious expansion of all his powers and interests. Culture, by contrast, "indefatigably tries, not to make what each raw person may like, the rule by which he fashions himself; but to draw ever nearer to a sense of what is indeed beautiful, graceful, and becoming, and to get the raw person to like that" (p. 50).

With neither an outward model of perfection to follow, nor an inward idea of perfection, the modern Englishman becomes preoccupied with such unevaluated enthusiasms as "British freedom, British industry, British muscularity" (p. 161), pursuing them as if they did represent such an idea or model. These mean master-concerns, as Arnold calls them, worshiped in isolation from any general, embracing ideal, resemble "machinery" in their rigidity and rawness. "Bodily health and vigour" do have a value in themselves, but "the moment we disjoin them from the idea of a perfect spiritual condition, and pursue them, as we do pursue them, for their own sake and as ends in themselves, our worship of them becomes as mere worship of machinery, as our worship of wealth or population, and as unintelligent and vulgarising a worship as that is" (p. 53).

Beneath such crude ritualization, beneath "our actual habits and practice," lies a basis in national temperament, a "preference of doing to thinking" (pp. 128-129). In his fourth chapter Arnold explores the sources of this disposition. He describes the force of energy and the force of intelligence as "rivals dividing the empire of the world between them" (p. 129), and the "most signal and splendid manifestation" of these forces as Hebraism and Hellenism, whose governing ideas are, respectively, strictness of conscience and spontaneity of consciousness (pp. 130, 132). So long has Hebraism, the energetic obedience to Law, been dominant, so long have the ideals of duty and action been supreme, that in the English character the Hellenic side, the natural desire for sweetness and light, has been stunted. Meanwhile, the spirit of doing has been narrowed, externalized, and fragmented.

The Hebraizing temperament (what Matthew's father called the Judaizing temperament), therefore, is still religious in spirit though not necessarily in its objects of devotion. Whether in politics, religion, or recreation, it is a tendency to reduce one's guiding principles to a single rule or law, which Arnold calls in chapter five the *unum necessarium*, and a life of zeal in accordance with that law. In his time the phrase "the one thing needful" had become proverbially linked with the idea of a single, fundamental requirement in the education of children. Dickens used it as the title of his first chapter in *Hard Times* (in which Gradgrind calls out for "nothing but Facts"). In *Culture and Anarchy* the phrase stands for a narrow conception of human development, especially one which encourages external action and physical well-being at the expense of physical growth: "Nothing is more striking than to observe in how many ways a limited conception of human nature, the notion of a one thing needful, a one side of us to be made uppermost, the disregard of a full and harmonious development of ourselves, tells injuriously on our thinking and acting" (p. 151).

A curious fact about *Culture and Anarchy* is that, despite Arnold's professional interest in schools, they are scarcely mentioned in one of the great Victorian works on the cultivation of mind. But education in the broadest sense is what the book is about, and it concerns education in much the same way in which Newman's *Idea of a University* does: it describes an ideal of cultivation which transcends any single discipline, a "philosophic habit," as Newman put it. We have seen how this ideal, and the method intended to achieve it, were directly opposed to those of Spencer's *Education*. Arnold may well have had Spencer in mind when discussing "the one thing needful," for that is a concept (and an expression) used frequently in *Education*. Spencer's rigidly utilitarian view of learning was that those subjects which have most directly to do with the preservation of life—with "health" in its strictest sense—should assume the most prominent place in schools. There was a time when "the getting of knowledge was thought the one thing needful," but we now know that "the first requisite to success in life, is to be a good animal." It is safe to assume that Arnold acquainted himself with these views, inasmuch as Spencer's work appeared in a book form at the very time that Arnold was submitting his own reports to the Duke of Newcastle's commission on education. He could not have been unaware of such a popular and influential work, nor of its contention that "knowledge which subserves direct self-preservation by preventing loss of health, is of primary importance."[46]

Spencer's pedagogic theories were directed wholly toward individual success and racial progress. He conceived of life as a contest between individuals and between races, in which the best prepared are the hardiest: "Hence it is becoming of especial importance that the training of children should be so carried on, as not only to fit them mentally for the struggle before them, but also to make them physically fit to bear its excessive wear and tear." Further, since physical attraction is the basis of sexual selection, in the human as well as the animal world, those who are robust will survive as a family line. The supreme end of Nature is "the welfare of posterity," and "in so far as posterity are concerned, a cultivated intelligence based on a bad *physique* is of little worth, seeing that its descendants will die out in a generation or two."[47]

It is in the name of progress, then, that Spencer calls for more physical education, even if some intellectual education must be sacrificed. The sense of moral urgency with which he speaks of pursuing what Arnold calls "bodily health and vigour" was becoming increasingly common. Arnold addresses it in *Culture and Anarchy*: "Culture does not set itself against the games and sports; it congratulates the future, and hopes it will make a good use of its improved physical basis; but it points out that our passing generation of boys and young men is, meantime, sacrificed" (p. 61).

As Arnold witnessed the spread of the gospel of health through large sections of the intellectual community, he saw reflected a distressing trend in cultural values: the ascendancy of a narrowly utilitarian concept of personal development founded on an exaltation of the natural—or, as he calls it, the "usual"—self. The zealots of robustness shared with those of political equality and commercial enterprise the conviction that the most visibly practical object in life should be pursued, and that individual freedom, the "natural" thing, was the best means to attaining this object. In *Education* Spencer declared that gymnastics have less value than "games of skill," for in the latter children not only strengthen their muscles, but teach themselves quickness of judgment, and so learn naturally how to deal with life's rigors.[48]

Although Arnold had never before written of gymnastics with much ardor, in *Culture and Anarchy* he uses them to exemplify the best in Hellenic culture. Why, he asks, have Greek freedom and Greek gymnastics drawn the admiration of all people, while British freedom and British games are admired by so few in other countries? "Surely because the Greeks pursued freedom and pursued gymnastics not mechanically, but with constant reference to some ideal of complete human perfection and happiness" (p. 162). As in all things, the Greeks guided themselves by "right reason" in these enterprises and used them as a means of training this faculty. British sport and British libertarianism, on the other hand, have developed from "a too exclusive worship of fire, strength, earnestness, and action" and so represent "the habits of unintelligent routine and one-sided growth" (p. 162).

To Arnold, as to Newman in *The Idea of a University*, Greek gymnastics embodies a different kind of freedom from that of British games, a spontaneity of consciousness rather than of will. Doing as one likes seems to be freedom but actually results in a slavish submission to some narrow enthusiasm or mean master-concern. The formal discipline of gymnastic exercise embodies true development, the harmonious play of mind and body, beauty and strength, whose study is an end in itself. Culture cannot be attained simply by letting loose the usual self. Excellence "dwells among high and steep rocks, and can only be reached by those who sweat blood to reach her" (p. 116).

Nor can true culture be inherited. The British aristocracy, the Barbarians, have little light and only "a kind of image or shadow of sweetness" in their "outward gifts and graces, in looks, manners, accomplishments, prowess": "The Barbarians . . . had the passion for field-sports; and they have handed it on to our aristocratic class, who of this passion too, as of the passion for asserting one's personal liberty, are the great natural stronghold. The care of the Barbarians for the body, and for all manly exercises; the vigour, good looks, and fine complexion which they acquired and perpetuated in their families by these means,—all this may be observed still in our aristocratic class" (pp. 102-103). Having survived as a class through the cultivation of the body (an example of Spencer's natural selection), the Barbarians have invested manly sports with social meaning and taken a special proprietary interest in them. To Arnold this signifies the Hebraic bent of mind they share with the other classes: "Hebraism makes its stand, as we have said, as something talismanic, isolated, and all-sufficient, justifying our giving our ordinary selves free play in bodily exercises, or business, or popular agitation, if we have made our account square with this master-concern; and, if we have not, rendering all other things indifferent, and our ordinary self all we have to follow, and to follow with all the energy that is in us, till we do" (p. 158). From generation to generation the aristocracy has passed on the raw self with its ritualized concerns. In a later essay, "An Eton Boy" (1882), Arnold comments on a description he had read of one Etonian who "showed himself to possess all the qualities of a keen sportsman, with an instinctive knowledge of the craft": "The aged Barbarian will, upon this, admiringly mumble to us his story how the battle of Waterloo was won in the playing-fields of Eton. Alas! disasters have been prepared in those playing-fields as well as victories; disasters due to inadequate mental training—to want of application, knowledge, intelligence, lucidity."[49] For Arnold the preoccupation with sport among the privileged was wasteful not because it misapplied energy and strength, but because it made primary virtues of them. British life at all levels had a sufficiency of these qualities, but they were not necessarily signs of vital growth. They nourished nothing but the outer and ordinary person, whereas "the idea of perfection at all points, the encouraging in ourselves spontaneity of consciousness, the letting a free play of thought flow around all our activity . . . may even, also, bring new life and movement into that side of us with which alone Hebraism concerns itself, and awaken a healthier and less mechanical activity there" (pp. 158-159). As a continuing process of expansion culture represents true health and growth: "It is in making endless additions to itself, in the endless expansion of its powers, in endless growth in wisdom and beauty, that the spirit of the human race finds its ideal" (p. 47).

CHAPTER 9

Two Staunch Walkers:
Tom Thurnall and Tom Tulliver

In november 1870, after he had read *Culture and Anarchy*, Charles Kingsley sent its author a note of congratulation and warm approval. It was "an exceedingly wise and true book, a moral tonic, as well as an intellectual purge." He even conceded that some of Arnold's remonstrances might have been aimed at men like him: "For me, born a barbarian, and bred a Hebrew of the Hebrews, it has been of solid comfort and teaching. I have had for years past an inkling that in Hellenism was our hope. I have been ashamed of myself, as a clergyman, when I caught myself saying to myself that I had rather have been an old Greek than an Englishman. Your book justified me to myself, where it showed me where I was ungrateful to God and wrong."[1] Kingsley had no doubt noticed Arnold's uncomplimentary reference to muscular Christianity, and he must also have observed that Arnold's description of the Hebraist fit him perfectly.

Matthew Arnold's Hebraist relies on "strictness of conscience," on a circumscribed vision and narrow philosophy. Instead of seeing things steadily and whole, he settles on one aspect of the universal scheme (for example, the idea of divine law) and interprets human conduct solely in terms of that. Because his vision is limited he can attain his ideal of perfection with relative ease. Once having reached it, he no longer wants to become anything, or to learn anything, only to act instinctively by the best light he has: "Christianity changed nothing in this essential bent of Hebraism to set doing above knowing. Self-conquest, self-devotion, the following not our own individual will, but the will of God, *obedience*, is the fundamental idea of this form, also, of the discipline to which we have attached the general name of Hebraism." If we add to all this a devotion to bodily health and vigor we have Kingsley's muscular Christianity. As a thinker, Kingsley always "walked staunchly." His habit was to push an idea as if any contrary view was absurd, to make his way roughly with it through all opposition. He believed that physical discipline promotes decisiveness and sensuality promotes inertia and weakness. His response to man's physical self meets Arnold's description of the Hebraic attitude: "The Greek quarrel with the body and its desires is, that they hinder right thinking, the Hebrew quarrel with them is, that they hinder right acting."[2] Kingsley's enthusiasm for Arnold's book therefore seems surprising. Was this a reconstructed Kingsley? The conclusion of his letter raises doubt, for it says that he had given himself up to physical science, "which is my business in the Hellenic direction." Inasmuch as his chief scientific interest at this time was hygienics, Arnold must have been perplexed to see it described as an "Hellenic" occupation.

A clarification of sorts came in an essay Kingsley wrote in 1873, titled "Nausicaa in London; Or, the Lower Education of Women." In it he showed what he had meant by the "Hellenic direction" his work had taken. His purpose was to convince readers that if, as was then being proposed, the education of girls was to be patterned after that of boys, the public school games should provide the example, not the public school learning. Although still the Barbarian with the Hebraic spirit, he offered his own conception of Hellenism in the example of Homer's Nausicaa. This young woman, playing ball on the beach when she met the shipwrecked Odysseus, Kingsley chose to illustrate Greek "healthfulness." If educators would develop in girls an admiration for such exemplary types, instead of making them read more books, do more sums, and learn Latin and Greek, they might witness the growth of a whole race of Nausicaas. This may be Kingsley's equivalent of Arnold's study of perfection, but his notion of perfection is somewhat different, and he was perfectly aware of this fact. He anticipates and answers the charge that Nausicaa is "a mere child of nature, and an uncultivated person": "So far from it, that her whole demeanour and speech show culture of the highest sort, full of 'sweetness and light.'—Intelligent and fearless, quick to perceive the bearings of her strange and sudden adventure, quick to perceive the character of Ulysses, quick to answer his lofty and refined pleading by words as lofty and refined, and pious withal."[3]

The essay is a skillful adaptation of Arnold's terms to Kingsley's views. In *Culture and Anarchy* the Hellenist and the Barbarian are two different types. This is not so in "Nausicaa in London"; whereas the nineteenth-century "civilized" Englishman must be reminded by a physiologist of the values of good health, "those old half-barbarous Greeks had found them out for themselves, and, moreover, acted on them."[4] For Arnold, a classical humanist, Greek civilization meant culture, cultivation. Kingsley, reflecting the romantic naturalism which underlay his belief in *mens sana*, enthusiastically commended "those old half-barbarous Greeks." A passage in *Culture and Anarchy* seems almost to anticipate Kingsley's creative reading of the work: "But, oh! cry many people, sweetness and light are not enough; you must put strength and energy along with them, and make a kind of trinity of strength, sweetness and light, and then, perhaps, you may do some good. That is to say, we are to join Hebraism, strictness of moral conscience, and manful walking by the best light we have, together with Hellenism, inculcate both, and rehearse the praises of both."[5]

In their fictional heroes Kingsley and Hughes attempted that sort of synthesis, blending the sweetness and light of the British gentleman with the strength of the Carlylean hero. The hero, to use Sidney Hook's phrase, is an "event-making man,"[6] one who by exceptional native talents can change the course of events, create order, and lead his people to salvation. The gentleman, on the other hand, is not a man apart, not the great man but a good one. His attribute is benevolence expressed in social grace rather than energy expressed in social activism. The gentleman-hero created by Kingsley and Hughes possessed more moral sweetness than intellectual light, and more strength and energy than either. Reflecting on such fictional types, a writer in the *Saturday Review* described the "new generation" of novelists as believing that "power of character in all its shapes goes with goodness, and that there is so intimate a connection between the various departments of life, physical and moral, that strength of mind may be expected to be closely connected with, or may perhaps be said to be reflected in, strength of body."[7] That idea, he added, signified a disposition to see life as a whole, to see the "great and good man" as having "great physical and mental endowments, all harmonized together and all directed toward good ends"—precisely the holistic, teleological concept of health being promulgated by the muscular Christians and fostered in some public schools. As Arnold pointed out, however, wholeness does not necessarily mean completeness. The healthy hero, for all his "strength of mind" and "strength of body," may well be wanting in that general and harmonious development of mind which distinguishes the cultivated self from the usual self.

In an astute study written fifteen years after Kingsley's death, M. M. Mallock observed that different aspects of Kingsley's varied personality were often "projected" or "materialized" in separate characters within the same novel, resulting in their one-sidedness: "In particular, where he affects the 'Muscular Christian,' or the sportsman pure and simple, this is very noticeable; and for the obvious reason that in so doing, he is endeavouring, for the time being, to make a portion, and a very small portion, of himself do duty for the whole."[8] Thus, Mallock declared, the almost feminine sweetness and the vague, passive spirituality which Kingsley's friends noticed underlying his more obvious common-sense heartiness[9] are represented in the Roman Catholic Eustace Leigh of *Westward Ho!*, while the masculine side is personified in the Protestant cousin, the muscular seaman-soldier Amyas. The same two facets appear in the central characters of *Two Years Ago*: the affected, ultraromantic poet Elsley Vavasour and the robust, pragmatic doctor Tom Thurnall. Free of the open economic and political campaigning of the earlier tales, *Two Years Ago* stands out more clearly as the sort of allegory of human nature described by Mallock, a study of the manly and unmanly temperaments. In its time this novel was a considerable success. It appeared the same year as *Tom Brown's School Days*, and reviewers easily recognized the spiritual kinship between the two works. Generally they applauded its "healthy" philosophy; even the usually hostile W. R. Greg adjudged it Kingsley's cleverest and most pleasant work.[10] The youthful Swinburne read it and admired it "almost as much as Westward Ho!"[11] Mudie's lending library placed an order large enough to enable Kingsley to clear his financial obligations.[12]

Because this sprawling narrative of several loosely gathered-together plots is seldom read today, a brief summary of its contents may be helpful. Tom Thurnall, a strapping young lad of high spirits, and John Briggs, an effeminate neighbor boy, are brought up together by Tom's father, Tom to be a physician and John a pharmacist. Tom leaves home to study medicine in London and Paris, then sets out to confront the world and the adventures it offers. After a number of challenging experiences, including an accidental involvement in a South American revolution and an Australian gold-mining venture, he sails for home. His vessel is wrecked in a storm near Aberalva, in the west of England. The townspeople heroically rescue Tom and many other passengers, but Tom comes to suspect one of the rescuers, an evangelical schoolmistress named Grace Harvey, of having stolen his money belt during the excitement. Also, he discovers that John Briggs is now living in Aberalva. Briggs, who has changed his name to Elsley Vavasour, has become a morbid, dandyish poet, the author of a collection titled *A Soul's Agonies*. Tom further perceives that the town will almost certainly be visited by a cholera epidemic sweeping England, though the townspeople and the local squire are too improvident to take preventive measures. Despite Tom's warnings the town is unprepared when the cholera arrives. Vavasour proves helpless in the crisis, but Tom's efforts, along with those of Frank Headley, the local curate, save many lives. Shortly after the epidemic ends, Vavasour begins to nourish an unjustified jealousy toward his wife, becomes a laudanum addict, and goes to London. There he suffers a steady disintegration of body and spirit and finally dies after an attempted suicide. Tom, now bitter and cynical, goes off to the Crimea. There he acquires a new humility, returns a devout Christian, recognizes his misjudgment of Grace Harvey, and marries her.

Unlike Kingsley's earlier novels, *Two Years Ago* offers no natural villain or villainous institution. The repressive economic system of *Alton Locke* and *Yeast* is missing, as is the equally repressive Catholic Church of *Westward Ho!* The chief crises faced by the characters spring from their own shortcomings. The deficiencies of Briggs/Vavasour are so manifold and fundamental that a personal conversion is impossible. Although these faults are evident enough from his actions, the author describes him variously as vain, discontented, moody, ambitious, melancholic, and effeminate. ("He is rather hard on that unlucky poet," Swinburne thought.)[13] In time of stress Elsley is useless. During the rescue of the shipwrecked passengers he has no thought of assisting, but considers the event only as a subject for poetic creation, "as if men were sent into the world to see, and not to act."[14] During the cholera epidemic a timid stomach and oversensitive temperament send him to bed for several days with "sanitary nightmares," leading the author to comment, "There was no work to be got out of him in that direction." Elsley's final crisis is more personal: he suspects the rugged and amiable Major Campbell of having an affair with his wife. Instead of confronting the issue directly, he tries to lose himself in opium dreams and in a Manfredian encounter with the natural wilds of the Welsh mountains.

Tom Thurnall disapprovingly assesses the poet's character as that of "a self-indulgent, unmethodical person, whose ill-temper was owing partly to perpetual brooding over his own thoughts, and partly to dyspepsia, brought on by his own effeminacy—in both cases, not a thing to be pitied or excused by the hearty and valiant Doctor" (p. 128). The chain of causality here is somewhat obscure, but Kingsley does make one point clear throughout the book: Elsley's moral failings and the unkempt condition of his body are closely related. "Believe me," Tom urges him, "it may be a very materialist view of things: but fact is fact—the *corpus sanum* is father to the *mens sana*—tonics and exercise make the ills of life look marvellously smaller. You have the frame of a strong and active man; and all you want to make you light-hearted and cheerful, is to develop what nature has given you" (p. 189). With the purpose of strengthening Elsley's muscles and opening his chest Tom prescribes shooting, fishing, and sailing ("nothing oxygenates the lungs like a sail"), and has a pair of dumbbells made, even taking the trouble to cover them with leather himself. The admonition to develop what nature had given him comes too late. "His *natural goodness* fades away," one reviewer put it, "as if mildewed, from the degeneracy of his turbulent and morbid fancy, which is sanctified by no spiritual faith, nor invigorated by the healthy exercise of a practical life."[15] Elsley's moral lapses arise from his progressively unnatural character; the foreign-sounding, vaguely aristocratic name he assumes is symptomatic of that process, as is his foppish way of dressing—a Byronic collar, lavender gloves, a "poetical cloak." Even more significant is his aesthetic attitude toward nature. The first time the youthful John Briggs appears in the novel he is gazing at the landscape, but "thinking not so much of it as of his own thoughts about it" (p. 20). Overwrought with self-concern, he is the pure embodiment of Ruskin's pathetic fallacy. Because of this sensitive, melancholic temperament, he draws farther and farther away from nature's simple reality. Once genuinely lofty and idealistic, his poetry grows superficial, fastidious, and sentimental.

During his frenetic tramp through the storm-swept Welsh mountains he persists in viewing nature not as it is, but through "the lurid glow of his distempered brain" (p. 379). Nature turns in revenge upon the perceptions of the wild fugitive, and the whole landscape becomes a nightmarish spectacle. At first he attempts to disjoin himself mentally from the surrounding wilderness: "Now he is safe at last; hidden from all living things—hidden, it may be, from God; for at least God is hidden from him. He has desired to be alone: and he is alone; the centre of the universe, if universe there be. All created things, suns and planets, seem to revolve round him, and he a point of darkness, not light. He seems to float self-poised in the centre of the boundless nothing, upon an ell-broad slab of stone—and yet not even on that: for the very ground on which he stands he does not feel" (p. 377). With the thunder booming about him, the lightning-illuminated landscape seems alive with fiends, giants, and enormous snake heads. Terrified by these apparitions, Vavasour attempts a real and symbolic disrobing in an effort to meet nature on her own ground, to be a creature among creatures. Fortunately, "merciful nature brought relief, and stopped him in his mad efforts," as his fingers stiffen with cold.

In a lecture delivered before the Royal Institution, Kingsley argued the unusual thesis that superstition is "altogether a physical affection, as thoroughly material and corporeal as those of eating or sleeping, remembering or dreaming."[16] Maintaining his usual dualistic epistemology, he declared that there are two kinds of fear—spiritual fear, that is, "fear of doing wrong; of becoming a worse man," and physical fear, fear of objects and their effect on the body. When a hunter is afraid of leaping a fence, what he fears is the unknown—the other side of the fence—and the images he has of the other side: of a ditch, perhaps, and of himself falling into it. Even a fear of demons is physical, for the image created in the mind is of these demons doing their harm according to physical, natural laws. Superstitious beliefs, no matter how elaborate and well-articulated, are all grounded in a fear of nature and natural law. To the degree that we see nature as an "unknown," we allow ourselves to be victims of this physical, superstitious cowardice. Spiritual fear is a fear of God and of moral laws, and of not measuring up to those laws. The physical coward, Kingsley argued, is by his superstition distracted from this higher, nobler awe. "And if anyone shall complain that I am talking materialism: I shall answer, that I am doing exactly the opposite. I am trying to eliminate and get rid of that which is material, animal, and base; in order that that which is truly spiritual may stand out, distinct and clear, in its divine and eternal beauty."[17]

As the case of Elsley Vavasour makes evident, superstition may arise in modern man, refined and sophisticated as he may be, through an overwrought imagination, which in turn may result from indifference to bodily health. "When one sees a man in the state of prostration in which you are," Tom warns, "common sense tells one that the body must have been neglected, for the mind to gain such power over it" (p. 189). If a man has good cause to feel secure in the natural part of himself, his body, he is unlikely to imagine that nature more generally is incomprehensible or hostile. The athletes Wynd and Naylor, who finally rescue Elsley from the mountaintop, have no fear for themselves or of nature's malevolence. Rugby products and Cambridge boating men (they were modeled after Kingsley's friends Tom Hughes and Tom Taylor), the two show even in their serious task a boyish lightheartedness, joking and singing as they go, in striking contrast to the poet and his fanciful ravings.

Also in contrast to the sickly Vavasour is of course the book's hero Tom Thurnall, who is "of that bull-terrier type so common in England;

sturdy, and yet not coarse; middle-sized, deep-chested, broad-shoul-
dered; with small, well-knit hands and feet, large jaw, bright grey eyes,
crisp brown hair, a heavy projecting brow" (p. 20). A twofold symbol of
bodily health, Tom is an athlete as well as a physician. In Paris he was
recognized as the best pistol-shot and billiard player of the Latin Quarter;
while studying medicine in London, he was the hospital's top boxer and
captain of the eight-oar. Like Wynd and Naylor he has a cheerful sportsman's philosophy: "Fall light, and don't whimper: better luck next
round." Combined with this unwillingness to take personal defeat seriously is the love of a good fight: "It's a sort of sporting with your true
doctor. He blazes away at a disease where he sees one, as he would at a
bear or a lion; the very sight of it excites his organ of destructiveness" (p.
223).

Tom's dominant traits—a healthy body, a love of sport, an unselfish
aggressiveness, and a cheerful stoicism—comprise his "manly" nature.
But as we follow his career in the novel, we can see that he was hardly intended, as some reviewers thought, as the perfect physical hero.[18] His
cocksureness is more beguiling than Elsley's hysterical timidity, but it is
nearly as dangerous. Viewing life as a game leads Tom at times into
heroic exploits, at other times into foolish, swashbuckling ones, mere
feats of empty valor to satisfy his vanity. On one occasion his pride,
cynicism, and strong but vague sense of "honor" all combine in his nearly
killing a man in a duel. After that he goes off to the Crimea, still with the
same vainglorious, sardonic spirit. "He has escaped once more," the
author observes, "but his heart is hardened still. What will his fall be
like?" (p. 482). Tom's conversion in the Crimea results not from further
immersion in physical action, but in exclusion from it. He suffers the
humiliation of being imprisoned on a mistaken charge of drunkenness before seeing any of the war. On his return to England he admits that his
adventurous life had been all along a contest with God to see who was
the stronger.

In Tom Thurnall and John Briggs, Kingsley has shown two varieties of
"self-conceit" and godlessness. If Briggs's failings are those of the hypo-
muscular temperament, Tom's are those of the hyper-muscular. Elsley
has the effeminate sentimentalism of a mind overawed by circumstances,
Tom the rough cynicism of a mind contemptuous of them. Tom is "one
of those men," Kingsley writes, "with whom the possession of power,
sought at first from self-interest, has become a passion, a species of
sporting which he follows for its own sake" (p. 90).

No doubt Kingsley tried to maintain a balance of sympathy between the two types, but the advantage is clearly on the side of the more robust figure. The man who lets himself slide downhill physically is less likely to be morally salvageable than the man who is always in training. "At least he is a man," Kingsley says of Tom, "and a brave one; and as the greater contains the less, surely before a man can be a good man, he must be a brave one first, much more a man at all" (p. 226). The healthy hero may be hard and misanthropic, but at least he has the sturdy foundation on which Christian humility may be grounded. The unhealthy man, on the other hand, will never be able to see anything right because he is always contemplating himself. The manly man only needs some theological straightening out.

THAT LINE OF thought did not have a universal appeal, nor in fact did Kingsley's novel. In his review for the *Westminster* George Meredith was less than enthusiastic about the author's craftsmanship, his moral teaching, and his main character. "The hero is, of course, Kingsleyan," he drily observed, "—a modern Amyas Leigh, adventurous, muscular, and Saxon—with whom, as with everyone else in the book, Kingsley does what he pleases."[19] When two years later a *Saturday Review* critic observed that *Adam Bede*'s author evidently "has sat at the feet of Mr. Kingsley, and Mr. Kingsley may in many points be proud of his follower,"[20] the novel's publisher, John Blackwood, was "riled." The review as a whole, he declared, was the work of a "damned presumptuous ass," and as to the Kingsley reference, "Why there is more sense in George Eliot's little finger than in Kingsley's whole carcase. With all his blustering, would-be manliness, I do not look upon Kingsley as a man of power and substance at all."[21] Nor could George Eliot herself have been pleased to have *Adam Bede* linked with Kingsley. In a review of *Westward Ho!* written in 1855 she had remarked on the peculiar paradox of Kingsley's nature, a "ferocious barbarism, which is singularly compounded . . . with the susceptibility of the poet and the warm sympathy of the philanthropist."[22] She was to become even less tolerant of the Canon of Eversley, for in 1864 she wrote of his "mixture of arrogant, coarse impertinence and unscrupulousness with real intellectual *in*competence."[23] The type of manliness Kingsley spoke for—the robust will schooled in self-denial—had as little charm for her as it had for Matthew Arnold. Her early novels show that the man who remains content with that concept of the healthy life may impoverish his own character while spoiling the lives of those closest to him.

Both physically and temperamentally the hero of *Adam Bede* bears a resemblance to Kingsley's robust protagonists. He has "an iron will, as well as an iron arm."[24] He "can walk forty miles a-day, an' lift a matter o' sixty ston' " (p. 15). His physique is solid and massive: "Such a voice could only come from a broad chest, and the broad chest belonged to a large-boned muscular man nearly six feet high, with a back so flat and a head so well poised that when he drew himself up to take a more distant survey of his work, he had the air of a soldier standing at ease. The sleeve rolled up above the elbow showed an arm that was likely to win the prize for feats of strength; yet the long supple hand, with its broad finger-tips, looked ready for works of skill" (p. 6).

Further, Adam has the personal philosophy of a muscular Christian. In a letter to Sara Hennell in 1843, George Eliot directed her to the words of St. Paul among the Romans, chapters 14 and 15.[25] No doubt one passage she had in mind was "We that are strong ought to bear the infirmities of the weak, and not to please ourselves" (15:1). This, at any rate, is the advice Adam quotes to himself during his father's spell of drunkenness; he continues: "Father's a sore cross to me, an's likely to be for many a long year to come. What then? I've got th' health, and the limbs, and the sperrit to bear it" (p. 43).

And yet, while Adam has sufficient fortitude to bear up under adversity, his noble strength has a "correlative hardness" (p. 179) which makes forgiveness of the erring difficult for him. He also, rather like Kingsley, has a mental inflexibility, a tendency toward fixed views: "Whenever Adam was strongly convinced of any proposition, it took the form of a principle in his mind: it was knowledge to be acted on, as much as the knowledge that damp will cause rust" (pp. 178-179). His strength is that of the plain, uneducated individualist—firm principle, "large-hearted intelligence" (p. 35), a keen sense of duty. Because his wisdom is of a simple, general kind, expressing itself in maxims conveniently applying to a range of situations, he is never perplexed by the peculiarities of individual situations: " 'There's nothing but what's bearable as long as a man can work,' he said to himself: 'the natur o' things doesn't change, though it seems as if one's own life was nothing but change. The square o' four is sixteen, and you must lengthen your lever in proportion to your weight, is as true as when a man's miserable as when he's happy; and the best o' working is, it gives you a grip hold o' things outside your own lot' " (p. 99).

Unfortunately Adam's grasp of people is not equal to his grasp of things. He can work on his father's coffin despite his grief ("and subdue sadness by his strong will and strong arm"), but he has little to offer his mother in her grief; during her lamentations he feebly leaves the room. He can walk in pursuit of the fallen Hetty "with swiftest stride" (p. 339), but becomes weak and helpless in the presence of her suffering: "This brave active man, who would have hastened towards any danger or toil to rescue Hetty from an apprehended wrong or misfortune, felt himself powerless to contemplate irremediable evil and suffering . . . Energetic natures, strong for all strenuous deeds, will often rush away from a hopeless sufferer, as if they were hard-hearted" (pp. 356-357).

Adam's constitutional rigidness can only be softened by a more vital inner life. Shortly after the novel opens, his previously hard but unperplexing life takes the kind of turning which makes his struggles internal ones: the death of his father, his passionate interest in Hetty, Arthur's betrayal of him and Hetty, the death of Hetty's child, and finally, his growing love for Dinah. As he is drawn more and more actively into the emotional lives of others, he comes to relax his "grip hold o' things" and to let his own consciousness subordinate itself to that of others. In his pain and sense of helplessness he grows resigned to the limitations of his own will: "For it is at such periods that the sense of our lives having visible and invisible relations beyond any of which either our present or prospective self is at the centre, grows like a muscle that we are obliged to lean on and exert" (p. 407).

In *The Mill on the Floss* it is Tom Tulliver's tragedy that this faculty of receptiveness never has a chance to develop. As a youth he is good at the things boys like to excel in, and so he finds his own sense of superiority easy to maintain: "At Mr. Jacobs' academy, life had not presented itself to him as a difficult problem: there were plenty of fellows to play with, and Tom being good at all active games—fighting especially—had that precedence among them which appeared to him inseparable from the personality of Tom Tulliver."[26] The early Tom Tulliver reminds us in some ways of that "robust and combative urchin," Tom Brown, though to John Blackwood he offered "a lifelike contrast to the sort of Tom Brown ideals of what boys are."[27] His combative urge is generally put to the service of his self-esteem. A case in point is his early acquaintance with Philip Wakem. At first the clever and artistic Philip threatens Tom's belief that the physically weak are in all ways inferior to the physically strong: "This Wakem was a pale, puny fellow, and it was quite clear that he would not be able to play at anything worth speaking of: but he handled his pencil in an enviable manner, and was apparently making one thing after another without any trouble" (pp. 143-144). When Philip further succeeds in impressing him with his knowledge of "fighting stories," Tom tries to regain dominance in a characteristic way: "I thrashed all the fellows at Jacobs'," he counters. "And I beat 'em all at bandy and climbing."

Conversations in this novel are often dynamic because the spirit of competition is so alive in them. There are certain people, the author says, "to whom predominance is a law of life" (p. 174). The book as a whole is a demonstration of this principle. As E. S. Dallas noted in his *Times* review, pugnacity is a leading trait of nearly all the characters: "Everybody in this tale is repelling everybody, and life is in the strictest sense a battle."[28] The first words spoken in the novel, Mr. Tulliver's "What I want" set the direction of the whole story. *The Mill on the Floss* is about people trying their best to do as they like and asserting their claims against other people's. The characters generally know what they want or don't want (Maggie's first words are "O mother, I don't *want* to do my patchwork"), but they seldom examine either their own motives or those of others. Like Mr. Tulliver they have the habit of not listening very carefully, partly because they are sure that since others are always trying to get the better of them, listening would be a waste of time. Nor do they often comprehend themselves, an understandable failing, since in any particular situation their motives are likely to be a confusing mixture of personal vanity, easy good will, and the desire, as Uncle Deane puts it, to "get on in the world" (p. 204). Mr. Tulliver wants Tom to be an engineer and a fine gentleman so that like Riley he can look "Lawyer Wakem i' the face as hard as one cat looks another" (p. 9). On the other hand, he is afraid that, should Tom learn the miller's trade, the time will eventually come when his son will turn him out. When Tulliver seeks Riley's advice on the matter of Tom's schooling, the auctioneer fashions his opinion from "pleasant little dim ideas and complacencies" (p. 24), which he never takes the trouble to sort out: he has a vague notion that sending a pupil to Stelling will help him out with his influential father-in-law; he wants to impress Tulliver; and above all he is pleased to be able to express an opinion emphatically. A strong opinion forcefully delivered is as much a sign of personal power and authority in the eyes of the St. Ogg's citizens as a resplendent linen closet or a full bank account. No matter how dubious its source, once formed it is a substantial possession. "You make it your own in uttering it," the author observes, "and naturally get fond of it" (p. 24).

In such an environment one learns to shoulder his way with the rest or else find himself trampled. This principle is illustrated when Tom visits Mr. Deane's office in search of a job. His mood as he sets out is buoyant, his mental energy expressed in his "firm, rapid step": "He would provide for his mother and sister, and make everyone say that he was a man of high character. He leaped over the years in this way, and in the haste of strong purpose and strong desire, did not see how they would be made up of slow days, hours, minutes" (p. 199). Tom is not long in his uncle's office, however, before he begins to learn the ease with which older, more settled people can shrink those who have nothing but high hopes. Mr. Deane not only refuses him but lectures him magisterially and at length on the virtues of application. While doing so he seems "to expand a little under his waistcoat and gold chain, as he squared his shoulders in the chair" (p. 205). Tom, now diminished in his own mind, returns home and finds in his sister someone at whose expense he can raise himself. When she makes the mistake of telling him that if she could learn book-keeping she might be able to teach him, Tom proceeds to put her in her place: "You should leave it to me to take care of my mother and you, and not put yourself forward." "Poor Tom!" the author comments; "he had just come away from being lectured and made to feel his inferiority: the reaction of his strong, self-asserting nature must take place somehow; and here was a case where he could justly show himself dominant" (p. 207).

If predominance is a law of life in St. Ogg's, a correlative law is that the strong grow stronger at the expense of the weak, who inevitably grow weaker. This same theory was advanced by Spencer in his *Principles of Psychology:* "That continued successes tend to bring about an habitual self-exaltation, and that a painful want of confidence follows perpetual failures, are familiar truths clearly implying that the sentiment of pride and the sentiment of humility are thus fostered in the individual. And seeing this, we cannot fail to see that they are thus evolved in the race."[29] In *The Mill on the Floss* strength of will derives from the feeling of righteousness, a feeling reinforced by the spectacle of weakness in others. When Mr. Tulliver visits his sister and brother-in-law in the prosperity-forsaken village of Basset, he is resolved against any appeal to his pity, "and a ride along the Basset lanes was not likely to enervate a man's resolution by softening his temper" (p. 70). Nothing fortifies the will so much as a general sense of the rightness of things as they are; and nothing fortifies that sense like prosperity: "Tom saw some justice in severity; and all the more, because he had confidence in himself that he should never deserve that just severity" (p. 199). In their own minds the Dodsons stand as living examples of justice triumphant. Each of them finds a bracing tonic in the frailties of others: "Mrs. Glegg had both a front and a back parlour in her excellent house at St. Ogg's, so that she had two points of view from which she could observe the weakness of her fellow-beings, and reinforce her thankfulness for her exceptional strength of mind" (p. 107).

Tom's early life is a succession of confrontations with people whom he dominates or who dominate him. His greatest asset in these episodes is an instinctive barrier against self-doubt and self-examination. He has little difficulty achieving superiority, at least in his own mind, over his play-mates—Bob Jakin, Philip Wakem, and Maggie—and with them he is cocksure and bullish. With adults, however, he tends to be circumspect and spiritless. He says little in the presence of his parents; under Stelling's "vigorous treatment" he sinks into helpless passivity; he withdraws silently after his defeat by Deane. But the longer his father remains im-mobilized by the apoplectic stroke, the more Tom begins to assert him-self, a process first noticeable immediately after Tulliver's first attack, when the lad sets out so eagerly to Deane's office. His humiliation there is but a temporary setback, and he becomes increasingly anxious to prove himself manly, to move in the world of adults with the same sustained energy which characterized his childhood experiences.

Until his illness Mr. Tulliver often displayed great force of personality, a force which maintained its intensity by being channeled in a single pre-occupation, his continual battle with Lawyer Wakem. But he is a man of fits and starts, alternately waxing emphatic and falling into a troubled dubiety. Although his energy of spirit is bolstered by his certainty about the sanctity of property rights, it is at times weakened by his "good-natured fibre" which, through sympathy for the weak, tends to under-mine the simple structure of his opinions. One scene in particular shows this divided nature. After firmly demanding from Moss the money owed him, he walks "abruptly" from the scene, gets on his horse, and prepares to ride away: "No man could feel more resolute till he got outside the yard-gate, and a little way along the deep-rutted lane; but before he reached the next turning, which would take him out of sight of the dilapi-dated farm-buildings, he appeared to be smitten by some sudden thought. He checked his horse, and made it stand still in the same spot for two or three minutes, during which he turned his head from side to side in a melancholy way, as if he were looking at some painful subject on more sides than one. Evidently, after his fit of promptitude, Mr. Tul-liver was relapsing into the sense that this is a puzzling world" (p. 75).

In temperament, then, Mr. Tulliver is sanguine and melancholy by turns, sometimes certain, energetic, and hopeful and sometimes confused, passive, and moody. When he learns that his enemy Wakem has come into possession of the Tulliver mortgage he has his first attack. The kind of illness he suffers is symbolic of the man himself: he alternates between periods of "spasmodic rigidity" and apathy. He is only roused to action when he believes that his deeds are being tampered with; as usual, the thought of holding onto his property gives him emotional as well as physical energy (p. 195).

At this time, as Tom begins to think of assuming responsibility for his father's debts, he begins to assume also his father's energy and single-mindedness: "For the first time Tom thought of his father with some reproach. His natural inclination to blame, hitherto kept entirely in abeyance towards his father by the predisposition to think him always right, simply on the ground that he was Tom Tulliver's father—was turned into this new channel by his mother's plaints, and with his indignation against Wakem there began to mingle an indignation of another sort. Perhaps his father might have helped bringing them all down in the world, and making people talk of them with contempt; but no one should talk of Tom Tulliver with contempt. The natural strength and firmness of his nature was beginning to assert itself, urged by the double stimulus of resentment against his aunts, and the sense that he must behave like a man to take care of his mother" (pp. 180-181). Even as a boy Tom "was rather a Rhadamanthine personage, having more than the usual share of boy's justice in him" (p. 48). Now, as with his father in the first half of the novel, the sense of justice is fortified by a sense of injured innocence. As the moral issue becomes crystal clear, his will strengthens and hardens and his determination becomes "channeled" in the particular direction of righting this injustice. The appearance of the bailiff in the Tulliver home and the ensuing self-complacent "family council" serve to threaten Tom's pride and fortify his will. His "practical sagacity" is "roused into activity by the strong stimulus of the new emotions he had undergone" (pp. 186-187). Leaving the physical and psychological care of his father largely to Maggie, he begins to form grandiose plans for regaining the family fortune. As with all the characters in the book, Tom's motives are a mixture of generosity and selfishness, but as they express themselves in sagacity and action they seem a single flow of energy: "Tom's strong will bound together his integrity, his pride, his family regrets, and his personal ambition, and made them one force, concentrating his efforts and surmounting discouragements" (p. 270). This unity of self expressed in purposeful activity is what goes for strength of character in St. Ogg's; it is what Tom has in mind when he wants everyone to say that he has a high character, and what the author means when she refers to Mrs. Glegg's "hereditary rectitude and personal strength of character" (p. 436). In *Culture and Anarchy* Arnold calls it an "energy driving at practice, [a] sense of the obligation of duty, self-control, and work, [an] earnestness in going manfully by the best light we have."[30]

George Eliot's early thoughts on the subject of character were much influenced by a once popular but now little-known essayist named John Foster, a man she regarded as a "genius."[31] Foster's *Essays* (1805), which by 1846 had gone into thirty editions, contain a piece titled "On Decision of Character" that might well have influenced Eliot's conception of Tom Tulliver. The most "striking distinction" of decision of character, Foster wrote, is "the full agreement of the mind with itself, the consenting cooperation of all its powers and all its dispositions." Given this kind of harmony of faculties and desires, the strong character focuses and conserves its vitality: "One signal advantage possessed by a mind of this character is, that the passions are not wasted. The whole measure of passion of which any one, with important transactions before him, is capable, is not more than enough to supply interest and energy for the required practical exertions; therefore as little as possible of this costly flame should be expended in a way that does not augment the force of action. But nothing can less contribute or be more destructive to vigour of action than protracted anxious fluctuation, through resolutions adopted, rejected, resumed, suspended; while yet nothing causes a greater expense of feeling."[32]

Maggie develops into the type of person described in the second part of this passage, but Tom, if anything, gains in vitality as he pursues his plans with fervid single-mindedness. His whole being becomes narrowed by a "practical shrewdness" which tells him that he must continue in "abstinence and self-denial." "Having made up his mind on that point, he strode along without swerving, contracting some rather saturnine sternness, as a young man is likely to do who has a premature call upon him for self-reliance" (pp. 270-271). He has now lost the tendencies to passiveness he once had. His "firm step becomes quicker"; he speaks with "energetic decision" (pp. 306, 307). Foster warned of the essential danger in this sort of temperament: "As it involves much practical assertion of superiority over other human beings, it should be as temperate and conciliating as possible in manner; else pride will feel provoked, affection hurt, and weakness oppressed . . . When [a strong man] can accomplish a design by his own personal means alone, he may be disposed to separate himself to the work with the cold self-enclosed individuality on which no one has any hold, which seems to recognise no kindred being in the world, which takes little account of good wishes and kind concern, any more than it cares for opposition; which seeks neither aid nor sympathy, and seems to say, I do not want any of you, and I am glad that I do not; leave me alone to succeed or die."[33]

Obviously this is Tom's disposition when he tells Maggie, "You should leave it to me to take care of my mother and you, and not put yourself forward." What young Tulliver gains in manliness he loses in humaneness. As a boy at Stelling's he is "a kind-hearted lad" with "the fibre that turns to true manliness, and to protecting pity for the weak" (p. 127). This is the better aspect of his strength, but he also has Adam Bede's "correlative hardness," a quality which circumstances conspire to make dominant. When he suggests to his uncles and aunts that they yield up the expected inheritance early to save the Tullivers' household goods, they are surprised at his "sudden manliness of tone" (p. 189). Here manliness means maturity, an assumption of responsibility, but the dismal truth is that in most cases maturing in St. Ogg's means developing that community's ethic of manliness—that is, resoluteness without sympathy or intellectual flexibility, or "that prudence and self-command which were the qualities that made Tom manly in the midst of his intellectual boyishness" (p. 242). As time goes by, Tom's manliness comes to display itself in asserting his prejudices "strongly and bravely" (p. 400).

By and large those who most influence the lives of Tom and Maggie are comfortably robust. Stelling is "well-sized, broad-chested" (p. 119); Mrs. Tulliver has always been "healthy, fair, plump, and dull-witted," "a woman of sparse tears, stout and healthy" (pp. 13, 82); Mr. Tulliver is "not dyspeptic" (p. 69); Aunt Glegg has a "well-formed chest" and never visits the doctor (pp. 49, 85); and although Aunt Pullet is a hypochondriac with a closet full of pills and boluses, she has the promise of a long life. In Eliot's novels those unacquainted with infirmity or any other personal grief tend to have short memories and little imagination. The mind will not grow to a strong comprehension of the past and the future if it is totally satisfied with present circumstances; conversely, as Dinah observes in Adam Bede, "the soul gets more hungry when the body is ill at ease" (p. 80). The blooming Hetty Sorel and the broad-chested Arthur Donnithorne in that novel exemplify the relation between physical prosperity and mental self-satisfaction. Even just before Arthur's deepest crisis, when he is about to learn that Hetty has been arrested for murdering their child, he faces the future as usual with "agreeable anticipation": "The level rays of the low afternoon sun entered directly at the window, and as Arthur seated himself in his velvet chair with their pleasant warmth upon him, he was conscious of that quiet well-being which perhaps you and I have felt on a sunny afternoon, when, in our brightest youth and health, life has opened a new vista for us, and long to-morrows of activity have stretched before us like a lovely plain which there was no need of hurrying to look at, because it was all our own" (p. 322).

George Eliot was always keenly interested in formal psychology, especially in theories of the relation between the bodily frame and the frame of mind. In accordance with the trends of the time she came to reject phrenology in favor of the new physiological psychology. One similarity, however, between the two approaches was the idea that functions of the mind had their basis in the condition of the body, so abandoning her faith in phrenology did not require abandoning that idea. "I am not conscious of falling off from the 'physiological basis,' " she wrote Charles Bray in 1855. "I have never believed more profoundly than I do now that character is based on organization."[34]

Her own circumstances gave her a special awareness of this whole subject. Anyone who reads her letters may follow the dreary story of her chronic debilities: hysteria, melancholy, hypochondria, severe headaches, gastric disorder. "How impossible it is," she wrote in 1863, "for strong healthy people to understand the way in which bodily malaise and suffering eats at the root of one's life." She was convinced, as were all the valetudinarians (and physicians) of her time, that physical disorder created a disorder of the mind. In 1849 she wrote that because her health was poor she suffered from "egoism and susceptibility." Once she confided to Sara Hennell that a current bout of melancholy, the "ill-favoured offspring of my character and circumstances," was the foster-child of a week-long physical indisposition.[35] For her ailments she had a grand variety of doctors and prescriptions—quinine, "alteratives" (medicines to improve the digestive process), Epsom salts, tonic, leeches, mercury, hydrochloric acid, "bluepill," and many others. But is it possible for someone in a chronically weakened physical condition to be mentally sound, especially if that person has the weaker "organisational" structure of a woman? Must one have a healthy body to have a healthy mind?

Eliot always considered herself to have a frail constitution. She wrote to the robust Charles Lewes, only half-playfully, that hers was a "feminine head, supported by weaker muscles, and a weaker digestive apparatus, than that of a young gentleman with a broad chest and hopeful whiskers." The idea which seems to have sustained her in her long and varied illnesses was outlined in a letter to John Sibree in 1848: "Alas! the atrabiliar [melancholy or hypochondrial] patient you describe is first cousin to me in my very worst moods, but I have a profound faith that the serpent's head will be bruised. This conscious kind of false life that is ever and anon endeavouring to form itself within us and eat away our true life will be overcome by continued accession of vitality, by our perpetual increase in 'Quantity of existence' as Foster calls it. Creation is the superadded life of the intellect; sympathy, all-embracing love, the superadded moral life. These given more and more abundantly, I feel that all the demons, which are but my own egotism, mopping and mowing and gibbering would vanish away and there would be no place for them—for

> Every gift of noble origin
> Is breathed upon by hope's perpetual breath.

Evil, even sorrows, are they not all negations? Thus matter is in a perpetual state of decomposition—superadd the principle of life, and there is a power of self-amelioration. The passions and the senses decompose, so to speak. The intellect by its analytic power, restrains the fury with which they rush to their own destruction, the moral nature purifies, beautifies and at length transmutes them."[36] Bodily affliction or infirmity can be countered by a growth and consequent increase in vitality of the higher faculties, a development of the moral and intellectual self, a "superadded life" more fortifying than purely physical well-being. It is much like what Arnold calls having the spirit "make endless additions to itself." "Where *thought* and *love* are active," Eliot wrote Bray, "—thought the formative power, love the vitalizing—there can be no sadness. They are in themselves a more intense and extended participation of a divine Existence. As they grow, the highest species of faith grows too—and 'all things are possible.' "[37]

Eliot may have found a support for these views in phrenology. Phrenologists like her friend George Combe held that the "organs" of the brain could be exercised and strengthened like the organs of the body; their size was considered a measure of their power and vitality, and their health contributed, through an increase in energy, to the health of the whole system: "The brain is the fountain of nervous energy to the whole body, and many individuals are habitual invalids, without actually labouring under any ordinary recognised disease, solely from defective or irregular exercise of the nervous system . . . Thought and feeling are to the brain what bodily exercise is to the muscles; they put it into activity, and cause increased action in its blood vessels, and an augmented elaboration of nervous energy . . . When . . . the cerebral organs are agreeably affected, a benign and vivifying nervous influence pervades the whole frame, and all the functions of the body are performed with increased pleasure and success. Now, it is a law, that the quantum of nervous energy increases with the number of cerebral organs roused into activity, and with the degree of that activity itself."[38]

This is the reverse of the proposition that the sound body makes the sound mind. In *The Mill on the Floss* it is illustrated by Philip Wakem. Deformed from birth and reduced to "a life in which the mental and bodily constitution [has] made pain predominate," he has a nature "half feminine in sensitiveness" (p. 289) and finds it difficult to make his way in the world as it is. His soul "vibrates," but its energies disperse themselves in random attempts to achieve small pleasures: "I think of too many things—sow all sorts of seeds, and get no harvest from any one of them. I'm cursed with susceptibility in every direction, and effective faculty in none" (p. 286). His physical peculiarities have made him a freak in healthy St. Ogg's; this in turn makes him so contemptuous of the "dead level of provincial existence" that he is constantly driven back into himself: "Perhaps there is inevitably something morbid in a human being who is in any way unfavourably excepted from ordinary conditions, until the good force has had time to triumph; and it has rarely had time for that at two-and-twenty. That force was present in Philip in much strength, but the sun himself looks feeble through the morning mist" (p. 290).

In the hurried disposition of Philip's story at the end of the book we find the "good force" now directing itself. When he goes abroad he writes Maggie to comfort her, "not with selfish wishes, but with a devotion which excludes such wishes" (p. 441). His account of his own transformation recalls George Eliot's description of the process of superadded life. Though still subjected to the enfeebling and painful consequences of his frail constitution, and still suffering from "nervous headaches," he is no longer "filled with selfish passion": "The new life I have found in caring for your joy and sorrow more than for what is directly my own, has transformed the spirit of rebellious murmuring into that willing endurance which is the birth of strong sympathy. I think that nothing but such complete and intense love could have initiated me into that enlarged life which grows and grows by appropriating the life of others; for before, I was always dragged back from it by ever-present painful self-consciousness. I even think sometimes that this gist of transferred life which has come to me in loving you, may be a new power to me" (p. 440).

The existence of this "new power" is probably manifested in the directness of that letter, and in the letter he writes to Dr. Kenn vindicating Maggie. In *Leaves from a Note-book* Eliot wrote that "feeling is energy." The most lasting kind of energy, she said, is energy of human sympathy which stimulates to "ardent co-operation."[39] Her novels show that this kind of force is all the more powerful because it can be passed from individual to individual. By contrast, the energy which begins and ends in simple strength of will—the Dodson type of energy—not only fails to enlarge itself, but tends to sap the strength in others.

Maggie Tulliver, described as a "small mistake of nature," appears to have a character in singular contrast with her mother's tendency to "feeble fretfulness" and "feeble remonstrance." Her gestures, like her father's, are quick and decisive. On the matter of the patchwork she speaks in a "vehemently cross tone"; when Mr. Tulliver praises her for her reading ability her cheeks "flush with excitement"; and when she talks about the illustration in the book she is reading her voice grows "louder and more emphatic." And yet, as the author says, we see in the young Maggie two "opposing elements, of which a fierce collision is imminent" (p. 261). These elements are the tendencies toward self-assertion and resignation. By nature (probably by heredity) she has the same "excessive delight in admiration and acknowledged supremacy" (p. 382), that Tom and her father have. As a girl, however, she has no way to feed this delight, no way to be admired. From the beginning she is "rather in awe of Tom's superiority" (p. 36) and allows herself to be dominated by him. The agonizing misfortunes of her father and the whole family, a sustained crisis in which she has no role except as a nurse, also tend to deaden her will. While Tom is vigorously going about the business of salvaging the family finances, she is afflicted by "that strange dreamy weariness which comes from watching in a sick-room through the chill hours of early twilight and breaking day—in which the outside day life seems to have no importance, and to be a mere margin to the hours in the darkened chamber" (p. 187). Nothing in her life has given her a firm contact with the active world about her, and she becomes more and more isolated in spirit, with a "blind unconscious yearning for something that would link her together with the wonderful impressions of this mysterious life, and give her soul a sense of home in it." Her emotional and creative life narrowed and shriveled by circumstances, she has not that additional "quantity of existence" which makes vital action possible: "There is no helplessness so sad as that of early youth, when the soul is made up of wants, and has no long memories, no superadded life in the life of others" (p. 208).

Under the circumstances, Tom's advice to his sister seems reasonable enough: "If you can do nothing, submit to those that can" (p. 304). Tom's strength and competency chasten and diminish her, and as her brother permits his will to flourish, she finds joy in subduing hers. Paradoxically, both Tom and Maggie begin to develop personalities based on negation. Tom has a "character at unity with itself—that performs what it intends, subdues every counteracting impulse, and has no visions beyond the distinctly possible—is strong by its very negations" (p. 271). The will which becomes fulfilled and fortified by narrowing itself to probabilities excludes that half of life over which it can have no dominance. In suppressing her own will, especially when she begins to read and emulate Thomas à Kempis, Maggie denies that part of her which could come to terms with probabilities. But what Philip says could apply to both brother and sister: "It is mere cowardice to seek safety in negations. No character ever becomes strong in that way" (p. 288). Maggie tries to reconcile the "contrast between the outward and the inward," between the ugliness of life as she sees it and the beauty of life as she feels it might be, by conceiving of her life "as an insignificant part of a divinely-guided whole." Just as Tom had found unity in his own character, Maggie finds it in the universe, but both attain it artificially. While Maggie seeks to reject the palpable world, and her desires in connection with it, Tom rejects the unknown possibilities in his own soul. For Maggie, reading Thomas is a "sudden vision," which makes all things clear, which dispels mysteries: "Here then was a secret of life that would enable her to renounce all other secrets—here was a sublime height to be reached without the help of outward things—here was insight, and strength, and conquest, to be won by means entirely within her soul" (p. 254).

As a young girl Maggie is described as having "at once the timidity of an active imagination and the daring that comes from an over-mastering impulse" (p. 96). In this her paradoxical nature is like her father's. Her passive moods throughout the book spring from her innate awe of the mystery of life. Her impetuousness is expressed in sudden acts of love or rebellion, all doomed to frustration. Therefore, that inner force weakens and she assents to a life of passive submission. Her dependence on Philip is understandable in light of Tom's growing coolness toward her: "What a dear, good brother you would have been . . . You would have loved me well enough to bear with me, and forgive me everything. That is what I always longed that Tom should do" (p. 287). From the time we first meet her to the climactic flood scene Maggie reacts immediately but erratically to strong judgments of her. Her response to Tom's charge that she wilfully pursues "perverse self-denial" while being too weak to resist error elicits a typical response: "she rebelled and was humiliated in the same moment: it seemed as if he held a glass before her to show her her own folly and weakness" (p. 343). Philip is the one person, after her father dies, capable of relieving her sense of guilt and self-abasement. But in addition to his affection, a love external to her, she also needs a strength and substantiality external to her, and this Philip does not have.

Stephen, on the other hand, fills the roles of father, brother, and lover. When, as they walk into the garden, he offers her his arm, she accepts it with her mind in a "dim dreamy state." The offer has a symbolic importance for her: "There is something strangely winning to most women in that offer of the firm arm: the help is not wanted physically at that moment, but the sense of help—the presence of strength that is outside them and yet theirs—meets a continual want of the imagination" (p. 356). That Stephen was intended as the embodiment of manly strength was pointed out by one displeased reviewer: "The *idea*, if it can be so called, of this unpleasant part of the book is, that a powerful physique, and the self-possessed nature which rarely goes with a diseased or delicate physique, is an essential to command the full passion of Maggie's heart, which Mr. Stephen strives for and obtains."[40] The tone of this comment is a little harsh, but the observation is accurate. With her father dead and her brother emotionally distanced from her, Stephen is Maggie's only present strength, or so she sees him. Also, she surrenders to him because she is, in effect, worn out. "All yielding is . . . the partial sleep of thought," the author observes; "it is the submergence of our personality by another." Throughout her life Maggie has had experience in submission without receiving much joy from it. Here is a kind of submission which is immediately gratifying and "enough to absorb all her languid energy" (p. 410). Exhausted both physically and emotionally, she drowsily luxuriates in Stephen's solicitude and, on the river trip with him, in an undemanding flow of life. The past vanishes from memory; the future seems at best a dim, melancholy prospect: "Behind all the delicious visions of these last hours, which had flowed over her like a soft stream, and made her entirely passive, there was the dim consciousness that the condition was a transient one, and that the morrow might bring back the old life of struggle" (p. 412).

The consequences of Maggie's river trip, especially the isolation from her familiar world, only serve to weaken her spirit further. She contemplates total self-negation in a life with Stephen "in which hard endurance and effort were to be exchanged for easy delicious leaning on another's loving strength" (p. 450). The flood restores her sense of self-identity. When the black tidal current sweeps the boat away from her lodgings she awakens to "fuller consciousness" (p. 452). For the first time she is vividly aware of her aloneness, and this restores in her a distinct sense of the past, of her family, and of her ties with both. She is "hardly conscious of any bodily sensations—except a sensation of strength, inspired by mighty emotion" (p. 453). Because the remnants of her past now seem palpable, so does the life around her—the livestock huddled forlornly on an isolated spot of dry land, the gray willows, the Scotch firs, the home chestnuts. It is as if only in the anarchy of nature can she get her bearings, and this orientation strengthens her to purposeful action: "More and more strongly the energies seemed to come and put themselves forth, as if her life were a stored-up force that was being spent in this hour, unneeded for any future" (p. 454).

In this closing scene Maggie is finally liberated from the enfeebling influences of life in a provincial community. The quiet, steady erosion of her soul, turning love into pity, wonder into perplexity, expansion and assertion of self into morbid self-consciousness—all of these vanish like the arrested symptoms of a disease. Her convalescence is rapid, dramatic—and tragic. But in the process she achieves the total reintegration of self under the dominance of will which signifies the healthy mind. If it is true, as George Eliot comments of the ailing Mr. Tulliver, that "feeble limbs easily resign themselves to be tethered" (p. 232), Maggie's brief career shows that tethered souls resign themselves to be enfeebled. In an age and in a community where the noblest ideal is respectability, where the only evils feared are "Catholics, bad harvests, and the mysterious fluctuations of trade" (p. 106), individualism dwindles into a choice between getting on and getting out, between petty assertion of self and pathetic withdrawal into self. Heroic behavior depends on the sort of grand vision of existence which a calamity supplies. Alone on the darkened, flooded plains, with her ties to home and past temporarily severed, Maggie for the first time sees herself as part of the larger order of things: "it was the transition of death, without its agony—and she was alone in the darkness with God" (p. 452).

Thus, just before her death Maggie has all those qualities of the thoroughly healthy mind—a tangible sense of things as things, a spiritual sense of the harmony of things, and the will or energy to accomplish good. That they come too late is the novel's tragedy. Circumstances have by that time accumulated, gathered together with an energy of their own, the blind purposeless energy of natural law and of a society which has not risen much above natural law. Like the tragic protagonist of a Greek drama, Maggie fights an internal contest between passion and duty, one which commands our attention and dominates the novel. Tom, like the conventional hero of Victorian popular fiction, struggles to save the family fortune, then fights to save his sister from drowning. With a fixed sense of duty and no knowledge of his own passion, all his contests are external ones. His heroism is the self-made manliness which was even more admired in Eliot's time than in the 1830s when the novel takes place. But if, as Newman says, the gentleman need not be a hero, it is equally true that the hero need not be a gentleman. Indeed Tom develops the heroic frame of mind at the cost of those qualities which, according to Newman, identify the gentleman: "a cultivated intellect, a delicate taste, a candid, equitable, dispassionate mind, a noble and courteous bearing in the conduct of life."[41] By nature and experience Tom possesses "the positive and negative qualities that create severity—strength of will, conscious rectitude of purpose, narrowness of imagination and intellect, great power of self-control, and a disposition to exert control over others" (p. 400). These are much the same traits found in the Kingsleyan gentleman-hero. In both Tom Thurnall and Tom Tulliver the negative qualities grow into contempt and distrust until purged by sudden revelation.

Tulliver, awed by the dramatic vision of Maggie's unselfish love in the midst of an incomprehensible natural destructiveness, experiences "a new revelation to his spirit, of the depths in life, that had lain beyond his vision which he had fancied so keen and clear" (p. 455). His former "manliness" vanishes, and the only word he can utter is "the old childish 'Maggsie.' " Thurnall too finds redemption in personal misery, with similar effect: "And so the old heart passed away from Tom Thurnall: and instead of it grew up a heart like his father's; even the heart of a little child" (p. 495). Unfortunately, in the process of losing the negative qualities of manliness Thurnall loses the positive ones as well. Confiding to Grace that he has become a physical coward, he relies on her to teach him a sure faith in God so that he can "be brave again." For the muscular Christian, theological certainty and physical self-assurance go hand in hand. The physical self derives its active strength from a confidence in the benevolent order of the physical world. In *The Mill on the Floss* that benevolence is largely an illusion, so conventional manliness is of less use than the less easily attained kind which makes possible love in a world of egoism and decisiveness in an enigmatic universe.

CHAPTER 10

The True Gentleman and the
Washed Rough in Broadcloth

No VICTORIAN WRITER was so instrumental in popularizing the ideal of the self-made man as Samuel Smiles, author of *Self-Help, Thrift, Character*, and other treatises on moral philosophy. An evangel of Success through Application—"honest force of will and steady perseverance"—Smiles was quite successful himself: 20,000 copies of *Self-Help* were sold the first year (1859), 150,000 altogether in the first thirty years of its publication. What so many readers must have found inspiriting in his works was that he taught redemption in positive terms: personal merit, along with a modest but satisfying eminence, lay within the reach of anyone willing to make full use of his natural gifts and were achieved through self-fulfillment, not self-denial.

The aim of his books, the *Spectator* stated, was "to show young men that they have first to lead a full and active life, developing all their faculties, bodily as well as mental, to the utmost extent compatible with their health."[1] Having been a physician himself, Smiles believed that the dynamic life results as much from bodily as from moral fitness; the two go hand in hand, for the "moral man lies concealed" in the physical.[2] His first book (published at his own expense) was titled *Physical Education*, and he frequently contributed articles on health to newspapers and periodicals. In all of his writings he pursued a theme stated in *Self-Help*, "Practical success in life depends more on physical health than is generally imagined." The true gentleman, according to Smiles, is a man of power rather than refinement: "His law is rectitude—action in right lines."[3] He need not emulate the affectations of the upper class, for robustness is the birthright of all classes.

When Smiles was writing, Victorian youth were being increasingly counseled to avoid sham gentility. An 1864 article in the popular sporting journal *Baily's*, titled "Mens Sana in Corpore Sano," argued that "the sinews of a country like England cannot depend on its aristocracy. A good wholesomely cultivated mind and body, taught to endure, disciplined to obedience, self-restraint, and the sterner duties of chivalry, should be the distinguishing mark of our middle-class youth." The article objected not only to such modish sartorial affectations as the turndown collar and the Zouave breeches-pocket, but to any sort of adopted style or manner. A man's bearing should be a natural expression of his own mind and body, and a program designed to train both of these would impart "a cheerful, active, confident tone, an upright carriage, and a graceful ease, instead of that lounging, semi-swaggering, confoundedly lackadaisical manner which they have adopted in compliment . . . to the real swell, and the man of fashion."[4] The true gentleman is recognized by his independent spirit, his unwillingness to be flattered or intimidated by the counterfeit gentleman; he is not a snob. If he remembers the principle of *mens sana in corpore sano*, his inner qualities—self-mastery, veracity, industriousness—will show through to the outer man.

Many Victorian writers strove to divest the "gentleman" of his traditional hallmarks—pedigree, wardrobe, or accent—and to insist instead on qualities of the soul. True gentlemen, Thackeray wrote in *Vanity Fair*, are "men whose aims are generous, whose truth is constant, and not only constant in its kind but elevated in its degree; whose want of meanness makes them simple: who can look the world honestly in the face with an equal manly sympathy for the great and small" (ch. 62). To him manliness, the mark of the true gentleman, was not the opposite of womanliness. Manly did not mean strong-willed, daring, or stoical, but humane, displaying natural human kindness and sentiment.[5] As evidenced in *The Mill on the Floss*, however, the word was developing those more limited connotations in the nineteenth century. When in 1879 Hughes declared that the "foundation of manliness" was courage, he referred to the distinctive qualities of the male.[6]

Because manliness was synonymous with "character" in the male, it is not surprising to find that word also developing specifically masculine connotations. In the broadest sense character was simply the sum of a person's qualities at any one time: a person's character was what made him unique. It was essentially the product of *self*-culture and reflected one's capacity to be himself. Mill declared in *On Liberty*: "A person whose desires and impulses are his own—are the expression of his own nature, as it has been developed and modified by his own culture—is said to have a character. One whose desires and impulses are not his own, has no character, no more than a steam-engine has a character."[7] One develops, strengthens, and supports his character by good habits, which are the enduring impressions left on his nature by his past actions, a sort of register or diary of his life; he literally is what he has done. "Indeed," according to *Self-Help*, "character consists in little acts, well and honourably performed; daily life being the quarry from which we build it up, and rough-hew the habits which form it." Every conscious, definite act builds decisiveness of character. Smiles terms this growth "self-culture" because it requires neither social position nor extraordinary natural gifts. He cites the case of the politician and economist Francis Horner, who "had neither rank, wealth, talents in great abundance, nor fascination of manner. It was the force of his character that raised him; and this character not impressed upon him by nature, but formed, out of no particular fine elements, by himself."[8] When Smiles wrote that in 1859, the phrase "force of character" was almost tautological, as character was coming to imply force.[9] In its older meaning, everyone had *a* character, just as he had *a* personality; today when we say someone "has character" it is a little like saying he "has personality." A particular, dynamic element is suggested. "Energy of will—self-originating force—is the soul of every great character," Smiles wrote. Where it is, there is life; where it is not, there is faintness, helplessness, and despondency."[10]

Because robust character was a national, and therefore classless trait, it was the natural sign of the true gentleman, not only a virtue but an emblem of virtue. "There may be homeliness in externals," Smiles wrote, "which may seem vulgar to those who cannot discern the heart beneath; but, to the right-minded, character will always have its clear insignia."[11] The discerning or right-minded, however, are never as numerous as they ought to be. "The great mass of men must have images," Macaulay once observed. "The strong tendency of the multitude of all ages and nations to idolatry can be explained on no other principle."[12] In the Victorian period the athlete, far from homely in externals, came to supply that sort of image and attract that sort of idolatry. Recalling the athletic aristocracy at his school in the 1860s, one old Harrovian declared, "No thinking man will blame us for idolising the athlete. The cricketer in his flannels was our hero, not the student immersed in his books. Can there ever be the question as to which is the more picturesque figure? Was there ever a race more intellectual than the ancient Greeks, and did they not worship the human form divine?"[13]

To a nation preoccupied with health, the athlete was the new hero and the "human form divine" the hero's clear insignia; had tradition not been so strong, robustness might have become also the distinguishing mark of a new gentleman class: an "aristocracy of Character," as the *Times* hopefully called it, rather than an aristocracy of blood.[14] But the idea persisted in Britain that virtue and breeding went hand in hand; in the later nineteenth century, words like "cad" and "lout" signified both ungentlemanly behavior and ungentlemanly position. While novelists and moral philosophers labored to redefine the "gentleman" more democratically, many who claimed the title were trying to give it a clearer meaning within the existing social hierarchy. As G. Kitson Clark has noted, the concept of the gentleman was then neither "precise enough or powerful enough to be the ruling principle in determining social position"; so the more tangible tests of education and profession were introduced.[15] The gentleman might at least be known by the school he attended and the vocation he followed—or by one other test: one might know him by the games he played and the terms on which he played them.

To the extent that sport is considered simple recreation or even an instrument of education, it tends to be nonaristocratic, even anti-aristocratic. It encourages a meritocracy based on strength and agility, courage and tenacity. But when considered a possession or attainment (as water-coloring was for Victorian ladies), it tends to become a proof of position and to be attached to considerations of social rank. In England sport has always played a considerable role in maintaining social distinctions, especially in distinguishing the gentleman from the non-gentleman. Authors of Renaissance courtesy books, for example, usually designated those athletic recreations befitting gentility. Roger Ascham wrote in *The Schoolmaster*: "To ride comely, to run fair at the tilt or ring, to play at all weapons, to shoot fair in bow or surely in gun, to vault lustily, to run, to leap, to wrestle, to swim, to dance comely, to sing and play of instruments cunningly, to hawk, to hunt, to play at tennis, and all pastimes generally which be joined with labor, used in open space and on the daylight, containing either some fit exercise for war or some pleasant pastime for peace, be not only comely and decent but also very necessary for a courtly gentleman to use."[16] Like the early Greek *kalos kagathos* the Renaissance Man was supposed to have spiritual beauty manifested physically, since the visible attainment was the symbol of the invisible soul. For this reason manuals of conduct were concerned about which activities were suitable not only intellectually but also socially and aesthetically. Attainments which were varied, aesthetically pleasing, and aristocratic were indications of a soul possessing these qualities. Castiglione's

Courtier tells us that the gentleman must be born of a noble and genteel family, endowed *by birth* "not only with talent and with beauty of countenance and person, but with that certain grace which we call an 'air,' which shall make him at first sight pleasing and lovable to all who see him." Certain activities are proper for such a man and certain others are not. Castiglione advises young men to be able to swim, jump, run, throw stones, play tennis, and vault on horseback; but he discourages "vaulting on the ground, rope-walking, and the like, which smack of the juggler's trade and little befit a gentleman."[17] The active pursuits recommended as gentlemanly varied from writer to writer. Whereas Castiglione praises wrestling, Henry Peacham (1622) advises that throwing and wrestling are "exercises not so well beseeming nobility, but rather soldiers in a camp or prince's guard."[18] Apparently there was some doubt as to whether the more strenuous exercises should be permitted, but riding was high on everyone's list. For Peacham riding a horse signified noble bearing, and Sir Thomas Elyot declared that it "importeth a majesty and dread to inferior persons."[19]

In the early nineteenth century certain sports were still largely associated with the upper classes. The Regency buck, though he may have gone gracefully in Mayfair, went strenuously at the turf or in the ring. *Vanity Fair's* Rawdon Crawley likes boxing, rat-hunting, fives, and coach-driving. George Osborne in the same novel is "famous in field sports," rides his own horse at major races, and can "spar better than Knuckles." "I know what it is to be a gentleman, dammy," boasts Rawdon's cousin Jem. "See the chaps in a boat-race; look at the fellers in a fight; aye, look at a dawg killing rats,—which is it wins? the good blooded ones."

In the Victorian period sport came to be commonly esteemed as a social leveler. Hughes records that he first exercised his "radical propensities" on the Rugby close. When the village "louts" were excluded from the school playing field, as captain of the cricket eleven he made a point of asking the best players among these outcasts to practice with him. He also arranged matches between them and the schoolboys, "to the great advantage . . . of school as well as town."[20] Needless to say, this did not result in total integration; the louts were still the louts, whether invited in or not. In *Pictures of Sporting Life* (1860) Lord William Lennox remarked that although his own experience in playing cricket had convinced him that the game "cements the friendly feeling which is so conducive to the interests of both classes," he had never seen "the deference to rank and wealth in the slightest degree lessened."[21] Though a peer might play beside a joiner or greengrocer, and might even sit down to dinner with him afterward, he need expect no insolent familiarity from the man the next day. Thus, sport might serve the function of temporarily inspiring feelings of camaraderie without weakening the awareness of class distinctions.

Not only did sporting enthusiasm fail to break up existing class attitudes, in some ways it actually fostered them. Sports like mountaineering, athletics, and rowing were essentially the property of the growing Victorian upper-middle class, requiring as they did at least some spare cash and a good deal of leisure time. They were appropriated by those who, financially at least, were somewhere near the top of the middle-class ladder. Given dignity by the people who pursued them, they became the perfectly respectable attainments of the gentleman. Prior to an 1860 cricket match in which twenty-two members of Parliament played the I Zingari club, the *New Sporting Magazine* observed that if fifty years previously any member of the Bar had "resorted frequently to manly games, with that spirit and enthusiasm with which a large majority of barristers now indulge," he would have found it impossible to pursue his calling. "It is daily apparent that the man who excels in manly games and exercises at his college, or in country sports and recreations, is the man who eventually excels at his profession."[22] Although gentlemen went in more and more for these manly recreations, they did not drive out those who were not gentlemen. Most of the sports of the mid-Victorian period, therefore, followed the example of cricket in carefully distinguishing the "gentleman amateur" from the mere professional. The Henley Regatta Committee and the Amateur Athletic Club declared ineligible anyone who was "by trade or employment for wages a mechanic, artisan, or labourer."[23]

Distinctions of rank became fixed in the very framework of athletic society. By various kinds of exclusion, some subtle, some more obvious, the enlarged "gentleman" class used sport to underline its own identity, to demonstrate, as Arnold said, its "class-instinct."[24] Therefore, it was unnecessary for the gentleman-hero to discard the insignia of the traditional gentleman—good clothes, coolness, a family name of substance—in favor of those of the "true" gentleman—personal integrity, robustness of will and body; he could combine all these in one grand presence. In the heroes of his immensely popular novels George Lawrence did just that, and resurrected the Dandy, Newman's "narrow or fantastic type," in a form appropriate to an age of Health.[25]

IN 1857, the year Tom Brown and Tom Thurnall made their appearances, Lawrence introduced his own muscular hero in a novel titled *Guy*

Livingstone; or Thorough. Like Tom Brown, Guy begins his career at Rugby, already a picturesque figure: "His features were dark and pale, too strongly marked to be called handsome; about his lips and lower jaw especially there was a set sternness that one seldom sees before the beard is grown. The eyes were very dark grey, nearly black, and so deeply set under thick eyebrows that they looked smaller than they really were; . . . their expression, when angered, was anything but pleasant to meet. His dress was well adapted for displaying his deep square chest and sinewy arms—a close-fitting jersey, and white trousers girt by a broad black belt; the cap, orange velvet, fronted with a silver Maltese cross."[26]

At school Guy is a devastating football player. The story's narrator recalls how the other boys, trying to conceal the pain caused by his vicious "hacks," would limp disconsolately out of the game, one by one. After leaving Rugby he becomes engaged, but there is a falling-out over a scandalous temptress, and his fiancée dies of consumption. With her death a change comes over him. Up to this time his behavior has been simple, raw self-assertion. Remorse gradually debrutalizes him. Putting his own life in jeopardy to rescue some shipwrecked Italian seamen signals the transformation, for his principle had always been that "a man who could not help himself was not worth helping."[27] Unfortunately, this softening of temperament produces a weakening of his athletic prowess. One day, while attempting a riding maneuver which once would have been easy for him, he is thrown beneath his horse, and his spine is crushed. With his lower limbs paralyzed he lingers on for a while, his "brave heart and iron nerve" struggling with his physical agony.

Guy became a folk hero. Young men copied his dress, and "even the chubbiest of the Adonises of the time affected 'to set his face like a flint,' and adopted to his sweetheart the tones of calm command, in place of the old ones of beseeching adoration."[28] There is much that is distinctly Byronic in Guy Livingstone—the pedigree, the aloofness, the adventuresome spirit. What makes him a new sort of hero is the combination of physical power and vehement feeling: "The pupils of Livingstone's eyes contracted ominously; a lurid flash shot out from under his black bent brows, and there came on his lip that peculiar smile that we fancy on the face of Homeric heroes—more fell, and cruel, and terrible than even their frown—just before they levelled the spear. He laid his broad hand, corded across with a net-work of tangled sinews, on the table before him, and the stout oak creaked and trembled."[29]

Only part of the appeal of Lawrence's novels is the heroes, such figures as Guy, or Royston Keene, the "Cool Captain" of *Sword and Gown* ("difficult perhaps to arouse, but more difficult to appease or subdue"), or Sir Alan Wyverne of *Barren Honour* ("The ruffle of brief emotion had passed away from his quiet face, and it had settled into its wonted calmness"). Also compelling is the milieu of the novels, a world where, as with the protagonists, there is a sense of bulk and solidity on the one hand, movement and danger on the other. A feudal primitive, the Laurentian hero functions as easily in a landscape of modern warfare and industrial power as among the stately homes of England. In *Barren Honour* the reader is introduced to the "big, black, busy town" of Newmanham, whose "pulse beats, now, sonorously with the clang of a myriad of steam hammers." A few miles away lies Dene, the ancient family home of the novel's hero. The building has "a huge irregular mass of vaulted roof, and [is] girdled by two tiers of elaborately carved galleries in black oak." Inside, in a "large, square, low-browed room" with walnut bookcases, marble fireplace adorned with family crest and arms, and large windows with "heavy stone mullions and armorial shields on every pane,"[30] the hero appropriately makes his first appearance.

Stolid and dignified, but also active and violent, the Laurentian hero seems to symbolize the world he inhabits. He partakes of the old and the new, of the traditional aristocratic order which maintains itself by right of its massive entrenchment and of the technological order whose values are mobility and power. "A terrible machine has possessed itself of the ground," Emerson had written of the new industrialism: "The mechanical might and organization requires of the people constitution and answering spirits: and he who goes among them must have some weight of metal."[31] Lawrence's world is one of latent and released energy, where female cousins are as sleek, willful, and dangerous as one's riding mares, where those who matter at all can trace their families back to the Heptarchy, and where, under its solid framework, passions rise slowly and consume quickly like the fires in the great baronial hearths or town factories.

Lawrence's imitators, chiefly women writing for a female audience, tended to confirm his observation in *Sword and Gown* that even a quite ordinary feat of strength has more interest for "the generality of our sisters" than any show of moral excellence.[32] These writers dwelt even more on the erotic appeal of the combined ruthlessness and melancholy in the muscular hero. Captain Dare Stames in Rhoda Broughton's *Not Wisely, But Too Well* is typical: he has broken the hearts of many; he has a powerful physical presence ("arms long and sinewy, with the muscles—much developed in many a boxing match or many a cricket field—rising in knotted cords above them; and a great columnar throat"); and he is constitutionally gloomy, "one who walked upon life's paths with his eyes glued to the crumbling dust-heaps of the earth, instead of raised in glad expectancy and awed contemplation of those skyey chambers, built all of pure, untarnished gold, which are waiting for us above the sun and the moon and the stars."[33]

Some of these novels portrayed two distinct types of manliness. With the first, exemplified by Vane Castleton in Ouida's *"Held in Bondage,"* physical power expresses an erotic diabolism, and a clear threat to the heroine's virtue: " 'Off! do not touch me!' cried Alma fiercely, as his hand worked towards the delicate form that he could crush in his grasp as a tiger's fangs a young gazelle." Castleton's aggressive sensuality is contrasted with the paternally protective strength of Major de Vigne, who repays that insult to his loved one by thrashing the offender senseless: "Then he lifted him up as one would lift up a dead rat or a broken bough, and threw him down the stone flight of the staircase: in his wrath he seemed to have the strength of a giant."[34]

Here the sides of the robust hero are divided as, perhaps, the morality of some Victorian women readers might divide them. More typically, however, the descendants of Guy Livingstone are unstable mixtures of brutal energy and moral will, the two elements struggling for control. In Ouida's *Strathmore* the hero intercepts a runaway coach by catching hold of the horses "with a strain enough to make every fibre break and snap." As he pulls them to a stop, "his eyes glittered and gleamed dark with a swift, dangerous passion—a passion that was evil."[35] Then he lashes the horses ferociously with his whip. In Lawrence's work especially, the line between moral and sadistic force is often almost indiscernible. Maurice Dering, in the novel of that title, is capable of astonishing savagery in the name of revenge, whether upon a drunken, insolent stable-groom, an enraged she-bear, or a group of Hindoo mutineers who have given themselves up to his mercy only to be shot down by his men. ("Every now and then one of the executioners came staggering out into the open air—drunk and faint with the scent of blood. And Dering stood by—with that dark pitiless look on his face.")[36] Thus, the muscular hero manages to subdue the energies about him but not those within him. Untamed physical force is met with untamed physical force and the moral will of the ego circumvented by the power of the unconscious. Deep-lying sexual and aggressive energies are directly expressed in physique, physiognomy, and the power of the controlling arm, rather than redirected by the intermediary faculties of the healthy mind.

Predictably *Guy Livingstone* was greeted with coolness in some quarters. When told that the anonymously published novel had been attributed to G. H. Lewes, George Eliot replied that although she had not read the book, reviews convinced her that "Mr. Lewes would be anything but gratified to have it fathered upon him."[37] In a review of the novel, Fitzjames Stephen mused that whenever he met the Guy Livingstone type in fiction he wished he could "put the whole batch of them into some convenient arena and let them fight it out."[38]

Across the Atlantic, Bret Harte included among his *Condensed Novels* a parody titled *Guy Heavystone.* Harte's hero, introduced as a schoolboy "cleaning out" the fourth form with a piston-rod, ultimately dies "as he had lived,—hard": he is shot, and in his death throes he pulls the manor house down about him. Here he is at fifteen: "His eyes were glittering but pitiless. There was a sternness about the lower part of his face,—the old Heavystone look,—a sternness, heightened, perhaps, by the snaffle-bit which, in one of his strange freaks, he wore in his mouth to curb his occasional ferocity. His dress was well adapted to his square-set and herculean frame. A striped knit undershirt, close-fitting striped tights, and a few spangles set off his figure."[39]

In *Tom Brown at Oxford* (1861) Hughes did his best to free his young hero from any association with the Laurentian value system. In a chapter called "Muscular Christianity" he noted that Tom had been enrolled in "the brotherhood of muscular Christians, who at that time were beginning to be recognized as an actual and lusty portion of general British life." Not quarreling with that designation itself, he cautioned against confusing the muscular Christian with the "muscleman," who has "no belief whatever as to the purposes for which his body has been given him, except some hazy idea that it is to go up and down the world with him, belabouring men and captivating women for his benefit or pleasure, at once the servant and fomenter of fierce and brutal passions which he seems to think it a necessity, and rather a fine thing than otherwise, to indulge and obey."[40]

Hughes's critics were not appeased. When *Memoir of a Brother* appeared in 1873 the *Saturday Review* balanced its praise for the book with a rebuke to its author for helping promote "the present outrageous worship of bodily strength and bodily skill."[41] Equally troublesome were the excesses of Hughes's admirers. In 1879 he received from the North of England a proposal for a society to be called the Christian Guild. In the belief that other Christian groups had neglected the manlier virtues, the Christian Guild proposed as one entrance qualification the winning of a town or district championship in running, wrestling, or rowing. Dismayed, Hughes at once set out to clarify his position. In an enormously popular book, *The Manliness of Christ,* he defended the cause of manliness while putting at rest the notion that manliness meant being good at games. "Athleticism is a good thing if kept in its place, but it has come to be very much over-praised and over-valued amongst us, as I think these proposals of the Christian Guild . . . tend to show clearly enough, if proof were needed." An athlete "may be a brute and a coward, while a truly manly man can be neither." Manliness has nothing to do with animal courage, nor does it consist in simple moral courage: "Tenacity of will, or wilfulness, lies at the root of all courage, but courage can only rise into true manliness when the will is surrendered; and the more absolute the surrender of the will the more perfect will be the temper of our courage and the strength of our manliness."[42]

Like Hughes, Kingsley had come under frequent attack from conservative clergymen for seeming to devote himself so much to bodily health and so little to spiritual, for being keener on muscularity than on Christianity. At length, in 1865, he was forced into the awkward position of defending that phrase he had always loathed. The occasion was the first of several sermons preached at Cambridge on the Biblical David. "We have heard much of late about 'Muscular Christianity,' " he said, beginning a lengthy digression on the subject.[43] "A clever expression, spoken in jest by I know not whom, has been bandied about the world, and supposed by many to represent some new ideal of Christian character." He offered two interpretations of the term, the preferred being "simply a healthy and manful Christianity, one which does not exalt the feminine virtues to the exclusion of the masculine." This ideal, he explained, was far from new. During the church's patristic period, and during the Middle Ages as well, persecuted Christians adopted the feminine virtues of gentleness, patience, self-sacrifice, and self-devotion. As one unsalutary result the monastic clergy became cunning, cowardly, and querulous (traits Kingsley tended always to attribute to Roman Catholics and in particular to Newman). Eventually the older, now decadent Christian ideal was replaced by a chivalric one which "consecrated the whole manhood, and not merely a few faculties thereof, to God." That, Kingsley insisted, was what muscular Christianity ought to mean. However, "there are those who say, and there have been of late those who have written books to show, that provided a young man is sufficiently brave, frank and gallant, he is more or less absolved from the common duties of morality and self-restraint." He then declared that obeying the spiritual laws of life was a more pressing duty than obeying the physical: "Better it would be for any of you to be the stupidest and ugliest of mortals, to be the most diseased and abject of cripples, the most silly, nervous, incapable personage who ever was a laughing stock for the boys upon the streets, if you only lived, according to your powers, the life of the Spirit of God." From this the Cambridge students—and Newman, perhaps, whose *Apologia* had appeared the previous year—were to understand that being humble and effeminate was preferable to being arrogant and masculine, but better than either was a manly humility.

The following year in his final novel, *Hereward the Wake*, Kingsley tried to dramatize this point with a new forcefulness, but he found that many still were unwilling to revise their standard view of him. During the nine years which had elapsed between this work and *Two Years Ago* the public had grown weary of muscular Christianity, and many had set Kingsley down as a pure and simple fanatic on the subject. When *Hereward* appeared in book form in 1866 the journals were cool, and most ignored it. A few praised it rather routinely, but on the whole the novel was not a critical success.

Two publications which had dealt quite kindly with *Two Years Ago* were openly hostile. The *Saturday Review* devoted much space to quarreling with Kingsley's use of sources, then turned critically to his choice of heroes and to the author himself: "Hereward, if a Christian at all, was certainly a muscular one, but the great muscular Christian of all had not yet arisen."[44] This line of attack was followed by the *Westminster* critic, who suggested that *Hereward* was written in Kingsley's "blood and thunder mood." "Instead of the picture of a patriot, we have a daub of a sensational ruffian. Instead of being gladdened with a tale of honour and high bearing, we are drenched with blood and sickened with villainy."[45]

It was widely held that Kingsley had reached the logical culmination of muscular Christianity in what Leslie Stephen was to call (humorously) the "Viking or Berserker" ideal.[46] There was a notion that as he had grown older, he had become more and more pugnacious. That Kingsley was retelling a semi-historical legend set in a less delicate age made no difference; critics insisted on reading the novel as a fable for the times and seeing its hero as a model for modern young men. The real Hereward was an eleventh-century Englishman who, with a company of English outlaws and marauding Danes, plundered Peterborough in 1070 and led a rising against King William. Although the rebellion was unsuccessful, the name of Hereward was for centuries a symbol of English resistance to foreign domination. In the course of time much legendary material grew up around this figure, and Kingsley drew heavily on apocryphal as well as substantiated history.

As a young man, Kingsley's Hereward is a jaunty highwayman, something of a Prince Hal. For stealing some church money he is driven from home by his father and declared an outlaw. After some adventures in Scotland and Cornwall he goes to Flanders, where he marries a woman named Torfrida. Hearing of William's invasion, he returns home with a vow that he will drive the foreigners out. While engaged in this rebellion he falls in love with another woman, Alftruda, whom he marries after divorcing his first wife. Finally his intrigues against William result in a determined effort against him by the King, and eventually he is defeated and slain.

Like other Kingsley heroes, Hereward has a strikingly developed frame, including the inevitable broad upper torso: "His face was of extraordinary beauty, save that the lower jaw was too long and heavy, and that his eyes wore a strange and almost sinister expression, from the fact that the one of them was grey, and the other blue. He was short, but of immense breadth of chest and strength of limb." He is an athlete as well as a muscular wonder. Reprimanding him for his thievery and brawling, his mother speaks contemptuously of him as "Hereward the leaper, Hereward the wrestler, Hereward the thrower of the hammer."[47] Nothing more is made of his abilities in this direction, however, and throughout the rest of the novel his muscularity is demonstrated only in battle scenes. Not only is Hereward muscular, he is also Christian, after a fashion—he does have himself knighted by English monks. But Kingsley obviously meant him to be the inferior type of muscular Christian he had recently described in the sermon on David—the man who, being honest and courageous, feels "more or less absolved from the common duties of morality and self-restraint."

One reason why Kingsley's aim was so thoroughly misunderstood was the common belief that he was a passionate and uncritical worshiper of everything Teutonic. In fact, his admiration for the primitive virtues of early Northern European cultures was most qualified, as any reader of his *The Roman and the Teuton* can ascertain. In this series of historical lectures the Teutons are represented as being more vigorous than the decadent Romans, but at the same time lacking in any system of positive values. In an elaborate allegory of the sacking of Rome with which Kingsley introduces the series, the Northern tribes are "forest children," who storm the fairy palace of the Trolls, but once inside fall to drunken orgies and quarrels, and ultimately lose the treasure they came for. Until Christianity bound them to "the holy bonds of brotherhood and law" these Teutons were "children in frankness, and purity, and affectionateness, and tenderness of conscience, and devout awe of the unseen; and children too in fancy, and silliness, and ignorance, and caprice, and jealousy, and quarrelsomeness, and love of excitement and adventure, and the mere sport of overflowing animal health."[48]

Kingsley delivered these lectures in 1864, probably when he was planning *Hereward*. Knowing his mental tendency toward fixed categories, it would be surprising if he did not make the hero of his new novel conform to what he had already decided were the characteristics of the early Teuton. Further, he had by now established a pattern of protagonists whose merits as well as faults were those of boys, as, for example, Amyas Leigh in *Westward Ho!* and Tom Thurnall of *Two Years Ago*. In *Hereward* Kingsley sets the stage for his main character with a discourse on the relation of primitive people to their primitive environment. Mountain people, he contends, are poetical but uncourageous; nature overwhelms their judgment by its power and sublimity: "For Nature among the mountains is too fierce, too strong for man. He cannot conquer her, and she awes him." The lowlander, on the other hand, possesses a stolid manfulness, but is usually unimaginative. Further, the very fact that he has been able to subdue Nature is likely to make him arrogant toward his fellows and scornful of the unseen: "Meeting with no visible superior, he is apt to become not merely unpoetical and irreverent, but something of a sensualist and an atheist . . . He may sink into that dull brutality which is too common among the lower classes of the English lowlands; and remain for generations gifted with the strength and industry of the ox, and with the courage of the lion, but, alas! with the intellect of the former, and the self-restraint of the latter." This description pretty well fits Hereward, who after slaying a bear reflects that like the old Viking he fears nothing and would even battle God if given the chance. "There he stood," Kingsley says of him, "staring, and dreaming over renown to come, a true pattern of the half-savage hero of those rough times, capable of all vices except cowardice, and capable, too, of all virtues save humility."[49]

Except for a sportsman's sense of fair play and a chivalrous respect for women, Hereward possesses few civilized virtues. He is described as intelligent and sagacious, but these qualities are limited to practical cleverness and an immense resourcefulness. Choosing to be knighted by the monks rather than by the secular nobility is for him purely a matter of propriety. His championing of liberty, ungrounded in firm and general principle, is strictly limited to people of his own kind. On one occasion he joins the Frankish nobility in harrying the Frisians, whose freedom he regards as a trifling consideration: "To him these Frieslanders were merely savages, probably heathens, who would not obey their lawful lord, a gentleman and a Christian; besides, renown, and possibly a little plunder, might be got by beating them into obedience. He knew not what he did; and knew not, likewise, that as he had done to others, so would it be done to him."[50]

Kingsley made Hereward stronger, cannier, and superficially nobler than the others in the story, whether English, Normans, Franks, or Frisians. Like the rest, however, he is only a "grown child," without the wisdom to foretell the consequences of acts committed when his moral judgment lies slumbering. In his personal affairs his morality is erratic, as shown by his desertion of his wife. His courage, as Henry James observed in an acute analysis of the book, is merely physical and is manifested only in violent action.[51] Once the battles are over he loses both pride and purpose. His self-discipline is toughened by danger; but when there is no danger, there is no discipline. After his second marriage he debauches himself with drink and becomes a braggart, living off the interest of his old valor. Every man "brings into the world with him a certain capacity, a certain amount of vital force, in body and in soul; and when that is used up, the man must sink down into some sort of second childhood; and end, like Hereward, very much where he began: unless the grace of God shall lift him above the capacity of the mere flesh, into a life literally new, ever-renewing, ever-expanding, and eternal."[52] Just as Hereward's higher instincts are those of the body, so are his baser instincts, and it is these which cause his downfall.

In *Hereward* Kingsley did his best to dispel the notion that he worshiped physical strength and "simple massive understanding." Of course he would not have taken issue with the reviewer who welcomed "this study of a ruder world" in the midst of all the "pictures of vicious modern life and social disease with which we have been of late satiated in fiction."[53] Although the world of the novel seems relatively uncomplicated, however, Kingsley's moral conception of the healthy hero was far from primitivistic: the impulsive act signifies constitutional health, a natural mind-body accord, but only a religious enlightenment will guarantee the ethical soundness of that act, the harmony of the self with the moral laws outside the self. Raw adventurers may train themselves to be heroic, but not to be humble. In his later years he liked to express his concept of manliness with the phrase "Divine discontent," a virtue he ascribed to F. D. Maurice in a eulogy published in May 1872: "But it was that very humility, that very self-distrust, combined so strangely with manful strength and sternness, which drew to him humble souls, who, like him, were full of the 'Divine discontent'; who lived—as perhaps all men should live—angry with themselves, ashamed of themselves, and more and more angry and ashamed as their ideal grew, and with it their consciousness of defection from that ideal."[54] Later that year, in a lecture published as "The Science of Health," Kingsley described "Divine discontent" as the state of being "ashamed with the noble shame."[55] Hereward, the muscular hero of Kingsley's final novel, like Tom Thurnall through most of *Two Years Ago*, has a nobility unblessed with shame.

There is a good chance that Kingsley's intentions would not have been so widely misinterpreted had he brought out his novel at any other time. In 1866 England was experiencing a general reaction against massive masculinity. Victorians were not giving up their sports or their admiration of the athletic type, but they were giving up the appearance of a too-obvious enthusiasm for either. Only five years before, William Hardman had written: "No doubt our tendency for many years was to apathy, peace, and squeamishness. Now our spirit has been aroused, and muscular Christianity, Volunteer movement, Alpine climbing, and the art of self-defense are in the ascendant. The affected Dandy of past years is unknown; if he exists he is despised . . . The standard or average English gentleman of the present day must at least show vigour of body, if he cannot display vigour of mind."[56] The "standard or average" gentleman of the *later* sixties might indeed train himself into athletic shapeliness, but his clothing concealed what his training had achieved. He wore a bowler, perhaps, or a "muffin hat," or a stovepipe hat; trousers which looked as if they had been rained on; a frock coat or a sack coat, or a jacket with tiny lapels, enormous pockets, and no particular shape. If he was a "heavy swell" he might affect a monocle, Dundreary whiskers, a gold watch-chain, and a fancy vest. But all of this was modified by severe colors elsewhere in his dress, as well as perpendicular lines in coat and trousers. He might swagger or lounge, but never bustle. He was unpressed and unruffled, baggy and "cool." Although he "cultivated muscle beneath that languor,"[57] he embodied the casual and the natural. The "muscular vigour" of Hardman's gentleman was still there, but masked by quiet detachment of expression. Visible strenuosity was shunned as much as visible elegance. By the seventies a young man who looked like an athlete might find himself spurned, as Alfred Lyttleton was at Eton, when his "swinging walk to the cricket-field" was mistaken for swagger by the lower boys.[58] "It has become impossible," Leslie Stephen wrote in 1870, "to hear a gentleman described as 'manly' or spoken of as a 'good fellow' without conceiving a certain prejudice against him; even those simple terms are beginning to connote a decided imbecility; whilst the still more exalted vocabulary of the true muscular Christians has been drawn upon too freely for further use."[59]

The popular weeklies *Punch* and the *Saturday Review* serve as convenient barometers of taste in this matter. Both tended to be John Bullish and hearty in outlook, both were slow to accept a novelty and quick to abandon it when it became outré. In the fifties and early sixties these journals were regarding athletic games as essentially English and "in the highest degree honourable and manly," as the *Saturday Review* put it.[60] *Punch* put aside its customary playfulness to applaud a French journalist's opinion that cricket had made the Englishman "a magnificent specimen of human kind."[61] The *Saturday Review* was running frequent pieces on physical education, sport, and mind-and-muscle; but by the end of the sixties, what that journal had once approvingly called "this gymnastic period"[62] was beginning to seem more and more bizarre. If things went on as they were, *Punch* prophesied, soon at the universities "Latin will be nowhere, Leaping everything; Geometry will yield to Gymnastics; Philosophy to Fencing; Paley to Pole-jumping; Homer to Hurdles; Co-sines to Calisthenics; Trigonometry to Training."[63] The *Saturday Review* made a similar observation: "Beside the boat-race and the cricket match and the athletics, there are inter-University billiard matches, tennis matches, racket matches, and steeple-chases; and, in a year or two, we suppose, if the velocipede mania spreads much in England, there will be inter-University bicycle matches also."[64] The University Boat Race, once described by the *Review* as reflecting that spirit "which held the slopes of Waterloo on a long summer day," now could draw but the confession of a "sneaking affection" from the journal.[65] A *Punch* contributor signing himself "Epicurus" reflected something of this new spirit when, taking notice of one of Archibald Maclaren's new books on training, he displayed a jocular alarm at the pictures of youths "flying with apparent ease over all sorts of bars and things."[66]

Now even articles on cricket and rowing were appearing only sporadically in the pages of the *Saturday Review*. "If there is any truth to the converse of the proverb," the journal predicted in 1869, "we ought to be not far off the sublime in athletics, for the ridiculous has been attained already." As an illustration it printed an account of a much-publicized event staged by the Thames Rowing Club. Contestants were to swim across a frigid lake, cross five hurdles spaced along a 150-yard course, surmount an "obstacle," then race to the finish. As to the obstacle there had been much speculation before the event. "One paper said it was an extraordinary obstacle; another said it would be an obstacle simply; another that no conception whatever could be formed about it." The object in question turned out to be a sort of nine-foot ladder made by fixing three horizontal bars to three vertical ones. Two men successfully completed the course, winning first and second prizes. Two others, having climbed to the top of the obstacle, found they could not descend. Soon they were joined on their perch by a third: "He also could not get down. He looked at the pair beside him, sitting fixed and motionless. *Sedent, aeternumque sedebunt*. Should he also abide on a perpendicular pole, crossed by a horizontal one? No. How then should he get down? Happy thought; tumble down. Accordingly he tumbled down, and the shock of the fall preventing him from reassuming the correct posture, crawled the remaining distance and won the third prize."[67]

The athletic mania also provoked more serious comment. There was concern over the amounts of money involved, both in betting and in prize-awards. One rowing cup was said to have been valued at £350, and a university undergraduate was reported to have risked losing £3,500 if his college's boat did not finish first in its race.[68] At this time expenditures on games at a single school could exceed £1,300 a year. Many people objected to the professionalization of certain sports. Professional players at the metropolitan cricket-fields were now asking £5 per match; since they were paid entirely out of ticket sales, the problem of gate-money had become, in the view of Frederick Gale, "past remedy."[69]

In the schools games were an expensive duty; elsewhere they were a business. "Many do not like to see athletics made so artificial," commented *Baily's*, the influential sporting magazine: "Instead of casually walking into a cricket-field, you now pass a policeman, and show a season ticket, or pay for entrance, into a ground furnished with a path of cinders, and fenced in with grim barriers, in order to look at athletes who have been training systematically, instead of runners who take off their coats, and go in with glorious uncertainty as to who's going to win what. Many look back with a sort of regret to the more primitive athletic times —the days of grass, when cinder paths were not yet dreamed of, when a stop-watch was talked of but not seen . . . and when people ran into the tent to look at the man who had run a mile under five minutes, or jumped over five feet."[70]

Sport was becoming not only more artificial, but more hazardous as well. This was the period of the "hacking" issue in football, and of controversies over other dangers involved in games. The *Lancet* ran frequent articles on the dangers of training for the University Boat Race. Stories appeared about boys who had broken arms and legs on the football field; one youth had his back broken in a football scrum.[71] The author of an 1873 book on rowing cited the story of a crew which rowed from Oxford to London one hot summer day. Although they were "all sturdy and robust men when that disastrous voyage was undertaken, five short years beheld them the sorry wreck of what they once had been, and in another five they were all consigned to an untimely grave."[72]

There were manifest reasons why thoughtful people were asking with Anthony Trollope whether "we are overdoing our Sports, and making it too grand in its outlines, and too important in its details."[73] The subject was considered of sufficient urgency to merit an entire article in the *Contemporary Review* in 1866. It was a topic, the author declared, not out of keeping with the "graver arguments" readers of that journal had become accustomed to. At issue were not only the problems of betting, prize-money, and overtraining, but the very character of the athletes themselves. Modern sport had lost sight of its meritorious purpose, "teaching a youth to fulfil his baptismal vow by keeping his body in temperance, soberness, and chastity"; instead, the boy was being urged "to keep himself temperate and strong, not that he may run well a manly and Christian course throughout the world, but that he may be better than A or B at the next Oxford and Cambridge sports, or that his school may beat some other school at cricket next season."[74] To John Ruskin the issue had developed broad social implications. In his books and lectures Ruskin often spoke warmly in favor of sport, but only insofar as it made the individual healthier in a Carlylean sense: engendering the instinct and the capacity for work.[75] To that end rowing, riding, and cricket might be the most useful things learned at public schools, though "it would be far better that members of Parliament should be able to plough straight, and make a horseshoe, than only to feather oars neatly or to point their toes prettily in stirrups."[76] When, in the winter of 1869-70, Trollope and E. A. Freeman were publicly debating the morality of fox-hunting, Ruskin took an immediate interest. In a letter to the *Daily Telegraph* he declared that while the sort of people who go hunting may well need the exercise, the sport more generally "wastes the time, misapplies the energy, exhausts the wealth, narrows the capacity, debases the taste, and abates the honour of the upper classes of this country."[77]

The cult of robustness was losing influence, at least among the intelligentsia. "Their brief day of general favour is over," Leslie Stephen wrote, "and we are now going through the familiar process of breaking in pieces the idol we had set up. The sect, indeed, flourishes and spreads as ever;

but it is no longer the object of universal petting and flattering."[78] Stephen's remarks were occasioned by the appearance in 1870 of Wilkie Collins' *Man and Wife*. Partly a plea for marriage-law reform, the novel also made the severest attack yet on the muscular ruffian. Collins tried to show that, as one of his characters puts it, there was no necessary connection between moral and physical wholesomeness. There was a direct connection between "the unbridled development of physical cultivation in England, and the recent spread of grossness and brutality among certain classes of the English population."[79] His symbol of physical culture was Geoffrey Delamayne, a young man flattered by servants, women, and fellow-athletes alike.

In appearance Delamayne recalls all the muscular heroes of popular fiction: "His expression preserved an immovable composure wonderful to behold. The muscles of his brawny arms showed through the sleeves of his light summer coat. He was deep in the chest, thin in the flanks, firm on the legs—in two words, a magnificent human animal, wrought up to the highest pitch of human development, from head to foot."[80] The college-trained son of a barrister, Geoffrey seduces a young woman and, with the promise of marriage, arranges to meet her at a country inn. Instead of appearing there himself he sends along a friend with a temporizing message. To protect the girl's reputation the friend represents himself at the inn as the girl's husband. Geoffrey, now aiming at a more socially advantageous attachment, tries to rid himself of the girl by means of the confused marriage laws of the time. He claims that the girl and the friend are in fact married, having spent a night as man and wife. When his strategy fails he is forced to marry her. He bitterly accepts his fate but torments his wife mercilessly. Meanwhile, against his physician's advice he has been in training for an important four-mile race. In the course of the race he collapses, his health permanently shattered. Finally, in a mood of vengeful frustration he plans to murder his wife, but is instead murdered by a woman he has been blackmailing.

Delamayne is the "washed Rough in broadcloth," the upper- or middle-class young man whose athletic education has taught him to take every advantage of his fellows: "There had been nothing in his training to soften the barbarous hardness in his heart, and enlighten the barbarous darkness in his mind. Temptation finds this man defenceless, when temptation passes his way. I don't care who he is, and how high he stands accidentally in the social scale—he is to all moral intents and purposes, an Animal, nothing more." Years at the university have left Geoffrey neither educated nor humane. When asked if he knows Dryden, he answers yes, he and Dryden trained and raced together. Though a member of the Christian-Pugilistic Association, he is not above fracturing a dog's ribs with a kick to stifle its barking. He lives for the adulation of his friends, the savage enthusiasm of his fans, and above all the fascinated adoration of women: "*He* was the first among the heroes hailed by ten thousand roaring throats as the pride and flower of England. A woman, in an atmosphere of red-hot enthusiasm, witnesses the apotheosis of Physical Strength. Is it reasonable—is it just—to expect her to ask herself, in cold blood, What (morally and intellectually) is all this worth?"[81]

As Stephen commented in his review of the book, Collins "lays on his colours pretty thickly." No doubt the melodramatic element in *Man and Wife* helps account for the fact that during its serialization in *Cassell's* the circulation of that magazine shot up to an amazing 70,000.[82] Collins had a bent for the sensational, and without question artistic subtlety in this novel is sacrificed in the warmth of crusading zeal. He was spurred to his contempt for what he calls "Muscular England" by two incidents which occurred within a year of each other. In June 1869 a gang of undergraduates broke up commencement at Oxford, forcing the Vice-Chancellor and faculty to leave the hall. The following May some other undergraduates entered the library of Christ Church College, carried off several works, and burned them. In both cases athletes were reported responsible.[83] These events seemed to confirm a growing view that the muscular ruffian was not simply a concoction of George Lawrence and his followers. Sir Patrick Lundie, Collins' spokesman in *Man and Wife*, is Geoffrey Delamayne's direct opposite. A man of middle age, a philosopher, and a connoisseur of food, he is an erudite reminder of a quieter, more gracious generation. As he observes the signs of deterioration of civilized life in the new spirit of Contest—as he watches a croquet match consume everyone's interest at a garden party and looks on while Geoffrey and his friends break fireplace equipment over their arms and necks—Sir Patrick is moved to protests like the following: "I don't like the model young Briton. I don't see the sense of crowing over him as a superb national production, because he is big and strong, and drinks beer with impunity, and takes a cold shower bath all year round. There is far too much glorification in England, just now, of the mere physical qualities which the Englishman shares with the savage and the brute. And the ill results are beginning to show themselves already! . . . Read the popular books; attend the popular amusements—and you will find at the bottom of them all a lessening regard for the gentler graces of civilized life, and a growing admiration for the virtues of the aboriginal Britons!"[84]

Those aboriginal Britons, Arnold noted in *Culture and Anarchy*, left to their social descendants as a principal legacy the cult of the body. They could not leave a similar respect for the mind because they themselves did not respect it. So the modern Barbarian, blessed with this dubious legacy, was rather an anomaly in man's evolutionary pattern: a man whose body had benefited from centuries of healthy breeding, but whose mind still had the inclinations of the savage.

CHAPTER 11

The Athlete as Barbarian:
Richard Feverel and Willoughby Patterne

GEORGE MEREDITH was in his early fifties when he began to develop the first symptoms of ataxia, a crippling spinomotor disease. For a year and a half, until it was properly diagnosed, he tried all the standard "cures." A visit to Brighton for a "change of air" left him "still of crazy construction." Then on his doctor's advice he stopped all writing, believing that "the seat of the malady is the pen." Next, convinced that "some course of water cure for unstrung nerves" would help, he journeyed to the spa at Evian in France. He tried the warm sea-baths at Eastbourne and also a "milk and fruit diet, meat and wine temporarily abjured." But his legs grew steadily weaker. Gradually he was forced to abandon his outings with the Sunday Tramps, the group of intellectuals organized by Leslie Stephen for twenty- and thirty-mile hikes. "I wish I could come to you," he wrote Robert Louis Stevenson in 1884, "I have developed a spinal malady and can walk not much more than a mile . . . I am a cripple." Some years later he lamented to a fatally ill Stephen, "We who have loved the motion of legs and the sweep of the winds, we come to this."[1]

Until the onset of his paralysis Meredith was an outstanding long-distance walker, who on an Alpine trip could boast a record of thirty miles a day. He "loved all manner of bodily exercises," Justin McCarthy recalled; "and, indeed, it amazed me when I first used to visit him, to see a man, no longer young, indulge in such feats of strength and agility. It delighted him to play with great iron weights, and to throw heavy clubs into the air and catch them as they fell, and to twirl them round his head as if they had been light bamboo canes."[2] Many of his friends were of similar spirit. There was Stephen, of course, and the London barrister William Hardman, a noted athlete in college and a sturdy walker (fifteen to eighteen miles a day) throughout his life. Another was the socialist Henry Mayers Hyndman, who met Meredith while a Cambridge undergraduate. At the time Hyndman was a varsity cricketer, and, as he says, "pretty good at rough-and-tumble." Still he was no match for Meredith, who was "always in training and very much stronger muscularly than he looked. In fact he was all wire and whipcord without a spare ounce of flesh upon him." One of his letters records his method and philosophy of training: "My best solitary exercise is, throwing the beetle—a huge mallet weighing 18 or nineteen pounds—and catching the handle, performing wondrous tricks therewith. The best in the world is *fencing*, which braces the nerves, tightens muscles, occupies brain, better than anything going: contains fit measure of excitement and is thorough exercise. Boxing is a little brutal, though good. Fencing brightens the eye without blackening it."[3]

Unlike many Victorian intellectuals Meredith was not plagued by nervous ailments. Occasional bouts with dyspepsia he usually ascribed to overwork as when, driving himself to finish *The Egoist*, he developed "catarrh of the stomach, owing to weakness in that region from a prolonged course of writing at night during winter." Blessed with habitual robustness, he assumed the role of authority in matters of fitness. He was always supplying advice about diet and exercise to his dyspeptic friend Frederick Maxse. He insisted that Maxse (who was a believer in the medical efficacy of water) not totally abstain from wine and counseled that all food, but especially meat, should be taken in moderation and that "ice, but not ice-water, is a specific for indigestion, though one to be rarely used." "I can cure you of you[r] dyspeptic ailment," he assured his patient, "and wash rose into your cheeks instead of yellow. Let me briefly say, take exercise, but not much walking. Open the chest vigorously, to give play to the vital organs. Above all things, see that you *sweat* daily, and not to a small degree . . . Do not, I entreat you, take what they call strengthening medicines."[4]

Meredith's life and writings are a kind of synthesis of Victorian attitudes and ideas about health. He kept current on all the latest methods for staying well and tried many of them himself: hydropathy, homeopathy, Change of Climate, vegetarianism, calisthenics. He followed closely the new theories of physical training, and at social gatherings his conversation was as likely to turn to "the maintenance of the British physique" as to literature or politics.[5] He tried to live by *mens sana in corpore sano*, and in his best novels—*The Ordeal of Richard Feverel* and *The Egoist*—expressed a physiologically based concept of culture more comprehensive than any we have encountered. And yet these same works, like the writings of Newman, George Eliot, and Matthew Arnold, also point to the dangers of adhering to a philosophy of health that sacrifices receptivity to robustness and fails to provide for the health of the perceiving mind.

IN THE *Ordeal* the woeful state of the Feverel line appears to confirm Sir Austin's view that a restorative system of health is needed. His brothers and sisters have all been hapless: Cuthbert was killed in an African adventure; Vivian, having made an improper marriage, is no longer welcome at Raynham Abbey; Doria's husband was more acceptable, but he died and left her widowed; Algernon, a bachelor, lost his leg as a result of a cricket accident; Hippias, another bachelor, is a chronic dyspeptic. The younger generation is hardly more promising: Adrian Harley is corpulent and lazy; Doria's daughter Clara is weak and unhealthy. When Sir Austin's wife runs off with the poet Diaper Sandoe, the "Sentimentalist jilted" develops a mistrust of all women and of the world at large. "Fit only for passive acting," he responds to life by means of cranky aphorisms which comprise a "system": a world-view and a special plan for rearing his son.

Sir Caradoc, Richard's grandfather, claimed that there was a blight in the family blood. Because the male Feverels have had chronic difficulties with women, Sir Austin diagnoses the trouble as a probable susceptibility to temptation: "Whether it was the Apple-Disease, or any other, strong constitutions seemed struggling in them with some peculiar malady."[6] The Baronet's answer is to make future constitutions stronger. As a start he determines that his son will grow up with "good blood" and teaches him that the body is a temple, of which physical health is the adornment and lust the desecration. His scheme is to inculcate a combination of moral innocence and bodily robustness, "that by hedging round the Youth from corruptness, and at the same time promoting his animal health, by helping him to grow, as he would, like a tree of Eden . . . there would be seen something approaching to a perfect Man" (pp. 11-12). In the manner of a retired boxer Sir Austin proceeds to train his young protégé, to "brace him up" for the inevitable ordeal of adolescence: " 'By giving him all the advantage of Science,' Sir Austin emphasized. 'By training him . . . It may be true that I sacrifice two or three little advantages by isolating him at present: he will be better fortified for his trial to come. You know my opinion, Doctor: we are pretty secure from the serpent till Eve sides with him. I speak, of course, of a youth of good pure blood' " (p. 39). In pitting science against the serpent Sir Austin enlists the aid of Richard's cousin Adrian, who is to keep the boy secure from temptation, and the disabled cricketer Uncle Algernon, another passive actor. Although Algernon's own sporting life has been confined to "horse, and card, exercise" and writing tedious articles on the Decline of Cricket, he teaches his charge fencing, shooting, and boxing. To assure himself that this program is working, that Richard is "physically sound" as well as "morally promising," Sir Austin conducts a ceremonial physical examination every seven years.

Although Sir Austin's "system" is evidently intended by Meredith to satirize Victorian moral physiology, in some particulars the Baronet's views parallel his own. When his own son Arthur reached the age of seven (the age of Richard's first physical examination), Meredith declared his intention to "keep him sound and to instil good healthy habits of mind and body." He placed him in a Norwich school where the boys were "healthy, gentlemanly fellows," and where he had observed "a fine river for rowing; a good cricket ground etc." In 1870 he wrote to Arthur, "You will note that I lay stress on the physical condition. I do so for the reason that it is the index to the moral condition in young men. It is ten to one that a healthy lad is of good general worth. If not physically healthy he will not be of much value."[7]

Unlike Sir Austin, however, Meredith trusted his son to flourish at a school, in a world of equals, rather than keeping him sequestered at home. A moral quack, the Baronet assumes the most dangerous disease to be worldly temptation, a theory apparently confirmed when he interviews some advocates of the Wild Oats school and discovers that one has consumptive daughters, another an imbecile son. Whereas the family physician, Dr. Clifford, advises sending Richard to school to take life on naturally, Sir Austin believes in keeping him at home and administering small, carefully regulated quantities of experience. "Perhaps our only difference after all," he tells the doctor, "is not a pathological one. I acknowledge your diagnosis, but mollify the prescription. I give the poison to my son in small doses; whereas you prescribe large ones. You naturally contend with a homoeopathist—Eh?" Dr. Clifford replies curtly, "With your permission, Sir Austin, I hate that humbug" (p. 40). The difference, of course, *is* pathological. Richard's real disease is not knowledge of the world, but a romantic vanity he learns at home. When Farmer Blaize catches him and Ripton Thompson poaching on his grounds he gives them a horsewhipping as a lesson. Richard instantly contracts "birch-fever"—a "horrible sense of shame, self-loathing, universal hatred, impotent vengeance"—and talks the less volatile Ripton into burning the farmer's ricks. When Sir Austin learns of the act he characteristically misinterprets the symptoms. Believing that Ripton was behind the plan, he temporarily "mollifies" his prescription by banishing the youth from Raynham: "The infinitesimal dose of THE WORLD which Master Ripton Thompson had furnished to the System with such instantaneous and surprising effect, was considered by Sir Austin to have worked quite well, and to be for the time quite sufficient" (p. 121).

Such systematic treatment is intended to see Richard safely through his "Magnetic Age," a phase of life about which Meredith himself warned his own son: a "perilous sensual period when the animal appetites most need control and transmutation."[8] Again the character appears to reflect the author's views, but the final two words of the Meredith passage reflect a concept of human growth more complex and more in tune with current scientific thought than the Baronet's. Like certain Victorian headmasters, Sir Austin believes in setting the body against itself, training "healthy" physical energies to expel "unhealthy" ones. To Meredith, all the energies of the body were healthy as long as they were directed toward the development of the supraphysical energies of mind and spirit.

Like Kingsley's "healthy animalism," Meredith's philosophy was not materialistic though it was grounded in materialism: no one, he held, can be generally healthy who is not physically fit. "The principle of health is this," he wrote Maxse, "to make good blood plentifully, and to distribute it properly. Exercise of the right sort, acting on seasonable diet, keeps the machine clear." His "customary specific of hard exercise" was a way of making good blood, of renewing vital energy.[9] But the animal part of man, the "blood," should be continually transformed into mind and spirit rather than simply subdued or harnessed. The healthy man converts a lower form of energy to a higher (Meredith's version of the nineteenth-century doctrine of the transformation of force): "Having mastered sensation—insane / At a stroke of the terrified nerve; / And out of the sensual hive / Grown to the flower of brain" ("A Faith on Trial"). In so doing he finds himself blessed with clarity of vision; he gains a better understanding of Nature and of his own role in the natural scheme: "This way have men come out of brutishness / To spell the letters of the sky and read / A reflex upon earth else meaningless" ("Hymn to Colour"). Nature, Meredith told an interviewer in 1904, "loves us no better than her other productions, but she signifies that the intelligence can make her subservient to our needs: and one proof of this is the joy in a healthy body, causing an increased lucidity of the mind. Therefore, exercise of the body is good, and sport of all kinds to be encouraged."[10] By the very process of physical awakening and development which imparts a sense of belonging to Nature, we gain that "increased lucidity of mind" which dispels the illusion of our being *nothing but* a part of nature. Since physical and conceptual well-being are interdependent, by training the body one helps train the mind. When a man leads a strenuous outdoor life, he shares in the process of constant renewal by which nature's energy reanimates all things. His spirit thus evolves in harmony with that spirit which pervades the Earth:

> Nor broken for us shows the mould
> When muscle is in mind renewed:
> Though farther from her nature rude,
> Yet nearer to her spirit's hold. ("Hard Weather")

The same vital energy which animates the body creates and nourishes the blossoming mind, and "the brutish antique of our springs may be tamed, / Without the loss of strength that should push us to flower" ("The Empty Purse"). As mind evolves, the old strength remains, though in a higher, more sophisticated form. Thus, quite literally, "muscle is in mind renewed." Conversely the body itself is renewed, made to feel younger, by what the mind comprehends; physical health depends on a mind lucid and balanced, not given over to specters of its own imagining. Meredith appears to have accepted the common nineteenth-century belief that unhealthy habits of thought may ultimately lead to acute physical illness. His diagnosis, when the skipper of Maxse's yacht died, was: "The typhus probably followed gastric fever, which one gets from fretting; it speedily sends us on."[11]

In Meredith's conception of the human constitution, Brain is the intermediary between Blood (or body), which is wholly material, and Spirit, that faculty (something like Pure Reason or religious sensibility) which unites the senses and the intellect in an intuitive recognition of the pattern and purpose of life. A synthesis of the best qualities of the lower faculties, a product of the Brain's and the Blood's energies, Spirit provides man with what emotional calm is possible in a life of struggle and change: "I see all round me how much Idea governs; and therein see the Creator; that other life to which we are drawn: not conscious, as our sensations demand, but possibly cognizant, as the brain may now sometimes, when the blood is not too forcefully pressing on it, dimly apprehend. Consciousness excites human felicity to kill it. Past consciousness, there may be a felicity eternal. These are not words, they are my excruciated thoughts—out of bloody sweat of mind, and now peaceful, imaging life, accepting what is there."[12] "Bloody sweat of mind"—hard intellectual labor—draws us ultimately to a spiritual conception of life and with that to the soul's serenity. To use Leslie Stephen's distinction between two kinds of knowing, if Brain comprehends natural laws, Spirit, lying beyond reason, apprehends the totality of nature, loves nature, and identifies with it: "I say but that this love of Earth reveals / A soul beside our own to quicken, quell, / Irradiate, and through ruinous floods uplift" ("My Theme").

The renewal of mind in body and body in mind—*mens sana in corpore sano* as a reciprocal process—is impossible without strife: both bodily sweat and "bloody sweat of mind." Since the basis of health is energy, the proof of health is energetic, self-impelled change. In his compact sonnet "The Garden of Epicurus" Meredith argues that the easeful life of Epicureanism is unrealistic and spiritually enervating.

> That Garden of Sedate Philosophy
> Once flourished, fenced from passion and mishap,
> A shining spot upon a shaggy map.
> Where mind and body, in fair junction free,
> Luted their joyful concord; like the tree
> From root to flowering twigs a flowing sap.
> Clear Wisdom found in tended Nature's lap
> Of gentlemen the happy nursery.
> That garden would on light supremest verge,
> Were the long drawing of an equal breath
> Healthful for Wisdom's head, her heart, her aims.
> Our world which for its Babels wants a scourge,
> And for its wilds a husbandman, acclaims
> The crucifix that came of Nazareth.

To the early Epicurean, mind and body were "in fair junction free" because both were composed of matter, differing only in the manner of composition. Disturbed by heat (the passions) or by chill wind (fear), they could be stabilized, Lucretius wrote, by the "calm and steady air" of reason—the "equal breath" of Meredith's poem.[13]

No doubt Meredith found much that was appealing in Epicurean materialism and in its idea that the mind was vivified by the movement of the same natural elements which animate the body. He wrote in 1864, "I hold that to be rightly materialist—to understand and take Nature as she is—is to get on the true divine highroad. That we should attain to a healthy humanity, is surely the most pleasing thing in God's sight." But he did not find credible the Epicurean's belief (or the equivalent idea in nineteenth-century thought) that the mind can be trained to ignore the

disquieting motions of the senses. As a "sedate" philosopher the Epicurean places great emphasis on mental calm. The garden in which Epicurus taught during his lifetime and which, on his death, he left to his followers, is for Meredith the symbol of any philosophy which detaches
itself from a universe of movement or seeks to eliminate, as Lucretius
said, "the lingering traces of inborn temperament."[14] To him there was
no wisdom except that gained in participation and contest:

> Behold the life at ease; it drifts.
> The sharpened sense commands its course.
> While [Earth] winnows, winnows roughly; sifts,
> To dip her chosen in her source:
> Contention is the vital force,
> Whence pluck they brain, her prize of gifts,
> Sky of the senses!   ("Hard Weather")

An athletic, joyful struggle with nature was to Meredith a ritualistic
striving against the more primitive aspects of one's own nature; to understand and accept the natural world in this struggle is to understand and
accept the totality of the self. A thunderstorm may be comprehended by
the philosopher or scientist, but is especially "beloved" by those who
tramp through it, "who fare / Lock-mouthed, a match in lungs and thews
/ For this fierce angel of the air, / To twist with him and take his bruise"
("Hard Weather"). In Meredith's poem "Manfred," the Byronic hero is a
romantic egoist who climbs mountains but is no athlete:

> Projected from the bilious Childe,
> The clatterjaw his foot could set
> On Alps, without a breast beguiled
> To glow in shedding rascal sweat.

Meredith's system of health, a humanistic naturalism, was philosophically comprehensive. As John R. Reed has shown in his perceptive analysis of the "digestive metaphor" in *Richard Feverel*, the novel attacks not
philosophical systems, but "abuses of systems, whether digestive or intellectual." Not only was Meredith himself an elaborate system-maker, he
believed that material nature operated entirely in accordance with system
or law. He spoke of the body's collective functions as "the system." He
approved of Archibald Maclaren's system of training the body; he advo-
cated systems of diet, writing to Maxse, "the system by which you are
correcting your troubled physical condition is I am sure quite sound."
During his period of homeopathic enthusiasm he urged Maxse to try "a
system of medicine . . . Nature's medicine!—as I repeat, the only *system*
in existence."[15]

Although always intrigued by systems, Meredith insisted that they should accord with the grand system of nature. "Our great error," he wrote Maxse, "has been (the error of all religion, as I fancy) to raise a spiritual system in antagonism to Nature." His own philosophy is wholly consistent with the then-current theories of physiological psychology (he especially admired the writings of G. H. Lewes and Alexander Bain).[16] By contrast, Sir Austin Feverel's "system," whatever its scientific pretensions, is grounded not in a study of science *or* nature but in personal whim and prejudice. A fusion of gloomy, old-fashioned puritanism (arising from his "Manichaean tendency") and optimistic, vaguely scientized nineteenth-century nature worship, it is not systematic at all. Here is his explanation of human growth: "Man is a self-acting machine. He cannot cease to be a machine; but, though self-acting, he may lose his powers of self-guidance, and in a wrong course his very vitalities hurry him to perdition. Young, he is an organism ripening to the set mechanic diurnal round, and while so he needs all the Angels to hold watch over him that he grow straight, and healthy, and fit for what machinal duties he may have to perform" (pp. 162-163). This, encapsulated, is the Baronet's philosophy of the Organism and the Mechanism: man is a self-*acting*, though not necessarily self-*guided* machine with "vitalities" which may speed it to "perdition." However, a young man is not a mechanism but a ripening organism which becomes a good mechanism only if its guardian "Angels" have done their work. This explanation comes nearer pure madness than science, and owing to Sir Austin's influence the world of Richard Feverel is one of bedlam. Adrian's analysis is acute: "In youth, 'tis love, or lust, makes the world mad: in age, 'tis prejudice. Superstition holds a province; Pride, an empire . . . There's a battle raging above us . . . If we are not mad, we should fight it for ourselves, and end it. We are, and we make Life the disease, and Death the cure" (p. 65).

Richard Feverel is a satiric tragedy, its satire the kind designated by Northrop Frye as Menippean. The type, Frye says, "deals less with people as such than with mental attitudes. Pedants, bigots, cranks, parvenus, virtuosi, enthusiasts, rapacious and incompetent professional men of all kinds, are handled in terms of their occupational approach to life as distinct from their social behavior."[17] Sir Austin is a real person with believable woes, but his distorted sensibilities have turned his mind fantastic. When he feels, he is pathetic; when he thinks, he resembles the intellectual zanies in a Peacock novel; his logic, metaphors, and even syntax are discomfortingly skewed: "You give human nature but a short tether. Our Virtues, then, are pigmies, Doctor, that daren't grow for fear of the sty?" (pp. 35-36). He has a turn for the emphatic, murky epigram: "It is the tendency of very fast people to grow organically *downward*" (p. 199). The more he enlarges on his system the more bizarre the result: "Sin is an alien element in our blood. 'Tis the Apple-Disease with which Nature has striven since Adam. To treat Youth as naturally sinful, is, therefore, false, and bad; as it is bad, and false, to esteem it radically pure. We must consider that we have forfeited Paradise, but were yet grown there.

Belonging, then, by birth to Paradise, our tendency should ever be towards it: allowing no lower standard than its Perfection. The triumph of man's intellect, the proof of his power, is to make the Serpent who inhabits us fight against himself, till he is destroyed" (p. 11). The small group of female admirers to whom these words are addressed are both fascinated and perplexed, as the reader is likely to be. Sin is both a disease and a serpent. As a disease it is chronic, yet it is also "alien" to the body. "Nature" strives against the disease, but the serpent strives against itself.

For Meredith there was an element of self-parody in this. He, too, was fond of combining images in a jarring and often perplexing way, as demonstrated in a passage from his poetry quoted earlier: "the brutish antique of our springs may be tamed, / Without the loss of strength that may push us to flower." These lines are perhaps as obscure, and certainly as awkward, as, for example, Sir Austin's pronouncement that love is the "ripe fruit of our animal being" (p. 225). Whereas Sir Austin thinks in terms of barren, unexamined analogies, however, Meredith's imagination moves rapidly within his conceptual world, abstracting, as G. M. Trevelyan has said, the essence of things to create a realm somewhere between idea and sensation.[18] Like the Woods of Westermain, it is a dark, "enchanted" world which challenges thought by baffling the vision, but through which we can see our way when we understand the mystery of Change:

> Then you touch the nerve of Change,
> Then of Earth you have the clue;
> Then her two-sexed meanings melt
> Through you, wed the thought and felt.
> Sameness locks no scurfy pond
> Here for Custom, crazy-fond:
> Change is on the wing to bud
> Rose in brain from rose in blood.   ("Woods of Westermain")

To Meredith, man literally changes his nature as he evolves, both as an individual and as a race. The inner beast, tamed, *becomes* the flower.

Although this "reading" of nature is done by Spirit, spiritual cognition is impossible without freedom of the body: "I have written always with the perception that there is no life but of the spirit; that the concrete is really the shadowy; yet that the way to spiritual life lies in the complete unfolding of the creature, not in the nipping of his passions. An outrage to Nature helps to extinguish his light. To the flourishing of the spirit, then, through the healthy exercise of the senses."[19] Clearly the System is an outrage to nature, but at least in making Richard a polished athlete it has visible success. His first fight, "witnessed and chronicled" by Algernon, is with a boy three years his senior, whom he defeats "with the aid of Science" (p. 28). He later takes on his friend Ripton, a boy with size and pluck but no Science: "He was all abroad, and fought in schoolboy style: that is, he rushed at the foe head foremost, and struck like a windmill. He was a lumpy boy. When he did hit, he made himself felt; but he was at the mercy of Science" (p. 47).

Richard belongs to that line of Victorian fictional boys who earn their place in life by beating other boys. Like Tom Tulliver, however, he develops only a counterfeit manliness. The "complete unfolding of the senses" is sacrificed to his desire for physical and psychological predominance. His usual self, to use Arnold's phrase, flourishes uninhibited. Ultimately Richard's senses break loose childishly in his adventure with Mrs. Mount, but for the time being his involvement with sport succeeds in keeping mind and body occupied. Science appears to be vanquishing the serpent. On one occasion early in the novel, however, Richard's "vitalities" rebel against the system and Science loses out. The event is his swimming race with Ralph Morton. Richard, who is by this time "tall, strong, bloomingly healthy" as well as superior in style, ought to win, but as he makes his dive he catches sight of Lady Blandish's bonnet. Undone by this symbol of the female enigma he falls ineptly into the water and is beaten by several lengths. "The Bonnet," Meredith comments, "typical of the mystery that caused his heart those violent palpitations, the Bonnet was his dear, detestable enemy" (p. 128).

"Why," Meredith asks, "will silly mortals strive to the painful pinnacles of championship?" (p. 127). The answer is egoism. Richard's swimming challenge is an attempt to repair a self-esteem damaged by earlier losses to Ralph in diving and cricket competition. The stakes are his little river-yacht, which of course he loses. Later, having acquired another boat, the *Blandish*, he enters that in a race, and this time the consequences are more serious. While the race is in progress Richard leaves his young bride Lucy with Adrian Harley rather than take her on board and jeopardize his chances of winning. Adrian convinces Lucy to let Richard return home alone after the event. So, although Richard wins the race by a good margin, the episode begins the process by which he loses his wife. Richard's romantic vanity causes that ordeal, for by winning the race he hopes to raise himself in the eyes of the glittering Mountfalcon party. When, after his escapade with Mrs. Mount, he learns of Mountfalcon's attempted seduction of Lucy, the same vanity moves him to challenge the peer to a duel, an incident which causes his alarmed wife's brain fever and death. In the series of competitive matches the stakes are successively raised as the play itself grows more dangerous.

To Meredith the value of sport was the mind's loss of self-consciousness in the body's unconscious apprehension of itself and its natural environment. "Nature is very kind to her offspring," he once remarked. "If you are a fine runner and your blood is up, you don't, in point of fact, feel a half of what you do when you are lying in bed or sitting in a chair thinking about it."[20] Simple exercise of that kind sweats out morbid egoism, while athleticism nourishes it. In a humorous piece which Meredith wrote for the *Wykehamist*, a muscular Christian headmaster named Thews complains to the mother of one of his pupils that the newspapers of the time were "fanning and puffing the young athletes to extremes, exciting the vanity of the lads." The Reverend Thews recalls some advice he has given the boys: "England wants men, and our Creator virtuous creatures. Your training is not an end but a means; you want no more than an established health up to the mark . . . Aim to be athletic, not an athlete; and shun Olympic laurels, they are not for our time." Meredith lamented the increasing popularity of training systems designed only to produce athletes. Reviewing Maclaren's *Training in Theory and Practice*, he agreed with the author's thesis that the real purpose of exercise is "to develop bodily strength and fitness for all forms of manly work": "Rowing, running, boxing, fencing, or hunting, or cricketing will do this, when combined with gymnastics, that is general exercise. But men who go into training merely for one determined object forget the principle."[21]

In *Richard Feverel* Sir Austin's program of training his son seems comprehensive, designed as it is to produce the Perfect Man. The ideal he envisions, however, is like a simplified version of Spencer's "good animal," a model of moral purity and physical fitness. "Health is the body's virtue," one of his aphorisms reads; "Truth the Soul's; Valour springs but from the unison of these twain" (p. 35). In Richard's case a superabundance of health is less an instrumental virtue than, as Dr. Clifford says, an "inductive Disease"—inductive in the clinical sense of producing a morbid change in the organism (p. 35). Sir Austin believes in developing the body, curbing the passions, and letting the mind more or less have its own way. As a result, Richard grows up almost wholly at the mercy of his instincts and imagination, with what Sir Austin calls the soul's virtue wholly undeveloped. He learns to be an accomplished liar, "a heathen as to right and wrong" (p. 39). The Baronet's vision extends only to the visible: if his son is sound physically, he must be so mentally as well.

The theory is tested when Richard is stricken ill for the first time. Having dashed out into the rain in pursuit of the exiled Lucy, he contracts a fever and is put to bed. Sir Austin is apprehensive but not alarmed. "He had looked forward to such a crisis as that point in the disease his son was the victim of, when the body would fail and give the spirit calm to conquer the malady, knowing full well that the seeds of the evil were not of the spirit . . . Anxious he was, and prayerful; but with his faith in the physical energy he attributed to his System" (p. 259). Richard's fever *is* of the mind, or at least partly so, according to the author's diagnosis: "Excitement of blood and brain had done its work on him." Like the brain-fever which kills both Clare and Lucy, the ailment is constitutional. Sir Austin, oblivious to psychological affliction, assures himself that the crisis will pass, for "the healthy nature is pretty safe." Richard does get well and marries Lucy secretly. As he sends daily letters home from London, where he is living with his bride, the Baronet reads them with typical lack of perception: " 'The letters of a healthy physique!' he said to Lady Blandish with sure insight. Complacently he sat and smiled, little witting that his son's Ordeal was imminent, and that his son's Ordeal was to be his own" (pp. 327-328). The Hope of Raynham survives his fever, his boxing matches, his swimming and yachting races, even his duel with Mountfalcon. His severest ordeal, the death of Lucy, he survives only physically. "I think Richard is safe," Lady Blandish reports. "Had we postponed the tidings till he came to his clear senses, it must have killed him. His father was right for once then. But if he saved his son's body, he has given the death-blow to his heart. Richard will never be what he promised" (p. 591).

Ultimately the System fails because of what it cannot accommodate: the natural attraction of the sexes for each other. Regarding woman as "the main bait: the sole to be dreaded for a youth of good pure blood" (p. 40), Sir Austin wants to drive Eve from the Garden and thereby drive out the serpent as well. As he discovers, however, the problem is not keeping Eve out, but keeping Adam in. When Richard does escape, he carries with him little knowledge of the world, and practically none of human nature. "O Richard of the Ordeal!" Adrian chides, "I'm sure you've had your lessons in Anatomy, but nothing will persuade you that an anatomical figure means flesh and blood" (p. 277).

Maturity, Meredith believed, is the mastery of the senses "under a firm grasp of the meaning of life." Unless the mind is strengthened by a comprehensive realism it cannot, so to speak, digest the raw energy of the body. Untransmuted, animal force overwhelms the mind, inducing a vaporish romanticism. The combination of undeveloped Brain and unrestrained Blood—or a "tyrranous delicacy of imagination" and a "grossness of developing appetites"—results in that paradoxical figure, the sentimental sensualist, a type Meredith rightly credited himself for introducing into British fiction.[22]

WHATEVER his appearance of fitness, the egoist is unwholesome both in himself and in his influence on those who believe in him. That point was made first in *Richard Feverel* and even more trenchantly twenty years later in a novel which Lionel Stevenson has aptly called a sequel to the *Ordeal*.[23] *The Egoist's* Willoughby Patterne is conceivably what Richard might have become at thirty-two had there been no ordeal earlier. Like Richard he is the Family Hope, protected and flattered by his elder kin, and chosen for his fitness and athletic temperament to be their champion in the struggle for survival.

Love, declares the opening sentence of *The Egoist*, is a game. Bred with the sporting instinct of the British upper class, Willoughby Patterne plays the game in earnest; he plays to win. "The secret of him is," declares his admiring tutelary spirit, Mrs. Mountstuart, "that he is one of those excessively civilized creatures who aim at perfection . . . He excels in manly sports, because he won't be excelled in anything, but as men don't comprehend his fineness, he comes to us."[24] Having reached young manhood, Willoughby has adapted his competitive drives to the politer world of garden and drawing room, where he finds contests as challenging as those of the playing field: "His admirable passion to excel . . . was chiefly directed in his youth upon sport; and so great was the passion in him, that it was commonly the presence of rivals which led him to the declaration of love" (p. 14). News of Captain Oxford's "hot pursuit" of Constantia Durham, therefore, spurs his own proposal of marriage. As it turns out, he is unequal to his competitor, and unequal also to Constantia, a girl who torments him by withholding her adoration. Constantia possesses health, money, and beauty, "the triune of perfect starriness, which makes all men astronomers" (p. 32). After losing her, the Egoist turns briefly to the anemic Letty Dale until he discovers Clara Middleton, a girl cast much in the same mold as Constantia but, at least initially, without her independent spirit.

Of the three attractions Willoughby seeks, physical health most interests him. "My bride must have her health," he tells Clara, "if all the doctors in the kingdom die for it!" (p. 51). His reasons tell us much about him. He needs a wife whose character will be "the feminine of his own," a "mirror of himself" (pp. 39, 38). He himself is good-looking and physically fit, "health incarnate," according to his aunts; his self-flattery demands a wife with similar qualities. Also, like his mother he is a believer in the principle of Selection; a sound mate will help assure the continuance of the Patterne line. Finally, like Sir Austin Feverel he cannot dissociate health and purity, for to an Egoist purity means perfect loyalty. "He looked the fittest; he justified the dictum of Science. The survival of the Patternes was assured. 'I would,' he said to his admirer, Mrs. Mountstuart Jenkinson, 'have bargained for health above everything, but she has everything besides . . . ' Miss Middleton was . . . the true ideal, fresh-gathered morning fruit in a basket, warranted by her bloom" (p. 34).

Although Clara is variously described in the novel as "young, healthy, handsome," "a healthy young woman," and "a healthy creature, an animal," her constitution cannot stand up to Willoughby's smothering ego. As he draws her farther and farther into the barren recesses of his personality she begins to assume the sickly mental hues of Laetitia Dale, a condition he dismisses as "vapourish confusion" (p. 65). But Clara's manifold confusions stem from a perplexity about the real nature of her fiancé. For example, his bizarre demand that she swear an oath to "love him beyond death" is so at odds with the suave manliness of his figure that she is revolted and bewildered, unable to reconcile her own insight with the impression he so forcefully imparts: "She watched him riding away on his gallant horse as handsome a cavalier as the world could show, and the contrast of his recent language and his fine figure was a riddle that froze her blood" (p. 44).

Clara's "quick nature"—the liveliness of her physical instincts—penetrates Willoughby's mask, but, as Meredith says, "the tempers of the young are liquid fires in isles of quicksand; the precious metals not yet cooled in a solid earth" (p. 101). Instead of trusting her own nature she suppresses it, retreating "more and more inwardly" (p. 78). As with Letty, this denial of her womanly response to Willoughby results not only in a "physical coldness" toward his coldness (p. 48) but also in a romantic idealization of him: "Well, perhaps it was good for the hearts of women to be beneath a frost; to be schooled, restrained, turned inward on their dreams. Yes, then, his coldness was desireable; it encouraged an ideal of him" (p. 64). She is much less comfortable than Letty, however, with this ideal. She cannot help vacillating between simple loathing and a guilty fear of loathing (pp. 162, 164)—guilty because she believes it is her duty as a woman to yield to his will. Even when her "irradiating brain" begins awakening to a conscious perception of the ugliness of Willough-by's mind she rejects the reality while unable to accept the illusion. Desperate to escape but trained in submission, she comes to doubt that she has a will and becomes a victim of emotional caprice.

The symptoms of Clara's crisis follow the pattern of Victorian nervous afflictions: she has alternating periods of tiredness and giddiness; she develops headaches, chills, and burning fever. In the chapter titled "Clara's Meditations" we see the nightmare of a soul divided in a state of semi-consciousness—a turbulence of petty wilfulness and lassitude, self-abasement and female pride. As she lies for a long period sleepless, "in a fever, lying like stone, with her brain burning," her reason tells her she must battle Willoughby, while her female training tells her she must battle instead her own accurate perceptions and pretend not to understand him: "The instinct of seeking to know, crossed by the task of blotting knowledge out, creates that conflict of the natural with the artificial creature to which [woman's] ultimately revealed double-face, complained of by ever-dissatisfied men, is owing" (p. 167). Thus, man's duplicity inspires an answering duplicity in women. Like a Prince Charming carrying around his own slipper in hopes of finding a Cinderella to wear it, Willoughby seeks a mate "in harmony with him, from the centre of his profound identity to the raying circles of his variations": "Know the centre, you know the circle, and you discover that the variations are simply characteristics, but you must travel on the rays of the circle to get to the centre. Consequently Sir Willoughby put Miss Middleton on one or other of these converging lines from time to time. Us, too, he drags into the deeps, but when we have harpooned a whale and are attached to the rope, down we must go; the miracle is to see us rise again" (p. 90). The miracle is also to know where we have been once we come up. For a unified picture of the man we must reconcile the center with the raying circles, but as Clara discovers, doing that is a mystifying task.

There is his enigmatically expressive "leg," which one is conscious of even when his trousers conceal it: "The leg of the born cavalier is before you: and obscure it as you will, dress degenerately, there it is for ladies who have eyes. You *see* it: or, you see that *he* has it" (p. 13). Mrs. Mountstuart's phrase *"he has a leg"* appears heavy with significance; the problem with such terse "phrases," however, as the novel's Vernon Whitford points out, is that they dazzle the penetration of the one who invents them (p. 252). As aspects of Willoughby's supposed splendor, his raying circle of variations, both the phrase and the leg may also dazzle the penetration of the observer.

The modern egoist is the fantastic embodiment of society's dearest illusions about itself. Willoughby's celebrated "leg" is no more than this borrowed style; it expresses not the inner self, but the slowly accumulated habits of an elegant but decadent upper class: "The Egoist is our fountain-head, primeval man: the primitive is born again, the elemental reconstituted. Born again, into new conditions, the primitive may be highly polished of men, and forfeit nothing save the roughness of his original nature. He is not only his own father, he is ours; and he is also our son. We have produced him, he us" (p. 322). As to the invention of Willoughby's "leg" by his admirers, Meredith comments ironically: "A simple-seeming word of this import is the triumph of the spiritual, and where it passes for coin of value, the society has reached a high refinement" (p. 12).

Walter F. Wright has observed that Willoughby "is not athletic; he expresses no force of character in his legs." That is true, but so also is Stevenson's description of the Egoist as "rich, handsome, athletic, aristocratic, and urbane."[25] Just as the leg symbolizes a counterfeit delicacy, it also symbolizes a false manliness. Despite Mrs. Mountstuart's assurance that Willoughby "excels in manly sports," he is never shown taking exercise, except "horse exercise." Clara, Vernon, and Crossjay are all runners or fast walkers, but "pedestrianism was a sour business to Willoughby, whose exclamation of the word indicated a willingness for any amount of exercise on horseback" (p. 26).[26] We see Vernon training for an Alpine tour and in a swimming race with Crossjay; we see Crossjay at hare and hounds and Clara rowing in a scull. Willoughby, however, is seen only at billiards. For an athletic man he has a peculiar distaste for strenuous activity. He refuses, for example, to join the others in their frequent pursuits of Crossjay, complaining that one "has to catch the fellow like a football" (p. 231). Watching Vernon set out after the truant lad "at full pedestrian pace," he remarks scornfully to De Craye, "A man looks a fool cutting after a cricket-ball; but putting on steam in a storm of rain to catch a young villain out of sight, beats anything I've witnessed" (p. 210).

Still, Willoughby's exploits throughout the story are metaphorically athletic. Among the many sporting metaphors in the novel are ones having to do with fishing, skating, fencing, foot-racing, horse-racing, cricket, shooting, swimming, chess, bowls, boxing, mountaineering, yachting, and hunting. Most of these are used to describe the Egoist's courting machinations, especially his treatment of rivals: "An English squire excelling his fellows at hazardous leaps in public, he was additionally a polished whisperer, a lively dialoguer, one for witty bouts." (p. 134). Before Mrs. Mountstuart's dinner party he encounters De Craye, verbally spars with him, and looks forward eagerly to a further match: "Willoughby had refreshed himself. At the back of his mind there was a suspicion that his adversary would not have yielded so flatly without an assurance of practically triumphing, secretly getting the better of him; and it filled him with venom for a further bout at the next opportunity . . . Sharing the opinion of his race, that blunt personalities, or the pugilistic form, administered directly on the salient features, are exhibitions of mastery in such encounters, he felt strong and solid, eager for the successes of the evening" (p. 244).

Willoughby mistakenly sees De Craye as his chief rival for Clara and thus a natural opponent in such games. Vernon, on the other hand, "was one of your men who entertain the ideas about women of fellows that have never conquered one: or only one, we will say in this case, knowing his secret history; and that one no flag to boast of" (p. 240). Whereas De Craye is charming and witty, Vernon is "not a bad talker, if you are satisfied with keeping up the ball" (p. 76).

Willoughby's strategy with De Craye—making the Colonel think that Clara is in love with him—is good gamesmanship but bad sportsmanship. The whole chapter (47) which relates the gulling of De Craye is sprinkled with games-metaphors. Willoughby plans his revenge believing that he has been "stale-mated" in some grand chess match; he then strips to "enter the ring" with his adversary; he envisions himself as a mountaineer sacrificing his own life to defend a peak against a rival climber; finally, after he throws out to De Craye some appealing hints, his "fish [gives] a perceptible little leap" and takes the bait. That the Colonel, discovering the ruse, refuses to exact his own revenge puzzles Willoughby; but in doing so De Craye is the better sportsman of the two. As he says to Mrs. Mountstuart on the last page of the novel, "revenge for a stroke in the game of love shows us unworthy to win."

Mrs. Mountstuart is a detached spectator at these polite contests, realizing that as a woman her role should be to stand by the playing field and watch with visible admiration. Her advice to Clara never to "play at

counter-strokes" with Willoughby exemplifies Meredith's theory that female duplicity is a response to male vanity: "They say we beat men at
that game, and so we do, at the cost of beating ourselves. And if once we
are started, it is a race-course ending on a precipice—over goes the winner. We must be moderately slavish to keep our place; which is given us in
appearance; but appearances make up a remarkably large part of life,
and far the most comfortable, so long as we are discreet at the right
moment" (p. 288).

Willoughby's games-playing is like his leg—it is athletic and nonath-
letic at the same time. Its form—its manner—is polite, gracious, and styl-
ized: it mirrors the overrefinement, the decadence, of an age. But to the
perceptive it also symbolizes a brutal, energetic hardness. The Egoist,
Meredith declares in a famous passage, stands in the midst of Society
"monumentally, a landmark of the tough and honest old Ages, with the
symbolic alphabet of striking arms and running legs, our early language,
scrawled over his person" (p. 322). Behind the symbolic alphabet of the
modern male Barbarian—his "leg"—is that of his ancestor, the language
of brute struggle; and when we learn to read both, we see the naked,
embryonic core of egoism which takes much longer to change than does
the external person.

Vernon Whitford also has a leg; indeed we are often reminded that he
has two legs and makes use of them. A dedicated mountaineer, this "un-
tiring pedestrian" spends two months each year in the Alps and as much
as nine and a half hours a day in training. Unlike Willoughby's, however,
Vernon's legs are real. They are in firm contact with the solid earth. Dif-
fident and wry, Vernon spends much of his time early in the novel hanging about, or tagging along, or leaving the scene for one of his long
walks. His actions, so far as the movement of the novel is concerned, are
inconsequential until the very end. But when we see him out-of-doors by
himself, he is transformed from this shadowy presence into a lively
Dionysian celebrant of nature, the embodiment of the healthy man as
participator in the life of the universe. As he pursues the frightened, fleeing Clara through a violent downpour his "noble coldness" gives way to
a "happy recklessness." His own energies and those of nature are one; his
mind quickens with freshly drawn perceptions of a natural scene renewing itself in the renewal of the perceiving mind: "A rapid walker poeti-
cally and humourously minded gathers multitudes of images on his way.
And rain, the heaviest you can meet, is a lively companion when the
resolute pacer scorns discomfort of wet clothes and squealing boots . . .
The watery lines, and the drifting, the chasing, the upsoaring, all in a

shadowy fingering of form, and the animation of the leaves of the trees pointing them on, the bending of the tree-tops, the snapping of branches, the hurrahings of the stubborn hedge at wrestle with the flaws . . . make a glory of contest and wildness without aid of colour to inflame the man who is at home in them from old association on road, heath, and mountain. Let him be drenched, his heart will sing" (pp. 213-214).

Vernon has not civilized his leg. He is an athlete but no gamesman: "He walked heroically, his pedestrian vigour being famous, but that means one who walks away from the sex, not excelling in the recreations where men and women join hands" (p. 62). His past and present hardships—the death of his wife, his poverty, his confinement at Patterne—have instilled a self-distrust and a fear of women. As Willoughby rightly says, "his shyness is his malady" (p. 114). Although responsive to Nature, he denies part of his own nature. He is sensitive about having his own feelings touched and insensitive about the necessity of touching Clara's: "Mr. Whitford meant well; he was conscientious, very conscientious. But he was not the hero descending from heaven bright-sworded to smite a woman's fetters off her limbs and deliver her from the yawning mouth-abyss" (p. 125). This stoic, decent, intellectual man of action cannot be anything but decent to the struggling woman. When he overtakes her in her flight from Willoughby he leads her to an inn, orders some medicinal brandy and water, takes her upstairs, and acts with perfect propriety: "He had done something perhaps to save her from a cold: such was his only consolatory thought. He had also behaved like a man of honour, taking no personal advantage of her situation; but to reflect on it recalled his astonishing dryness. The strict man of honour plays a part that he should not reflect on till the fall of the curtain, otherwise he will be likely sometimes to feel the shiver of foolishness at his good conduct" (p. 224).

Although Vernon's heroic walking is his way of enlivening his mind, of making good blood, as Meredith would say, it is also his way of fleeing emotionally disturbing situations, much in the manner of Adam Bede. The most telling instance is the scene in which he wakens from a nap beneath the double-blossomed wild-cherry tree and sees Clara standing above him, her "fair head circled in dazzling blossom." He stoically refuses to yield to the "vapourish rapture" brought on by the vision: "He jumped to his feet, rattled his throat, and attacked the dream-giving earth with tremendous long strides, that his blood might be lively at the seat of his understanding . . . He had not much vanity to trouble him, and passion was quiet, so his task was not gigantic. Especially be it remarked, that he was a man of quick pace, the sovereign remedy for the dispersing of the mental fen-mist. He had tried it and knew that nonsense to be walked off" (p. 95).

Leslie Stephen, on whom the character of Vernon was based, wrote that walking is "the best of panaceas for the morbid tendencies" of writers.[27] The idea was a commonplace among Victorian intellectuals. The young Kingsley used "a day in the roaring Fen wind" as his "panacea" for thinking too much. Meredith himself believed in that sort of natural mind-body therapy, but apparently recognized its danger in inhibiting that "complete unfolding of the senses" necessary to total health. Illumination for Vernon comes later in the novel, in an uncomfortable scene with Laetitia. As he listens to her praise his conscientiousness and "pure self-abnegation" (p. 270), he realizes that these qualities, when inspired by a fear of failing, are but another kind of egoism, and that it is no consolation to be a good loser if one has lost by default. As he sees himself a "grisly Egoist" he begins the descent from his glacial mountain. When next he visits the Alps it is with Clara, as a lover rather than a mountaineer.

Although the athlete Vernon finally rescues Clara from Patterne Hall, it is her own healthy nature which first has to rescue her from Willoughby's spell. Since her "disease" is merely "the longing for happiness" (p. 94), in that disease lies the cure: "Her personal position . . . was instilling knowledge rapidly, as a disease in the frame teaches us what we are and have to contend with. Could she marry this man?" (p. 92). Thus, even as her illness develops, her convalescence is taking place. The enlightenment comes in stages, but nearly every contact with him increases her intellectual distrust and clarifies her objective vision. On one occasion, in the presence of Vernon, Dr. Middleton, and some impercipient aunts, Willoughby blandly warns her against marrying an egoist: "None of them saw the man in the word, none noticed the word; yet this word was her medical herb, her illuminating lamp, the key of him . . . Egoist! She beheld him—unfortunate, self-designated man that he was!—in his good qualities as well as bad under the implacable lamp, and his good were drenched in his first person singular . . . He was in his thirty-second year, therefore a young man, strong and healthy, yet his garrulous return to his principal theme, his emphasis on I and me, lent him the seeming of an old man spotted with decaying youth" (p. 81).

Clara has the sort of nature which assures its own mending. She is sensitive, observant, and perhaps above all, lively. She is too spirited to remain long in Willoughby's prison or in the prison of her own self-conception: "With her body straining in her dragon's grasp, with the savour of loathing, unable to contend, unable to speak aloud, she began to speak to herself, and all the health of her nature made her outcry womanly, — 'If I were loved!'—not for the sake of love, but for free breathing" (p. 84). As Clara, struggling to be free, regains her health, Willoughby begins to lose his. He succumbs to jealousy, a disease he had thought contracted only by "luckless fellows" (p. 187). He starts wearing a haggard smile, like "a convalescent child the first day back to its toys" (p. 254). When Mrs. Mountstuart observes that he is not looking well, he responds ruefully, "Don't take away my health, pray!" (p. 281). Ultimately he begins to worry that his ordeal will expose him to "some organic malady, possibly heart-disease" (p. 310).

Generally in *The Egoist* poor health is the outward sign of obtuseness, and good health the sign of quick intelligence. Letty Dale and her father are semi-invalids; both harbor their illusions about Willoughby longer than Clara or Vernon. When Letty does come to perceive his essential selfishness she begins to look "fresher and younger; extremely well" (p. 281). Her father, however, has difficulty understanding Letty's refusal of Willoughby, having "but strength for the slow digestion of facts" (p. 375). Digesting a fact means more than just having it in mind: it means letting it change one's nature, using it as the body uses food, in the process of growth. As Dr. Middleton observes, we are all slow to digest facts and "make good blood of the fact of our being" (p. 376). In this, Willoughby, with his youthful agility and "brilliant health," ought to have an advantage over some of the other characters. As in all other ways, however, his appearance belies his soul. His mind is extremely anemic, owing to its being sheltered by guardians and admirers from the rigors of life. As a boy he was never birched; as a man he has never really been challenged. Dr. Middleton describes the type: "They are ill-balanced men. Their seat of reason is not a concrete. They won't take rough and smooth as they come. They make bad blood, can't forgive, sniff right and left for approbation, and are excited to anger if an East wind does not flatter them" (p. 65).

As the novel proceeds, Willoughby must gradually face up to the conceptual problem posed by a girl who, though young, sound, and virginal, will not maintain a thorough devotion to him: "The fact that she was a healthy young woman returned to the surface of his thoughts like the murdered body pitched into the river, which will not drown and calls upon the elements of dissolution to float it. His grand hereditary desire to transmit his estates, wealth and name to a solid posterity, while it prompted him in his loathing and contempt of a nature mean and ephemeral compared with his, attached him desperately to her splendid healthiness. The council of elders, whose descendant he was, pointed to this young woman for his mate. He had wooed her with the idea that they consented. O she was healthy! And he likewise: but, as if it had been a duel between two clearly designated by quality of blood to bid a House endure, she was the first who taught him what it was to have sensations of his mortality" (p. 190).

Never having needed to confront the world before, Willoughby's habit has been to despise it as, "if you will allow, gross . . . a beast" (p. 39). His defense has been to create a holy temple of his own psyche and bid others worship there. When Clara shows unmistakable signs of apostasy, he begins to see her as worldly and therefore bestial: "a healthy creature and an animal; attractive, but capricious, impatient, treacherous, foul; a woman to drag men through the mud" (p. 315). The sequence of epithets which run through his mind is significant. He has been willing to accept some capriciousness in Clara for the sake of her attractiveness; she cannot be healthy without being spirited. But impatience, and the skepticism it signifies, is a scourge to his ego: "Sir Willoughby by no means disapproved of a physical liveliness that promised him health in his mate; but he began to feel in their conversations that she did not sufficiently think of making herself a nest for him" (p. 74). When he sees the hope of that snug nest irrevocably vanishing he is driven to regard even her health as "treacherous, foul." This equation of health with impurity, a philosophical about-face, gives him the excuse for proposing to the sickly Laetitia. He takes modest consolation in the fact that while sacrificing "a shape of youth and health" (p. 395), he has at least gained a wife with intelligence: "But he had the lady with brains!" (p. 419) The marriage is appropriate. Both Willoughby and Letty have devoted themselves to protecting their illusions about him. And, as Clara tells him, Laetitia's patient adoration has destroyed in her "the health you demand as one item on your list" (p. 106). Now Laetitia has lost her illusions and might help him to lose his as well.

Clara is fundamentally healthy in a way that Willoughby is not. She is "rooted in earth" like the wild-cherry tree, so whatever disunion there might be between trunk and blossom—body and mind—it is foreign to her nature and therefore temporary. Willoughby is *essentially* unnatural. He is a Patterne, the pattern or type of the British upper class. His body and manner are exquisite; his soul is that of a cave dweller. Long generations have gone into producing this freak of evolution. According to

Clara's father, the English are "barbarians, on a forcing soil of wealth, in a conservatory of comfortable security; but still barbarians" (p. 372). Like Matthew Arnold, Meredith believed that the upper classes reflected this heritage in their traditional love of competitive sport. Also like Arnold he saw this sporting instinct as descended from the old barbarian's love of war. In modern times, he tells us (p. 14), the aristocracy may, without the stimulus of warfare, become enervated. This has happened on the continent, but "happily our climate and our brave blood precipitate the greater number upon the hunting-field, to do the public service of heading the chase of the fox, with benefit to their constitutions. Hence a manly as well as useful race of little princes, and Willoughby was as manly as any." One can see a sort of evolution in Willoughby: he has refined his warring instinct to a passion for outdoor sport, and that still further to an indoor gamesmanship. Twenty years after *The Egoist* appeared, Thorstein Veblen, whose wit and angular discursive style recall Meredith's, remarked: "Sports—hunting, angling, athletic games, and the like—afford an exercise for dexterity and for the emulative ferocity and astuteness characteristic of predatory life. So long as the individual is but slightly gifted with reflection or with a sense of the ulterior trend of his actions—so long as his life is substantially a life of naïve impulsive action—so long the immediate and unreflective purposefulness of sports, in the way of an expression of dominance, will measurably satisfy his instinct of workmanship."[28] The barbarian Willoughby is Meredith's caricature of sham "healthy" gentility. His health, his athletics, and his gentlemanly manner are all superficial and counterfeit, all external, inherited, and therefore retrogressive. He never grows; he never learns. Vernon Whitford, the "lean long-walker and scholar," is the embodiment of *mens sana in corpore sano*, Meredith's version of the gentleman-hero. He has the true gentleman's modesty and thoughtfulness, and he ultimately develops the hero's capacity for courageous, direct and effective action. Early in the novel Meredith compares him with Willoughby as the two cousins appear to foreigners during their grand tour: "Vernon seemed a sheepish fellow, without stature abroad, glad of a compliment, grateful for a dinner, endeavouring sadly to digest all he saw and heard. But one was a Patterne, the other a Whitford. One had genius; the other pottered after him with the title of student. One was the English gentleman wherever he went; the other was a new kind of thing, produced in England of late, and not likely to come to much good himself, or do much good to the country" (p. 23).

Meredith viewed the healthy growth of the individual as a reflex of the pattern of historical evolution, a process of "transmutation" in which one's purely sensual and selfish side becomes absorbed in those higher faculties which distinguish the adult from the child and the genuinely civilized man from the savage. Vernon, the "new kind of thing," exemplifies that healthy growth. Sir Willoughby, with a healthy body and an unhealthy mind, is, like his literary predecessor Richard Feverel, a case of progress arrested at an early stage.

CHAPTER 12

Conclusion

In the last book of the *Prelude* Wordsworth tells how, one foggy summer night, he "panted up" Mt. Snowdon with a friend and a guide. He was leading the way, and suddenly as he climbed above the fog the brilliant moonlight showed him a vision as much imaginative as real. "Headlands, tongues, and promontory shapes" of mist encroached even into the distant Atlantic, yet the bright heavens, while seemingly sensible to the roaring of unseen "waters, torrents, streams / Innumerable," remained serenely uncontaminated. Later, in "calm thought," he read this vision as emblematic of "a mind sustained / By recognitions of transcendent power, / In sense conducting to ideal form, / In soul of more than mortal privilege." Such minds, touched but unshaken by the darker aspects of life, turning perception into felt vision and felt vision into concept, can both know themselves and "deal / With the whole compass of the universe." Therefore,

> the highest bliss
> That flesh can know is theirs—the consciousness
> Of Whom they are, habitually interfused
> Through every image and through every thought,
> And all affections by communion raised
> From earth to heaven, from human to divine.

For Wordsworth, man's greatest happiness is to know who he is and how he belongs, and to know these so intensely that all feelings, images, and ideas reflect the knowledge. Such a concept of "bliss" is not unique in the nineteenth century; it is assumed by most Romantics and nearly all the Victorian writers we have been studying. What distinguishes Victorian thought, however, is the implied or explicit designation of the state as "healthiness" and the persistent use of bodily health as a means of understanding it.

The two kinds of health, physical and spiritual, are similar in their effects on the mind. Bodily health imparts a sense of physically belonging, of being at home with physical things and laws. Spiritual health imparts a sense of spiritually belonging, of being in harmony with nonphysical laws, whether divinely or societally ordained. Both types result in, or are characterized by, feelings of ease, comfort, and freedom from anxiety. Victorian intellectuals tended to see the process of growing up as moving from the lower, natural kind of health, to the higher, cultivated kind without of course losing the first. "The highest and healthiest state," Ruskin wrote, "which is competent to ordinary humanity appears to be that which, accepting the necessity of recreation, and yielding to the impulses of natural delight springing out of health or innocence, does, indeed, condescend often to playfulness, but never without a deep love of God, of truth, and of humanity."[1] Health in its limited sense—mindless, youthful vitality and joy—is here defined within the framework of a higher healthiness, a clearly spiritual state. Although the expression of spiritual or moral health is seen as something quite different from the "playfulness" of mere bodily health, both conditions represent contentment.

Most commonly Victorians used physical health as the model for a higher human excellence, a way of envisioning it. As definitions of the one state varied from writer to writer, so did those of the other state, but the practice of analogically or metaphorically connecting the two was habitual in Victorian epistemology. Writers like Meredith and Stephen went further: to them the healthy body was not just an aid to mental cognition, but was itself a direct means of cognition. For Meredith, Blood, Brain, and Spirit were all faculties of knowing: the body understands life physically, the brain intellectually, and the spirit emotionally and imaginatively. Without the body's knowledge neither the mind's concept-making nor the spirit's image-gathering is possible. Therefore, we need not only the mind's knowledge *of* the body, and a foundation for a knowledge of life which that provides, but a knowledge *by* the body—not just, in Stephen's terms, comprehension of self and experience, but apprehension as well.

Sometimes when climbing in the Alps, Stephen would roll a large rock down a precipice and imagine that he was that rock. This kinetic, bodily vision would bring home to him "the real majesty of an Alpine cliff." Mountain climbing supplied him with "what theologians call an experimental faith in the size of mountains." In measuring nature's magnitude "in terms of muscular exertion instead of bare mathematical units" it substituted "a real belief for a dead intellectual assent."[2] Whereas Wordsworth grasped nature visually and then mentally, Stephen began by apprehending it with his whole body. This measurement by muscular exertion, using healthy will and body together as means of cognition, gives one a sense of his own reality as well as that of his environment. The athlete who reduces by ten seconds the time it takes to run a mile has measured his own will against the limitations of his body and his whole person against the track he runs on. Simultaneously he grows aware of the reality of a mile of dirt track and of his own body in relation to it. Like Hopkins' windhover, he displays "the achieve of, the mastery of the thing," a mastery both of the act and of the circumstances which resist the act. Physical exertion, pitting one's own force against external forces and obstacles, supplies the sense of conquest out of which identity emerges. The idea that the self and the environment are conceptually created in personal action runs through Victorian thought from Carlyle onward. Health might even be defined as that state in which reliable cognition and purposeful action continually reinforce each other. This notion was basic to Hughes's philosophy of educative play and Meredith's philosophy of sport. Sartre refers to this process of significant striving as the appropriative aspect of sport: " That pure-in-itself, comparable to the absolute, intelligible plenum of Cartesian extension, fascinates me as the pure appearance of the not-me; what I wish precisely is that this in-itself might be a sort of emanation of myself while still remaining in itself . . . Before descending this snowy slope, I must climb up it. And this ascent has offered to me another aspect of the snow—resistance. I have realized that resistance through my fatigue, and I have been able to measure at each instant the progress of my victory. Here the snow is identical with *the Other*, and the common expressions 'to overcome,' 'to conquer,' 'to master,' *etc*. indicate sufficiently that it is a matter of establishing between me and the snow the relation of master to slave. This aspect of appropriation we find in the ascent, exists also in swimming, in an obstacle course, *etc*."[3]

In *Mountaineering in 1861* the scientist John Tyndall made some pertinent observations along this line. Without external resistance, man is "a mere *capacity*, if such a thing is conceivable alone; potential, but not dynamic; an agent without an object." The mountain climber, grappling physically with tangible resistance, gains a consciousness of himself as a palpable existence—he discovers himself. During one particularly taxing ascent Tyndall suddenly realized, "The fingers, wrist, and forearm were my main reliance, and as a mechanical instrument the human hand appeared to me this day in a light which it had never assumed before. It is a miracle of constructive art." In forcing the body to respond to demanding physical exigencies one gains a permanent cognition of both self and nature: "In places where the danger is not too great, but where a certain amount of skill and energy are required, the feeling of self-reliance is inexpressibly sweet, and you contract a closer friendship with the universe in virtue of your more intimate connection with its parts."[4]

Victorians thus used the healthy body indirectly, as a concept, and directly, in itself, to gain that knowledge deemed necessary to what Wordsworth called the "highest bliss" and Ruskin the "highest and healthiest state." Bodily health was also considered a sign of a more general personal health and therefore a direct means of personal evaluation. Some writers further adopted into their philosophies the view that physical fitness was an agent of moral or spiritual fitness. As to how accurate a sign it was, and how effective an agent, there was far from general accord. Newman, Arnold, and George Eliot, for example, insisted that the truly healthy mind had a vital power sufficient to compensate for bodily weakness. They also insisted, in opposition to men like Spencer and Kingsley, that in considering the human constitution, the health of the mind, by itself, should be given priority over bodily well-being.

Victorians found in the ideal of personal health a way of grasping the proper relation between the self as a whole—*mens sana in corpore sano*—and the unity of moral and physical laws which transcend the self. "We ought to feel," F. D. Maurice declared, "that all God's judgments by fever and cholera are judgments for neglect of His physical laws, but that *they* will not be obeyed till men obey His moral laws, by ceasing to live to themselves, by feeling that it is their business to care for their fellows and for the earth."[5] The accord between one's physical and moral health signified a like accord between external physical and moral principles and therefore the ethical justness of natural occurrences. Thus, the state of health offered not only a sense of reality, of intimacy with the physical universe, but what Arnold termed a *satisfying* sense of reality, a feeling of being spiritually as well as physically at home among things.

This search for a satisfying reality underlies the Victorian intellectual's body-consciousness. According to Maurice, the quest for unassailable certainty of knowledge was indispensable to healthy human growth, but in modern times those who most passionately yearn for "some spiritual object" develop "feelings and consciousnesses . . . which are uneasy, feverish, tormenting, precisely because that which they seek they cannot

find, and because some faint, obscure image is offered to them as a substitute for it." Although the healthy body in itself or as a model was not
usually deemed a spiritual object, it was a cognitive aid in identifying
spiritual goals and had the advantage of not being faint and obscure.
Physiologists, he wrote, were then insisting that the "knowledge which
we have attained respecting men's physical condition is the only secure
knowledge, the only knowledge upon which we can act."[6] That is, the
laws of the body were more definite, more verifiable, than those of the
mind. Just as important, to the individual the body's health seemed more
easily evaluated than that of the mind or soul.

It may seem today that Victorians had very inadequate information
about the nature of the body and its health. Even so, the physical effects
of health and disease were clear enough to provide a tangible basis for a
more general knowledge of self. Spiritual progress or backsliding could
at least be grounded in, measured by, and defined in terms of a condition
about which there was reliable subjective knowledge. Physical health, a
kind of certainty about one's body, offered a starting point for other certainties. There could be "no mistake," Kingsley wrote, about the saving
of lives—or of course one's own life. Since health was obviously, as
Newman said, a good in itself, the search for it had clear value.

Chronically wearied by the mental struggle with imponderables, Victorian intellectuals found relief in a plainer agon, one in which at least
the issues were comprehensible. Although sickness and other kinds of
physical hardship were a person's "inseparable companions," Charlotte
Brontë wrote, "these real, material dangers, when once past, leave in the
mind the satisfaction of having struggled with difficulty, and overcome
it. Strength, courage, and experience are their inevitable results; whereas,
I doubt whether suffering purely mental has any good result, unless it be
to make us by comparison less sensitive to physical suffering."[7] Physical
strife, whether in the sickroom or on a mountain peak, was a battle with
adversity which, because its progress was knowable, provided a degree
of mental certainty. Edward Whymper, conqueror of the Matterhorn,
declared that climbing gives a more than physical strength. Although we
"glory in the physical regeneration" the effort provides, "we value more
highly the development of manliness, and the evolution, under combat
with difficulties, of those noble qualities of human nature—courage, patience, endurance, and fortitude."[8]

All of these qualities are noble, and therefore healthy in a moral sense,
in that they imply a higher purpose to life than one's own happiness. The
conscious struggle to attain them is obviously different from what Ruskin

calls "natural delight" and "playfulness," though Victorian concepts of health often sought to relate the two: the ethical pleasure of behaving well and improving oneself and the aesthetic pleasure of feeling well and enjoying oneself. The notion of a "highest state of health" assumes a very demanding view of life, in which all personal states and activities are envisioned teleologically in terms of duties, goals, and significant challenges. To be truly healthy a person must always be reaching out morally and intellectually, even trying to reach what is beyond the grasp. All life, therefore, involves work, not just labor but work in the Carlylean sense: socially useful and personally creative labor. Duty often centers on the compelling choice between the intrinsic healthiness of play and the extrinsic healthiness of work. It teaches a preference for the second over the first, for self-improvement over self-awareness. "A man perfects himself by working," Carlyle wrote. "The whole soul of man is composed into a sort of harmony, the instant he sets himself to work!" With self-perfection comes enlightenment: "Properly, thou hast no other sort of knowledge but that thou hast got by working. The rest is yet all a hypothesis of knowledge."[9]

Ruskin believed that the highest state includes a lower state to which the healthy man "condescends." Without occasional playfulness, man's constant search for meaning would be overburdensome, Dr. Arnold insisted in desiring "pure play." Eugen Fink writes, "If we compare play to the rest of life with its impetuous dynamism, its provoking orientation toward the future, play appears as a serene 'presence' with a meaning sufficient to itself. It is like an oasis of happiness found in the desert of our questing . . . The activity of play has only internal finalities which do not transcend it." Lacking what Sartre calls "serious thought"—an awareness of self in relation to the Other—play asserts the self *as* self. In Sartre's words, "the desire to do is . . . reduced to a certain desire to be . . . The function of the act is to make manifest and present *to itself* the absolute freedom which is the very beginning of the person."[10]

Many Victorian intellectuals insisted on carefully distinguishing work and play, the two expressions of the healthy nature. Ruskin declared: "Play is an exertion of body or mind, made to please ourselves, and with no determined end. You play, as you call it, at cricket, for instance. That is as hard work as anything else; but it amuses you, and has no result but the amusement. If it were done as an ordered form of exercise, for health's sake, it would become work directly. So, in like manner, whatever we do to please ourselves, and only for the sake of pleasure, not for an ultimate object, is 'play,' the 'pleasing thing,' not the useful thing."

Play is aesthetic, work is ethical. Play has a limited, personal value, work a higher personal value as well as a social value. If play has some external object, then, with its added purposefulness, it is work. In *The Crown of Wild Olive* Ruskin scolds the wealthy "playing class" for being absorbed in such "games" as war and mercantilism as well as in field and athletic sports. Like football, the pursuit of wealth is "absolutely without purpose; no one who engages heartily in that game ever knows why." London, the center of British finance and commerce, is "a great city of play; very nasty play, and very hard play, but still play. It is only Lord's cricket-ground without the turf:—a huge billiard table without the cloth, and with pockets as deep as the bottomless pit; but mainly a billiard table, after all."[11]

In their sports, however, Victorians turned play into work, investing it with just those higher meanings Ruskin claimed it lacked. In so doing they found a way of reconciling the pleasure of bodily self-awareness with the duty of moral self-improvement. Any game, of course, has an inherent ethical structure. Its completion, with a clear separation of winner from loser, is a goal achievable only by strict observation of the rules of play. If, as Anatol Rapoport says, a player assumes for the time being that his opponent is a rational creature (an assumption he cannot make in a fight), he must also assume him to be an ethical being, who will not cheat.[12] Unless the society of the game is a moral one, there can be no game. The game is an expression of society's ethical ideals in such a way that they are made secure from erosion. In the nineteenth century this aspect was consciously emphasized, and the style of play became ethically meaningful in itself. The phrases "fair play," "playing the game," and "It's not cricket" reflect the strict moral environment which came to surround sport in Victorian England. Even the solitary climber or walker might feel that he had to choose between what he would like to do and what he ought to do. Since the decision is entirely his own, he feels "a severe strain on his moral energies" as he tries to live up to a general standard as well as a particular one set by himself. "Why not break the mountaineer's code of commandments?" Leslie Stephen asked himself during one outing. "Why not sit down in the first bit of shade, to smoke my pipe and admire the beauties of nature? . . . I struggled, however, against the meshes of false reasoning which seemed to be winding themselves tangibly round my legs, and toiled slowly upwards. I raised my feet slowly and sleepily; I groaned at the round, smooth, slippery pebbles, and lamented the absence of water. At length I reached a little patch of snow, and managed to slake my parched lips and once more to toil more actively upwards."[13]

In this account spiritual and physical healthiness go hand in hand. To the Victorians any activity was spiritually healthful which included the component of work, which "appropriated" the world, ordering it conceptually, mastering it with the mind. All great vital literature, according to Richard Le Gallienne, deals with experience in "its relations to health, to the great vital centre of things." It seeks essential, comprehensive, and absolute meaning: "The theme, great or small, is considered in its relation to the sum-total of things, to the Infinite, as we phrase it."[14] Healthy thought is serious, pointed toward the world, not the self.

In a sense, the institutionalization of games in the later nineteenth century made them more healthful—worklike. Sport moved toward an external "vital centre," the center of culture, and derived its meanings from that. The center it sought to identify with was not the "Infinite" or the "sum-total of things," but merely the social code, and very often only the code of a particular class, or even of a particular school. Therefore, in playing the game, the moral faculty took over entirely from the cognitive. The healthy body was an instrument not for understanding the ineffable, but for ritualizing an obedience to the reasonable. Applying Arnold's terminology, the difference was between a Hellenistic and a Hebraistic use of the body. The one discipline, Arnold says, lays its main stress "on clear intelligence, the other on firm obedience; the one, on comprehensively knowing the grounds of one's duty, the other, on diligently practising it."[15] Even Carlyle's duty-oriented concept of healthy action, Hebraistic as it was in some respects, emphasized knowing and clear-sightedness. These qualities tended to be less important in popular versions of the healthy hero, which stressed heroic action but not heroic knowledge. The "grounds of one's duty" were assumed, not sought for comprehensively. In this sense sport became the perfect ritual embodiment of the life of action within a framework of assumed values, and to the extent that the game thus became a model for the healthy life, it blurred distinctions between life and not-life, tautness and relaxation, work and play, the battle and the game.

This blurring was most evident in the schools. Headmasters were turning play into a duty, and some, like Edward Bowen of Harrow, tried to infuse the whole life of the school with the spirit of the game. He did not encourage rifle-corps or gymnastics because, his nephew and biographer says, "they neither of them supplied a game." Cricket and football did supply it, so he encouraged them. He was often found on the playing fields and organized special matches for small boys so that all could play. Later in his life he wrote a satirical essay on earnestness at school; the subject was "Arnoldides Chiffers," a master in the Arnold tradition: "Work with him was work, and play was play. No lounging or smiling before the desk of such a teacher; every pupil feared him while at class, but, the lesson over, had nothing to fear . . . In a word, he studied day by day to bring his own moral influence to bear on the characters of those entrusted to him, he made his approval their standard, and he taught them to regard one another, not from the point of view of fleeting popularity or schoolboy honour or social gifts, but from the eternal point of view of right and wrong."[16]

Bowen believed in developing a proper balance between boyishness and manliness, "the good temper, cheerfulness, gaiety, if you will, the disposition to make the best of things, the absence of suspicion, the forbearance, the unity." Something of this spirit can be found in *Tom Brown*, which looked back to Arnold as it looked forward to Bowen. Under the latter's system the mood of the classroom was identical with that of the playground. A boy would not need to be punished for whistling in class for the simple reason that he would not think of whistling; it would not be, in one of Bowen's favorite phrases, "playing the game." A boy "doesn't need punishments any more than he needs them when fielding at cricket; he ought to feel the suggestion of such a thing . . . as an affront."[17] What he really meant was that life should be taken as seriously as the game. Playing the game is acting instinctively with the same sense of purpose, the same moral decisiveness, off the playing field as on.

The phrase "play the game" was immortalized in Henry Newbolt's poem "Vitaï Lampada." An ex-schoolboy soldier, his regiment under bloody siege, rallies his comrades with inspiriting words recalled from his days on the cricket field:

> This is the word that year by year,
>   While in her place the School is set,
> Every one of her sons must hear,
>   And none that hears it dare forget.
> This they all with a joyful mind
>   Bear through life like a torch in flame,
> And falling fling to the host behind—
>   "Play up! play up! and play the game!"[18]

By the nineties, when this poem was composed, the cricket match had become symbolic of gentlemanly life outside the school. The process begun with *Tom Brown* culminates with "Vitaï Lampada": the highest values of the schoolboy become the guiding principles of the adult.

The imposed moral imperatives of the game are few and simple: one does not cheat, take unfair advantage, shirk, or give up. Although this represents a type of seriousness, it is nothing like Arnold's "high seriousness." The player who lives by these lights on or off the field does not need the developing vision, the mental receptivity, or the imaginative or philosophic grasp—qualities most Victorian intellectuals considered necessary for a healthy mind. Those qualities he does need—tenacity, daring, and moral decisiveness—are not so much mental traits as traits of the mind-body, constitution, or "character."

Symbolized by the British athlete—the player as gentleman-hero—strong character was popularly considered the basis of true manliness. As Arnold might have said, however, strength of character may be adequate for running staunchly on the football field but inadequate for walking in the world at large. In "Notes on the English Character" E. M. Forster describes the public-school types who, having been taught that the school is a microcosm of the world, enter the world with the incomplete vision of schoolboys: "They quote the remark that 'the battle of Waterloo was won on the playing-fields of Eton.' It is nothing to them that the remark is inapplicable historically and was never made by the Duke of Wellington, and that the Duke of Wellington was an Irishman. They go on quoting it because it expresses their sentiments; they feel that if the Duke of Wellington didn't make it he ought to have, and that if he wasn't an Englishman he ought to have been. And they go forth into a world that is not entirely composed of public-school men or even of Anglo-Saxons, but of men who are as various as the sands of the sea; into a world of whose richness and subtlety they have no conception. They go forth into it with well-developed bodies, fairly developed minds, and undeveloped hearts."[19]

If the Victorian age created that manly ideal, Victorian intellectuals initiated the protest against it. They did so, not because it equated health and manliness, but because it envisioned both of these so narrowly. Encouraging a contentment with the raw self, it neglected that aspiration toward a higher healthiness, an endless expansion of one's powers.

Notes

Chapter 1
Introduction: Victorian Health

1. "They Taught the World to Play," *Victorian Studies*, 2 (1959), 211.

2. *The Physiology of Common Life*, 2 vols. (1860; New York: Appleton, 1864), II, 378.

3. *A Short History of Medicine* (New York: Oxford University Press, 1928), p. 203.

4. A. H. T. Robb-Smith, "Medical Education at Oxford and Cambridge Prior to 1850," in *The Evolution of Medical Education in Britain*, ed. F. N. L. Poynter (Baltimore: Williams and Wilkins, 1966), pp. 49-50.

5. Brian Abel-Smith, *The Hospitals, 1800-1948: A Study in Social Administration in England and Wales* (Cambridge, Mass.: Harvard University Press, 1964), p. 16.

6. Ibid., p. 17.

7. *Charles Kingsley: His Letters and Memories of His Life*, ed. [Frances Kingsley], 4 vols. (1877; London: Macmillan, 1901), II, 232.

8. *An Introduction to the History of Medicine*; 2nd ed. (Philadelphia: W. B. Saunders, 1917), p. 408.

9. N. C. Macnamara, *Asiatic Cholera: History up to July 15, 1892; Causes and Treatment* (London: Macmillan, 1892), p. 219.

10. Quoted by W. T. Gairdner, *Public Health in Relation to Air and Water* (Edinburgh: Edmonston and Douglas, 1862), pp. 15-16.

11. E. Symes Thompson, *Influenza or Epidemic Catarrhal Fever: An Historical Survey of Past Epidemics in Great Britain from 1510 to 1890* (London: Percival, 1890), p. 471.

12. Charles Creighton, *A History of Epidemics in Britain*, 2 vols. (Cambridge: University Press, 1891, 1894), II, 380, 381.

13. Ibid., II, 198, 606.

14. Ibid., II, 208, 206, 391.

15. Rollo Russell, *Epidemics, Plagues and Fevers: Their Cause and Prevention* (London: Stanford, 1892), p. 58.

16. Creighton, *History of Epidemics*, II, 198; René and Jean Dubos, *The*

White Plague: Tuberculosis, Man and Society (Boston: Little, Brown, 1952), p. 65.

17. Edwin Chadwick, *Report on the Sanitary Condition of the Labouring Population of Gt. Britain,* ed. M. W. Flinn (1842; Edinburgh: University Press, 1965), p. 78.

18. Sir George Newman, *The Rise of Preventive Medicine* (London: Oxford University Press, 1932), p. 158.

19. R. Thorne Thorne, *On the Progress of Preventive Medicine during the Victorian Era* (London: Shaw, 1888), p. 4.

20. Chadwick, *Report,* p. 225. The figure given is for 1840.

21. Frederick Engels, *The Condition of the Working-Class in England* (1844; London: Swan Sonnenschein, 1892), pp. 39-40.

22. Edwin Chadwick, *The General History of Principles of Sanitation* (London: Cassell, 1899), p. 10.

23. *Typhoid Fever: Its Nature, Mode of Spreading, and Prevention* (London: Longmans, 1873), p. 139.

24. Thompson, *Influenza,* pp. 275-276.

25. J. C. Drummond and Anne Wilbraham, *The Englishman's Food: A History of Five Centuries of English Diet* (London: Cape, 1939), p. 363.

26. "Training in Relation to Health," *Cornhill,* 9 (1864), 219.

27. *The Collected Letters of Thomas and Jane Welsh Carlyle,* ed. Richard Sanders et al. (Durham, N.C.: Duke University Press, 1970-   ), II, 479; IV, 152.

28. *New Letters of Thomas Carlyle,* ed. Alexander Carlyle, 2 vols. (London: John Lane; The Bodley Head, 1904), I, 201.

29. *The Letters of Thomas Carlyle to His Brother Alexander, With Related Family Letters,* ed. Edwin W. Marrs, Jr. (Cambridge, Mass.: Belknap Press of Harvard University Press, 1968), p. 680.

30. See Thea Holme, *The Carlyles at Home* (London: Oxford University Press, 1965), pp. 49-57.

31. *The Life and Letters of Charles Darwin,* ed. Francis Darwin, 2 vols. (New York: Appleton, 1888), I, 318.

32. *Life and Letters of Thomas Henry Huxley,* ed. Leonard Huxley, 3 vols. (London: Macmillan, 1900), I, 159; II, 65, 79, 80, 289.

33. *The George Eliot Letters,* ed. Gordon S. Haight, 7 vols. (New Haven: Yale University Press, 1954-55), II, 255.

34. *New Letters and Memorials of Jane Welsh Carlyle,* ed. Alexander Carlyle, 2 vols. (London: John Lane, 1903), I, 93.

35. *Quacks and Quackery: A Remonstrance Against the Sanction Given by the Government, the Press, and the Public* (London: Simpkin, Marshall, 1844), p. vii.

36. James Morison, *Morisoniana; or, Family Adviser of the British College of Health* (1829; 3rd ed., London: Sherwood and Gilbert, 1831), p. iv.

37. "The Function of Criticism at the Present Time," *Complete Prose Works,* ed. R. H. Super, 11 vols. (Ann Arbor: University of Michigan Press, 1960-77), III, 279-280.

38. *Morisoniana,* p. vii.

39. Arthur Penrhyn Stanley, *The Life and Correspondence of Thomas Arnold, D.D.* (1844; 2 vols. in 1, New York: Scribner's, 1892), II, 42-43. Neville

M. Goodman remarks, "Medical diagnosis and treatment had hardly advanced since Harvey—or indeed Hippocrates"; *Medicine and Science in the 1860's,* ed. F. L. N. Poynter (London: Wellcome Institute, 1968), p. 135.

40. *Aequanimitas, With Other Addresses to Medical Students, Nurses and Practitioners of Medicine* (London: H. K. Lewis, 1946), p. 254.

41. *Morisoniana,* p. 12.

42. Wilhelm Ameke, *History of Homoeopathy: Its Origins; Its Conflicts,* trans. Alfred E. Drysdale (London: E. Gould, 1885), p. 106.

43. *Taking the Cure* (London: Michael Joseph, 1967), p. 193.

44. *Testimonies to the Efficiency of Hydropathy in the Cure of Disease,* ed. Richard Metcalfe (London: W. Tweedie, [1878]), p. 136.

45. Ibid., p. 143.

46. Quoted by Henry E. Sigerist, *On the History of Medicine,* ed. Félix Martí-Ibáñez (New York: MD Publishers, 1960), p. 16.

47. *Manual of the Turkish Bath,* ed. Sir John Fife (London: John Churchill, 1865), p. 16.

48. *Education: Intellectual, Moral, and Physical* (Amer. ed. 1860; repr. New York: Appleton, 1896), pp. 282-283.

49. *The Philosophy of Health; or, An Exposition of the Physiological and Sanitary Conditions Conducive to Longevity and Happiness* (1835; 11th ed., London: Longman, Green, 1865), p. xi.

50. *The Idea of Nature* (1945; New York: Oxford University Press, 1960), p. 44.

51. *Ancient Medicine,* ch. xx; quoted by Benjamin Farrington, *Greek Science: Its Meaning for Us* (Baltimore: Penguin, 1953), p. 74.

52. *Collected Essays;* 9 vols. (New York: Appleton, 1917), I, 164; italics mine.

53. *Man Adapting* (New Haven: Yale University Press, 1965), p. 333.

54. Carlyle was fond of reminding his audience of this point: "You should always look at the *heilig,* which means 'holy' as well as 'healthy.' " "Inaugural Address at Edinburgh," *The Works of Thomas Carlyle,* ed. H. D. Traill; Centenary ed., 30 vols. (London: Chapman and Hall, 1896-1899), XXIX, 480.

55. *The Use of the Body in Relation to the Mind* (London: Longman, Brown, Green, 1846), p. 255.

56. *A System of Physical Education, Theoretical and Practical* (Oxford: Clarendon Press, 1869), p. 24.

57. "Health," *Cornhill,* 3 (1861), 333.

58. *Body and Will* (London: Kegan Paul, 1883), p. 254.

59. "Inaugural Address," *Works,* XXIX, 479.

60. *Education,* p. 222.

Chapter 2
Mens Sana in Corpore Sano: Victorian Psychophysiology

1. *Times,* October 24, 1857.

2. J. Milner Fothergill, *The Maintenance of Health: A Medical Work for Lay Readers* (London: Smith, Elder, 1874), pp. 25-26.

3. *Mind and Body: Psychosomatic Pathology; A Short History of the Evo-*

lution of Medical Thought, trans. Aurelio M. Espinosa, Jr. (London: Harvill, 1955), p. 64.

4. Ilza Veith, "On Hysterical and Hypochondriacal Afflictions," *Bull. Hist. Med.,* 30 (1956), 233-240.

5. Walther Riese, "An Outline of a History of Ideas in Neurology," *Bull. Hist. Med.,* 23 (1949), 115.

6. Edward Theodore Withington, *Medical History from the Earliest Times: A Popular History of the Healing Art* (1894; repr. London: Holland Press, 1964), p. 345.

7. Max Neuberger, "British and German Psychiatry in the Second Half of the Eighteenth and the Early Nineteenth Century," *Bull. Hist. Med.,* 18 (1945), 139; italics mine.

8. E. C. Gaskell, *The Life of Charlotte Brontë,* 2 vols. (New York: Appleton, 1857), II, 190-191, 196, 197, 199.

9. "Hypochondriasis," Robert Hooper, *Lexicon Medicum, or Medical Dictionary* (7th ed., rev. by Klein Grant; London: Longman, Orne, 1839).

10. Thomas Hawkes Tanner, *An Index of Diseases and Their Treatment* (4th ed., rev. by Percy Boulton; London: Henry Renshaw, 1892), p. 155.

11. *Life and Letters of Thomas Henry Huxley,* ed. Leonard Huxley, 3 vols. (London: Macmillan, 1900), I, 143.

12. "Hysteria," *Lexicon Medicum.*

13. Clark, *The Sanative Influence of Climate* (1829; 4th ed., London: John Murray, 1846), pp. 155, 102; Lionel J. Beale, *The Laws of Health in Relation to Mind and Body* (London: John Churchill, 1851), pp. 269, 271.

14. "Temperaments," *The Cyclopaedia of Practical Medicine,* ed. John Forbes, Alexander Tweedie, John Conolly (London: Sherwood, Gilbert, and Piper; and Whittaker, Treacher, and Co., 1833-35); Beale, *Laws of Health,* p. 153.

15. George Moore, *The Use of the Body in Relation to the Mind* (London: Longman, Brown, Green, 1846), p. 264.

16. Robert Hutchinson Powell, *A Medical Topography of Tunbridge Wells* (London: John Churchill, 1846), p. 62.

17. *Laws of Health,* p. 152.

18. "Inflammation of the Brain," *Cyclopaedia of Practical Medicine.*

19. Beale, *Laws of Health,* p. 269.

20. *A Monograph on Fever and Its Treatment,* ed. W[illiam] C[ourt] G[ully] (London: Simpkin, Marshall, 1885), esp. pp. 36 ff.

21. "On the Practical Administration of Mineral Waters," *British and Foreign Medical Review,* 14 (1842), 313.

22. *Philosophy and Medicine* (London: Tavistock Publications, 1970), p. 27.

23. *Darwin and Henslow: The Growth of an Idea: Letters 1831-1861,* ed. Nora Barlow (Berkeley and Los Angeles: University of California Press, 1967), pp. 163-164; *Testimonies to the Efficiency of Hydropathy in the Cure of Disease,* ed. Richard Metcalfe (London: W. Tweedie, [1878]), p. 142.

24. Hallam, Lord Tennyson, *Alfred, Lord Tennyson: A Memoir,* 2 vols. (New York: Macmillan, 1911), I, 241.

25. Joan Evans, *John Ruskin* (New York: Oxford University Press, 1954), p. 125.

26. "Disease as Biography," *The Crystal Arrow: Essays on Literature, Travel, Art, Love, and the History of Medicine* (New York: Clarkson N. Potter, 1964), p. 416.

27. Spearman, *Psychology down the Ages*, 2 vols. (London: Macmillan, 1937), I, 51.

28. "Mr. Noble on the Brain and Its Psychology," *British and Foreign Medical Review*, 22 (1846), 544.

29. Robert M. Young, *Mind, Brain and Adaptation in the Nineteenth Century* (Oxford: Clarendon Press, 1970), p. 211.

30. The discovery was made independently in France by François Magendie.

31. *The Senses and the Intellect* (London: John W. Parker, 1855), p. v.

32. Laycock, *Mind and Brain*, 2 vols. (1860; 2nd ed., London: Simpkin, Marshall, 1869), I, 18-19. *The Works of Sir Benjamin Collins Brodie, Bart.*, coll. and arranged by Charles Hawkins, 3 vols. (London: Longman, Green, 1865), I, 159.

33. Young, *Mind, Brain and Adaptation*, p. vii.

34. Brodie, *Works*, I, 366.

35. *The Human Mind and Its Relations with the Brain and Nervous System* (London: John Churchill, 1858), p. 157.

36. "On Descartes' 'Discourse . . . Truth,' " *Collected Essays*, 9 vols. (New York: Appleton, 1917), I, 189.

37. *The Study of Psychology: Its Object, Scope, and Method* (London: Trübner, 1879), pp. 57-58.

38. Alexander Bain, *Mind and Body: The Theories of Their Relation* (London: Henry S. King, 1873), p. 132. *The Emotions and the Will* (London: Parker, 1859), p. 478.

39. *Principles of Mental Physiology* (London: Henry S. King, 1874), pp. ix-x.

40. Noble, *The Human Mind*, pp. 152-153.

41. Ibid., p. 151.

42. Carpenter, *Principles of Mental Physiology*, p. 25.

43. *Chapters on Mental Physiology* (London: Longman, Brown, Green, and Longmans, 1852), p. 113.

44. Carpenter, *Principles of Mental Physiology*, p. 24; Brodie, *Works*, I, 150.

45. *The Causational and Free Will: Theories of Volition* (London: Williams and Norgate, 1877), p. 62.

46. *The Physiology and Pathology of Mind* (London: Macmillan, 1867), p. 157.

47. Roback, *The Psychology of Character* (3rd ed., London: Routledge and Kegan Paul, 1952), p. 182; Maudsley, *The Pathology of Mind* (London: Macmillan, 1879), p. 98; Laycock, *Mind and Brain*, II, 323.

48. *On the Study of Character* (London: Parker & Son, 1861), pp. 205-206, 199.

49. *Autobiography of John Stuart Mill*, ed. J. J. Coss (New York: Columbia University Press, 1944), p. 119; italics mine. He later used it as the basis of his chapter on liberty and necessity in his *System of Logic*.

50. Tuke, *Illustrations of the Influence of the Mind upon the Body* (London: J. & A. Churchill, 1872), p. 327; Maudsley, *Physiology and Pathology of the Mind*, p. 158.

51. Maudsley, *Body and Will* (London: Kegan, Paul, Trench, 1883), pp. 96-97; Beale, *Laws of Health*, p. 7.

Chapter 3
The Thoroughly Healthy Mind: Victorian Criticism

1. Macaulay, "Horace Walpole," *Literary Essays Contributed to the Edinburgh Review* (London: Oxford University Press, 1937), p. 250. Carlyle, *Heroes and Hero Worship; The Works of Thomas Carlyle*, ed. H. D. Traill; Centenary ed., 30 vols. (London: Chapman and Hall, 1896-99), V, 187. Hutton, "Arthur Hugh Clough," *Literary Essays* (3rd ed., London: Macmillan, 1888), p. 288. Stephen, *Swift*, ed. John Morley; English Men of Letters (New York: Harper, [1887]), p. 177.

2. "Tennyson's Idylls," *The Collected Works of Walter Bagehot*, ed. Norman St. John-Stevas (London: The Economist, 1965-   ), II, 181.

3. Stephen, "Balzac's Novels," *Hours in a Library* (1st ser.; London: Smith, Elder, 1874), p. 219. Roe, *Thomas Carlyle as a Critic of Literature* (New York: Columbia University Press, 1910), p. 32. Stephen, "Art and Morality," *Cornhill*, 32 (1875), p. 94.

4. Alexander Bain, *Mental and Moral Sciences* (London: Longmans, Green, 1868), p. 395. Henry Maudsley, *Responsibility in Mental Disease* (London: Henry S. King, 1874), p. 34.

5. *Past and Present; Works*, X, 274.

6. *Modern Painters*, V; *The Works of John Ruskin*, ed. E. T. Cook and Alexander Wedderburn, 39 vols. (London: Allen, 1903-12), VII, 263-264.

7. Hutton, *Literary Essays*, pp. 185, 176; Ruskin, *Modern Painters*, III; *Works*, V, 61; Stephen, "Fielding's Novels"; "Wordsworth's Ethics," *Hours in a Library* (3rd ser.; London: Smith, Elder, 1879), pp. 79, 186; Bagehot, "Mr. Clough's Poems," *Works*, II, 250; Arnold, "Maurice de Guérin," *The Complete Prose Works of Matthew Arnold*, ed. R. H. Super, 11 vols. (Ann Arbor: University of Michigan Press, 1960-77), III, 31.

8. *Complete Prose Works*, III, 12-13, 33, 32.

9. *The Letters of Matthew Arnold to Arthur Hugh Clough*, ed. Howard Foster Lowry (Oxford: Clarendon Press, 1932), p. 97; "Wordsworth," *Complete Prose Works*, IX, 44; "Preface to First Edition of Poems, 1853," *Complete Prose Works*, I, 15.

10. Bagehot, "Mr. Clough's Poems," *Works*, II, 243.

11. Bagehot, *Works*, II, 244, 246.

12. Bagehot, "Charles Dickens," *Works*, II, 81.

13. Bagehot, "The Waverly Novels," *Works*, II, 66.

14. Arnold, "On the Modern Element in Literature," *Complete Prose Works*, I, 20.

15. Stephen, "Wordsworth's Ethics," *Hours in a Library*, 3rd ser.; p. 226.

16. Bagehot, "Charles Dickens," *Works*, II, 106.

17. Arnold, *Letters to Clough*, p. 97.

18. "Tennyson's Poems," *Essays*, ed. W. G. Clark (Cambridge: Macmillan, 1858), pp. 78-79.

19. Stephen, "Wordsworth's Ethics," *Hours in a Library*, 3rd ser.; p. 185.

20. "Tennyson's Poems," *John Stuart Mill: Literary Essays*, ed. Edward Alexander (Indianapolis: Bobbs-Merrill, 1967), pp. 101-103.

21. Ruskin, *Works*, V, 201-220.

22. Ruskin, *Stones of Venice*, II; *Works*, X, 203, 240, 238.

23. Ruskin, *Stones of Venice*, III; *Works*, XI, 187.

24. Stephen, *Hours in a Library*, 3rd ser.; pp. 178-229. Subsequent page references in my text are to this edition.

25. *Mind and Brain*, 2 vols. (2nd ed., London: Simpkin, Marshall, 1869), II, 39.

26. *Conversations of Goethe with Eckermann and Soret*, trans. John Oxenford (1850; new ed., London: George Bell, 1874), p. 510; *Letters of Thomas Carlyle to John Stuart Mill, John Sterling, and Robert Browning*, ed. Alexander Carlyle (London: Unwin, 1923), p. 292; Stephen, "Wordsworth's Ethics," *Hours in a Library*, 3rd ser.; p. 183; Ruskin, "On the Relation of National Ethics to the National Arts," *Works*, XIX, 165; Carlyle, *Heroes and Hero Worship; Works*, V, 104.

27. Quoted by F. W. Roe in *Thomas Carlyle as a Critic of Literature*, p. 42. Ruskin, *Modern Painters*, III; *Works*, V, 127.

28. *Miscellanies*, 2 vols. (London: Parker, 1859), I, 279-280.

29. Carlyle, *Heroes and Hero Worship; Works*, V, 170.

30. *Mill's Essays on Literature and Society*, ed. J. B. Schneewind (New York: Collier Books, 1965), p. 28.

31. "Disease and Social Criticism: A Contribution to a Theory of Medical History," *Bull. Med. Hist.*, 10 (1941), 5-15.

32. *Mill's Essays on Literature and Society*, p. 34.

33. Carlyle, "Characteristics," *Works*, XXVIII, 21.

34. *Essays Chiefly Literary and Ethical* (London: Macmillan, 1889), p. 49.

35. Arnold, *Complete Prose Works*, I, 21-22, 20. Subsequent page references in my text are to this edition.

36. Arnold, *Complete Prose Works*, I, 2-3.

37. Stephen, *Cornhill*, 43 (1881), 42.

38. Mill, "The Two Kinds of Poetry," *Literary Essays*, p. 66.

39. Frederic William Maitland, *The Life and Letters of Leslie Stephen* (London: Duckworth, 1906), p. 32.

40. Maitland, *Life and Letters*, p. 57.

41. "Mr. Stephen and Mr. Ramsay: The Victorian as Intellectual," *Partisan Review*, 19 (1952), 667.

42. "Rowing," *British Sports and Pastimes*, ed. Anthony Trollope (London: Virtue, 1868), p. 236.

43. *Essays Chiefly on Poetry*, 2 vols. (London: Macmillan, 1887), II, 130-131.

44. Macaulay, "The Life and Writings of Addison," *Literary Essays*, p. 656.

45. *Alexander Pope*; English Men of Letters, ed. John Morley (New York: Harper, 1880), pp. 209, 119.

46. "Life of Tennyson," *Studies of a Biographer*, 4 vols. (1898-1902; New York: Putnam's, 1907), II, 208-209.

47. Ruskin, *Lectures on Art*; *Works*, XX, 79.

48. Ruskin, *Works*, IX, 444-448.

49. Ruskin, *Academy Notes, 1859*; *Works*, XIV, 233.

50. Ruskin, *Modern Painters*, III; *Works*, V, 233.

51. Stephen, *Studies of a Biographer*, III, 248.

52. Leslie Stephen, "Art and Morality," *Cornhill*, 32 (1875), 93.

53. Stephen, *Cornhill*, 43 (1881), 42; italics mine.

54. *The Fleshly School of Poetry and Other Phenomena of the Day* (London: Strahan, 1872), pp. 83, 54, 65.

55. Stephen, "Art and Morality," pp. 100-101.

Chapter 4
Obeying the Laws of Life: Carlyle and Spencer

1. *Mill's Essays on Literature and Society*, ed. J. B. Schneewind (New York: Collier Books, 1965), pp. 386-388.

2. *The Social & Political Ideas of Some Representative Thinkers of the Victorian Age*, ed. F. J. C. Hearnshaw (1933; repr. New York: Barnes & Noble, 1967), p. 53.

3. In chapter 45 Lydgate reports that the epidemic has reached Danzig; the "horrors of Cholera" become an "exciting" topic in chapter 56; in chapter 63 Lydgate prepares a new fever ward; in chapter 67 the town takes sanitary measures; and finally the first case of cholera in Middlemarch occurs in chapter 71.

4. J. A. Froude, *Thomas Carlyle: A History of the First Forty Years of His Life, 1795-1835*, 2 vols. (New York: Scribner's, 1882), II, 183, 178.

5. Ibid., II, 185.

6. Page references to "Characteristics" are to *The Works of Thomas Carlyle*, ed. H. D. Traill; Centenary ed.; 30 vols. (London: Chapman and Hall, 1896-99), vol. XXVIII.

7. *Nature and Life* (1934; New York: Greenwood Press, 1968), p. 36.

8. Carlyle, *Works*, I, 211, 51.

9. *Body, Soul, Spirit: A Survey of the Body-Mind Problem*, trans. Hubert H. Hoskins (London: Oxford University Press, 1966), pp. 102-103.

10. I am paraphrasing Guenter Risse, "Kant, Schelling, and the Early Search for a Philosophical 'Science' of Medicine in Germany," *Bull. Hist. Med.* 27(1972), pp. 155-156.

11. F. W. J. von Schelling, *On University Studies*, trans. E. S. Morgan; ed. Norbert Guterman (Athens: Ohio University Press, 1966), pp. 66-67.

12. Carlyle, *Works*, I, 57.

13. Ibid., I, 176.

14. *The Letters of Thomas Carlyle to His Brother Alexander, With Related Family Letters*, ed. Edwin W. Marrs, Jr. (Cambridge, Mass.: Belknap Press of Harvard University Press, 1968), p. 310.

15. Carlyle, *Works*, XXVII, 81; I, 132; X, 271.

16. Carlyle, "Signs of the Times," *Works*, XXVII, 80-81.

17. *Carlyle and German Thought, 1819-1834* (New Haven: Yale University Press, 1934), pp. 61-63. See also Karl E. Rothschuh, *History of Physiology*, trans. and ed. Guenter B. Risse (Huntington, N.Y.: Robert E. Krieger, 1973), pp. 158-161.

18. Carlyle, *Works*, I, 172, 184-185.

19. *Selected Writings of Florence Nightingale*, ed. L. R. Seymour (New York: Macmillan, 1954), pp. 123-124 (*Notes on Nursing: What It Is and What It Is Not*, 1859).

20. Froude, *Thomas Carlyle*, II, 194; *Letters of Thomas Carlyle to His Brother*, p. 303; *Thomas Carlyle*, II, 210.

21. This and subsequent page references to *Past and Present* are from *Works*, vol. X.

22. Quoted in Wolfgang Kayser, *The Grotesque in Literature and Art*, trans. Ulrich Weisstein (Bloomington: Indiana University Press, 1963), p. 55.

23. On Morison see chapter 1. Carlyle misspells the name.

24. Noel Gilroy Annan, *Leslie Stephen: His Thought and Character in Relation to His Time* (Cambridge, Mass.: Harvard University Press, 1952), p. 115.

25. "Physiology as an Inductive Science," repr. in *Nature and Man: Essays Scientific and Philosophical* (London: Kegan, Paul, Trench, 1888), p. 157.

26. *First Principles* (1862; 4th ed., 1880; repr. New York: DeWitt Revolving Fund, 1958), pp. 136-137.

27. *Nothing But or Something More* (Seattle: University of Washington Press, 1971), p. 5; *Man Adapting* (New Haven: Yale University Press, 1965), pp. 331-333.

28. *The Positive Philosophy of Auguste Comte*, trans. and condensed by Harriet Martineau, 3 vols. (1853; London: George Bell, 1896), II, 260; italics mine.

29. Comte did not go as far in this as Spencer. Comte believed that while the laws of human behavior followed generally those of biological science, they cannot simply be reduced to those laws. See William Coleman, *Biology in the Nineteenth Century: Problems of Form, Function, and Transformation* (New York: Wiley, 1971), p. 111.

30. *Social Statics; or, The Conditions Essential to Human Happiness Specified, and the First of Them Developed* (1851; New York: Appleton, 1888), p. 498.

31. *Education: Intellectual, Moral, and Physical* (Amer. ed. 1860; New York: Appleton, 1896), p. 139.

32. Spencer, *First Principles*, pp. 394, 370; *Social Statics*, p. 497.

33. *Reasons for Dissenting from the Philosophy of M. Comte and Other Essays* (1864; repr. Berkeley: Glendessary Press, 1968), p. 22. See also Norman Fruman, *Coleridge, the Damaged Archangel* (New York: Braziller, 1971), pp. 121-134.

34. Spencer, *First Principles*, p. 362.

35. Spencer, *Social Statics*, pp. 488, 483; italics mine.

36. Spencer, *Social Statics*, p. 121; Buckle, *History of Civilization in England*, 3 vols. (London: Longmans, Green, 1901), I, 232, 1, 2-3.

37. John William Draper, *History of the Intellectual Development of Europe*, 2 vols. (rev. ed., New York: Harper's, [1876]), I, 20, iii, 20.

38. Spencer, *First Principles*, p. 538.

39. "On the Mutual Relations of the Vital and Physical Forces," *Philosophical Transactions of the Royal Society of London* (1850), p. 752.

40. *Principles of Mental Physiology* (London: Henry S. King, 1874), p. 696; Laycock, *Mind and Brain*, 2 vols.) 2nd ed.; London, Simpkin, Marshall, 1869), I, 382-383.

41. James Hinton, "Physiological Riddles, III," *Cornhill*, 2 (1860), 167-168; Maudsley, "The Theory of Vitality," *British and Foreign Medico-Chirurgical Review*, 32 (1863), 422.

42. Spencer, *First Principles*, pp. 218, 199-200.

43. *The Principles of Psychology*, 2 vols. (1855; New York: Appleton, 1896), I, 627.

44. Spencer, *First Principles*, p. 223.

45. Spencer, *Education*, p. 268.

46. Ibid., p. 282; italics mine.

47. Ibid., p. 32. Page references in the following discussion are to the edition cited in note 31.

48. This situation was rapidly changing, perhaps owing partly to Spencer's exhortations.

49. *The Study of Sociology* (1873; New York: Appleton, 1874), p. 21.

50. Spencer, *First Principles*, pp. 492, 494.

51. Walter Bagehot, *Physics and Politics* (2nd ed., 1872; Boston: Beacon Press, 1956), p. 9; Spencer, *Illustrations of Universal Progress; A Series of Discussions* (1864; rev. ed., New York: Appleton, 1888), p. 325.

Chapter 5
Types of Healthy Christianity: Newman and Kingsley

1. *The Educational Writings of John Locke*, ed. James L. Axtell (London: Cambridge University Press, 1968), p. 115.

2. *The Idea of a University Defined and Illustrated*, ed. C. F. Harrold (1852, 1859, 1873; new ed., New York: Longmans, Green, 1947), p. 143. Subsequent page references are to this edition.

3. *An Essay in Aid of a Grammar of Assent*, ed. C. F. Harrold (1870; new ed., New York: Longmans, Green, 1947), p. 265.

4. *Biology in the Nineteenth Century: Problems of Form, Function, and Transformation* (New York: Wiley, 1971), p. 12.

5. Charles Singer, *A Short History of Medicine* (New York: Oxford University Press, 1928), p. 33.

6. *Education: Intellectual, Moral, and Physical* (1860; New York: Appleton, 1896), p. 113.

7. "The Relation of Ancient Philosophy to Medicine," *Ancient Medicine: Selected Papers of Ludwig Edelstein*, ed. Oswei Temkin and C. Lilian Temkin, trans. C. Lilian Temkin (Baltimore: Johns Hopkins University Press, 1967), p. 361.

8. *The "Art" of Rhetoric*, with trans. by John Henry Freese; Loeb Classical

Library (London: Heinemann, 1926), p. 61.

9. See A. Dwight Culler, *The Imperial Intellect: A Study of Newman's Educational Ideal* (New Haven: Yale University Press, 1955), p. 187.

10. "Lord Bacon," *Literary Essays Contributed to the Edinburgh Review* (London: Oxford University Press, 1937), p. 369. Subsequent page references in my discussion of Macaulay's essay are to this edition.

11. *The Republic of Plato*, trans. and ed. F. M. Cornford (New York: Oxford University Press, 1945), pp. 312, 97; *The Politics of Aristotle*, trans. and ed. Ernest Barker (Oxford: Clarendon Press, 1946), p. 339.

12. *The Politics of Aristotle*, ed. W. L. Newman (Oxford: Clarendon Press, 1887-1902), I, 349.

13. Aristotle, *Politics*, ed. Barker, p. 338; Plato, *Republic*, pp. 100, 93.

14. Edith Hamilton, *The Greek Way* (New York: Norton, 1930), p. 25. *The Nichomachean Ethics*, with trans. by Harris Rackham; Loeb Classical Library (rev. ed., London: Heinemann, 1934), pp. 61, 365.

15. Aristotle, *The "Art" of Rhetoric*, pp. 62-63.

16. *Past and Present; Works*, ed. H. D. Traill; Centenary ed., 30 vols. (London: Chapman and Hall, 1896-99), X, 26. *Heroes and Hero Worship; Works*, V, 13.

17. A. N. Whitehead, *Nature and Life* (1934; New York: Greenwood Press, 1968), pp. 26-27.

18. Walter Bagehot, *Physics and Politics* (2nd ed., 1872; Boston: Beacon Press, 1956), p. 107. Carlyle, *Heroes and Hero Worship; Works*, V, 217. "Boswell's Life of Johnson," *Works*, XXVIII, 114.

19. Carlyle, *Heroes and Hero Worship; Works*, V, 155. Newman, "The Tamworth Reading Room," *Essays and Sketches*, ed. C. F. Harrold, 3 vols. (New York: Longmans, Green, 1948), II, 207.

20. Walter Houghton, "The Issue between Kingsley and Newman," *Victorian Literature: Selected Essays*, ed. Robert O. Preyer (New York: Harper, 1967), pp. 1-12. Newman, "Wisdom and Innocence," *Sermons and Discourses, 1839-57*, ed. C. F. Harrold (new ed.; New York: Longmans, Green, 1949), p. 115; italics mine. *Newman's Apologia Pro Vita Sua: The Two Versions of 1864 & 1865, Preceded by Newman's and Kingsley's Pamphlets*, ed. Wilfred Ward (London: Oxford University Press, 1913), pp. 34, 385; *Grammar*, p. 188.

21. *Charles Kingsley: His Letters and Memories of His Life*, [ed. Frances Kingsley], 4 vols. (1877; London: Macmillan, 1901), III, 18. Fitzjames Stephen, "Tom Brown's Schooldays," *Edinburgh Review*, 107 (1858), 190.

22. Spencer, *Education*, p. 223.

23. "Two Years Ago," *Saturday Review*, Feb. 21, 1857, p. 176. And see Merle M. Bevington, *The Saturday Review, 1855-1868* (New York: Columbia University Press, 1941), p. 188.

24. Fitzjames Stephen, "Tom Brown's Schooldays," pp. 190, 193.

25. *Charles Kingsley: His Letters and Memories of His Life*, [ed. Frances Kingsley], 2 vols. ("abridged ed."; London: Kegan Paul, 1879), II, 74; 1901 ed., III, 191.

26. *Yeast: A Problem* (4th ed.; London: Parker, 1859), pp. xii-xiii. *Letters and Memories*, 1901 ed., III, 191.

27. *Letters and Memories*, "abridged ed.," II, 74.

28. *Letters and Memories,* 1901 ed., I, 54, 64.

29. Ibid., I, 48, 53-54.

30. Ibid., I, 151, 267.

31. See Margaret Thorp, *Charles Kingsley 1819-1875* (Princeton: Princeton University Press, 1937), p. 22.

32. Kingsley, *Letters and Memories,* 1901 ed., I, 118. "Novalis," *Works,* XXVII, 29, 28, 39.

33. *Letters and Memories,* 1901 ed., I, 117.

34. *Works,* I, 23.

35. *Letters and Memories,* 1901 ed., I, 87.

36. Ibid., I, 91.

37. "Kingsley's Miscellanies," *Saturday Review,* Nov. 12, 1859, p. 583.

38. *Letters and Memories,* 1901 ed., I, 106-107.

39. Righteousness is "primarily an inward quality, the presupposition of right action, which makes healthful, wholesome, and harmonious community life possible." See *An Encyclopedia of Religion,* ed. Vergilius Ferm (Paterson, N.J.: Littlefield, Adams, 1959), p. 663.

40. "Superstition," *Scientific Lectures and Essays* (London: Macmillan, 1880), p. 207. "Grots and Groves," *Health and Education* (New York: Appleton, 1874), p. 324. *Letters and Memories,* 1901 ed., I, 118.

41. "The Natural Theology of the Future," *Scientific Lectures and Essays,* p. 325.

42. *Letters and Memories,* 1901 ed., II, 234-235.

43. "The Massacre of the Innocents," *Sanitary and Social Lectures and Essays* (London: Macmillan, 1880), p. 266. "The Two Breaths," *Sanitary and Social Lectures and Essays,* p. 64. *Letters and Memories,* 1901 ed., III, 29.

44. *Autobiography and Other Writings,* ed. Jack Stillinger; Riverside ed. (Boston: Houghton Mifflin, 1969), p. 320. Kingsley, "A Mad World, My Masters," *Sanitary and Social Lectures and Essays,* p. 278.

45. Carlyle, *Sartor Resartus; Works,* I, 203-204. *Past and Present; Works,* X, 273-274.

46. [J. K. Laughton], review of "*Charles Kingsley: His Letters and Memories of His Life,*" *Edinburgh Review,* 145 (1877), 438.

47. *Letters and Memories,* 1901 ed., I, 225.

48. *Letters and Memories,* "abridged ed.," II, 88. "The Massacre of the Innocents," p. 259.

49. "Kingsley and Carlyle," *Literary and Social Judgments* (London: N. Trübner, 1868), p. 150.

50. "North Devon I," *Fraser's,* 40 (1849), 6-7; Carlyle, *Past and Present; Works,* X, 291; "Boswell's Life of Johnson," *Works,* XXVIII, 90. Kingsley, "Heroism," *Sanitary and Social Lectures and Essays,* pp. 254, 252.

51. *Newman's Apologia,* pp. 47-48.

52. Kingsley, "Nausicaa in London," *Health and Education,* p. 86.

Chapter 6
The New Era: Victorian Sport and Training

1. J. A. Froude, *Thomas Carlyle: A History of the First Forty Years of His Life,* 2 vols. (New York: Scribner's, 1882), II, 183.

2. Quoted in Maurice J. Quinlan, *Victorian Prelude: A History of English Manners, 1700-1830* (New York: Columbia University Press, 1941), p. 213.

3. Quoted in J. L. and Barbara Hammond, *The Bleak Age* (London: Longmans, Green, 1934), pp. 181-182.

4. According to the *Oxford English Dictionary*, the use of the word "sport" to mean "participation in games and exercises, esp. those of an athletic character or pursued in the open air" was a late development. The examples given are both later nineteenth century. In his valuable *Sports and Pastimes of the People of England* (1801) Joseph Strutt describes the recreations of his time. Strutt's subtitle is significant, suggesting as it does that no important distinction is to be made among "Rural and Domestic Recreations, May Games, Mummeries, Pageants, Processions and Pompous Spectacles." They are all diversions.

5. "Athletic Sports," March 27, 1869, p. 413.

6. *The Boy's Own Book: A Complete Encyclopedia of All the Diversions, Athletic, Scientific, and Recreative, of Boyhood and Youth* (London: D. Bogue, 1855; Crosby, Lockwood, 1880).

7. *British Sports and Pastimes* (London: Virtue, 1868), pp. 2-4.

8. In addition to works separately cited, material on cricket has been drawn from the following sources: H. S. Altham, *A History of Cricket* (London: George Allen & Unwin, 1926); R. J. Evans, *The Victorian Age, 1815-1914* (2nd ed., London: Edward Arnold, 1968); Frederick Gale, *Echoes from the Old Cricket Fields* (London: Simpkin, Marshall, 1871); Frederick Gale, *Modern English Sports: Their Use and Abuse* (London, Sampson Low, 1885); A. G. Moyes, *A Century of Cricketers* (London: Harrap, 1950); [James Pycroft], *Cricketana* (London: Longmans, Green, 1865); Edward Rutter, *Cricket Memories* (London: Williams & Norgate, 1925); and various issues of the *Annual Register*.

9. "The Sporting Press," Nov. 22, 1856, p. 658.

10. Edward Lyttelton, "Athletics in Public Schools," *Nineteenth Century*, 7(1880), 45.

11. In addition to works separately cited, material on rowing has been drawn from the following: "Argonaut" [pseud. E. D. Brickwood], *The Arts of Rowing and Training* (London: Horace Cox, 1866); John E. Morgan, *University Oars* (London: Macmillan, 1873); and Caspar W. Whitney, *A Sporting Pilgrimage* (London: Osgood, 1895).

12. *Times*, March 30, 1873.

13. *Times*, April 1, 1873.

14. Lyttelton, "Athletics," p. 45.

15. *Sporting Gazette*, April 8, 1865.

16. *Times*, March 8, 1869.

17. "The University Boat Race," *Saturday Review*, April 23, 1859, p. 494.

18. *Times*, March 8, 1869.

19. Henry Hayman in *The Dark Blue*, March-August 1871.

20. *Bell's Life in London*, July 3, 1859.

21. Gale, *Modern English Sports*, p. 42.

22. *London Society*, 5(1864), 381.

23. In addition to works separately cited, material on athletics has been drawn from the following: H. M. Abrahams and J. Bruce-Kerr, *Oxford Versus Cambridge: A Record of Inter-University Contests from 1827-1930* (London:

Faber & Faber, 1931); "Athletic Sports," *Encyclopaedia Britannica*, 11th ed.; R. J. Evans, *The Victorian Age; The Athlete for 1866*, ed. W. Pilkington (London: Chapman & Hall, 1867); Montague Shearman, *Athletics and Football*; The Badminton Library (3rd ed.; London: Longmans, 1889); F. A. M. Webster, *Athletics of Today* (London: Frederick Warne, 1929); the *Annual Register*; and the *Sporting Gazette*.

24. Melvyn Watman, *A History of British Athletics* (London: Hale, 1968), p. 40.

25. *A New Book of Sports: Reprinted from the "Saturday Review"* (London: Richard Bentley, 1885), p. 156.

26. In addition to works separately cited, material on mountaineering has been drawn from: Ronald Clark, *The Victorian Mountaineers* (Boston: Branford, 1954); R. L. G. Irving, *A History of British Mountaineering* (London: Batsford, 1955); James Ramsey Ullman, *High Conquest: The Story of Mountaineering* (London: Gollancz, 1942); and Edward Whymper, *Scrambles Amongst the Alps in the Years 1860-69* (2nd ed., London: John Murray, 1871).

27. "Alpine Climbing," *British Sports and Pastimes*, p. 264.

28. In addition to works separately cited, material on football has been drawn from: W. L. Burn, *The Age of Equipoise* (New York: Norton, 1965); Frederick Gale, *Modern English Sports*; Morris Marples, *A History of Football* (London: Secker & Warburg, 1954); B. Fletcher Robinson, *Rugby Football*; The Isthmian Library (London: Innes, 1896); Montague Shearman, *Athletics and Football*; and U. A. Titley, "For Gentlemen Only: 100 Years of Football," *Country Life*, Oct. 1, 1970, pp. 841-842.

29. Alfred Gibson and William Pickford, *Association Football and the Men Who Made It*, 4 vols. (London: Caxton, 1905, 1906), I, 5-7.

30. Gibson and Pickford, *Association Football*, I, 40.

31. In addition to works cited separately, material on miscellaneous sports has been drawn from: Vernon Bartlett, *The Past of Pastimes* (London: Chatto & Windus, 1969); Robert Browning, *A History of Golf* (New York: Dutton, 1955); T. H. S. Escott, *Social Transformations of the Victorian Age* (London: Seeley, 1897); Leonard B. Williams, *Croquet*; The Isthmian Library (London: Innes, 1899); Norman Wymer, *Sport In England: A History of Two Thousand Years of Games and Pastimes* (London: Harrap, 1949); the *Annual Register*; and the *Illustrated London News*.

32. M. G. L. Bruce, Baron Aberdare, *The Story of Tennis* (London: Stanley Paul, 1959), pp. 110, 114; and Walter Wingfield, *The Game of Sphairistikè* (5th ed., London: Harrison, 1876).

33. "Lusio Pilaris and Lawn Tennis," *Edinburgh Review*, 141 (1875), 53, 72.

34. *Croquet* (Boston: Ticknor and Fields, 1863), p. iv.

35. "Cavendish," "The Science of Croquet," *Gentleman's Magazine*, 1 (n.s., 1868), 225-239, 338-351, 497-513.

36. "The Ancient Rinking Man," *Idyls of the Rink* (London: Hardwicke & Bogue, 1877).

37. Alfred E. T. Watson in his preface to *The Poetry of Sport*, ed. Hedley Peek; Badminton Library (London: Longmans, Green, 1896), p. xii. Golf was, of course, a Scottish institution long before this period. The Royal and Ancient Golf Club of St. Andrews had been operating since 1754.

38. *Bicycling 1874* (1874; rpt. of *Bicycling: Its Rise and Development*; London: David & Charles, 1970), preface.

39. *Times*, Oct. 6, 1874.

40. F. Napier Broome, "English Physique," *Macmillan's*, 22 (1870), 133.

41. *Illustrated London News*, Nov. 5, 1859, p. 442.

42. *Studies in Conduct* (London: Chapman and Hall, 1867), p. 258.

43. Feb. 18, 1860, p. 149.

44. July 9, 1867, p. 20.

45. July 2, 1867, p. 9.

46. Ibid.

47. *Thoughts upon Sport* (London: Simpkin, Marshall, 1895).

48. J. Wesley Bready, *Lord Shaftesbury* (New York: Frank-Maurice, 1927), p. 112.

Chapter 7
Growing Up Healthy: Images of Boyhood

1. *Sermons Preached in the Chapel of Rugby School with an Address before Confirmation* (London: B. Fellowes, 1845), pp. 117-118.

2. Reviewing *Tom Brown's School Days*, Fitzjames Stephen wrote of Arnold, "To him and his admirers we owe the substitution of the word 'earnest' for its predecessor 'serious' "; *Edinburgh Review*, 107 (1858), 183.

3. See David Newsome's *Godliness and Good Learning: Four Studies on a Victorian Ideal* (London: John Murray, 1961), which traces the change in the public school ideal from "godliness and good learning" to "godliness and manliness."

4. Ibid., p. 53.

5. Arnold, *Sermons*, p. 119.

6. Arthur Penrhyn Stanley, *The Life and Correspondence of Thomas Arnold, D. D.* (1844; 2 vols. in 1, New York: Scribner's, 1892), I, 331.

7. Stanley, *Life and Correspondence*, I, 118; II, 85.

8. Arnold, *Sermons*, pp. 126-127.

9. Stanley, *Life and Correspondence*, I, 52, 95.

10. "On the Discipline of Public Schools," *The Miscellaneous Works of Thomas Arnold, D.D.*, ed. A[rthur] P[enrhyn] S[tanley] (London: B. Fellowes, 1845), p. 368.

11. Stanley, *Life and Correspondence*, I, 376.

12. Arnold, *Sermons*, p. 117.

13. Stanley, *Life and Correspondence*, I, 377.

14. Quoted in *The Book of Rugby School; Its History and Its Daily Life*, ed. E. M. G[oulburn] (Rugby: privately printed, 1856), p. 54.

15. Author's preface to the sixth edition. *Tom Brown's School Days* (New York: Harper, 1871), pp. viii-ix.

16. "Thomas Hughes and Septimus Hansard," *Economic Review*, 6 (1896), 306.

17. In their assessments of *Tom Brown* both the *Edinburgh* and the *Saturday Review* compared it to *Sandford and Merton*.

18. T[homas] Day, *The History of Sandford and Merton* (1783-89; rev. ed.,

London: Henry G. Bohn, 1860), p. 286.

19. *Tom Brown's Schooldays;* Everyman ed. (London: Dent, 1952), p. 218. Page numbers in my text refer to this often reprinted and widely available edition.

20. W. Lucas Collins, "School and College Life: Its Romance and Reality," *Blackwood's*, 89 (1861), 131-132.

21. *A God Within* (New York: Scribner's, 1972), p. 76.

22. "Play, the Game and the Generalized Other," *Sport and the Body: A Philosophical Symposium*, ed. Ellen W. Gerber (Philadelphia: Lea & Febiger, 1972), p. 105.

23. Dubos, *A God Within*, p. 78.

24. Lionel Trilling remarks that Carlyle might well have called Thomas Arnold "the Hero as Schoolmaster"; *Matthew Arnold* (New York: Norton, 1939), p. 63.

25. *An Essay on Man* (1944; New York: Doubleday Anchor, 1953), p. 72.

26. *Works*, ed. H. D. Traill; Centenary ed., 30 vols. (London: Chapman and Hall, 1896-99), I, 196.

27. *The Scouring of the White Horse* (Boston: Ticknor and Fields, 1859), p. 299.

28. "Fragments of an Autobiography," ed. Henry C. Shelley, *Cornhill*, 58 (n.s., 1925), 563-564.

29. "Sport and Play: Suspension of the Ordinary," *Sport and the Body*, pp. 29-30.

30. *Notes for Boys (and Their Fathers) on Morals, Mind and Manners* (London: Elliot Stock, 1885), pp. 22-23.

31. "The Guilty Vicarage," *The Dyer's Hand and Other Essays* (New York: Random House, 1962), p. 151.

32. On the relation of obligation and cultural function in sport see Johan Huizinga, *Homo Ludens: A Study of the Play Element in Culture* (1950; Boston: Beacon Press, 1955), p. 8.

33. Stanley, *Life and Correspondence*, I, 165.

34. *Quarterly Review*, 102 (1857), 333.

35. "Tom Brown's Schooldays," *Edinburgh Review*, 107 (1858), 190.

36. "Arnold and His School," *North British Review*, 28 (1858), 137-138.

37. Preface to sixth edition, pp. viii-ix.

38. *Eric; or Little by Little: A Tale of Roslyn School* (1858; 25th ed., Chicago: A. C. McClurg, 1891), p. 26.

39. Farrar, *Eric*, p. vii.

40. Ibid., p. 337.

41. *Julian Home: A Tale of College Life* (Edinburgh: Adam and Charles Black, 1859), p. 277.

42. R. A. Farrar, *Life of Frederic William Farrar* (London: James Nisbet, 1904), p. 78.

43. *Responsibility in Mental Disease* (London: Henry S. King, 1874), p. 298.

44. Farrar, *Eric*, p. 196.

45. Farrar, *Life*, p. 33.

46. Quoted by Harold Nicolson, *Good Behaviour* (New York: Doubleday, 1956), p. 265.

47. *St. Winifred's; or The World of School* (Edinburgh: Adam and Charles Black, 1862), p. 285.

48. Hugh Kingsmill [pseud. H. K. Lunn], *After Puritanism, 1850-1900* (London: Duckworth, 1929), p. 33.

49. *A Critical History of Children's Literature: A Survey of Children's Books in English*, ed. Cornelia Meigs et al. (rev. ed., London: Macmillan, 1969), p. 250.

50. G. Manville Fenn, *George Alfred Henty: The Story of an Active Life* (London: Blackie and Son, 1907), p. 321.

51. *Out on the Pampas; or, The Young Settlers. A Tale for Boys* (London: Griffith and Farrar, 1871), p. 12.

52. *The Gorilla Hunters: A Tale of the Wilds of Africa* (1861; London: T. Nelson, 1873), pp. 27-28.

Chapter 8
Anarchy and Physical Culture

1. "The Public School Matches," *Saturday Review*, Aug. 8, 1857, p. 128.

2. A brief but helpful account of the games movement in Victorian Public Schools may be found in Peter C. McIntosh, *Physical Education in England Since 1800* (London: G. Bell, 1952; rev. and enlgd., 1968). Those interested in the same subject treated within the larger context of nineteenth-century educational issues should consult E. C. Mack's fine two-volume study, *Public Schools and British Opinion* (New York: Columbia University Press, 1939, 1941).

3. Edward Lockwood, *The Early Days of Marlborough College* (London: Simpkin, Marshall, 1893), p. 89.

4. A. G. Bradley, A. C. Champneys, and J. W. Baines, *A History of Marlborough College* (London: John Murray, 1893), pp. 126-130.

5. George F. Berkeley, *Wellington College: The Founders of the Tradition* (Newport, Mon.: R. H. Johns, 1948), pp. 27-28.

6. J. L. Bevir, *The Making of Wellington* (London: Edward Arnold, 1920), p. 12.

7. L. S. Milford, *Haileybury College: Past and Present* (London: Unwin, 1909), pp. 19, 25.

8. Ibid., p. 34.

9. Sir Lionel Cust, *A History of Eton College* (London: Duckworth, 1899), p. 244. Wasey Sterry, *Annals of the King's College of Our Lady of Eton beside Windsor* (London: Methuen, 1898), pp. 321-322.

10. Great Britain, Parliamentary Papers, vol. XX (*Report of Public Schools Commission*, 1864), vol. I ("Report"), p. 97.

11. L[udwig] A[dolf] Wiese, *German Letters on English Education*, trans. W. D. Arnold (London: Longman, Brown, Green, 1854), pp. 47, 56. C. F. R. de Montalembert, *The Political Future of England*, trans. H. Barrow[?], rev. J. W. Croker (London: John Murray, 1856), pp. 140, 143-144.

12. Bevir, *The Making of Wellington*, p. 116.

13. Sir George R. Parkin, *Edward Thring: Headmaster of Uppingham School*, 2 vols. (London: Macmillan, 1898), II, 160.

14. J[ohn] Percival, *Some Helps for School Life: Sermons Preached at Clif-*

ton College 1862-1879 (London: Rivingtons, 1880), p. 41.

15. *Nineteenth Century,* 34 (1893), 902-903.

16. "Public School Education," *Quarterly Review,* 108 (1860), 415.

17. *Report of Public Schools Commission,* vol. III ("Evidence"), pt. I, p. 183. Clement Dukes, *Health at School* (1883; new ed., London: Cassell, 1887), p. 197.

18. "Arnold and His School," *North British Review,* 28 (1858), 138. Parkin, *Edward Thring,* II, 161.

19. Edward Lyttelton, *The Causes and Prevention of Immorality in Schools* (privately printed; London: Spottiswoode, [1887]), p. 11.

20. Edith Lyttelton, *Alfred Lyttelton: An Account of His Life* (London: Longmans, 1917), pp. 19-20.

21. *Ibid.,* p. 34.

22. "Public School Education," *Quarterly Review,* p. 415.

23. "The Influence of Athletic Sports on Health," *Lancet,* April 9, 1870, p. 514.

24. William H. G. Kingston, *Ernest Bracebridge; or, School Days* (London: Sampson Low, 1860), p. 75.

25. *The Boys of Bircham School; Young Englishman's Journal,* June 1867, pp. 162-163.

26. *Times,* April 6, 1868.

27. According to Philip Guedalla, Wellington revisited Eton once and, on seeing a ditch he used to jump over to reach a neighboring garden, remarked that such schoolboy tricks had taught him "the spirit of enterprise"; *Wellington* (New York: Harper, 1931), pp. 22-23.

28. Montalembert, *The Political Future of England,* p. 145.

29. "Private Schools for Boys: Their Management," *Macmillan's,* 9 (1864), 389.

30. Lionel J. Trotter, *The Life of Hodson of Hodson's Horse* (1901; London: J. M. Dent, 1910), p. 9.

31. "Major Hodson's Life," *Edinburgh Review,* 109 (1859), 547; and Trotter, *Life of Hodson of Hodson's Horse,* p. 8 (quoting from *The Book of Rugby School*).

32. "Athletic Sports," *"The Field" Quarterly,* 1 (1870), 40.

33. Thomas Hughes, *Memoir of a Brother* (London: Macmillan, 1873), p. 45; and Sir Joshua Fitch, *Thomas and Matthew Arnold and Their Influence on English Education* (London: Heinemann, 1897), p. 105.

34. Quoted in G. W. E. Russell's *Matthew Arnold* (London: Hodder & Stoughton, 1904), p. 65.

35. "A French Eton or Middle-Class Education and the State," *Complete Prose Works,* ed. R. H. Super, 11 vols. (Ann Arbor: University of Michigan Press, 1960-77), II, 268.

36. *Ibid.,* II, 276, 315, 316.

37. *Schools and Universities on the Continent,* in *Complete Prose Works,* IV, 351 (editor's note).

38. Arnold, *Complete Prose Works,* IV, 249, 91.

39. *Aspects of Education,* Monographs of the Industrial Education Associ-

ation, vol. I, no. 5 (New York, 1888), p. 74.

40. *Memories of Sixty Years at Eton, Cambridge, and Elsewhere* (London: John Lane, 1910), p. 87.

41. "Mr. Matthew Arnold's Report on French Education," *Quarterly Review*, 125 (1868), 482. Browning was, as his biographer records, one of the early members of the Alpine Club. See H. E. Wortham, *Oscar Browning* (London: Constable, 1927), p. 67.

42. Browning, "Mr. Matthew Arnold's Report," p. 482.

43. Arnold, *Schools and Universities; Complete Prose Works*, IV, 92.

44. *Culture and Anarchy*, ed. J. Dover Wilson (Cambridge: University Press, 1963), p. 9. Subsequent page references are to this edition.

45. *Works*, ed. H. D. Traill; Centenary ed., 30 vols. (London: Chapman and Hall, 1896-99), XXVIII, 8.

46. *Education: Intellectual, Moral, and Physical* (Amer. ed., 1860; New York: Appleton, 1896), pp. 103, 42.

47. Ibid., pp. 223, 280.

48. Ibid., pp. 38-39.

49. Arnold, *Complete Prose Works*, X, 26.

Chapter 9
Two Staunch Walkers: Tom Thurnall and Tom Tulliver

1. *Charles Kingsley: His Letters and Memories of His Life*, ed. [Frances Kingsley], 4 vols. (1877; London: Macmillan, 1901), IV, 77-78.

2. *Culture and Anarchy*, ed. J. Dover Wilson (Cambridge: University Press, 1963), pp. 132, 131.

3. *Sanitary and Social Lectures and Essays* (London: Macmillan, 1880), pp. 125, 112, 113.

4. Ibid., p. 113.

5. Arnold, *Culture and Anarchy*, p. 148.

6. *The Hero in History* (Boston: Beacon Press, 1943), p. 154.

7. "Physical Strength," *Saturday Review*, Dec. 10, 1859, p. 701.

8. "Charles Kingsley," *Dublin Review*, 24 (3rd ser., 1890), 15-16.

9. See G. A. Simcox, "Charles Kingsley," *Fortnightly Review*, Jan. 1, 1877, p. 16: "Kingsley's muscles and senses were far more vigorous than the rest of his constitution: looking only to his strength, he was fit for an athlete; looking only at his temperament, he was fitter for a monk . . . Hence all who were really intimate with him were struck by the union of the most exquisite tenderness with a manliness that often seemed aggressive."

10. *Literary and Social Judgments* (London: Trübner, 1868), p. 170.

11. *The Swinburne Letters*, ed. C. Y. Lang, 6 vols. (New Haven: Yale University Press, 1959-62), I, 10.

12. Robert Bernard Martin, *The Dust of Combat: A Life of Charles Kingsley* (London: Faber and Faber, 1959), p. 206.

13. *The Swinburne Letters*, I, 10.

14. *Two Years Ago* (4th ed.; Cambridge: Macmillan, 1871), p. 61. Subsequent page references in the text are to this edition.

15. "Two Years Ago," *British Quarterly Review*, 25 (1857), 409.

16. Kingsley, *Scientific Lectures and Essays*, p. 202.

17. Ibid., p. 216.

18. T. C. Sandars, "Two Years Ago," *Saturday Review*, Feb. 21, 1857, p. 176.

19. "Belles Lettres," *Westminster Review*, 2 (n.s.; 1857), 609.

20. *George Eliot: The Critical Heritage*, ed. David Carroll (New York: Barnes & Noble, 1971), p. 76. The unsigned review appeared in the issue of Feb. 26, 1859.

21. *The George Eliot Letters*, ed. Gordon S. Haight, 7 vols. (New Haven: Yale University Press, 1954-55), III, 28.

22. "[Westward Ho! and Constance Herbert]," *Essays of George Eliot*, ed. Thomas Pinney (New York: Columbia University Press, 1963), p. 126.

23. *Letters*, IV, 158-159.

24. *Adam Bede*, ed. John Paterson; Riverside ed. (Boston: Houghton Mifflin, 1968), p. 143. Subsequent page references to *Adam Bede* will be to this edition.

25. *Letters*, I, 163.

26. *The Mill on the Floss*, ed. Gordon S. Haight; Riverside ed. (Boston: Houghton Mifflin, 1961), p. 118. Subsequent page references will be to this edition.

27. *Tom Brown's Schooldays*; Everyman ed. (1857; London: Dent, 1952), p. 15. *Letters*, I, 163.

28. *George Eliot: The Critical Heritage*, p. 133.

29. *The Principles of Psychology*, 2 vols. (1855; 3rd ed., New York: Appleton, 1895), II, 589.

30. Arnold, *Culture and Anarchy*, p. 129.

31. *Letters*, I, 227.

32. *Essays in a Series of Letters to a Friend* (1805; New York: Robert Carter, 1848), pp. 114, 89.

33. Ibid., pp. 118-119.

34. *Letters*, I, 210. At one time, in 1855, she was reading both Gall and Spurzheim's *Physiology*—a phrenological work—and Carpenter's *Mental Physiology*. See *Letters*, II, 220. For a phrenologist's view of the relation of character to organization see George Combe's *The Constitution of Man*, chs. ii, iv.

35. *Letters*, IV, 89; I, 304, 146.

36. *Letters*, III, 242; I, 251. Haight in his edition of the letters has "servant" for the twenty-fifth word, but "serpent," as printed in Cross, must be intended. See J. W. Cross, *George Eliot's Life as Related in Her Letters and Journals*, 3 vols. (Edinburgh: Blackwood, 1885), I, 176. Eliot's reference is to Genesis 3:15.

37. Ibid., I, 265-266.

38. *The Constitution of Man Considered in Relation to External Objects* (1828; 3rd ed., New York: Harper, 1859), pp. 112-113, 115.

39. *Essays of George Eliot*, p. 450.

40. "The Novels of George Eliot," *National Review*, 2 (1860), 217.

41. *The Idea of a University*, ed. C. F. Harrold (1852, 1859, 1873; new ed., New York: Longmans, Green, 1947), p. 107.

Chapter 10
The True Gentleman and the Washed Rough in Broadcloth

1. Quoted by Thomas Bowden Green, *The Life and Work of Samuel Smiles* (London: Betterment of London Printing and Publ. Co., 1904), p. 22.

2. *The Autobiography of Samuel Smiles, LL.D.*, ed. Thomas Mackay (New York: Dutton, 1905), p. 62.

3. *Self-Help* (1859; rev. ed., New York: Harper, 1899), pp. 349, 432.

4. *Baily's*, 7 (1864), 330, 334.

5. Thackeray in *Vanity Fair* credits Rawdon Crawley with having "certain manly tendencies of affection in his heart" (ch. 37). This is also Pip's use of the word in *Great Expectations* when he speaks of Joe Gargery's "manly heart" (ch. 27).

6. Hughes, *The Manliness of Christ* (London: Macmillan, 1879), p. 6.

7. *On Liberty* (ch. 3, "Of Individuality"), *Autobiography and Other Writings*, ed. Jack Stillinger (Boston: Houghton Mifflin, 1969), p. 407.

8. Smiles, *Self-Help*, pp. 425, 418.

9. "Moral qualities strongly developed or strikingly displayed," as the *Oxford English Dictionary* defines it; "distinct or distinguished character; character worth speaking of."

10. *Character* (London: John Murray, 1871), pp. 15-16.

11. Smiles, *Self-Help*, p. 429.

12. "Milton," *Literary Essays Contributed to the Edinburgh Review* (London: Oxford University Press, 1937), p. 18.

13. J. G. Cotton Minchin, *Old Harrow Days* (London: Methuen, 1898), p. 150.

14. Quoted by Smiles, *Self-Help*, p. 416.

15. *The Making of Victorian England* (New York: Atheneum, 1967), pp. 254 ff.

16. *The Schoolmaster*, ed. Lawrence V. Ryan; Folger Documents on Tudor and Stuart Civilization (Ithaca: Cornell University Press, 1967), p. 53.

17. Baldesar Castiglione, *The Book of the Courtier*, trans. Charles S. Singleton (New York: Doubleday Anchor, 1959), pp. 29, 38-39.

18. *The Complete Gentleman, The Truth of Our Times, and The Art of Living in London*, ed. Virgil B. Heltzel; Folger Documents on Tudor and Stuart Civilization (Ithaca: Cornell University Press, 1962), p. 137.

19. *The Book Named the Governor*, ed. S. E. Lehmberg; Everyman ed. (London: Dent, 1962), p. 64.

20. *True Manliness; from the Writings of Thomas Hughes*, ed. E. E. Brown (Boston: Lothrop, 1880), p. xi.

21. *Pictures of Sporting Life and Character* (London: Hurst and Blackett, 1860), II, 181.

22. "The Cricketers of England," *New Sporting Magazine*, 40 (n.s., 1860), 19.

23. Quoted by Peter McIntosh, "The British Attitude to Sport," *Sport and Society: A Symposium*, ed. Alex Natan (London: Bowes & Bowes, 1958), p. 20.

24. *Culture and Anarchy*, ed. J. Dover Wilson (Cambridge: University Press, 1963), p. 109.

25. For a commentary on Lawrence's Guy Livingstone as a dandy see Ellen Moers, *The Dandy: Brummell to Beerbohm* (New York: Viking, 1960), p. 255.

26. *Guy Livingstone; or Thorough* (1857; new ed., London: Elkin, Mathews, & Marrot, 1928), pp. 16-17.

27. Ibid., pp. 16, 269.

28. "The Late George Lawrence and His Work," *Spectator*, Oct. 28, 1876, p. 1346.

29. Lawrence, *Guy Livingstone*, p. 125.

30. *Barren Honour: A Tale*, 2 vols. (London: Parker, 1862), I, 16-17.

31. *English Traits* (Boston: Phillips, Sampson, 1857), p. 107.

32. *Sword and Gown* (London: Parker, 1859), p. 169.

33. *Not Wisely, But Too Well: A Novel*, 3 vols. (London: Tinsley, 1867), I, 68, 70.

34. *"Held in Bondage"; or, Granville de Vigne*, 3 vols. (London: Chapman and Hall, 1863), III, 23.

35. *Strathmore: A Romance*, 3 vols. (London: Chapman and Hall, 1865), I, 47-48.

36. *Maurice Dering; or, The Quadrilateral*, 2 vols. (London: Tinsley, 1864), I, 68.

37. *The George Eliot Letters*, ed. Gordon S. Haight, 7 vols. (New Haven: Yale University Press, 1954-55), II, 444.

38. "Guy Livingstone, or Thorough," *Edinburgh Review*, 108 (1858), 533.

39. *Condensed Novels* (Boston: Osgood, 1871), pp. 128-129.

40. *Tom Brown at Oxford*; Nelson's Classics (1861; London: Nelson, [1908]), pp. 121-122.

41. *Saturday Review*, May 3, 1873, p. 594.

42. Hughes, *The Manliness of Christ*, pp. 24-26.

43. *David: Four Sermons Preached before the University of Cambridge* (Cambridge: Macmillan, 1865), pp. 5-14.

44. "Kingsley's Hereward," *Saturday Review*, May 19, 1866, p. 595. The writer was probably the historian E. A. Freeman. See Merle M. Bevington, *The Saturday Review, 1855-1868* (New York: Columbia University Press, 1941), p. 190.

45. "Belles Lettres," *Westminster Review*, 30 (n.s., 1866), 268.

46. "Charles Kingsley," *Hours in a Library* (3rd ser.; London: Smith, Elder, 1879), p. 408.

47. *Hereward the Wake, "Last of the English,"* 2 vols. (London: Macmillan, 1866), I, 38, 43.

48. *The Roman and the Teuton: A Series of Lectures Delivered before the University of Cambridge* (Cambridge: Macmillan, 1864), p. 2.

49. Kingsley, *Hereward the Wake*, I, 3, 4-5, 89-90.

50. Ibid., I, 209-210.

51. "Kingsley's 'Hereward,'" *Notes and Reviews*, ed. Pierre de Chaignon la Rose (Cambridge, Mass.: Dunster House, 1921), p. 143.

52. Kingsley, *Hereward the Wake*, II, 372.

53. "Hereward the Wake, 'Last of the English,'" *Athenaeum*, April 14, 1866, p. 493.

54. "Frederick Denison Maurice. In Memoriam," *Macmillan's*, 26 (1872), 88.

55. *Sanitary and Social Lectures and Essays* (London: Macmillan, 1880), p. 40.

56. S. M. Ellis, *A Mid-Victorian Pepys: The Letters and Memoirs of Sir William Hardman* (London: Palmer, 1923), pp. 26-27.

57. Cecil and Phillis Cunnington, *Handbook of English Costume in the Nineteenth Century* (London: Faber & Faber, 1959), p. 253.

58. Edith Lyttelton, *Alfred Lyttelton: An Account of His Life* (London: Longmans, 1917), pp. 32-33.

59. "Athletic Sports and University Studies," *Fraser's*, 82 (1870), 692.

60. "Prizefighting," *Saturday Review*, Nov. 2, 1856, p. 658.

61. *Punch*, May 31, 1862, p. 221.

62. "Mind and Muscle," *Saturday Review*, April 21, 1860, p. 494.

63. *Punch*, Mar. 20, 1869, p. 112.

64. "Athletics," *Saturday Review*, Mar. 27, 1869, p. 414.

65. "The University Boat-Race," *Saturday Review*, April 23, 1859, p. 494; Mar. 20, 1869, p. 386.

66. *Punch*, Feb. 6, 1869, p. 47.

67. "Athletics," *Saturday Review*, Mar. 27, 1869, p. 413.

68. "Athletics," *Contemporary Review*, 3 (1866), 378, 380.

69. *Echoes from the Old Cricket Fields* (London: Simpkin, Marshall, 1871), pp. 64-65.

70. "The Present Aspect of Athletics," *Baily's*, 18 (1870), 203.

71. In his autobiography Frederick Harrison tells of a boy in his family who was incapacitated for over a year after having been forced by school authorities to run in a five-mile race; another was made to play football on threat of expulsion, even though a doctor had testified regarding the boy's bad heart. *Autobiographic Memoirs*, 2 vols. (London: Macmillan, 1911), I, 64-65.

72. John E. Morgan, *University Oars* (London: Macmillan, 1873), p. 3.

73. *British Sports and Pastimes* (London: Virtue, 1868), pp. 6-7.

74. "Athletics," p. 389.

75. See, for example, *Sartor Resartus; Works*, ed. H. D. Traill; Centenary ed., 30 vols. (London: Chapman and Hall, 1896-99), I, 73.

76. "*A Joy for Ever*," *The Works of John Ruskin*, ed. E. T. Cook and Alexander Wedderburn; 39 vols. (London: Allen, 1903-12), XVI, 111.

77. Ruskin, *Works*, XXXIV, 498.

78. "Athletic Sports and University Studies," p. 692.

79. *Man and Wife: A Novel*; 3 vols. (London: Ellis, 1870), preface.

80. Ibid., I, 76-77.

81. Collins, *Man and Wife*, preface; I, 336; I, 104-105.

82. Kenneth Robinson, *Wilkie Collins: A Biography* (New York: Macmillan, 1952), p. 236.

83. Collins, *Man and Wife*, preface.

84. Collins, *Man and Wife*, I, 90.

Chapter 11
The Athlete as Barbarian: Richard Feverel and Willoughby Patterne

1. *The Letters of George Meredith*, ed. C. L. Cline, 3 vols. (Oxford: Clarendon Press, 1970), II, 647, 650, 652, 657, 662, 704, 730-731; III, 1491.

2. Justin McCarthy, *Reminiscences*, 2 vols. (New York: Harper, 1899), I, 330.

3. Hyndman, quoted in Lionel Stevenson, *The Ordeal of George Meredith* (New York: Scribner's, 1953), p. 127. Hyndman, *The Record of an Adventurous Life* (New York: Macmillan, 1911), p. 72. *Letters*, I, 201.

4. *Letters*, II, 570; I, 325, 328, 345, 198.

5. See James Sully, *My Life & Friends: A Psychologist's Memories* (London: Unwin, 1918), p. 326.

6. *The Ordeal of Richard Feverel* (1859; New York: Modern Library, 1927), p. 14. Subsequent page references are to this edition.

7. *Letters*, I, 80, 166, 429.

8. Ibid., I, 466.

9. Ibid., I, 201; II, 569.

10. J. A. Hammerton, *George Meredith: His Life and Art in Anecdote and Criticism* (rev. ed., Edinburgh: John Grant, 1911), p. 64.

11. *Letters*, I, 371.

12. Ibid., II, 744.

13. *On the Nature of the Universe*, trans. Ronald Latham (Baltimore: Penguin, 1951), pp. 104-105.

14. *Letters*, I, 247. Lucretius, *On the Nature of the Universe*, pp. 105-106.

15. John R. Reed, "Systemic Irregularity: Meredith's *Ordeal*," *PLL* 7 (1971), 61. Meredith, *Letters*, I, 345, 315.

16. *Letters*, I, 93; II, 578.

17. *Anatomy of Criticism: Four Essays* (Princeton: Princeton University Press, 1957), p. 309.

18. *The Poetry and Philosophy of George Meredith* (2nd imp.; London: Constable, 1907), p. 78.

19. *Letters*, II, 910.

20. Quoted in J. B. Priestley, *George Meredith*; English Men of Letters (New York: Macmillan, 1926), p. 74.

21. Robert E. Sencourt [pseud., Robert E. G. George], *The Life of George Meredith* (London: Chapman and Hall, 1929), p. 48. *The Works of George Meredith*; Memorial ed., 29 vols. (Scribner's, 1909-12), XXIII, 91.

22. *Letters*, II, 841; I, 306.

23. Stevenson, *The Ordeal of George Meredith*, p. 228.

24. *The Egoist*, ed. Lionel Stevenson (Boston: Riverside Press, 1958), p. 288. Subsequent references are to this edition.

25. *Art and Substance in George Meredith* (Lincoln: University of Nebraska Press, 1953), p. 65. Wright comments that the "leg" is "identical with feudal and courtly prestige." One of the older, specialized meanings of the word is a manner of bowing gracefully. The *Oxford English Dictionary* quotes Selden: " 'Tis good to learn to dance, a man may learn his Leg, learn to go handsomely." *The Ordeal of George Meredith*, p. 226.

26. In 1904 Meredith, then paralyzed, recalled: "I preferred walking to riding; it sent the blood coursing to the brain, and besides, when I walked, I could go through the woods and footpaths, which I could not have done if I had ridden"; Hammerton, *George Meredith*, p. 74.

27. "In Praise of Walking," *Studies of a Biographer*, 4 vols. (New York: Putnam's, 1907), III, 249.

28. *The Theory of the Leisure Class: An Economic Study of Institutions* (1899; New York: New American Library, 1953), p. 173.

Chapter 12
Conclusion

1. *Stones of Venice; The Works of John Ruskin*, ed. E. T. Cook and Alexander Wedderburn, 39 vols. (London: George Allen, 1903-12), XI, 152-153.

2. *The Playground of Europe* (London: Longmans, Green, 1871), pp. 196, 276-277.

3. *Being and Nothingness: An Essay on Phenomenological Ontology*, trans. Hazel E. Barnes (New York: Philosophical Library, 1956), pp. 582, 585.

4. *Mountaineering in 1861; A Vacation Tour* (London: Longman, Green, 1862), pp. 5-6, 53, 81.

5. *Theological Essays* (1853; 5th ed., London: Macmillan, 1905), p. 210.

6. Ibid., pp. 184-185, 183.

7. E. C. Gaskell, *The Life of Charlotte Brontë*, 2 vols. (New York: Appleton, 1857), I, 260-261.

8. *Scrambles Amongst the Alps in the Years 1860-69* (2nd ed., London: John Murray, 1871), p. 407.

9. *Past and Present; The Works of Thomas Carlyle*, ed. H. D. Traill; Centenary ed., 30 vols. (London: Chapman and Hall, 1896-99), X, 196, 198.

10. Eugen Fink, "The Ontology of Play," *Sport and the Body: A Philosophical Symposium*, ed. Ellen W. Gerber (Philadelphia: Lea and Febiger, 1972), pp. 79-80. Sartre, *Being and Nothingness*, p. 581.

11. Ruskin, *The Crown of Wild Olive; Works*, XVIII, 405-406.

12. *Fights, Games, and Debates* (Ann Arbor: University of Michigan Press, 1960), p. 9.

13. Stephen, *The Playground of Europe*, pp. 206-207.

14. Quoted by Karl Beckson, *Aesthetes and Decadents of the 1890's* (New York: Vintage Books, 1966), p. 134.

15. *Culture and Anarchy*, ed. J. Dover Wilson (Cambridge: University Press, 1963), p. 137.

16. W. E. Bowen, *Edward Bowen: A Memoir* (London: Longmans, Green, 1902), p. 369.

17. Ibid., p. 370.

18. *The Island Race* (London: Elkin, Mathews, 1898), p. 82.

19. *Abinger Harvest* (1936; New York: Meridian Books, 1955), pp. 4-5.

Index